938

Alexander the Gr
in Fact and Ficti

D1375657

Alexander the Great in Fact and Fiction

EDITED BY

A. B. Bosworth
and
E. J. Baynham

OXFORD
UNIVERSITY PRESS

OXFORD

UNIVERSITY PRESS

Great Clarendon Street, Oxford OX2 6DP

Oxford University Press is a department of the University of Oxford.
It furthers the University's objective of excellence in research, scholarship,
and education by publishing worldwide in

Oxford New York

Auckland Cape Town Dar es Salaam Hong Kong Karachi Kuala Lumpur
Madrid Melbourne Mexico City Nairobi New Delhi Shanghai Taipei Toronto

With offices in

Argentina Austria Brazil Chile Czech Republic France Greece
Guatemala Hungary Italy Japan South Korea Poland Portugal
Singapore Switzerland Thailand Turkey Ukraine Vietnam

Oxford is a registered trade mark of Oxford University Press
in the UK and in certain other countries

Published in the United States
by Oxford University Press Inc., New York

© Oxford University Press 2000

British Library Cataloguing in Publication Data

Data available

Library of Congress Cataloging in Publication Data

Alexander the Great in fact and fiction / edited by A. B. Bosworth and E. J. Baynham.
"This book originated in a symposium on Alexander the Great, held at the University of
Newcastle (NSW, Australia) in July 1997"–Prelim. p.
Includes bibliographical references and index.
1. Alexander, the Great, 356-323 B.C.–Influence–Congresses. 2. Alexander, the Great,
356-323 B.C.–In literature–Congresses. 3. Myth in literature–Congresses. 4. Greece–
History–Macedonian Expansion, 359-323 B.C.–Congresses. I. Bosworth, A. B. II.
Baynham, Elizabeth, 1958-
DF234.2 .A394 200
938.07'092–dc21 99-057300
ISBN 0-19-925275-0

3 5 7 9 10 8 6 4

Typeset in Imprint
by Regent Typesetting, London
Printed in Great Britain on acid-free paper by
Biddles Ltd., King's Lynn, Norfolk

Preface

THIS book originated in a symposium on Alexander the Great, held at the University of Newcastle (NSW, Australia) in July 1997. It was largely funded by a generous grant from the Australian Research Council, which was designed to encourage 'greater collaboration among researchers . . . and thus enhance the quality and effectiveness of outcomes of that research'. Collaboration and co-operation were the operative words. The symposium brought together established scholars, students both graduate and undergraduate, and interested members of the public. The papers which were presented each had a designated respondent, and there was ample time for formal and informal discussion. In the aftermath a number of selected papers were revised and refereed, and the outcome is this present volume, which we hope will be a stimulus to scholarship on the Alexander period.

We have many obligations. The symposium could not have taken place without significant financial support, and we are grateful to the Australian Research Council for a Strategic Research Initiative Grant, which provided optimal conditions for the occasion. The University of Newcastle provided excellent facilities and generous hospitality; and significant and strategically vital resources were committed by Dr Fran Flavel, the Director of Marketing and Media Services, and the Department of Classics from its Roos–Ashworth fund. We also extend a warm note of thanks to Hugh and Catherine Lindsay for hosting a most convivial occasion in the wilds of Wallalong.

We are grateful for the contributions of all symposiasts and their respondents, in particular the postgraduate participants, Ingrid Hastings, Elias Koulakiotis, Lara O'Sullivan, and Pat Wheatley. We acknowledge too the contributions of the Heads of Department, past and present, Harold Tarrant and Godfrey Tanner, who emerged as the *arbiter elegantiae* and public orator for the symposium, and the many devoted and unpaid helpers, in particular Robyn Gay, Kay Hayes, Renée Wilkinson, and Marguerite Johnson.

The preparation of the volume has necessarily been protracted, and we should like to thank all contributors for their patience in the face of delay and their responsiveness to deadlines. It has made the editorial work easier, as have the labours of Pat Wheatley, who has unified the referencing in the disparate papers and imposed the Harvard system upon some rather recalcitrant material. Finally, we should express our gratitude to Oxford University Press and its readers for careful and helpful criticism, which has materially improved the collective work.

A.B.B.
E.J.B.

April 1999

Contents

Abbreviations

THIS list comprises the abbreviations used in the body of the volume, other than those in the Bibliography, which follow conventions of *L'Année Philologique*.

FD	*Fouilles de Delphes*
FGrH	F. Jacoby, *Die Fragmente der griechischen Historiker* (Berlin and Leidon, 1923–)
IG	*Inscriptiones graecae* (1st edn.: Berlin, 1873– ; 2nd edn.: Berlin, 1913–)
Moretti, *ISE*	L. Moretti, *Iscrizioni storiche ellenistiche* (Florence, 1967–)
OGIS	*Orientis graeci inscriptiones selectae*, ed. W. Dittenberger (Leipzig, 1903–5)
RE	*Realencyclopädie der classischen Altertumswissenschaft*, ed. Pauly, Wissowa, Kroll (Stuttgart, 1893–1980)
SEG	*Supplementum Epigraphicum Graecum*
SIG³	*Sylloge inscriptionum graecarum*, ed. W. Dittenberger (3rd edn.: Leipzig, 1913–24)

I

Introduction

BRIAN BOSWORTH

The passionate popular interest in Alexander has never flagged. It may even be intensifying in this age of mass communication. Web sites proliferate on the Internet, where a plethora of aficionados advertise their fascination with the Macedonian conqueror. In the most powerful medium of all, television, there has been an enthusiastic response to Michael Wood's recent series with its striking visual images of the route of conquest, accompanied by a terse, energetic commentary on the more colourful episodes of the reign.[1] Translated into book form (Wood 1997) it has become a best-seller. Fact and fiction are here intertwined, and the result is a new Alexander Romance with all the fascination of the old. The object of the series is entertainment—in which it has succeeded admirably. It has also raised public interest in the charismatic figure of Alexander and challenged specialists to give new answers to old questions. That is the purpose of the present volume, to take new approaches, to analyse and explain some of the huge body of romance that has adhered to the historical Alexander and to address the perennial problems of kingship and imperialism. We cannot claim to be unveiling universal truth. Given the state of the evidence that is impossible. What is more feasible is to identify distortion and myth-making, to provide a general context of historical interpretation, and to clear the obstacles preventing a dispassionate and balanced assessment of the few questions which can be profitably discussed.

The besetting problem of Alexander scholarship is the dearth of contemporary sources. That has not changed in

I am grateful to Elizabeth Baynham, Michael Flower, and Olga Palagia for their advice and helpful criticism.

[1] One may also mention Antony Spawforth's BBC production, 'Alexander the Great: the God-King' (1996), with its ironically sceptical treatment of the newest piece of Alexander fiction, the supposed tomb at Siwah.

the last decades. There has been no influx of new documentary material like the marvellous bronze inscriptions
from Spain which have so enriched our knowledge of early
Imperial Rome.[2] The corpus of contemporary inscriptions
has been increased by a handful of documents from Macedonia which raise interesting questions about Alexander's
relations with his subjects in the distant homeland but leave
us more perplexed than enlightened.[3] The same applies to
the study of Alexander's prolific and enigmatic coinage.
New issues have been discovered, predominantly in the
great Babylon hoard; we now have more (and more reveal-
ing) examples of the Porus decadrachms and a whole series
of tetradrachms with Indian themes.[4] However, the
problems of dating and provenance remain as controversial
and intractable as ever. There have been sensational
archaeological discoveries, but again they are the subject of
intense academic debate. More than twenty years after their
discovery the contents of the Vergina Tombs are still incom-
pletely documented, and there remains deep disagreement
about their dating; the once conventional attribution of
Tomb II to Philip II has come under increasing attack,
and archaeological and historical arguments have combined
in different patterns without any accepted dating peg
emerging. That has been the stimulus for Olga Palagia's
contribution[5] in which iconographic analysis is combined
with historical interpretation to secure a late dating (after the
eastern campaigns of Alexander) for the hunting fresco on
Tomb II. Such progress is, however, rare. The gaps in our
knowledge are usually too extensive for us to resolve the
problems presented by the material evidence.

The history of the period remains based on literary evidence. Here too there is a lack of contemporary material
which has not been rectified by papyrological discoveries.

[2] In particular the *Lex Irnitana*, the *Tabula Siarensis*, and, above all, the great
Senatus Consultum recording the condemnation of Cn. Piso. It has been observed
by Miriam Griffin that 'The Spanish inscriptions on bronze are making a fair bid to
rival the Egyptian papyri in their contribution to our knowledge of the ancient
world'.

[3] The definitive edition with full bibliography is Hatzopoulos 1996: 25–8, no. 6;
84–5, no. 62. See also Hatzopoulos 1997; Errington 1998: 77–90.

[4] See Price 1982; 1991. For recent summaries and bibliography see Lane Fox
1996 and Le Rider 1995–96: 856.   [5] Below, Ch. 6.

The one piece of evidence which has emerged (a fragmentary account of the Thracian campaign of 335 BC) is an enigma, elusive in genre and only explicable through extant literature.[6] It adds little or nothing in its own right. The basic evidence is what it always has been: derivative writings from the Roman period which draw upon the lost contemporary historians of Alexander. There is general agreement that this source material falls into two families. On the one hand we have the history of Arrian which is explicitly based on Ptolemy, Aristobulus, and (to a lesser degree) Nearchus, and on the other a tradition common to Diodorus, Curtius Rufus, and Justin, which is thought to derive from the popular Hellenistic writer, Cleitarchus of Alexandria. There is also the biography of Plutarch, which drew upon a mosaic of sources, and the voluminous geography of Strabo, which adapted significant passages of major historians, predominantly Onesicritus, Nearchus, and Aristobulus. This canonical list now has an extra member in Polybius, whose references to Alexander are analysed (amazingly for the first time) by Richard Billows, who argues that he drew upon Hieronymus and ultimately Demetrius of Phalerum.[7]

It is one thing to put a name upon a lost source, quite another to identify how that source was adapted in its extant context. Paradoxically one of our most powerful research tools, Jacoby's monumental collection of the fragments of the lost historians, is responsible for many misapprehensions. Direct quotations are identified by Sperrdruck, but the vast majority of 'fragments' are paraphrases by secondary writers, and we have no indication how faithfully they reproduce the content of the original or even how much of the context is attributable to the named author.[8] As a result

---

[6] Published by Clarysse and Schepens 1985. The text has been interpreted as part of a history or, less probably, a fragment of Strattis' commentary on the Royal *Ephemerides* (Hammond 1987; 1993: 201–2). I suspect that the work was a very detailed campaign history, which gave a full account of the movements of Alexander and his lieutenants, correlating the invasion of Triballian territory with simultaneous actions in Eordaea and Elimeia, in Macedonia proper. Unfortunately Arrian's account (1. 2. 1) is compressed to the last degree, and the papyrus is too defective to reconstruct any continuous narrative. All that remains is a tantalizing miscellany of familiar names without a meaningful historical context.

[7] See below, Ch. 10.

[8] See the cautionary remarks of Brunt 1980 and Flower 1997: 4–9.

there has been a strong tendency to take what Jacoby prints as the work of the cited author, not the actual writer. The extant intermediary tends to be forgotten, and it is assumed that the text of Arrian, say, is a reflecting mirror for Ptolemy. That tendency has now been obviated by studies dedicated to the literature that has survived. Detailed commentaries on Arrian and Curtius have shown how complex and sophisticated their composition was.[9]

Arrian, for instance, does not merely transpose material from his sources. He engages in an allusive dialogue with the great historical masters of the past: Herodotus, Thucydides, and Xenophon. There are subtle echoes of vocabulary; familiar themes from earlier periods are reworked in the context of Alexander's campaigns. There is also explicit literary rivalry. As a self-conscious stylist, by his own claim the equal of Alexander in the field of literature, he surpasses the writers of the past—in his own eyes at least. Consequently he subjects his source material to a counterpoint of allusive commentary. His description of the aftermath of Alexander's wounding at the Malli town is a good example. He drew on Nearchus for the vivid scene of the king's generals reproaching him for his excessive recklessness, but he dresses the scene in terminology that recalls Xenophon: Alexander's soldiers are made to represent their plight if their king died in language reminiscent of the Ten Thousand after the execution of their generals.[10] The implicit comment leads to an explicit statement of opinion by Arrian (6. 13. 4), that the criticism was justified: Alexander's thirst for glory drove him to embrace danger. That in turn looks forward to the complex passage at the beginning of book 7, in which Alexander's insatiate desire for glory is treated from several aspects. His ambition for further conquest is represented as inherently plausible, because of the underlying passion for glory; if there were no one else to surpass, he would compete with himself.[11]

---

[9] Bosworth 1980a, 1995 on Arrian; Atkinson 1980, 1994 on Curtius.

[10] Arr. 6. 12. 1–3; Xen. *Anab*. 3. 1. 2–3; for detailed discussion see Bosworth 1996a, 54–6.

[11] Arr. 7. 1. 4. The general sentiment was expressed by Aristobulus (Strabo 16. 1. 11 (741) = *FGrH* 139 F 56), and Arrian (7. 19. 6) duly records it as his own view (ὥς γέ μοι δοκεῖ). However, Arrian sharpens the comment, and expresses himself in

The theme is then illustrated by three vignettes from different sources: the criticisms by the Indian gymno-sophists, the meeting with Diogenes, and finally Mega-sthenes' account of Alexander's conversation with the Indian sage, Dandamis.[12] This last scene is also reported by Strabo, who gives essentially the same substance but places it in a different context, a formal contrast between Dandamis and his rival, Calanus.[13] The contrast is brought out by Arrian, but it is subordinate to the main theme, Alexander's failure to overcome his desire for fame. Dandamis' admonitions are an explicit commentary on the king's imperial ambitions, and form a bridge to the next episode in the history, the suicide of Calanus, who is portrayed as unconquerable (ἀνίκητον) in his resolution to die, as much so as Alexander in his determination to achieve world empire (Arr. 7. 3. 4). Here Arrian uses his sources with considerable sophistica-tion. He does not misrepresent them, but he uses them discriminatingly to illustrate and underpin his view of Alexander. What is more, the material is not chosen with an eye solely for historical veracity. It is selected because it gives the most vivid illustration of his theme, and allows him to express his judgements both implicitly and explicitly. One cannot use his exposition as a primary source without taking account of his narrative perspective and indeed the tastes and expectations of his audience in the second century AD.

The same is true of the other extant writers. There is now a flourishing industry devoted to research on Plutarch, and

Thucydidean style (Högemann 1985: 130); where Strabo merely states that Alexander 'desired to be lord of all things', Arrian has a more vivid turn of phrase: Alexander 'was for ever insatiate of conquest'. The phrase is probably a deliberate reminiscence of Herodotus' Cyrus, who was 'insatiable of blood' (Hdt. 1. 212. 2–4; cf. 1. 187. 5), and implicitly compares the two conquerors (note also the warning against insatiable exploitation of good fortune in Xen. *Cyrop.* 4. 1. 15). The termi-nology recurs in the final summation of Alexander, where Arrian insists that his hero was most continent with respect to bodily pleasures and when it came to the pleasures of the mind he was completely insatiate—of fame alone (ἐπαίνου μόνου ἀπληστότατος). The lust for conquest was central in Arrian's picture of Alexander; it fascinated him, and despite himself a note of admiration underlies his moral censure.

[12] Arr. 7. 1. 5–2. 1 (gymnosophists); 7. 2. 1 (Diogenes); 7. 2. 2–4 = *FGrH* 715 F 34b (Dandamis).

[13] Strabo 15. 1. 68 (718) = *FGrH* 715 F 34a. On this episode see Bosworth 1998: 181–90.

the richness and diversity of his biographical method are widely recognized. The *Life of Alexander* has played an important role in that evaluation. It was the subject of one of the earliest and best modern commentaries (Hamilton 1969), and the programmatic utterance in its preface ('we are not writing histories but Lives') with its insistence on the value of the illustrative anecdote and apophthegm has been widely recognized as the key to the interpretation of the biographies.[14] Now there is less of a tendency to see a strict chronological sequence, more appreciation of the generic construction and the huge range of sources that Plutarch draws upon to illustrate Alexander's character. There is more to be done, of course. We still await a formal cross-comparison between the *Alexander* and its companion bio-graphy, the *Caesar*, to determine the degree of parallelism and the extent to which the interpretation of the one character has affected that of the other. However, there is probably more appreciation of the complexity of Plutarch than of any other source, and it is to be hoped that his rhetorical extravaganza in the first treatise, *On the Fortune or Virtue of Alexander*, will no longer be taken as the basic explanatory text for Alexander's treatment of his subject peoples.[15]

There are related problems in tackling the rest of the tradition. It is agreed (as, with rare exceptions, it has been for the last two centuries) that there is a common source which is drawn upon selectively by Diodorus, Curtius Rufus, Justin's epitome of Pompeius Trogus, and miscellaneous late sources, the most important of which is probably the so-called *Metz Epitome*.[16] This tradition,

---

[14] Plut. *Alex.* 1. 1–2. On the comparable passage in the *Nicias* (1. 5) see Pelling 1992: 10–11, an essay in a collection which repeatedly invokes the opening of the *Alexander* (pp. 56, 109). On Plutarch's literary presentation of Alexander see Mossman 1988.

[15] On this Badian 1958a: 433–40 remains primary. For the continuing influence of Plutarch's rhetoric see Bosworth 1996a: 2–5.

[16] On the history of this discovery, perhaps the single most important contri-bution to the source criticism of Alexander's reign, see Bosworth 1976. There have been protests against the use of the label 'vulgate' (particularly Hammond 1983: 1–3; the term is defended by Bosworth 1988b: 8–9), but even the most confirmed critics of the terminology accept that there is a common tradition, used selectively and in different ways by a large proportion of our extant sources.

usually labelled the Alexander Vulgate, is plausibly ascribed to Cleitarchus of Alexandria, writing towards the end of the fourth century BC.[17] Large segments can be identified, when we have parallel narratives in two or more extant accounts, but there remain intractable problems in assessing the degree to which the material is adapted and embellished. Diodorus has traditionally been treated as the most authentic conduit for the vulgate, since elsewhere he can be shown to have relied on a single source, sometimes over several books. But even he imposes his own style. Throughout his Universal History his vocabulary is uniform and recurrent; he has a preference for specific types of episode, which he describes in remarkably similar terms. Material from completely different sources is presented with the same terminology, and no distinctive stylistic fingerprints survive from the original works.[18] He is also capricious in his selection. Known fragments of Cleitarchus are often not included in his work, and that has encouraged speculation that Cleitarchus was at best one of several sources. But we do not know Diodorus' reasons for choosing his material. It should be remembered that he wrote at a politically volatile period, during the Triumvirate, and there were episodes which he would treat with caution. Cleitarchus mentioned that Alexander received a Roman embassy shortly before his death in 323,[19] but that incident was best omitted by Diodorus, who was writing in the Roman west at a time when the last of the Ptolemaic dynasty was threatening to hold sway in Rome itself (or so Octavian's propaganda asserted).[20] The omission

---

[17] This seems now agreed: cf. Badian 1965; Schachermeyr 1970: 211–24; Hammond 1983: 84–5; Prandi 1996: 66–71.

[18] See the detailed analysis in J. Hornblower 1981: 263–79. Perhaps the best example is his penchant for describing fighting in relays (ἐκ διαδοχῆς) in siege warfare throughout his history. It seems to have been his personal imposition upon his source material (cf. Sinclair 1966). On Diodorus' literary shaping of his sources see particularly Sacks 1994.

[19] Pliny, *NH* 3. 57–8 = *FGrH* 137 F 31, on which see Bosworth 1988a: 85–91. The Romans are not named in the list of foreign embassies reported in Diod. 17.΄113. 1–2 and Just 12. 13. 1 (the corresponding passage in Curtius is not extant).

[20] So, memorably, Hor. *Od.* 1. 37. 5–8 (cf. Prop. 3. 11. 45–6; Ovid, *Met.* 15. 827–8). Cleopatra's favourite prayer was allegedly to dispense justice on the Capitol (Dio 50. 5. 4; cf. Florus 2. 21. 2). In those circumstances it would have been an effective gibe to point out that the Romans had in effect offered submission to Alexander. In the context of the Triumviral period the only options were to rebut

cannot be shown to prove that Diodorus did not use Cleitarchus at this point of his narrative.

What matters is the material that Diodorus shares with Curtius and Justin. But here too there is a tendency to divide the tradition into what is favourable or unfavourable to Alexander; the campaign narrative can be precise, detailed, and informative or sensational and slapdash. This variation in narrative tone encourages the inference that there are two distinct sources at issue, a slovenly, romanticizing scandal-monger (Cleitarchus) and a much more scrupulous and impartial historian, who has been variously identified as Diyllus of Athens or Duris of Samos.[21] But most of these peculiarities can be explained by Diodorus' own style and practice. He tends to abbreviate drastically and capriciously, and he has a marked taste for the sensational. What is more, sober fact and sensationalism can coexist in the same work; the same Cleitarchus could write a vivid and compelling account of the siege of Tyre and an equally vivid description of the visit of Thalestris, the supposed Amazon queen. One could find an inexhaustible hoard of such anomalies in Herodotus or even Polybius. The record of 'great and marvellous deeds' (ἔργα μεγάλα τε καὶ θωμαστά) embraced the plausible and implausible alike.

The most enigmatic and frustrating of all the extant authors is Curtius Rufus, who has probably been more excoriated by modern scholars than any writer on Alexander.[22] His work is shockingly transmitted. The first

the tradition with indignation, as Livy was to rebut the insinuations that Rome would have been conquered by Alexander, or to pass over the detail silently; since Cleitarchus merely mentioned the Romans without elaborating on their presence, it was easy merely to omit the embarrassing detail.

[21] See particularly Hammond 1983 (conclusions 160–5). This has the corollary that Diodorus and Curtius were using the same pair of sources, in which case one must assume that Cleitarchus and Diyllus were a canonical pair in the early Empire. Tarn 1948: ii. 116–22 had used similar arguments to reach the conclusion that Curtius drew directly upon Diodorus. In contrast Prandi, who believes that Diodorus supplemented Cleitarchus with Duris, takes it as axiomatic that Curtius cannot have used exactly the same pair of sources as Diodorus. She argues that Curtius did not use Duris, and consequently uses disagreements between Diodorus and Curtius as a tool to identify passages where Diodorus is supposedly dependent upon Duris (Prandi 1996: 125–6, 138–40).

[22] On Curtius see now the detailed bibliographical survey by Atkinson (Atkinson 1998). See too his commentaries (Atkinson 1980, 1994), and in brief the useful Penguin translation by John Yardley and Waldemar Heckel (1984).

two books are missing; there are numerous lengthy lacunae, and corruptions abound in the truncated corpus that remains. We lack any statement of the historian's aims and methods, and there are only two passages where sources are cited by name: Cleitarchus, Timagenes, and (perhaps indirectly) Ptolemy.[23] Since nothing outside Curtius is known of Timagenes' account of Alexander, this is not particularly helpful.[24] There is no way to isolate his contribution or even to determine whether Curtius used him at all outside the context of Ptolemy and the Malli town. It can be shown that Curtius' narrative follows sources identical or akin to those used by Ptolemy and Arrian, but it is well-nigh impossible to show how they have been adapted and transformed. It is agreed that he had a political agenda of his own, and interpreted the events of Alexander's reign, in particular the disturbances after his death, against the context of his own time under the Roman Empire. Unfortunately Curtius' own date is a notorious crux: practically every emperor from Augustus to Septimius Severus has been suggested at some time as the recipient of Curtius' eulogy in book 10 (some scholars have gone even later, suggesting Constantine or even Theodosius),[25] and it is difficult to give a precise political motivation if one cannot relate the text to any specific period. There is also Curtius' demonstrable penchant for rhetorical exaggeration, his punctuation of the narrative with rhetorical, moralizing comment, and his love of set speeches, long and short. What cannot be denied is that he has used every device at his disposal to make his narrative vivid and sensational. He also has recurrent themes which determine his choice and shaping of material. A recent study by Baynham has shed light on his treatment of prevailing motifs: the omnipresent influence of *fortuna*; kingship and its corollary, the autonomy of the individual in a despotism.[26] The overriding ideas explain the choice of material and much of the

---

[23] Curt. 9. 5. 21 = *FGrH* 137 F 24 (Cleitarchus) and 88 F 3 (Timagenes); Curt. 9. 8. 15 = *FGrH* 137 F 25. See Atkinson 1998: 3458–65 for traditional approaches to source identification.

[24] On the general character of Timagenes' work see Yardley and Heckel 1997, 30–4 and the discussion in Atkinson's essay, Ch. 11 below.

[25] For summaries of the manifold suggestions see Atkinson 1980: 19–57; 1998: 3451–6; Baynham 1998a: 201–19.   [26] Baynham 1998a,

emphasis. That and the traditional historians' preoccupation with dramatic narrative account for many of the apparent anomalies of his account. In Baynham's view Curtius tailors the source material at his disposal to create a wider interpretative pattern, but does not fabricate pseudo-historical material. Others have been less charitable, and Curtius has been credited with deliberate invention to improve his story.[27] Much has still to be done in this area. One needs more of the sober, systematic comparison with Diodorus that Hamilton used in his discussion of the Indian narrative, to determine what Curtius may have added and why.[28] As it is, approaches to Curtius have varied sharply, and the variation is reflected in the differing treatment in several of the essays in this collection.

Other sources too have received rather more attention in recent scholarship. Justin's Epitome has been intensively studied, and it has been established that even Justin makes his own editorial contribution; he does not merely transcribe at random, but imposes his own vocabulary and perhaps at times his own ideas.[29] Consequently, his original, Pompeius Trogus, becomes even more elusive. What we have is a partial, distorted echo of his text, which makes it desperately difficult to establish the sources he used for his account of Alexander (other than the vulgate) and the contemporary pressures which might have determined his treatment of Alexander. Once we take into account the contribution of the intermediary, the problems of historical analysis become sharper and more complex. In the past the tendency was to isolate, or purport to isolate, the original authority for an assertion in the extant sources. One identified the authority, and judged the material on the basis of the authority's reputation—and the reputation was often based upon its attitude to Alexander, favourable or unfavourable. Arrian, based as he was on Ptolemy and Aristobulus, would automatically gain preference if he disagreed with other sources. But this principle ruled out much of the available source tradition.

---

[27] Some instances are given by Atkinson 1998: 3475; see also Baynham 1998a: 5–6.

[28] Hamilton 1977: 129–35; cf. Bosworth 1988a: 9.

[29] Yardley and Heckel 1997: 8–19, 333–43.

With some episodes, notably the arrest, trial, and execution of Philotas, there is a gross imbalance: Arrian's report (3. 26. 1–2), explicitly based on Ptolemy and Aristobulus, is perfunctory and unilluminating, little more than a dogmatic statement of Philotas' guilt. What he deals with in a dozen lines is the subject of a very extended narrative in Curtius which engrosses over twenty pages of Budé text.[30] It is a story of conspiracy and betrayal, replete with names and detail and housing a series of direct speeches which contain material otherwise unattested in the tradition of the reign.[31] This is an extreme case where one cannot simply accept the evidence of the 'good' sources, because it is practically non-existent, and, whatever one may think of individual details in Curtius, one can hardly reject the entire account as fiction.

The most suspect of sources may on occasion record unique and authentic data. One particularly intriguing detail comes from the so-called *Metz Epitome*, a late (tenth-century) manuscript, which preserves part of an epitome of a history of Alexander's reign. The style of the *Epitome* is late, best attributed to the fourth or early fifth century AD, but its unknown author was digesting a much earlier history which largely followed the vulgate tradition common to Diodorus, Curtius, and Justin.[32] On occasion it records details which are not attested elsewhere. For instance, it states that Alexander lost a son borne by Rhoxane while his river fleet was being built on the Hydaspes.[33] This is not attested elsewhere, but it is plausible enough. The incident is placed late

[30] Curt. 6. 7. 1–11. 40. Other sources are less detailed, though in most cases more informative than Arrian (Diod. 17. 79–80; Plut. *Alex.* 48. 1–49. 13; Justin 12. 5. 2–3 (garbled)).

[31] In particular the detail that Philotas gave his sister in marriage to Attalus, Alexander's bitter enemy (Curt. 6. 9. 17). This is accepted in standard reference works (e.g. Berve 1926: ii. 94, 298; Heckel 1992, 23). On the political implications see Badian, Ch. 3 below, p. 63, who rightly accepts the evidence of Curtius while conceding (n. 24) that the context is highly suspect. 'That the speeches at Philotas' trial are not authentic does not need to be argued.'

[32] See particularly Baynham 1995, with references to earlier literature. The Teubner text, by P. H. Thomas, is unfortunately prone to adventurous emendation. A translation and commentary is being prepared by J. C. Yardley and E. J. Baynham.

[33] *Metz Epit.* 70. The incident is usually ignored in histories of the reign, but it was picked up and accepted as fact by Berve 1926: ii. 347, no. 688.

in 326 BC, about eighteen months after the marriage, and it comes at a juncture where the rest of the source tradition is very thin. Alexander was stationary around the Hydaspes between September and November, but Arrian has no record of anything between Alexander's arrival at the Hydaspes and the departure of the fleet.[34] In contrast the Vulgate account, common to Curtius, Diodorus, and the *Epitome*, has a series of events; the arrival of reinforcements from the west, the building of the fleet (with rough agreement on numbers), and the reconciliation of the Indian kings, Porus and Taxiles.[35] The details are consistent, but not every episode is recorded in every source; Diodorus, for instance, has nothing about the reconciliation. Now, the *Metz Epitome* places the death of Alexander's son between the completion of the fleet and the reconciliation, and it seems that it was part of the so-called vulgate, an authentic detail passed over by Diodorus and Curtius. There is no obvious reason for the invention of a fictitious son of Alexander at this stage, and the death of a child in infancy or at birth may have seemed too unimportant to warrant notice in Curtius and Diodorus, in an age of high infant mortality.

Our most effective tool is critical cross-comparison. If we cannot accept or reject material on the basis of the reputation of its supposed source, we are faced with a much more complex exercise, examining the whole range of evidence in detail, assessing the extent of agreement, isolating the disagreements, and looking for explanations of the rejected variant traditions. Such explanations are rarely simple; we may be faced with deliberate distortion in the primary, contemporary tradition, misunderstanding by a secondary writer, adaptation and modification for purely literary purposes—or most often a combination. One of the most complex problems (and one which surfaces repeatedly in these

[34] Alexander arrives at the Hydaspes towards the end of the monsoon season, and can repair the rain-damaged buildings at Bucephala and Nicaea (Arr. 5. 29. 5); this was around the rising of Arcturus (Strabo 15. 1. 17 (691) = Aristobulus *FGrH* 139 F 35). Arrian then digresses to describe Alexander's earlier investigations on the course of the Indus, and then moves directly to the start of the Ocean voyage. Apart from the funeral of Coenus (6. 2. 1) there is no reference to any event by the Hydaspes.

[35] Diod. 17. 95. 4–5; Curt. 9. 3. 21–2; *Metz Epit.* 70.

essays)³⁶ is Alexander's burning of Persepolis. As is well known, there are two conflicting traditions, one regarding the conflagration as an act of policy, vengeance for the sack of Athens in 480,³⁷ and the other as a virtual accident, the culmination of a drinking party in which the Athenian courtesan Thais led the Macedonian revellers in an orgy of impromptu arson.³⁸ There are two main directions in which the argument can be directed. The first is to accept the role of Thais,³⁹ which is explicitly attributed to Cleitarchus, and can be interpreted as in part a tribute to Thais herself. She was one of the more powerful figures in the early Ptolemaic court; her children by Ptolemy were important pieces in the dynastic game by 308 BC.⁴⁰ She was present at the conflagration, and Cleitarchus could make her the chief agent, avenging the injuries of her city.⁴¹ In that case the other tradition must be interpreted as apologetic. The wanton destruction was seen as an embarrassment,⁴² and Ptolemy may not have welcomed Thais' association with it. Instead he (and Aristobulus) represented the destruction as a conscious plan, one which provoked dissent with Parmenio, who is shown presenting rational arguments to counter the king's dogmatic insistence upon vengeance, an insistence which even Arrian (3. 18. 12) finds irrational. The second approach is to accept that Alexander did indeed destroy Persepolis out of policy, and that the exchange with Parmenio represents genuine disagreement on the Macedonian staff. In that case Cleitarchus' account of Thais'

---

³⁶ Flower, Ch. 4, pp. 113–15; Fredricksmeyer, Ch. 5, pp. 145–50; Carney, Ch. 9, p. 265.

³⁷ Arr. 3. 18. 12; Strabo 15. 3. 6 (730).

³⁸ Athen. 13. 576d = Cleitarchus, *FGrH* 137 F 11; Plut. *Alex.* 38; Diod. 17. 72; Curt. 5. 7. 2–11.

³⁹ So, for instance, Schachermeyr 1973: 289–90, and most recently Bloedow 1995.

⁴⁰ According to Athenaeus (13. 576e) she was actually married (ἐγαμήθη) to Ptolemy (Plut. *Alex.* 38. 2 describes her simply as his *hetaira*). At all events her children by Ptolemy were figures of distinction. A daughter, Eirene, was married to Eunostus, king of Cypriot Soli (Athen. 576e; cf. Seibert 1967: 77–8); one son, Leontiscus, ranked alongside Ptolemy's brother, Menelaus, among the Ptolemaic captives who fell into Demetrius' hands after the battle of Salamis (Justin 15. 2. 7); and the other, Lagus, won the chariot race at the Arcadian Lycaea while his father held court at Corinth in the summer of 308 (*SIG*³ 314, B V, lines 8–10).

⁴¹ So Plut. *Alex.* 38. 2–4; Diod. 17. 72. 2; Curt. 5. 7. 3.

⁴² As suggested by Curt. 5. 7. 10–11 (so Plut. *Alex.* 38. 8; see also Arr. 6. 30. 1).

actions could be seen as a colourful fabrication.[43] Whichever line of argument one takes there are secondary arguments to be deployed. If the burning was policy, what was behind it? Was Alexander symbolizing the end of the Persian Empire or declaring to the world at large that vengeance was a serious issue, not to be compromised?[44] And why would Cleitarchus give Thais a role that she never played? On the other hand, if one accepts Cleitarchus' version, one has to explain why the burning was still an embarrassment some thirty years after the event, and why the fictitious debate between Alexander and Parmenion arose. The problem is the lack of a firm starting point, the difficulty of excluding anything as a priori impossible; could Cleitarchus, writing under Ptolemy, have given a totally false report about Thais, and could Ptolemy (if he is the source of Arrian) have retailed a debate which he and many others knew was unhistorical? One is faced with an intricate balance of probability, and not surprisingly judgements about what is possible and probable vary dramatically. There is no simple key to interpretation, and as a result there is no consensus. Indeed, given the state of the evidence, it is unlikely that a satisfactory resolution of the problem will ever be achieved.

There is another important point, often overlooked in traditional scholarship. Alexander's death does not form an absolute divide. His reign cannot be studied in isolation from what follows. That is clearly the case with the Lamian War, where the disturbances created by Alexander's decree restoring Greek exiles escalated at the news of his death and led to full-scale war within a matter of weeks. Similarly the tensions and rivalries generated by the court intrigues under Alexander erupted into open conflict, first during the turbulent political settlement at Babylon and then during the first civil war, when Perdiccas' extravagant dynastic ambitions drove Craterus and Antipater to war. One is constantly looking back to Alexander's reign to explain what happened after his death and conversely interpreting his reign by reference to later events. It is the main weakness of Helmut Berve's

[43] So, for instance, Wilcken 1932: 145; Tarn 1948: ii. 48; Pearson 1960: 218–19; Hammond 1992: 363.

[44] For the various suggestions see Bosworth 1980*a*: 331–2; Atkinson 1994: 120–4; Chapters 4 and 5 by Flower and Fredricksmeyer.

still indispensable prosopography that it closes with Alexander and has the briefest of references to events after his death, and the strength of Waldemar Heckel's study of Alexander's marshals (Heckel 1992) is that it pays particular attention to the period of transition, the years between 323 and 319, when the dynastic struggle was at its height. It can be argued that the enmities that determined the wars of the period also affected the historical tradition. Service under Alexander was a potent element in dynastic propaganda. Alexander's generals had helped acquire world empire, and they considered themselves entitled to a share in it, the share commensurate with their achievements.[45] If we examine the historical record, it is not surprising that Ptolemy bulks so large; Cleitarchus, the source of the vulgate tradition, wrote under his regime, and Ptolemy himself was the main source of Arrian. It is not surprising that there is a constant stress on his exploits, a consistent insinuation that many of the great successes of the reign were directly due to his efforts.[46] On the other hand his enemies in the civil wars, notably Perdiccas, receive very grudging mention, and there are strong indications that some of the rare military setbacks of the reign were laid at his door.[47] Such animus is not easy to detect, and the evidence is far from uncontrovertible. However, it is a striking fact that the figures who are most prominent in the military narrative (apart from Ptolemy himself) are men who were dead within a few years of Alexander himself: Hephaestion, Craterus, and Leonnatus. Practically nothing is recorded of Ptolemy's contemporaries and rivals, Lysimachus and Seleucus,[48] despite the fact that one was a

[45] The classic instance is Seleucus' declaration to Antigonus that Babylonia was his by right in return for his services to the Macedonians during Alexander's lifetime (Diod. 19. 55. 4). Shortly before Antigonus had had problems removing Peithon from Media 'for it was no easy matter to arrest a man by force who had gained preferment while serving under Alexander' (Diod. 19. 46. 3). Cassander, who like Antigonus, played no role in the conquest of Asia, faced the same dilemma in removing Aristonous, 'seeing that he was respected because of the preferment he had received from Alexander' (Diod. 19. 51. 1). Both Peithon and Aristonous had been Bodyguards under Alexander, and it gave them dangerous prestige.

[46] See the recent discussion in Bosworth 1996a: 41–53.

[47] The fundamental discussion is Errington 1969; see also Bosworth 1976: 9–14. For more sceptical views see Roisman 1984; Hammond and Walbank 1988: 29, 61; Hammond 1993: 166–9.

[48] Lysimachus is mentioned at the crossing of the Hydaspes and, shortly after, at

royal Bodyguard and the other a hypaspist commander, both
holding positions which would keep them constantly in the
front. This is deliberately selective treatment by a royal
author who was not disposed to publicize the achievements
of competing dynasts, even dynasts who were for many years
his allies against Antigonus.

Ptolemy has deeply affected both the history and the
historical tradition of the period. He was also, it seems,
influential in devising the propaganda which evolved over
the centuries into the Alexander Romance. The inspiration
was the gossip and slander which circulated in the aftermath
of Alexander's death. The prolonged fever which took him
off after ten days was unsurprisingly attributed to poison
administered by the family of Antipater, which was in deep
disfavour during the last months of the reign, and the
rumours were later exploited to discredit the regent and his
sons. Olympias was to desecrate the grave of Iolaus, who had
been Alexander's cupbearer and, as such, was the prime
target of the calumny.[49] In the vulgate these stories are
recounted with some reserve, as though Cleitarchus was
unwilling to present them as fact but wished them to be
known and to circulate.[50] The most elaborate treatment of
the scandal is in the so-called *Liber de Morte*, an extensive
account of Alexander's last days with a full reproduction of
his purported testament.[51] This story ends all versions of the
Alexander Romance, and despite the deeply corrupt textual

the siege of Sangala (Arr. 5. 13. 1, 24. 5), while Seleucus only figures at the
Hydaspes, where he is attested close to Alexander (Arr. 5. 13. 1, 4; 16. 3). I would
not agree with a recent biographer 'that Lysimachus only reached military prominence in the latter years of the expedition' (Lund 1992: 5; so Heckel 1992: 274:
'Lysimachos attained his rank before Alexander's accession, his fame and power
after, and as a result of, Alexander's death.')

[49] Diod. 19. 11. 8; Plut. *Alex.* 77. 2. The orator Hypereides had earlier voted
honours for him at Athens for his part in the alleged poisoning ([Plut.] *Vit. X Orat.*
849f).

[50] Diod. 17. 118. 1 (φασὶ γάρ); Curt. 10. 10. 14 ('credidere plerique'); Justin 12.
13. 10–14. 8 has the same story, but he chooses to present it as fact, suppressed by
the affected parties (so Curt. 10. 10. 18). Onesicritus had already written that
Alexander died of poison, but he shrank from naming the conspirators (*Metz Epit.*
97 = *FGrH* 134 F 37).

[51] The document was preserved on the same manuscript as the *Metz Epitome*,
and standard editions run them together with sequential paragraphing. However,
there has never been any doubt that two separate and unrelated documents are at
issue (cf. Merkelbach 1977: 122; Baynham 1995: 62–3).

transmission there is substantial agreement in detail.[52] Although our extant texts come from late antiquity, there is little doubt that the nucleus of what became the *Liber de Morte* originated close to Alexander's death. Some of the material recurs on Egyptian papyri of a relatively early date,[53] and the narrative contains traces of the propaganda war which followed Alexander's death. Unfortunately the details are controversial, and it has hitherto proved impossible to anchor the document in any one historical context. However, Ptolemy appears in an extraordinarily favourable light, and the provisions of the testament can be shown to favour his interests and damage those of his dynastic enemies. Two of the contributions to this volume[54] examine the premiss that the propaganda that resulted in the *Liber de Morte* originated in Ptolemy's court around 309 BC, and that it was designed simultaneously to present him as the champion of the deceased Alexander and his family and to denigrate his enemies at that time, Antigonus and Cassander. Ptolemy, then, was circulating material which presented as fact what Cleitarchus had retailed as rumour— and which in his history (written in a different political context) he was to ignore or reject. For good and ill, in fact and fiction, our view of Alexander has been primarily determined by material emanating from him or his court.

The contributions to this volume represent almost all the approaches which have been described. They form a sequence, beginning with political analysis, progressing to the historical interpretation of iconography and literary propaganda, and ending with issues of historiography. Bosworth's essay on Alexander and Cortés sets the scene. It presents an interpretative model, arguing that the historical tradition of the conquest of Mexico in the early sixteenth century can shed light on the actions of Alexander in the far east (and vice versa), and also introduces some basic issues of

---

[52] The text is printed in composite form by Merkelbach 1977: 253–83, and the separate versions are presented sequentially in Heckel 1988: 96–107. Stoneman 1991: 148–55 supplies an English translation.

[53] *P. Vindob.* 31954 (first cent. BC) contains the same material as *Metz Epit.* 116 (Merkelbach 1977: 151, 166; Baynham 1998*b*: 113–14).

[54] Bosworth, Ch. 7, and Baynham, Ch. 8.

imperial ideology—attitudes towards the subject peoples
and justification of conquest. The dark side of monarchy is
further explored in Badian's detailed examination of conspiracies at the Macedonian and Persian courts. The conflicting source material is analysed on the basis of cumulative
probability, and a pattern gradually emerges: Alexander
systematically exploited the tensions at his court, using
conspiracies, both genuine and fictitious, to suppress opposition (in a manner only too reminiscent of the present
century), while Darius was acutely conscious of the ever-
present and real danger of conspiracy. He ultimately fell
victim to a plot by his own nobles which he had virtually
created by the very measures he had taken to prevent such
intrigues (the noble hostages whom he had taken with him
on campaign fell into Alexander's hands with disastrous
consequences). Alexander, on the other hand, survived and
prospered, the supreme political puppet master.

From political manœuvring we progress to ideology.
Flower's contribution examines the political impact of panhellenism, the principle that Greek *poleis* should reconcile
their differences and turn their united forces against Persia.
A new examination of the evidence presents the case that
panhellenism was a more potent ideal than has been recognized, and that it was far more than a pretext for war in the
eyes of both Philip and Alexander. It was the ultimate
justification for the burning of Persepolis, and, contrary to
what is usually thought, it continued to be an element of
policy throughout Alexander's reign, not incompatible with
the promotion of selected Iranian nobles. Panhellenism and
'Verschmelzungspolitik'[55] could coexist, even in the political
philosophy of Isocrates, and parallels could be drawn with
the actions of Agesilaus earlier in the century. Fredricksmeyer by contrast provides us with a deep analysis of
Alexander's concept of kingship. He attacks a firmly held
view that Alexander assumed the Achaemenid monarchy
and presented himself as Darius' successor. On the contrary,
he aimed at something higher and more ecumenical, a

---

[55] Meaning literally 'Policy of Fusion', a term invented to encapsulate
Alexander's supposed plan of blending together Macedonians and Persians as a
ruling elite (cf. Bosworth 1980*b*).

kingdom of Asia which transcended the boundaries of the old Persian Empire. On this reading Alexander had evolved the concept as early as 332. He consistently promoted himself as King of all Asia, both replacing and superseding the Great King, and his destruction of Persepolis gave a clear signal that he considered the Persian Empire to be extinct.[56] Once again the orientalizing traits at Alexander's court can be reconciled with the larger picture. It was necessary that the Persians felt some affinity with the new regime, and so Alexander adopted dress and ceremonial which would appeal to them, but the orientalism stopped short of the full assumption of Persian court ceremonial. It was part of the larger picture, the absolute and unrestricted Kingship of Asia.

Palagia's contribution marks a transition from purely literary evidence to the interpretation of visual propaganda. She begins by arguing for the basic authenticity of Diodorus' description of Hephaestion's pyre, which she compares with the late fourth-century funerary pyre at Cypriot Salamis. The description of the animal hunt frieze in Diodorus becomes the starting point for an investigation of hunting scenes in early Hellenistic art. Such scenes are not attested in the western Greek world before Alexander, and it is argued that they were inspired by the epic hunts which Alexander staged in the Persian game reserves. That leads in turn to a reinterpretation of the famous fresco on the façade of Tomb II at Vergina. The hunting scene there portrayed belongs to an Asian context and dates to the reign of Alexander. From that perspective it is compatible with the solemn reburial which Cassander accorded Philip Arrhidaeus, Eurydice, and Cynnane in 316 BC, and can be interpreted as a joint commemoration of Arrhidaeus himself and the family of Cassander. The point of reference has been changed. The lion hunt theme establishes a date for the fresco no earlier than Alexander's eastern conquests, and once that is accepted, the supporting evidence that Tomb II post-dates Alexander becomes irresistible. Bosworth's chap-

---

[56] This reading, it should be emphasized, is not in formal contradiction with Flower. Both interpretations can be accepted, and it could be argued that the conflagration was simultaneously the triumph of panhellenism and the end of the Achaemenid monarchy.

ter on the *Liber de Morte* adopts a similar method. Previous attempts to give a political context to the document (in 321 or 317 BC) had resulted in internal contradictions which could only be resolved on the assumption that it was heavily interpolated. However, these contradictions are largely resolved if we accept a precise dating to the year 309/8, when Ptolemy was paying court to Alexander's sister, Cleopatra, and championing the liberty of the Greeks against joint threats from Cassander and Antigonus. He is represented as the true heir of Alexander, the natural successor to the kingship after the murder of Alexander's son and the destined husband of Cleopatra. The propaganda can then be seen to promote Ptolemy's regal aspirations, which can be traced in literary and epigraphic evidence long before his formal assumption of the diadem. Baynham's chapter also addresses the *Liber de Morte*, and shows that the sensational portent with which it begins makes perfect political sense in the years after the death of Alexander IV but can be fitted to no other historical context. What is more, the portent fits nicely into the general tradition of the omens of Alexander's death and displays some knowledge of Babylonian mantic procedure. It comes in a literary context reminiscent of Xenophon's historical romance, the *Cyropaedia*, and the anonymous author can be seen to be working simultaneously in a literary and propagandist tradition, creating a novel with a strongly political purpose.

The remaining chapters tackle issues of source criticism. Carney deals with the complex relationship between fact and reported fact. She addresses two recurrent themes, the series of exchanges between Alexander and his senior general, Parmenio, and the three dramatic occasions when the king isolated himself from his troops. Here the analysis reaches contrasting conclusions, but in both cases there is an interplay between literature and life. The tradition of a hostile exchange between Alexander and Parmenio may have originated in the propagandist history of Callisthenes, who necessarily treated Parmenio as an opposition figure, but it has been elaborated by later writers who had their own propagandist objectives or were deliberately casting Parmenio in the Herodotean role of the warning adviser. The whole tradition is fundamentally warped and poisoned, and it is dangerous to accept any of the episodes as historical. On the other hand, the interplay between Alexander and his troops may have been affected by literary models: he, the new Achilles, was sulking in his tent, and his men reacted in a hysterical mode which recalls the figure of the excluded lover. Here the sources underscore the Homeric parallels, but the literary embellishment is justifiable; it enlarges on traits which were actually present. Alexander acted as Achilles, and the sources supply a counterpoint of allusion and rhetoric. In contrast, Billows focuses on a single historian, Polybius, whose references to Alexander have received very cursory attention in the past. However, his treatment of the king is interesting in that it is sober, free from apologia, recognizing atrocities like the sack of Thebes while keeping a generally favourable view of Alexander's generalship and character. The perspective is totally different from that of the extant Alexander sources, and several possible influences may be traced: the view of Alexander as the favourite of fortune may go back to Demetrius of Phalerum and his treatise *Peri Tyches*, and some of the historical detail could be ascribed to Hieronymus of Cardia, whose monumental history of the Successors repeatedly reached back into the reign of Alexander.

The final contribution by Atkinson takes the spotlight away from Alexander and concentrates upon the concerns of the primary historians. No writer can reconstruct the past without being influenced by his or her contemporary environment. That was clearly the case in antiquity. Atkinson shows how the interpretation of Alexander's reign was influenced by the wisdom of hindsight and the classical theory of the transmission of Empire, which began with Herodotus and was extended as each successive imperial power (Mede, Persian, Macedonian, and Roman) bit the dust. The interpretation can be in macrocosm, as with the sequence of empires, or in microcosm, when the actions of dominant contemporary individuals can be seen to be foreshadowed. In particular Curtius' description of the roles of Arrhidaeus and Perdiccas at Babylon is highly coloured by his experience of political intrigue and judicial murder in the early Empire. The past thereby becomes a vehicle for indirect and oblique comment upon the present. With that we come full circle. The history of Alexander remains anchored to the literary sources, and each student must establish his or her attitude to the extant tradition. The papers in this volume provide a rich variety of approaches and collectively, it is to be hoped, they make it more feasible to recapture something of that most elusive of figures, the historical Alexander.

2

A Tale of Two Empires: Hernán Cortés and Alexander the Great

BRIAN BOSWORTH

Imperialism is a strangely uniform phenomenon. The modes of acquiring empire tend to be similar, as do the arguments justifying its acquisition. That is not surprising. Imperial powers have a tendency to look over their shoulders at their predecessors, emulate the achievements of the past, and absorb the traditional philosophies of conquest. Cicero on the just war or Aristotle on natural slavery were texts familiar to the expansionists of the Renaissance and early modern periods.[1] The ancients provided convenient doctrines of racial superiority, which could be buttressed by appeals to the divinity. A typical example of complacent optimism is provided by a certain Daniel Denton, who observed in 1670 'that where the English come to settle a Divine Hand makes way for them by removing or cutting off the Indians, whether by wars one with the other or by some raging, mortal disease'.[2] God, then, was on the side of the English, and they could provide time-hallowed justification for their presence in North America. But can the reverse process be

---

[1] On these concepts and their exploitation see in general Clavedescher-Thurlemann 1985; Russell 1975, esp. 4–20; and Pagden 1995, esp. 19–28. In the immediate context of this chapter there is a fascinating collection of material in Hanke 1959: 44–73; the great debate at Valladolid in 1550 between Juan Ginés de Sepúlveda and Bartolomé de Las Casas focused on the twin issues of natural slavery and the just war. The theory was invoked from the early days of conquest by the formal reading of the *Requerimiento* (see below, n. 76) before battle was joined (Thomas 1993: 71–5; Bosworth 1996a: 159–61), and the doctrine of natural slavery underlies Cortés' attitude to the Chichimecas (see below, pp. 40–1).

[2] Daniel Denton, *A Brief Description of New York: Formerly Called New Netherlands* (London, 1670), 7, quoted by Pagden 1995: 105. A few years later John Archdale of Southern Carolina was to congratulate the English for shedding little Indian blood in contrast with the Spaniards: 'the Hand of God was eminently seen in thining the Indians to make room for the English . . . it at other times pleased Almighty God to send unusual sicknesses amongst them, as the Smallpox, to lessen their numbers' (quoted by Hanke 1959: 100).

justified? Can we, so to speak, call upon the New World to explain or illuminate the empires of the past? There are indeed similarities, notably between the conquests of Alexander the Great and those of the Spaniards in Central America. In both cases the spectacular campaigns of a handful of years changed the political map of the world. Alexander invaded Asia Minor in the spring of 334 BC, and a mere four years later he had overrun the greater part of the Near East, occupied the central capitals of the Persian Empire, and annexed the accumulated treasure of the imperial people he defeated. As a direct result of the campaigns the world from Macedon in the north to Egypt in the south and to Afghanistan in the east came under the control of a Graeco-Roman elite. Similarly between 1519 and 1522 a group of Spaniards under Hernán Cortés extended the rule of the Spanish crown from the east coast of Mexico over almost all Central America. They occupied and destroyed the Aztec capital and exploited its wealth to sustain the pretensions of the Spanish monarchs to domination in Europe. An élite of Spanish settlers moved in, supported by vast encomiendas, and maintained their domination for almost the length of the Hellenistic monarchies.

So far the similarities, if roughly drawn, are clear enough. The same can be said for the sources. For the Spanish conquest there is a rich tradition, predominantly from the conquerors' perspective. We have the Narrative Letters (*Cartas de Relación*) in which Cortés himself justified his actions to his master, Charles V.[3] We have several other memoirs from participants, notably the remarkable work by Bernal Díaz del Castillo, written at the ripe old age of 76, some fifty years after the events, and significantly entitled *The True History of the Conquest of New Spain*.[4] (A work that so openly professes its truth one automatically suspects

[3] Translated and edited by Pagden 1986; the parallel with Ptolemy is drawn by Bosworth 1996a: 34–5.

[4] *Historia verdadera de la Nueva España*, written c.1555 and published over 75 years later. The only full English translation is that of Alfred Maudslay (5 vols.: 1908–16); a slightly abbreviated version of the narrative to the fall of Tenochtitlan is also available (Maudslay 1928), as is a more truncated Penguin Classics version (Cohen 1963). One should also mention the largely derivative work of Cortés' secretary, Francisco López de Gómara (Simpson 1965), and other writings of the early Conquistadors collected in de Fuentes 1993.

of falsehood: think of Lucian.) All this was supplemented by documentation from the royal investigations into the conduct of Cortés and his lieutenant, Pedro de Alvarado.[5] There are also Mexican versions of the conquest, admittedly written under the supervision of Spanish priests, but which, however dimly, represent the perspective of the conquered people.[6] Nothing comparable exists from the period of Alexander, no testimony direct or indirect from the peoples he conquered. On the surface there appears a rich vein of contemporary memoirs, accounts by Alexander's lieutenants and humbler contemporaries. Ptolemy, Aristobulus, Nearchus, Onesicritus, and Cleitarchus all wrote significant works, but all are known solely through derivative authors writing centuries later, when the objective was literary embellishment, not factual reportage.[7] We may suspect bias and misinformation, but it is rare that we have solid evidence. The historical record of the Spanish conquest can perhaps be used as an explanatory matrix, showing how historians of the first generation differ in their record of fact, what they suppress for their convenience and how they slant the narrative to suit their political interests. Similar motives are at work, and the subject matter is often startlingly pertinent to the history of Alexander.

We may begin, as is appropriate, with the leaders of the conquests, Alexander of Macedon and Cortés of Castile. Both were complex characters, enigmatic and elusive to contemporaries and posterity alike, and both quickly became less the stuff of history than symbols of national aspiration, to be evoked in an amazing range of contexts. Anthony Pagden has written of the many personae which Cortés has assumed in modern writings: 'the soldier-scholar of the Renaissance, a bandy-legged syphilitic liar and, most improbable of all, a humane idealist aiding an oppressed people against tyranny'.[8] If one substitutes 'alcoholic'

[5] On the Spanish archives see the checklist in Thomas 1993: 784–90.

[6] Thomas 1993: 774–84, drawing upon the full bibliography by José Alcina Franch, *Códices Mexicanos* (Madrid, 1992). There is a useful anthology of material in Leon-Portilla 1962.

[7] For brief description of the source tradition of Alexander's reign see Bosworth 1988a: 1–15; Bosworth 1988b: 295–300. Pearson 1960 and Pédech 1984 give more extended accounts of the first-generation historians.

[8] Pagden 1986: xlv.

for 'syphilitic', one has a fair, if incomplete, spectrum of modern views of Alexander, the humanitarian champion of Hellenic culture, the promoter of the brotherhood of mankind, the sinister Machiavellian schemer, the alcohol-drenched debauchee. One creates one's picture, and the sources, if selectively exploited, will confirm it—provided that one ignores the vast bulk of the evidence. The undeniable similarity comes in the career of conquest. Despite the differences in their ages (Cortés was 35, already older than Alexander at his death, when he set foot in Mexico) and the size of their armies, both had spectacular and largely unbroken successes against much larger forces. Our sources are explicit. For Bernal Díaz 'the plain name Cortés was as highly respected in Spain and throughout the Indies as the name of Alexander in Macedonia or those of Julius Caesar, Pompey and Scipio among the Romans or Hannibal in Carthage'.[9] Alexander and Cortés alike were endued with an aura of invincibility, and both exploited the concept for self-glorification. The Macedonian king made victory inseparable from his person. The great silver decadrachms which he struck to commemorate his Indian victories depict him holding the thunderbolt of Zeus and receiving a crown from the hands of personified Victory.[10] Even at Athens his erstwhile enemies proposed erecting a statue to him as god invincible; they had an informed opinion of what would appeal to him and framed their motion accordingly.[11] Unfortunately for Cortés the immense proprietary interest of the Catholic Church prevented his claiming godhead, but he made the most of his invincibility. Just before his death he was portrayed with his arms as Marquis of the Valley of Oaxaca, and the legend proclaims him *dux invictissimus*.[12]

[9] Ch. 19: Maudslay 1908–16: i. 72; Cohen 1963: 47.

[10] For discussion and bibliography (to which add Lane Fox 1996; Le Rider 1995–6: 856) see Bosworth 1996*a*: 6–8, 166–9. The epithet ἀνίκητος was particularly associated with Alexander's purported forefather, Heracles (Tyrtaeus F 8. 1 Diehl; Diod. 8. 9. 1; App. *BC* 2. 76). That helps explain Alexander's interest in it from his earliest years.

[11] Hyp *Dem*. col. 32; cf. Din. 1. 94; Athen. 6. 251b; Ael. *VH* 5. 12. On the background see Badian 1981: 54–9, Bosworth 1988*b*: 288–9; Habicht 1995: 41–6 and the rationalizing interpretation of Cawkwell 1994: 301–6. The hero cult of Hephaestion, which was contemporaneous and apparently mandatory, is now attested on a 4th-cent. relief from Macedonia (Voutiras 1990).

[12] Reproduced in Pagden 1986: 7 and Thomas 1993: 269. Díaz (ch. 212:

His invincibility was truly superlative. The sceptics might point to the *Noche triste*, the night of sorrows (1 July 1520) when Cortés had to fight his way out of the Mexican capital with the loss of at least 500 of his Castilian troops (he admits to no more than 150).[13] They might also point to Alexander's first disastrous attempt to storm the passes into Persia, when his phalanx was smashed by missiles from the hillsides and withdrew demoralized, leaving its dead in the narrows.[14] However, both disasters were retrieved, Alexander's in a matter of days, that of Cortés only by the capture and destruction of Tenochtitlan over a year later. In the long view they could both be considered unconquered, and their military abilities are beyond question.

We can extend and deepen the investigation by the study of two parallel episodes, which to me are remarkably similar. Both Alexander and Cortés were prone to *folies de grandeurs*, and in both cases it led to near disaster and massive suffering. In the autumn of 325 Alexander returned from what is now southern Pakistan. His elephants and some of the heavy infantry and veterans he had sent on an alternative route through Afghanistan and southern Iran, while he took the bulk of the army, at least 30,000 strong, through the bleakly inhospitable Makran. It was an appalling hardship, a march of 750 kilometres over sixty days, plagued by sand drifts, monsoonal floods in the east, and thirst and famine in the west; and the army which limped into the Gedrosian capital of Pura had eaten its baggage animals and was reduced to the last stages of exhaustion.[15] The parallel in the career of Cortés is his march through Honduras. It began in October 1525 and took at least six months to cover a distance

Maudslay 1908–16: v. 301) reports Cortés' boast to Charles V 'that he had such valiant and brave captains and comrades that he believed none more spirited had been heard of in past history' and adds that he, Díaz, was present 'fighting in more battles than the great Emperor Julius Caesar'.

[13] On Cortés' figures see Pagden 1986: 139, 479 n. 94. By contrast, Díaz claims that over 860 soldiers were killed or sacrificed in the retreat (ch. 128: Maudslay ii. 255; Cohen 1963: 305); even the eulogistic Gómara admits to the death of 450 Spaniards and 4,000 Indian auxiliaries (Simpson 1965: 221).

[14] Diod. 17. 68. 2–3; Curt. 5. 3. 17–23 (cf. 22: *invictus ante eam diem fuerat*); cf. Arr. 3. 18. 3 (less dramatic); Polyaen. 4. 3. 27.

[15] See the recent discussion in Bosworth 1996a: 166–85, with the earlier excellent article of Schepens 1989.

comparable to Alexander's passage of Gedrosia. The hardships were also comparable: starvation and exhaustion predominating. Cortés' forces were often stranded for weeks at a time, while his Indian followers were impressed into engineering works, constructing vast log bridges and causeways at great human cost. Not surprisingly Cortés himself minimizes the hardships. In his detailed Fifth Letter he insinuates that the forces with him were minute (93 horsemen and some 30 foot soldiers) and emphasizes the care with which he provisioned the expedition, sending a small fleet of supply ships to the Tabasco River.[16] He somewhat weakens the effect by adding that, as his road lay inland, the supplies were of very little use. In his description of the march he does not deny that there were problems with hunger, particularly while building the bridge over the San Pedro Mártir,[17] but they were promptly relieved once his forces crossed over into Acalan. Hunger began in earnest only when he reached his destination at Nito and had to care for the handful of destitute and starving Spanish settlers whom he found there[18]—and it was the herd of pigs which Cortés had collected for the journey (or the few survivors) that prevented disaster. He had prepared carefully for the march, acquiring maps from the chiefs of Tabasco and Xicalango,[19]

[16] Pagden 1986: 342–3. Pagden 514 n. 15 observes that the numbers are wrong, but suggests that the copyist was at fault. But 93 is a remarkably precise figure for a copyist's error. It is more likely, I think, that Cortés deliberately minimizes the losses and stresses that he had the prudence to take 150 horses, allowing for remounts.

[17] Pagden 1986: 360: the Spaniards fatigued by having eaten nothing but the roots of trees, but an abundance of food to be found in Acalan. The bridge-building, then wholly delegated to the Indian auxiliaries, caused a large number of deaths.

[18] Pagden 1986: 387 'we had eaten no bread for eight days when we arrived in Tanyha'. For conditions at Nito see 388–90, esp. 390: 'if it had not been for some few pigs left over from the journey . . . we should all have ended our days there'. Gómara (Simpson 1965: 366) repeats Cortés' claims, as he does in his description of the bridge-building (351–2); his narrative is scarcely more than a literary elaboration.

[19] Pagden 1986: 340. Cortés is vague, referring to a map of the whole country, indicating where the Spanish settlement would be found. Gómara (Simpson 1965: 345) dutifully represents the map as covering the whole route from Xicalango to Naco and Nito and extending as far afield as Nicaragua. Cortés himself admits that the map only gave general directions, since the natives travelled by water and did not know which route to take overland.

and it was his initiative which ensured that the route was followed even though the natives professed ignorance of it.

Díaz, however, provides a complete contrast.[20] For all his admiration of Cortés his resentment gives his narrative an acid edge. The march was folly, ruined by Cortés' obstinacy in ignoring the advice of his lieutenants (including Díaz himself) who advocated a direct route through the Sierras.[21] His detailed account reveals that Cortés took over 250 Spaniards, including most of the settlers in the town of Coatzacoalcos, who were forced against their will to join the expedition[22]—and their absence led directly to a native revolt. Cortés' preparations are denigrated; his famous map described the lands only as far as Acalan,[23] and within a few days the expedition was lost; the road they laboriously cut went round in a circle and after two days intersected itself ('when Cortés saw this he was like to burst with rage'). The situation was hardly improved when the two guides he had brought with the expedition disappeared, and it transpired that they had been eaten by the starving Indian auxiliaries, some three thousand of whom followed in his train: Cortés showed his displeasure at the atrocity by having one of the culprits burned alive.[24] In Díaz' account starvation is an ever-present threat. A few days out from Iztapa the Spaniards were subsisting on herbs and roots, and were busy at heavy construction work.[25] When the great bridge over the San Pedro Mártir was built, there were numerous deaths from hunger, and the situation was only alleviated by a successful

[20] Díaz' account is unfortunately not contained in the abbreviated translations of Cohen 1963 and Maudslay 1928. It must be consulted in the original or in Maudslay's earlier full translation.

[21] Ch. 204: Maudslay v. 217 ('I told him many times that we ought to go by the Sierras'). This is one of only two criticisms that Díaz has to lay against Cortés' leadership.

[22] Ch. 175: Maudslay v. 8–9. The numbers seem generally agreed. Even Gómara (Simpson 1965: 346) concedes '150 horse and an equal number of foot, in battle trim'.

[23] Maudslay v. 12–13. Cortés himself admitted that he had to acquire another map during the journey (Pagden 1986: 365), precisely in Acalan.

[24] Maudslay v. 15–16. Cortés mentions the burning, but he treats it as repression of cannibalism, ignoring the prevailing hunger and implying that there was only the single isolated case; nor does he mention that the guides were eaten (cf. Pagden 1986: 351–2).

[25] Maudslay v. 13 ('we were three days building it and had nothing to eat but herbs and some roots . . . which burned our tongues and mouths').

foraging raid led by Díaz himself.[26] In fact Díaz represents
himself as the saviour of the expedition, the only person
capable of finding supplies in the native villages near by—
he was as indispensable as Xenophon to the Ten Thousand
and as shameless in recounting his services. By contrast,
Cortés kept his herd of pigs five days to the rear, and his
quartermaster spread the rumour that they had been eaten
by alligators.[27] He became the butt of the troops' mounting
exasperation. They seized the supplies brought by Díaz,
refusing to reserve anything for their leader, and Díaz had to
undertake yet another trip to relieve the situation, accompanied this time by Cortés' lieutenant, Gonzalo de Sandoval
('he went with me himself to bring his share of the food, and
would trust no one else, although he had many soldiers
whom he could have sent').[28] For Díaz the whole affair was
a bizarre catalogue of extreme hardship, and even Cortés
himself was 'regretful and discontented'.[29] It contrasts sharply with the bland, minimalist account of the leader of the
expedition.

The same variation occurs in our tradition of Alexander's
march through the Makran. There are two main accounts,
both resumed in the work of Arrian.[30] First there is a relatively matter-of-fact description of the journey from Oreitis
(Las Bela) to Pura (Bampur). The hardships are mentioned
but not stressed: the night marches, shortages of water, lack

[26] Ch. 176: Maudslay v. 21; cf. 23–4.

[27] Ch. 175: Maudslay v. 16.

[28] Ch. 176: Maudslay v. 21–3. Cortés naturally says nothing of this embarrassing
episode, nor of the fact that his reconnaissance team had failed to investigate the
swamps beyond the bridge (so Díaz in Maudslay v. 19). He states that after the
crossing he sent ahead 'some Spaniards', who returned with 80 Indian bearers
laden with supplies (Pagden 1986: 361). It comes as no surprise when Díaz
identifies himself as the leader of the foraging party and increases the number of
bearers to over one hundred.

[29] Ch. 177: Maudslay v. 29. A few pages earlier Díaz had given a bitter picture of
deaths by hunger and the desertion by three Spanish soldiers who 'had taken their
chance of a state of war along the road by which we had come, and preferred to die
rather than continue the advance'.

[30] Arr. 6. 23–27. 1. Here, as in earlier discussions (Bosworth 1988*b*: 143–6;
1996*a*: 169–73) I follow the exemplary treatment of the sources by Strasburger
1982–90: i. 451–9. I shall discuss the problems of attribution in the third volume of
my *Historical Commentary on Arrian*. For the present argument it does not matter
whether the narrative of horror comes from Nearchus, as I believe, or from
Aristobulus. In either case the analogy with Díaz holds good.

of provisions.[31] Even so, it is maintained, Alexander was able to acquire a surplus of grain which he sent to the coast to provision the fleet which was to sail along the coast in his wake after the monsoon southerlies abated. One of these convoys was devoured by its escort (and the source underlines the desperate state of hunger),[32] but it is implied that the bulk of the consignments reached the coast unscathed. What emerges is a rational scheme to provision the fleet, a scheme which was in part successful. The undoubted hardships were not catastrophic and did not take place in the immediate entourage of Alexander. Once again there is a second version. Nearchus, the actual commander of the Ocean fleet, gave a vivid account of privation:[33] deaths through flash floods in the early part of the march, extreme difficulties with the shifting sand dunes, chronic thirst and starvation. As the march continued the draught animals were gradually slaughtered and the army's baggage was necessarily discarded.[34] There was also trouble with the route. Alexander's guides may not have been eaten, but they were baffled by the configuration of the terrain after a sandstorm and led the army astray.[35] Finally, the attempt to provision the fleet was totally ineffectual. If any supplies reached the coast, they did not remain to be consumed by Nearchus' men. No supply depot is reported between the coast of Oreitis and Hormuz.[36] The difference between the two versions is palpable, however much Arrian may have

[31] Arr. 6. 23. 1, a very dry and succinct statement of the difficulties: ὁδὸν χαλεπὴν καὶ ἄπορον τῶν ἐπιτηδείων, τῶν τε ἄλλων καὶ ὕδωρ πολλαχοῦ τῇ στρατιᾷ οὐκ ἦν· ἀλλὰ νύκτωρ ἠναγκάζοντο γῆν πολλὴν πορεύεσθαι.

[32] Arr. 6. 23. 4–5.

[33] Recounted in a context dominated by Nearchus in Strabo 15. 2. 5–6 (721–2) with the statement of motivation (below, n. 43) anticipated at 15. 1. 5 (686) and ascribed directly to Nearchus. The same material is found, more rhetorically elaborated, in Arr. 6. 24. 1–27. 1, and again Nearchus is mentioned as a source (6. 24. 2).

[34] Arr. 6. 25. 1–2: Arrian adds that Alexander pretended ignorance, as he was unable to stop what was happening and unwilling to give it his licence.

[35] Strabo 15. 2. 6 (722); Arr. 6. 26. 4–5 (embellished with echoes of the journey through the Sahara to Siwah; cf. Arr. 3. 3. 4).

[36] Arr. *Ind.* 23. 6 (Oreitis). *Ind.* 26 describes the transit of the coast south of Alexander's route through the Makran, and it is clear that the fleet had to dig its own wells and subsist on dates and meat supplied by natives. By that stage most of the supply of grain had been exhausted (*Ind.* 26. 9). The only depot of provisions which Alexander supplied is recorded west of Persis on the Persian Gulf (*Ind.* 38. 9).

intensified the lurid details of Nearchus for rhetorical effect, and it is exactly the contrast we find in the reports of Cortés' march to Honduras. One account, which in all probability derives from Ptolemy, placed the emphasis on Alexander's leadership. He coped with impossible conditions with a degree of success, and he treated the one lapse of discipline with compassionate understanding. That account does not derive from Alexander himself, but it was written by one of his Bodyguards, one of the elite marshals of his court, who would have been involved in the planning of the expedition and shared any opprobrium for the hardships of the march. He would not have made a feature of the human misery and casualties it incurred. On the other hand, Nearchus had the same perspective as Díaz. He was making the most of a situation which he had not created. He could stress the miseries of the march which made it impossible for any provision to be made for him. It was almost a miracle that the land forces escaped with such comparatively small losses to the fighting forces. By contrast he was instrumental in saving the fleet—just as Díaz claims he delivered Cortés and his men from starvation. Despite the lack of provisions, the hostile coast, an incompetent head steersman, he brought the fleet to Hormuz practically untouched. It was his stratagem that extorted food from the natives on the Gedrosian coast, his initiative that coped with the threat from a school of whales, his foresight which saved the fleet from disaster when Onesicritus proposed extending the voyage west to the Arabian peninsula.[37] The hardship and near catastrophe suffered by the land forces served to highlight Nearchus' achievement. At the least he had vindicated his proud boast to Alexander that he would bring ships and men safe to Persis—and on his own account he had surpassed Alexander himself.

The similarities extend beyond the sources to the motivation of the two expeditions. All writers are somewhat baffled by the reasons for Cortés' march to Honduras. On the surface it is transparent enough. Cortés was infuriated by

---

[37] *Ind.* 27. 7–28. 9; cf. Bosworth 1996a: 184–5; *Ind.* 30. 1–7; Strabo 15. 2. 12 (725) (Onesicritus, *FGrH* 134 F 31 also mentioned the whales, as do Diod. 17. 106. 6 and Curt. 10. 1. 12); *Ind.* 32. 6–13; *Anab.* 7. 20. 9–10.

the defection of one of his captains. Cristóbal de Olid, whom he had dispatched to establish a settlement in Honduras, had gone over to his mortal enemy, Diego Velázquez, the governor of Cuba.[38] That was a violation of Cortés' authority as governor of New Spain, authority which had been only recently conferred (Cortés received the news in September 1523, only four months before Olid's betrayal). It is not surprising that Cortés reacted with fury, and imprudently threatened to cross to Cuba and arrest Velázquez,[39] and it is only natural that he sent a punitive force, a flotilla of five ships with a complement of conquistadors under his relative, Francisco de Las Casas. It is understandable, as Díaz states, that he had suspicions that Las Casas would fail and decided upon a second expedition led by himself.[40] What is not explained is why he went overland and took the route he did. Díaz maintains that he might have gone far more easily by way of the uplands, from Coatzacoalcos to Chiapa, from Chiapa to Guatemala, and from Guatemala to Olid's base at Naco. Instead Cortés insisted on the coastal route, although he knew that there were substantial rivers to cross as well as unforgiving marshy terrain and heavy jungle. Even Díaz gives no explanation for the march, and the only hint we have is Cortés' remark to his emperor that 'I had been for a long time idle and attempted no new thing in Your Majesty's service'.[41] He would not rest indefinitely on his laurels after the capture of Tenochtitlan, but would carry out an epic march through the most difficult of terrain to crush a rebel against his authority. The route was chosen precisely because it was the most difficult and challenging.

[38] For a lucid account of the complex political intrigues see the introductory essay by J. H. Elliott in Pagden 1986: xxxi–xxxvi.

[39] Cf. Pagden 1986: 332 (Cortés' Fourth Letter): 'I am of a mind to send for the aforementioned Diego Velázquez and arrest him and send him to Your Majesty; for by cutting out the root of all these evils, which he is, all the branches will wither . . .'.

[40] Ch. 174: Maudslay v. 1–2. Díaz adds that Cortés was excited by reports that the land was rich in gold mines. All the more reason for him to take the most direct route. Gómara (Simpson 1965: 338) has an interesting story of the royal officers in Mexico attempting to dissuade Cortés from the journey because of the danger of insurrection during his absence. 'Besides, they told him, the journey was long, difficult, and profitless.' It is strongly reminiscent of Alexander's briefing on the perils of the Makran.

[41] Pagden 1986: 339.

In the event it nearly killed him. He and his men arrived at the Honduran coast in the last stages of exhaustion, in no condition to crush any rebel, and he was lucky that Olid had already been captured and beheaded—through a combination of good luck and incompetence.[42]

Alexander's motivation is on record. According to Nearchus, Alexander went into the Makran in full knowledge of the difficulties of the terrain because he wished to eclipse the achievements of Semiramis, the legendary conqueror-queen of Babylon, and Cyrus the Great, the founder of the Persian Empire.[43] Both had allegedly come to grief in the Makran, escaping with a handful of survivors. By contrast, Alexander intended to bring his own army through intact. Like Cortés he had political reasons for concern. There were reports of insubordination among the governors of the western satrapies of his empire, and he took the first steps to quash the unrest before he embarked on the desert march. When he arrived in Carmania, he was met by the generals from Media who had completed a 1,700-kilometre march the length of Iran[44] and had obviously been summoned while he was still in India, as, it seems, was Apollodorus, the military commandant in Babylonia.[45] Alexander conducted a full investigation, and had the Median generals executed for insubordination and misgovernment. Apollodorus remained under suspicion.[46] The king had every reason to return and restore order among his errant subordinates, but, like Cortés, he chose the route which was most challenging and he did so to prove his pre-eminence as a leader of armies. He would bring his forces intact through the desert which had beaten Cyrus. In that he was partially

---

[42] For Cortés' version of events see Pagden 1986: 409–12; cf. Díaz, ch. 173: Maudslay iv. 368–73; Gómara in Simpson 1965: 335–7.

[43] Strabo 15. 1. 5 (686): φησὶ γοῦν Νέαρχος κτλ.; cf. 15. 2. 5 (722). Arr. 6. 24. 1 confirms, stating that Nearchus alone alleged that Alexander made the journey in full knowledge of its difficulties. The parallels for the construction (τοῦτο μέν used resumptively), particularly 7. 14. 7 and *Ind.* 10. 8–9, show that the whole preceding clause is to be understood, including the negative; Nearchus did *not*, as has been often argued, state that Alexander acted in ignorance of the route. I argue this more fully in my forthcoming commentary.

[44] Arr. 6. 27. 3–4; Curt. 10. 1. 1–9. See below, n. 47.

[45] Arr. 7. 18. 1 = Aristobulus, *FGrH* 139 F 54; Plut. *Alex.* 73. 3–5; cf. Bosworth 1996a: 23–4.

[46] Arr. 7. 18. 4–5; Plut. *Alex.* 73. 4.

successful. The casualties he sustained were largely suffered by the camp followers, the women and children in the army's train, and, though his troops arrived in Pura in an exhausted and demoralized state, they were soon rehabilitated and their military efficiency was unimpaired.

Alexander was also free to clean up the pockets of insubordination. At first he was cautious and calculating. While his men were still weak he treated the satrap of Carmania, Astaspes, with affable courtesy, only later catching him off guard and executing him (so sparking a local revolt).[47] That contrasted with the savagery with which he greeted Abulites, the satrap of Susa, berating him at their first meeting and personally spearing his son with a *sarisa*.[48] Then his troops were fully recovered, and the satrap was helpless. But the desert march had been a great miscalculation. It inflicted prodigious hardship, more, we are told, than the sum total of the other tribulations which the Macedonians endured in Asia.[49] It must have increased the resentment at Alexander's unceasing pursuit of glory, and his emulation of the heroic figures of the past was no more than extravagant bravado.

We have then two episodes of personal self-indulgence, both potentially disastrous. For Cortés the march to Honduras came when he was at the height of his glory, governor of the whole of New Spain and owner of vast estates which allegedly brought an income of 200 million pesos. His authority lapsed during his long absence, when rumours of his death were rife, and, although he was able to re-establish himself temporarily on his return, he was suspended from his governorship, subjected to an official investigation, and returned to Spain in 1528. For Alexander the consequences were less harmful. He was able to restore his authority by systematic execution of his subordinates, and he neutralized the resentment of the army by mass demobilization of his veterans. Perhaps the most damaging

[47] According to Curtius (9. 10. 21, 29–30), Astaspes was suspected of having plotted rebellion while Alexander was in India, and he was duly executed. For the rebellion which his death instigated see Arr. *Ind.* 36. 8–9.

[48] Plut. *Alex.* 68. 7; Arr. 7. 4. 1; cf. Badian 1961: 17, 21, and, more recently, Lane Fox 1996: 105–8.

[49] Arr. 6. 24. 1; *Ind.* 26. 1; all sources to some extent stress the hardships; for Strabo (15. 2. 5 (721–2)) 'Alexander was in great distress throughout the whole journey'.

aspect of the affair was its demonstration of the lengths to which he would go to rival the great exploits of history and mythology. If he had traversed Gedrosia in order to outdo Semiramis and Cyrus, would he not follow Heracles to the Straits of Gibraltar? The limits of his ambition were boundless, as were the sacrifices he demanded to reach them, and it was only a matter of time before disaster struck. He had no overlord to impose curbs on his ambition. He could not be demoted or recalled. He could, however, be killed if he presented too much of a threat to those around him, and the Gedrosian episode was a stark illustration of the magnitude of the dangers he voluntarily embraced.

We can extend the narrative similarities beyond the personae of the conquerors. In more general ways the sources echo each other and reveal comparable values, comparable modes of thought. One of the most striking phenomena is what can only be termed a sanitization of the military carnage. Both Cortés and Alexander led forces which were technically superior to anything they encountered. The firearms, crossbows, plate armour, and Toledo steel of the conquistadors were set against the obsidian clubs and quilted cotton armour of their Indian adversaries, while Alexander found nothing to match the six-metre long *sarisae* of his Macedonian phalanx or the discipline of mass engagement which he and his father had inculcated. Singly and collectively they outstripped their adversaries in all branches of military technology. Not surprisingly we read of epic combats in which the invaders were outnumbered many times and still won without significant losses. In his description of the first battle against the Tlaxcalans (later his most loyal allies) in September 1519 Cortés claims to have fought all day with half a dozen guns, five or six harquebuses, forty crossbowmen, and thirteen horsemen against a host of Indians which he modestly estimates as 100,000 strong, and did so without damage 'except from exhaustion and hunger'.[50] Díaz describes the same engagement with more reticence: there were only 3,000

---

[50] Pagden 1986: 59–60. The following day allegedly saw a renewed engagement with 'more than 149,000 men' (an amusingly precise figure), and the Spaniards were again unscathed.

Tlaxcalans, and they inflicted severe wounds with their obsidian 'broadswords'. Four Spaniards were hurt, one fatally, while the Indians left seventeen dead.[51] The epic scale of Cortés' narrative has been much reduced, but Díaz is still impressive in describing the lethal effects of the obsidian weapons which, he claims, literally decapitated one of the Spanish horses.[52] The enemy is represented as formidable, and the achievement of the conquerors is maximized. The same thinking almost certainly underlies the commemorative coinage of Alexander, which displayed the archers, elephants, and war chariots of his Indian adversaries, showing all with eyes to see the fearsome qualities of the troops which had defeated them.

What is not stressed is the effect of the fighting upon the conquered. Our sources for Cortés and Alexander alike write of huge casualties, but there is no attempt to spell out what those casualties implied. For that we need to turn to the records of the Indian informants whose testimony was compiled by Fray Bernadino de Sahagún in 1555. The most vivid description concerns the mysterious episode in 1520 when Cortés' lieutenant, Pedro de Alvarado, violated the national festival held by his permission in the capital, and massacred the largely defenceless celebrants. The results were gruesome, luridly illustrated in picture and prose:

They attacked all the celebrants, stabbing them, spearing them, striking them with their swords. They attacked some of them from behind, and these fell instantly to the ground with their entrails hanging out. Others they beheaded: they cut off their heads, or split their heads to pieces. They struck others in the shoulders and their arms were torn from their bodies. They wounded some in the thigh and some in the calf. They slashed others in the abdomen and their entrails all spilled to the ground. Some attempted to run away, but their entrails dragged as they ran . . .[53]

---

[51] Díaz, ch. 62: Maudslay i. 229; Cohen 1963: 143. The following day's battle was fought against two armies 6,000 strong, with the loss of 15 wounded, one of whom died.

[52] Díaz, ch. 63: Maudslay i. 231; Cohen 1963: 145–6. Gómara (Simpson 1965: 99) described the decapitation of two horses at a slightly earlier juncture; Díaz may be deliberately setting the record straight, and takes pains to identify the rider, Pedro de Moron, who died of his wounds after the battle.

[53] Conveniently translated in Leon-Portilla 1962: 74–6. There are gruesome

There could not be a more telling description of the effect of finely honed Toledo steel upon human flesh, and it is not surprising that the Spanish sources do not dwell on the details of the carnage. The battles would lose their heroic aura, and the conquistadors would appear more like abattoir workers. For Alexander's campaigns there is nothing to compare with the Indian testimony. Nobody describes what it was like to be spitted by a *sarisa* with its ferocious leaf-shaped blade fifty centimetres long (although the Alexander mosaic gives a visual representation). As a result one becomes immune to the casualty figures. Alexander's men may have killed countless thousands, but one gets the impression that nobody was really hurt, just as in some Disney cartoon. However, there must have been scenes of slaughter which made Alvorado's massacre at Tenochtitlan look tame. Consider the final scene at the Granicus, when the 20,000 Greek mercenaries were left stranded on the battlefield to be surrounded by Alexander's victorious army, the phalanx pressing their front, the cavalry harrying the sides and rear. The king disregarded their appeal for quarter, and a massacre ensued.[54] Whether or not 90 per cent were cut down, as Arrian and Plutarch imply, there is no doubt that many thousands fell, and the circumstances would not have been pretty. Given the large circular shields of the Greeks and their massed formation, the wounds inflicted by the *sarisae* would have been predominantly in the face and throat—otherwise in the groin. There was a similar scene at the end of the battle of the Hydaspes, when the Indian battle line was entrapped by the phalanx and a cordon of

illustrations in *Codex Duran* and the *Codex Florentino*, containing Sahagún's *Historia General*. Cortés himself was away from the scene of the massacre, but even so he considered it prudent to omit it from his Second Narrative Letter, stating only that the Indians were in revolt. Gómara (Simpson 1965: 208) has no hesitation in blaming Alvarado, who acted 'cruelly and pitilessly'; Díaz (ch. 124: Maudslay ii. 124; Cohen 1963: 283) adds that he attacked 'for no reason at all'. Even so none of the Spanish authorities attempts to depict the horror of the scene; 'he killed and wounded many' is all that Díaz says.

[54] Arr. 1. 16. 2; Plut. *Alex.* 16. 13–14. Plutarch alone mentions the mercenaries' attempt to surrender and reports substantial Macedonian casualties. Arrian has the mercenaries rooted to the ground with astonishment at the routing of their cavalry, and says nothing about Macedonian losses (later at 1. 16. 4 he implies that there were only 30 infantry casualties), but he does not minimize the horror of the slaughter: 'no one escaped unless he escaped notice among the corpses'.

Macedonian cavalry, and the horror of the slaughter was intensified by maddened elephants caught within their own disorganized mass of infantry and trampling indiscriminately everything in their path.[55] Few commanders have been more expert than Alexander in creating the conditions for mass slaughter, and his troops developed a terrible efficiency in killing. The conquest came at a high price in blood and agony. Vast areas in the west may have fallen to him without serious resistance, but from the great rebellion in Sogdiana in the summer of 329 to his invasion of the Makran in October 325 there was almost continuous fighting, scores of towns destroyed and whole populations, civilian and military alike, massacred.

The human cost is something best ignored by those who inflict it. Conquerors are in a position to control the record and take the high moral ground. If they attack, it is because they have been provoked and threatened, and the people they subjugate have a tendency to submit themselves voluntarily to their yoke. If they then change their mind, it is an act of rebellion; reprisals and condign punishment are justified. All these are common phenomena, too familiar to require illustration. What is, however, notable in the record of the Spaniards in the Americas and the Graeco-Macedonians in the far east is an atmosphere of wonder, a stress upon the marvels of the new territories.[56] In part it is sheer curiosity, sometimes tinged with a modicum of nostalgic admiration, but there is also a demonstrable tendency to depict the conquered as alien. However wonderful they may be, they are different from us and can therefore be treated differently. For the Spaniards in Mexico it was a simple matter. The natives were not Christian; their deities were portrayed in alarming and revolting imagery, and, worst of all, they practised human sacrifice, eating the remains of the victims after their palpitating hearts had been torn out and offered to the sun. The suppression of such practices was easy enough to justify, and Cortés' narrative letters are full of the complacent sermons he allegedly

---

[55] Arr. 5. 17. 7. Cf. Bosworth 1996a: 18–20.
[56] For the early European attitudes to the Americas see the wonderful compilation of material in Greenblatt 1991.

delivered, denouncing the twin evils of human sacrifice and sodomy. These were easy targets; the vice of the natives justified wholesale iconoclasm, massacre, and the burning alive of recalcitrants.[57] But in other ways the Spaniards have strongly traditional reactions to more familiar situations. They have the same prejudice in favour of agriculture and against nomadic populations that had prevailed since antiquity. In the Alexander authors we find the traditional admiration of the Saka nomads of the north-east as exemplars of the virtues of poverty,[58] but there is also the traditional exasperation against the depredations of the nomadic peoples of the Zagros. The marauding Cossaeans, who lived between Media and Babylonia, had a bad reputation for brigandage and received presents from the Great King to ensure safe passage when he moved court from Ecbatana to Babylon.[59] That alone justified Alexander's unprovoked attack late in 324. The Cossaeans were terrified into temporary submission and were subjected to a colonizing policy in which the new settlers would transform them from nomads into 'ploughmen and labourers on the land', as Nearchus coyly puts it.[60] In other words they ceased to be free herdsmen and became serfs labouring to support an alien military population. Cortés displays exactly the same attitude when he promises Charles V that he will subjugate the nomad Chichimeca peoples of the north. They are said to be very barbarous and less intelligent than the rest of the natives. He has therefore sent a small expedition to pacify them and settle if they show some aptitude. If not, they will be reduced to slavery. 'By making slaves of this barbarous people, who are almost savages, Your Majesty will be served

---

[57] In the debate at Valladolid Sepúlveda was to harp upon the practices of human sacrifice, cannibalism, and idolatry as proof of Indian inferiority and justification of the Spanish conquest: 'How can we doubt that these people, so uncivilized, so barbaric, so contaminated with so many sins and obscenities . . . have been justly conquered by such an excellent, pious, and most just king . . . and by such a humane nation which is excellent in every kind of virtue?' (Hanke 1959: 46–7).

[58] Arr. 4. 1. 1; Curt. 7. 6. 11; on this episode see Bosworth 1995: 13–15; 1996a: 151–2.

[59] So Nearchus, *FGrH* 133 F 1(g) = Strabo 11. 13. 6 (524); Arr. *Ind.* 40. 6–8.

[60] Arr. *Ind.* 40. 8. On the campaign see Arr. 7. 15. 1–3; Diod. 17. 111. 4–6 (confirming the establishment of cities); Plut. *Alex.* 72. 4; Polyaen. 4. 3. 21, and on the Cossaeans in general see Briant 1982b: 64–81.

and the Spaniards will benefit greatly, as they will work in the gold mines, and perhaps by living among us some of them may even be saved.'[61] The Aristotelian doctrine of natural slavery shines out here. The Chichimecas were too uncivilized to be anything but slaves and could therefore be enslaved and transported without any qualms. It is pleasant to record that in actuality they retained their independence for over a century, and improved their nomadic way of life by stealing Spanish horses and firearms.[62]

Traditional prejudice was matched by traditional curiosity. It is amusing to find Cortés invoking time-hallowed interest in Amazons, which had been stimulated by the recent publication of the romance of Amadis. That vastly popular work dealt with the exploits of the warrior queen Calafia, who held sway in the rugged but gold-rich island of California, 'on the right side of the Indies'. Diego Velázquez had originally commissioned Cortés to search for Amazons, and some years later Cortés was able to report to Charles V that there was a distant island off the Pacific coast which was inhabited by women, without a single man. Mating took place only at certain seasons, when sexual partners were allowed on the island, and only the female offspring were retained.[63] A kinsman, Francisco Cortés, was given a modest force of horse, crossbowmen, and artillery and sent to investigate this intriguing story; but the Amazons remained as stubbornly elusive as the pot of gold at the rainbow's end. Alexander received very similar information when he was approached by Pharasmanes, the ambitious ruler of Chorasmia, just south of the Aral Sea. Pharasmanes allegedly claimed to be a neighbour of the Amazons and their homeland near Colchis, and volunteered to lead Alexander on an expedition against them.[64] The political aims are transparent in both cases: Pharasmanes wished to harness the curiosity

---

[61] Pagden 1986: 446, 526 n. 118.

[62] It has been estimated that in the period between 1564 and 1574 more Spaniards died at the hands of the Chichimecas than had fallen in the original Mexican conquest (Powell 1944: 580 n. 1). Alexander's plans to 'civilise' the Cossaeans were equally abortive. Less than a decade later they were able to embarrass Antigonus when he traversed their territory (Diod. 19. 19. 2–8; cf. Billows 1990: 92–3).

[63] Pagden 1986: 298–300, 502 n. 21; Leonard 1944.

[64] Arr. 4. 15. 4–7; Bosworth 1995: 104–7.

of the Macedonians into the expansion of his own kingdom, while Cortés wished for an unlimited brief for exploration and conquest—as far as the Moluccas and Cathay, if it could be managed.[65] The Amazons were the prime drawcard, the ultimate appeal to prurient male curiosity, but in both cases the motivation of the informants was blatantly obvious and the reports were disregarded. However, there was much that was completely new, that could not be accommodated to traditional beliefs and prejudices. In the literature of the Spanish conquest the most moving expression of wonder is Bernal Díaz' panegyric over the marvels of Tenochtitlan. The city on the water with its great pyramids was almost the stuff of fairy-tales, 'like an enchanted vision from the tale of Amadis . . . It was all so wonderful that I do not know how to describe this first glimpse of things never heard of, seen or dreamed of before.' Díaz proceeds to a rapturous description of the palaces of stone and cedar wood, the fragrant orchards and rose gardens, the birds of all breeds and varieties. But then he ends on a chilling note: 'But today all that I then saw is overthrown and destroyed; nothing is left standing.'[66] The marvels did not protect the Mexican from the holocaust, and in some ways they were responsible for it. However wonderful and exotic the environment of Tenochtitlan, it was proof of the otherness of its inhabitants. They were different from the Spaniards, and the norms of western civilization did not apply to them.

Some of the same type of thinking can be found in the Alexander historians, particularly in their description of India, which they saw as a land of marvels, with curiosities known from past literature and an apparently inexhaustible supply of novelties. Perhaps the closest analogy to Díaz' outpouring is the description which Onesicritus gave of the realm of Musicanus, an Indian prince who held sway on the middle Indus, in the vicinity of the modern town of Alor. Musicanus was slow to submit to Alexander, but once he did so, admitting his error ('the most potent method with

[65] Pagden 1986: 326–7, 445.

[66] Díaz, ch. 87: Maudslay ii. 37–8; Cohen 1963: 214–15. There are some pertinent remarks in Greenblatt 1991: 132–4, who argues that it was the very act of destruction which gave the Spaniards possession of their empire; it transferred them from the imaginary to reality.

Alexander for anyone to obtain what he might desire'), he was confirmed as ruler with a supervisory garrison of Macedonians.[67] Alexander, so Arrian states, wondered at the city and its hinterland.[68] What he found to marvel at is not explicitly on record. However, Onesicritus, the head steersman of his fleet, gave a rhapsodic description of the land, which abounded with all the necessities of life.[69] Its inhabitants lived a frugal and healthy life, attaining an age of 130 years. They abjured the use of gold and silver, considered excessive practice in military science iniquitous and had no procedures of civil law. Above all there was no slavery; young men carried out menial domestic tasks, and the rural population had almost the serf status of the Laconian helots but was content with its lot.[70] Without a doubt Onesicritus is idealizing, and he may have the self-sufficiency advocated by his master, Diogenes the Cynic, at the back of his mind. However, he is explaining and interpreting Indian phenomena, like the social position of the *śūdras*, who were serf-like but free members of the society—the concept of caste no Greek appears to have fully appreciated. His explanation is cast in polar opposites: everything that the invaders cherished, banquets, precious metals, chattel slaves, litigation, and military expertise, were disdained by the people of Musicanus. Onesicritus praised their institutions highly, but he could not make it plainer that they were the antithesis of everything Hellenic.[71] They may have been successful, virtuous, and admirable but they were also alien. Accordingly their institutions no more saved them from disaster than did the beauties of Tenochtitlan. Once Alexander had left to deal with the stubborn resistance in the mountains to the west, Musicanus rebelled, encouraged by his Brahman advisers. We need not explore his motives here. What matters is the consequences. Alexander sent the satrap of

[67] Arr. 6. 15. 5–7; Curt. 9. 8. 8–10; Diod. 17. 102. 5.

[68] καὶ τὴν πόλιν ἐθαύμασεν Ἀλέξανδρος καὶ τὴν χώραν.

[69] Strabo 15. 1. 34 (701) = Onesicritus *FGrH* 134 F 24. On this passage see Brown 1949*b*: 54–61; Pearson 1960: 102–3; Pédech 1984: 114–23.

[70] The text is difficult and perhaps defective. On reading and interpretation see Bosworth 1996*a*: 85–6.

[71] The similarities almost prove the rule; the comparisons Onesicritus made were with the least typical of Greek states, Sparta and Crete.

Sind, Peithon, son of Agenor, to deal with the rebels. The cities of Musicanus were destroyed or turned into garrison centres, and their inhabitants were enslaved en masse. Musicanus and his Brahman advisers were crucified as an example to the rest—a terrible and perhaps deliberate flouting of Indian custom which exempted Brahmans from any sort of capital punishment.[72] We have the paradox of a realm admired for its peculiar institutions, but ruthlessly destroyed once it proved recalcitrant. Those very institutions were a proof of the otherness of the conquered, and the otherness was some justification for the savagery with which they were treated.

The conquered, however, could not be portrayed as totally alien. They had to understand their conquerors and converse with them in a meaningful way. Above all they had to offer submission and understand what submission meant. Whether Greek or Roman, Spaniard or English, a conqueror could not simply annex land by unprovoked violence. There had to be some act of recognition, some voluntary acceptance of the authority of the invaders. That is clearly illustrated in another fragment of Onesicritus, his famous account of his meeting with the Brahman sages outside Taxila.[73] This is an elaborate and complicated passage in which Onesicritus retails Brahman doctrine in a significantly Greek dress. It is hardly reportage of a specific exchange but a literary re-enactment, and an anthology of Indian doctrine which Onesicritus had assimilated in his years of interaction with the court sage, Calanus. For our purposes what is significant is Onesicritus' report of the doctrine of the senior Brahman, Dandamis. For Dandamis Alexander shows the interest in 'philosophy' which is the mark of a true king, and he retains it even in his military calling. He can therefore inculcate the virtues of temperance in his subjects. Dandamis in fact welcomes Alexander, and he adds that he

[72] Arr. 6. 17. 1–2; Curt. 9. 8. 16. The revolt is discussed by Bosworth 1998: 198–200.

[73] Strabo 15. 1. 63–5 (715–16) = Onesicritus, *FGrH* 134 F 17a; Plut. *Alex.* 65. 1–5. The Indian parallels are given in Bosworth 1998, contesting the view propagated by Schwartz 1896: 83–5 (cf. Brown 1949b: 41; Pédech 1984: 106) that Onesicritus is merely delivering a Cynic sermon. For more neutral approaches see Schwarz 1980: 108; Stoneman 1995: 103–4.

had encouraged the local prince, Taxiles, to receive him.[74] Taxiles had indeed invited Alexander into India long before Alexander was in a position to invade, and had sent a delegation to the western frontiers to welcome him into the Indian lands.[75] His submission is reinforced by the senior Brahman of northern India, who is represented hailing Alexander almost as an ideal king. Taxiles, it would seem, recognized the suzerainty of Alexander, based on his conquest of the Persian Empire, to which his princedom had once belonged, and Dandamis conferred moral legitimacy. However alien these Indians may have been, they recognized their natural sovereign and accepted his authority in unambiguous terms—or so Alexander's historians implied.

There is a striking counterpoint in the accounts of the Spanish conquest, which show the native chiefs accepting a state of vassalage to the Spanish crown, even though they can have had no inkling what the Spanish crown was or what the state of vassalage implied. Nevertheless their statements of submission were translated into Spanish and solemnly engrossed in legal form by a Spanish notary.[76] The most famous submission is that of Montezuma himself in November 1519, when he first received Cortés into Tenochtitlan. What he actually said we shall never know. What all sources represent him delivering is explicit recognition of the Spaniards as his legitimate overlords. Even the Indian accounts of the meeting have Cortés' coming predicted by previous Aztec rulers; they were merely representatives, and Montezuma surrenders his stewardship: 'Rest now, and take possession of your royal houses. Welcome to your lands, my lords.'[77] This acknowledgement was a moral necessity, and Sahagún, the Spanish editor,

---

[74] Strabo 15. 1. 65 (716): καὶ δὴ καὶ Ταξίλῃ νῦν συμβουλεύσειε δέχεσθαι τὸν Ἀλέξανδρον.

[75] Arr. 4. 22. 6; 5. 3. 5–6; Diod. 17. 86. 4; Curt. 8. 12. 5; *Metz Epit.* 49. On the problems of the tradition see Bosworth 1995: 2. 146–7, 220–1.

[76] For a typical instance see Bosworth 1996a: 159–60. The legalities observed by the Spaniards could verge on the bizarre, as with the famous 'Requirement', which was supposed to be read to Indians before any combat and presented the Spanish claims to empire (Gibson 1968: 58–60; Thomas 1993: 71–5).

[77] Leon-Portilla 1962: 64. On the Indian tradition see Thomas 1993: 283. There is an interesting essay (Hornung 1966: 30–47) which argues that the Mexican chronicles described the events of the conquest as a playing out of myth, almost in terms of ritual performance.

cannot have allowed any variant to stand in the record. The Spaniards are even more explicit, most of all Cortés, who put in Montezuma's mouth what is almost a classical foundation myth, reminiscent of the return of the Heraclidae. His people, he says, were brought into the Valley of Mexico by an overlord, who was in due course rejected by the Aztecs and disappeared into the east. Since Cortés and his men come from the rising sun and claim to be the servants of a great lord, they are clearly the descendants of the Aztec foundation hero and the Aztecs are their vassals. Consequently 'all that we own is for you to dispose of as you choose'.[78] A very comfortable doctrine for the Spaniards, expressed in terms that are totally unambiguous to them. And it is not surprising that other sources record Montezuma making much the same statement. Bernal Díaz mentions the prophecies of Montezuma's ancestors that some day rulers would come from the rising sun, and Francisco de Aguilar claimed that the emperor's submission was recorded by a notary.[79] All this is very suspicious. It will not do to argue (as Hugh Thomas has recently done) that the unanimity of the reports confirms that Montezuma did perform some act of submission, and that writers who wished to reduce the stature of Cortés would have had no hesitation in exposing a fiction. Perhaps not; but this fiction was the master lie which legitimized the Spanish conquest. Montezuma declared the invaders to be the proper rulers of Mexico and surrendered all his possessions to them. Such a fiction could not be exposed without undermining the position of the authors, the beneficiaries of the conquest. On the contrary, their interest was to strengthen and embellish it, and that they seem to have done. As a result Montezuma not only understands his guests, but acknowledges their lordship in terms that sound almost biblical ('See that I am flesh and blood like you and all other men, and I am mortal and substantial').[80] However alien his culture, however repulsive and outlandish his religion, when it comes to the

[78] Pagden 1986: 85–6, 467–9 n. 42. Cortés' version is not surprisingly repeated by his secretary Gómara (Simpson 1954: 141–2).

[79] Díaz, ch. 90: Maudslay ii. 57–8; Cohen 1963: 222–3; Aguilar, in de Fuentes 1993: 147.

[80] Cortés in Pagden 1986: 86; cf. Frankl 1962: 7–12, contra Thomas 1993: 286.

important issue Montezuma expresses himself with perfect clarity, accepting vassal status explicitly and categorically.

So far I have concentrated on the similarities of ideology and action. I shall end with an important difference. What is notorious in the career of Alexander is his willingness to collaborate with and use the conquered Persian aristocracy. There is nothing comparable in the annals of the Spanish conquest. Cortés may have used the local Indian peoples like the Tlaxcalans, and confirmed their chiefs as vassals of Spain, but he used them as auxiliaries to destroy the Mexican empire. The Mexica themselves were ruthlessly crushed: Montezuma's successor, Cuahtémoc, may have been named ruler of Tenochtitlan by the victorious Cortés, but he was put to torture to reveal his reserves of treasure, was dragged in Cortés' train to Honduras, and ended up hanging on a tree in Acalan, convicted of complicity in a mythical conspiracy. On the other hand, Alexander treated the Persian royal family with extreme deference; the brother of the deceased king became a Companion,[81] Persian nobles governed some of the more important satrapies, and at least seven younger sons of the nobility were admitted into the prestigious Macedonian Royal squadron.[82] Alexander himself took on some items of Persian court regalia and absorbed some of the traditional features of Persian court life; Peucestas, his satrap of Persia, actually assumed full Persian dress and learned Persian.[83] There is nothing remotely similar in the Spanish conquest. The explanation is simple but informative. For the Spaniards their new subjects were vassals of their own European emperor and submitted themselves to his supreme authority. Alexander, however, was taking over an empire and replacing the Great King. He was leading a war of revenge against Persia and simultaneously claiming to be the rightful occupant of the Persian throne.[84] There was no inherent contradiction. For Alexander's guest friend, Demaratus of Corinth, the greatest punish-

---

[81] Plut. *Alex.* 43. 7; Curt. 6. 2. 11; cf. Bosworth 1980*b*: 6, 12–13.

[82] Arr. 7. 6. 4–5. If 7. 29. 4 is taken literally, there were also admissions of Persian nobles into the infantry guard (*agema*).

[83] Arr. 6. 30. 2–3; 7. 6. 3; Diod. 19. 14. 5. Cf. Bosworth 1980*b*: 12; Hamilton 1988: 475–6.

[84] See the discussion of Michael Flower, below, pp. 107–15, 123–5.

ment for the Persians was to see him seated on the throne of the Achaemenids.[85] These claims to empire originated early. Our sources depict him representing himself as the proper king of Asia immediately after the battle of Issus in late 333,[86] and he had the mythological justification in that Perses, the supposed eponymous hero of the Persians, was the son of Perseus, Alexander's own remote ancestor. Herodotus had represented Xerxes appealing to the genealogy and respecting the Greek city of Argos as his kin.[87] For Alexander it was a tailor-made foundation myth, akin to the legend which the Spanish sources put in the mouth of Montezuma. This time it was an invader from the west coming to claim the monarchy which was his prerogative. But Alexander did not come to destroy, rather to make the Persian Empire his own. He accepted enough of the customs of the conquered to identify himself with the Persian monarchy, and took princesses from the Persian aristocracy as his wives. He was simultaneously King of Macedon and King of Kings.

The differing perspective made little difference in practice. The behaviour of Alexander to his subjects was not dissimilar from that of the Spaniards. Where there was opposition and what he saw as rebellion, he acted with total ruthlessness, as Musicanus and countless other magnates in Central Asia and India found to their cost. Although he had no god-sent visitation of smallpox to devastate the conquered populations, there were whole areas where the conquest came close to depopulation, thanks to the tactics of terror which he used. What for instance would have been the sequel in the oases of the Zeravshan valley (around Bukhara) after Alexander systematically ravaged the agricultural land as far the surrounding salt desert?[88] And the campaign against the Malli was deliberately planned to inflict the greatest possible number of casualties. After the slaughter Arrian describes the embassy of submission 'from those of

[85] Plut. *Alex.* 37. 7, 56. 1; *Ages.* 15. 4; *Mor.* 329d.

[86] Arr. 2. 14. 8–9; Curt. 4. 1. 14. See the observations of Ernst Fredricksmeyer, below, pp. 139–44.

[87] Hdt. 7. 150. 2.; cf. 6. 43; 7. 61. 3; Hellanicus, *FGrH* 4 F 59–60.

[88] Arr. 4. 6. 5–6.

the Malli who survived';[89] there is a clear implication that the majority had perished—and the grossly overused label of genocide may not here be inappropriate. For large areas of Asia the advent of Alexander meant carnage and starvation, and the effects were ultimately as devastating as that of the Spaniards in Mexico. The conquerors created a desert and called it empire.

[89] Arr. 6. 14. 1: τῶν Μαλλῶν τῶν ὑπολειπομένων. On the details of the campaign see Bosworth 1996a: 133–41.

3

Conspiracies

E. BADIAN

Plots, true or false, are necessary things
To raise up commonwealths and ruin kings.

Dryden, *Absalom and Achitophel*

No age has been a stranger to conspiracies and suspicion of conspiracies, least of all our own. Even in the USA, surely the most open society in history, conspiracies both by and against the government or members of it keep occurring and, at least as often, keep being suspected where they cannot be proved. In our age, in democratic societies, a new motive for allegations of conspiracy has been added to the traditional ones: the hope for lucrative publicity. This may have been one of the motives in charges used by lawyers defending O. J. Simpson to secure their client's acquittal, and certainly (one would think) in a recent conspiracy theory regarding the sinking of the Titanic, advanced around the release of the successful film.[1] Although that motive did not exist in this form in antiquity, we may compare the desire on the part of some historians to enliven their narratives and appeal to a wider audience by juicy allegations of this kind. Indeed, it sometimes seems that no prominent man was deemed by all who wrote about him to have died a natural death—whether he died relatively young, like Alexander the Great, or in middle age, like Aratus of Sicyon, or in extreme old age, like the Emperor Tiberius.

Dryden's verses were written in the light of his own experience of the Civil War and the 'Popish plots'. The conspirators we shall examine would never (like two of the

I should like to thank Professor Bosworth for searching questions and stimulating suggestions, which have made this essay longer and (I hope) better.

[1] Robin Gardner and Dan van der Vat, *The Titanic Conspiracy* (1997): essentially, that a damaged ship was made up to look like the 'unsinkable' *Titanic* and put under the command of a captain with a bad record, for financial gain by the owners. It may yet make a film.

imaginary ones in Herodotus' 'constitutional debate' among the Persian conspirators: 3. 80 ff.) have thought of 'raising up a commonwealth'; at most they aimed at substituting a better king for one whom they thought worse. Where Dryden was right for all ages, however, even if he intended it satirically, was in stressing that tyrannies cannot be overthrown except through conspiracies. What did not fit into his scheme (although he only had to look at earlier English history to notice it) was that kings can plot against their subjects (any of them whom they think too wealthy or too powerful) and that, from their position of supreme power, they are much more likely to succeed. Conspiracies do not always ruin kings, as we shall see: they often make them more secure.

Under an autocratic regime, which maintains its power in part through its ability to conspire against its subjects, conspiracies are more often formed as 'necessary things'—and more often alleged, as pretexts for conspiracies by the ruler. The Emperor Domitian said that no one believes there has been a conspiracy against a ruler unless he is killed (Suet. *Dom.* 21. 1). To the extent that this was so, he had only himself to blame, because of his use of allegations of conspiracies in order to carry out his own. Those of us who have lived through the age of Stalin and Hitler will find plenty of examples of this, as well as some of real conspiracies against those rulers—though surprisingly few that can be documented and none that succeeded. One result is that public opinion is likely to suspect conspiracies where in fact there were none. The Reichstag, as it turns out, was indeed set on fire by an unbalanced Dutchman, not by either the Communists (as the Nazi government claimed) or the Nazis themselves (as most of the rest of the world believed), even though neither of these charges was implausible in view of the records of the parties concerned.

This conspiracy theory is unlikely to be revived. But where there is powerful motivation—psychological or, often linked with it, financial—mere evidence will not necessarily allay such theories: witness a commercially successful recent pseudo-historical film on the death of John F. Kennedy; or the continuing allegations, ignoring the evidence provided by the Russian archives, that charges of treason against

Alger Hiss or I. F. Stone were conspiracies made up by right-wing enemies.

The historian, trying to arrive at the truth, must follow the hard evidence. Unfortunately the historian of Alexander rarely, if ever, has such hard evidence. He must rely on deductions from character and situations: analysis of an individual situation in the light of parallels that can be adduced to elucidate it—in short, the kind of evidence that can never be conclusive and (it must be stressed) that can in perfectly good faith be differently interpreted by different interpreters.

At this point another consideration must be added, which further confuses judgement. A ruler given to conspiring will be inclined to suspect the existence of conspiracies against him, especially when such suspicions suit his purpose. Hitler no doubt genuinely believed in a conspiracy by international Jewry. Stalin, after ordering the assassination of Kirov, may have believed in a conspiracy (which would not have been unjustified) against him by leading members of the party and by the general staff under Tukhachevski. Yet, did Stalin seriously believe, after the War against Germany, that Zhukov and a dozen other generals were preparing to betray the Soviet Union? Or, later, that Molotov and Voroshilov were, and even some of his own relatives? If he did, what does that tell us about his mental state? As we shall see, these questions are not irrelevant to Alexander.

Alexander, in one known case, did believe in a conspiracy that did not exist, on the part of supporters of Cleitus. Whether he genuinely believed this in some other cases is part of the impenetrable mystery of his psychology. The plotter does seem ultimately to have come to believe that he was surrounded by conspiracies. In some cases, this factor can obviously lead the historian into error. But unless it is well documented, the historian cannot allow for it, but, whether in Stalin's case or in Alexander's, must follow where the evidence of character and previous actions leads. Anyone accused of suspecting conspiracies on the part of Alexander, where some do not see them, can only reply that, like the Emperor Domitian, Alexander has only himself to blame if we approach his claims, as transmitted by court historiography, with some suspicion. This may, in individual cases, be mistaken, but I would reject any claim that it is unjustified.

The war of Alexander against Darius III and the continuation of Alexander's campaign is marked by a series of conspiracies, allegations of conspiracy, and attempts to anticipate conspiracy unequalled in any other war I know about. The two protagonists were heirs to a long history of conspiracies in their respective dynasties, and each of them had come to the throne through a conspiracy. Only two of Alexander's predecessors in the fourth century BC, Amyntas III and Perdiccas III (who died in battle), had not died by assassination, and only three among all the successors and destined successors of Darius I (Artaxerxes I, Darius II, Artaxerxes II) who preceded Darius III. In the Persian case, the monarch who had the longest reign and died peacefully in extreme old age, Artaxerxes II, had had to contend with conspiracies throughout his reign: from the well-supported revolt of his brother Cyrus at its beginning, through the Satraps' Revolts, to the conspiracies near the end of his life that began with that by (or against) his chosen successor and joint King Darius (who should really be called Darius III, had the numeral not become immovably attached to Alexander's opponent) and ended with Artaxerxes Ochus' bloody way to the throne.

Whether Darius III was involved in the conspiracy that led to the murder of his predecessor Artaxerxes Arses we cannot tell for certain. The only positive allegation comes in Alexander's supposed first letter to Darius (Arr. 2. 14. 5); and we need not even discuss the question of whether the letter is authentic or a historian's rhetoric to see that it cannot be used as evidence proving Darius' real guilt. In either case, it merely offers *ta deonta* ('what was required by the occasion'). Since our sources are not remiss in attacking Darius' actions and character, I think we may confidently exclude at least any Greek knowledge of his having participated in the removal of Ochus and Arses. However, since he had lived, as one of the King's 'friends', through the time of these plots, he could not fail to learn from the experience, in his case (it seems) a wholly passive one.

E. Badian

That Alexander was involved in the conspiracy that led to the death of Philip II seems to me as clear as when I first wrote about the subject;[2] although we cannot tell whether he initiated and led it. In any case, each of the protagonists had good reason to fear conspiracies—and to anticipate them.

Alexander put his experience to good use right from the start. The sons of Aëropus of Lyncestis were accused of having participated in the plot to kill Philip[3]—an implausible charge, since they had nothing to gain by his death. They were not Argeads, hence had not the slightest chance of seizing the Macedonian throne—and only two of the three were executed. The third, Alexander, who was Antipater's son-in-law and apparently had had warning of what was to happen, at once paid homage to Alexander as king and (although he was guilty, so Arrian states) was not only spared, but entrusted with important commands as long as Alexander was close to Antipater (Arr. and Curt., locc. citt.).[4]

That Antipater had master-minded Alexander's accession, hence must have known about the plot to kill Philip, is not attested by any good source. But it is clear from his prompt action, and even more so from that of his son-in-law—as we noted, the only one of the three sons of Aëropus who was fully prepared for the event. No other source for his foreknowledge is conceivable. Antipater's association with Alexander under Philip is attested: they were both sent by Philip to Athens to conclude peace after Chaeronea (Just. 9. 4. 5). There is no record of his having sought any contact with Attalus after the domestic coup that brought Attalus to

---

[2] Badian 1963. The replies, of varying quality, called forth by that article contain nothing to make me change my mind on either my interpretation of the train of events or the conclusions I drew from it. But this cannot be argued here.

[3] See esp. Arr. 1. 25. 1, cf. Curt. 7. 1. 6 (on Alexander son of Aëropus). See Berve 1926: no. 144 (Arrhabaeus) for balanced discussion, except that he believes Alexander saw them as rivals for the throne (against: Bosworth 1980a: 159). What Alexander may have feared was that they would raise Lyncestis against him: it was probably not regarded as certain that Philip's integration of the Upper Macedonian states would survive his death. See Bosworth 1971c: 93–105; and 1980a: 159.

[4] Diodorus' statement that the Lyncestian Alexander was related to Antigonus (17. 80. 2) is a mistake, but should be left in the text. There is no need to emend, as (e.g.) Goukowsky (in the Budé edition) does, following Freinsheim's old suggestion. Diodorus can confuse the Tigris with the Euphrates (2. 3. 2—surely not in Ctesias!).

power. (In this he contrasts with Parmenio, who married one of his daughters to Attalus.)[5] It was presumably on the occasion of the mission to Athens that Antipater was made a citizen and *proxenos* of Athens, an unusual combination (Harpocration, s.v. Ἀλκίμαχος, quoting Hyperides, *Against Demades*: we do not know when Alcimachus received the same grants, but perhaps also on a mission to Athens).[6] Antipater's patent involvement, incidentally, is another argument against the view (still sometimes advanced, perhaps on the basis of some of Plutarch's sources) that Olympias was involved in Philip's assassination. Not only was she away in Epirus at the time, but it is difficult to picture her collaborating with Antipater on such a project.

Having disposed of the two sons of Aëropus, Alexander could deal with Attalus. He could not be forgiven for wresting power from Olympias and for an insult to Alexander that had had disastrous consequences for the prince's life. His murder was also justified by a charge of conspiracy (Diod. 17. 2. 5; cf. Plut. *Demosth.* 23. 2), which some modern Alexander worshippers have seen fit to extend far beyond what even the hostile sources allege.[7] It was co-operation with the king in this plot against his own son-in-law that secured Parmenio's position and power under the new king, at the price of setting a precedent that Parmenio would have cause to regret. Alexander's cousin Amyntas, who had real claims to the throne, was also at once eliminated, not surprisingly on a charge of having conspired against

[5] Curt. 6. 9. 17. It is sometimes said (correctly, I must admit) that we do not actually know whether the marriage preceded or followed the elevation of Attalus and his niece-ward. I have assumed the latter. But if the former is true, it creates an even more sinister picture: in that case, it would be difficult to avoid the conclusion that it was Parmenio, Philip's most trusted general and adviser, who engineered Philip's marriage to Cleopatra. Attalus was probably not close enough to Philip to do so on his own, and we can hardly assume that Philip came across a noble girl of marriageable age by pure chance.

[6] That Philip was made an Athenian citizen is also attested (Plut. *Demosth.* 22. 4). I have not found any attestation that Alexander was, but it may not have been necessary, since the grant to Philip would presumably, in the usual manner, include his descendants. The grant to Philip should be put about the time of the treaty after Chaeronea.

[7] See Berve 1926: no. 182 for the modern charge of a treasonable understanding with Memnon, cited with apparent approval. Berve also accepts the charge of treasonable correspondence with Demosthenes, which is at least in the sources, but is implausible for various reasons.

Alexander.[8] It is significant that we do not hear of any trials in any of these cases, even where evidence was later alleged. Alexander could not yet trust the army to accept his word and his evidence against the denials of men who had been loyal to Philip. In total control of what was reported to the army, he had, however, shown real genius in using charges of conspiracy to make the elimination of men he feared politically acceptable.[9] This is one of the factors to be borne in mind when we evaluate later charges of conspiracies against him.

I must here repeat my warning that no reconstruction can claim certainty: anyone may believe that some or all of these 'conspirators' did conspire, against either Philip or Alexander. Thus, for example, Berve doubts the conspiracy of the sons of Aëropus, but seems to believe the others; Bosworth believes some but not others; Brunt seems not to believe any of them.[10] There are scholars who will even believe, with Plutarch (*Alex.* 10. 8), that Alexander disapproved of the murder of Cleopatra and her daughter.[11] Since I see no reason why the sons of Aëropus should have conspired to kill Philip, and I think it unlikely that Amyntas, with no known backing among the Macedonian nobles (and presumably no support in the army, which would hardly know him), would have tried to kill Alexander, I share Brunt's view and regard these executions merely as early indications of Alexander's methods. They could be refined later, when he could confidently resort to show trials.

The 'conspiracy' of Alexander son of Aëropus fits into this context and follows on smoothly. It was discovered in Asia Minor when Alexander was near Phaselis.[12] We do not

[8] See Berve 1926: no. 61, again apparently accepting the accusation, although we hear of no other member of the aristocracy involved in this 'conspiracy'.

[9] For the chronology see Bosworth 1980a: 159 f. (not accepting the charge against Amyntas).

[10] For Berve see above, nn. 7 and 8. Bosworth 1980a: 159 f. *et al.* Brunt 1976 (Arrian I, Loeb edn.), p. lxi.

[11] e.g. Berve 1926: no. 434, though aware of Just. 12. 6. 14, putting Cleopatra and her brothers (?) in a list of Alexander's victims.

[12] This is where it is placed by Arr. 1. 25 (early 333). The vulgate seems to have agreed with this. Just. 11. 7. 1 ff. puts the affair between Granicus, followed by fighting and the capture of other cities in Asia Minor, and Alexander's arrival in Gordium. For Curtius, see Atkinson 1980, 78: the account was in book 2, apparently following the fall of Halicarnassus. Diodorus is the odd man out: he

have Curtius' actual account. It appears to have been based on a different version from the one we have in our other sources (Arrian, Diodorus, and Justin), but that divergence must arouse our suspicion. Caution is indicated: it may be the same tradition, reworked by Curtius himself.[13]

Arrian gives the only full account: a Persian called Sisines[14] was captured by Parmenio as he carried a letter from Darius to the satrap of Phrygia—a circumstantial detail that ought to be accepted (the obscure Atizyes is named as the satrap) and that shows Arrian's date to be correct: by the time Alexander had reached the area of the Cilician Gates (as in Diodorus) Greater Phrygia no longer had a Persian

puts it (17. 32) after the incident involving Philip the physician (17. 31). See further, n. 23 below. The view I expressed in Badian 1960, that an interval elapsed between the deposition of Alexander the Lyncestian and his being taken into custody, is not seriously tenable.

[13] Diodorus mentions the 'evidence' of Sisines and Olympias' letter; Justin writes of an *indicium captiui* (i.e. clearly Sisines), ignoring the letter; Arrian too has only Sisines' evidence. Curtius' two *indices*, if taken literally, are unparalleled. I suspect, however, that he merely combined Sisines' evidence (as in Justin and Diodorus) with Olympias' letter (as in Diodorus), and, for dramatic effect, changed what might fairly be called two *indicia* to two personal *indices*. The fact that the reference to the two *indices* is repeated (7. 1. 6, 8. 8. 6, 10. 1. 40) merely shows that Curtius remembered what he had written (note *sicut supra diximus*, 7. 1. 6). Although Arr. 1. 25. 9 makes it just possible, I doubt that the swallow that, in an anecdote reported by Arrian (1. 25. 6 ff.), warned Alexander of danger facing him would count as an *index*. It is not to be excluded that Curtius told the story (obviously of vulgate origin). The supposed letter of Alexander, proving his guilt, was imported by Hedicke (Teubner) into the text at 8. 8. 6 by fanciful emendation. (Compare, e.g., Bardon (Budé), with much simpler and convincing intervention.)

[14] We do not know whether this Sisines is identical with the son of Phrataphernes (Berve 1926: no. 709). Berve's attempt to identify him with the hero of a fanciful story in Curt. 3. 7. 11 ff., whose existence is difficult to credit (no. 710), is worthless. These are the only three individuals by this name who occur in the Alexander historians. Berve's comment that no. 709 may have been too young in 330, when his father joined Alexander, even to meet the king can only be called 'aus der Luft gegriffen'. We are not told where this Sisines was between 330 and 324, when he entered the *agema* of the Companions, together with his brother, who had joined Alexander only a few months before (Phradasmanes, Berve 1926: no. 812; Arr. 7. 6. 4). As Berve himself says, 'all' those admitted to the *agema* on that occasion will have been with Alexander 'längere Zeit' (and all will have acquired military distinction (sub no. 526)). Since Phradasmanes clearly had not been with Alexander at all long, we must conclude that it was Sisines who secured his brother's admission along with his own. It follows further that he will not have left Alexander's entourage after joining him in 330. As for military distinction, it is quite likely that he had acquired some: our sources simply do not record the military activities of Persians in Alexander's service (of which there must have been many), except for one or two satraps.

satrap. Sisines, when interviewed by Parmenio (needless to say, through interpreters), is said to have revealed that his real mission was to contact Alexander the Lyncestian, said to have approached Darius to offer treason, and to promise him the throne of Macedon and 1,000 talents in gold if he assassinated his king.

The story, as it stands, is worthless. Parts of it may even have been excogitated for Alexander's show trial in 330, for which we have no details.[15] In the first place, we must ask: why did Sisines, unlikely to have to save himself from torture or death, reveal the 'plot' instead of confining himself to his prima-facie mission, which was perfectly plausible? Next, it is difficult to believe that Sisines was expected to meet in secret, and hold secret conversations through interpreters, with the commander of the Thessalian cavalry: one might even wonder (though an answer to this is possible) what πίστεις (physical pledges of good faith) Sisines could offer him.[16]

The story of the divine warning, this time transmitted through a swallow, is (as we shall see) not unparalleled in the tales of conspiracies against Alexander. However, the kernel of truth is the capture by Parmenio of an envoy from Darius to his governor of the province about to be invaded by Alexander, and Parmenio's sending him on to Alexander, who would want to hear Darius' message to his governor at first hand. The 'conspiracy of Alexander son of Aëropus' was grafted on to this authentic incident.

I think it was done at the time, not later. The opportunity was too good to be allowed to pass. Alexander had at the start of his reign had to accept and even honour Antipater's son-in-law. By now he was far enough away from Antipater, and sufficiently secure in his own power, to remove the man, provided a plausible reason could be found. With his

---

[15] See Bosworth 1980a: 161 ff. (As will appear, I think more of the details authentic than he does.)

[16] Robson's Loeb translation (copied by Brunt, as usual) certainly mistakes the meaning of πίστεις δοῦναι/λαμβάνειν. But although it always means a physical pledge *confirming* an assurance, it can be weakly used, so that the word may be acceptable here. It may mean only an explicit promise over the King's seal (thus probably Arr. 3. 6. 7; 1. 4. 7 is not clear). Xenophon rarely uses the phrase, but see for an amusing instance *Anab.* 1. 2. 26 (a 'strong' meaning). For Thucydides Bétant explains it as *fidei pignora*.

usual genius for recognizing and seizing an opportunity, Alexander at once saw that the capture of a Persian messenger would serve his purpose. We may even conjecture (although this is not a necessary or even a secure hypothesis) that Parmenio was informed of Alexander's plan. However, it was the opportunity of needing interpreters to transmit Sisines' message to Greeks and Macedonians that invited exploitation. It provided a perfect setting. Interpreters could be made to perform as instructed. If they were slaves, they obviously had no choice. If (as is quite possible) Alexander called on Laomedon and his staff (cf. Arr. 3. 6. 6), there can be no doubt of his devotion to Alexander: after all, he had suffered for that devotion under Philip (Arr. 3. 6. 5) and he would not let him down on an important occasion. The interpreters would produce the required message, and Sisines would never know about it (there is no reason to think he understood Greek), nor would the Greeks and Macedonians who, even if they heard them, would not understand Sisines' own words.[17] Parmenio's loyalty, whether or not he knew of the plot, was not in doubt: the man who had organized the murder of his own son-in-law would not hesitate to act against the son-in-law of Antipater. From what we know of the Macedonian court, there was probably no love lost between those two: Parmenio had at once joined what appeared to be the winning faction of Attalus, while Antipater had stayed with Alexander, awaiting his chance. Nor need we be surprised at Olympias' letter, which we can accept as genuine. I think it had arrived some time before and could be effectively produced at this point.[18] Olympias'

---

[17] It is relevant to refer to a famous translation scene in comedy: Aristoph. *Acharn.* 100 ff. The Persian there, called 'gibberish' by Sommerstein (agreeing with West 1968: 5–7 ff., with fanciful reconstruction of the OP), has been taken seriously by Iranologists. See Brandenstein and Mayrhofer 1964: 91, with a reference to a more detailed discussion (unknown to the two Hellenists). They produce an acceptable OP original, with minimal textual changes. (Noted already, with speculative discussion, Francis 1992: 337–9.)

[18] We cannot tell when Olympias' letter was received. Diodorus' aorist (17. 32. 1: ἔγραψε) is non-specific: either 'Olympias wrote' (without specification of time) or, following a common use of the aorist, 'Olympias had written'. His use of an aorist (συνδραμόντων) for the corroborative evidence prima facie suggests an earlier time. Of course, it may mean that that evidence had become known before Olympias' letter arrived, but the run of the narrative does not suggest this. I am therefore inclined to translate: 'when many other plausible points had come together to

feelings towards Antipater do not need documentation. That in Pella she could have acquired information about a plot by the Lyncestian that was not accessible to Alexander surely does not merit serious discussion. Her letter presumably was based on distrust for Antipater and merely contained an injunction to Alexander to be on his guard against the Lyncestian. At the most, it may have given Alexander the idea of staging his namesake's 'treason'.

The story of the 'conspiracy of Alexander son of Aëropus' is instructive. It adds considerably to our perception of Alexander's methods. The next suspicion of conspiracy, that of Philip the Acarnanian, acts as a foil (Arr. 2. 4. 7 ff.). Berve has shown that it was at the least novelistically expanded by reminiscences of the 'conspiracy' of Alexander. Although (as Bosworth has shown, 1980*a*: 191 f.) not all of Berve's arguments are sound, enough remains. Even as Arrian tells the tale (we do not know from what source), it shows features of dramatic embellishment characteristic of vulgate anec- dotes.[19] Arrian at least does not go as far as Curtius (3. 6. 3), where the feverish king is made to wait three days before he can take the 'medicine' (surely a duplicate of the three days it later took him to recover) and so has plenty of time, while near death, to do an elaborate cost-benefit analysis regarding confidence in Philip. In Arrian, who implies no long interval, but rather seems to envisage Philip mixing his potion by Alexander's bedside, we dramatically see Alex-

support the charge'. The letter would then be pulled out and acted upon when the time seemed right (Welles's addition, in his Loeb translation, that the letter arrived 'at this time', is pure fiction). It is interesting that Alexander did not have his name- sake tried at this time: obviously, that was because he could not. Sisines would have to appear as a witness, and the accusation would not have survived his testimony.

[19] Berve 1926: 388 n. 2 is wrong in stating that the story was not in Aristobulus. But he is essentially right in rejecting the story as we have it. The Philotas affair is not a parallel for Arrian's reluctance to use direct speech: he there explicitly tells us (3. 26. 2) that he is following Ptolemy, hence indirect speech is mandatory. There are no clauses in the indicative, except where the infinitive was precluded by grammar. In 4. 8. 8 (the Cleitus affair) we do see Arrian briefly changing to direct speech for vivid effect, as Bosworth says. Bosworth is surely right in explaining the indirect narrative of that episode by Arrian's reluctance to counter his encomiastic purpose. It would follow that he would have embraced the story of Philip the physician with open arms, and nowhere more so than in its conclusion. I must suggest that he did not do so because he not only did not find it in his main sources, but realized that Ptolemy's account left no room for it, and perhaps that it con- tained elements that did not make sense.

ander drinking the supposedly poisoned cup 'at the same
time' as Philip reads Parmenio's warning letter.[20]

Some major questions impose themselves. First, where
was Parmenio? In 2. 4. 4 Arrian has just told us that
Alexander's 'whole force' was with him just before this incident. Surely Parmenio is included, and there is no indication
of his being at once sent away. On the contrary, at the beginning of the very next sentence after the Philip story (2. 5. 1),
Arrian reports that ἐκ δὲ τούτων ('after this') Alexander sent
Parmenio ahead to seize the Gates. Of course, Parmenio
might have been somewhere else and then sent on from
there. A scenario can easily be constructed ad hoc that puts
Parmenio either in advance of the point Alexander had
reached or behind. But any such conjecture cannot refute

---

[20] Plutarch, who has precisely the same story as Arrian (presumably not from
Ptolemy but from a vulgate source), adding dramatic detail and wording of his own,
describes the scene of the reading of the letter as θαυμαστὴν καὶ θεατρικήν ('astonish-
ing and fit for the stage'): here, for once, he did not need to add to the dramatic
colouring.

Curtius does not call the remedy a purge, which may be to his credit. For the
three days' wait, see Atkinson 1980: ad loc. Rolfe (Loeb) and Bardon (Budé) make
nonsense worse by mistranslation: they take *praedixit* to mean that Philip *ordered*
Alexander to wait, while near death, for three days before he could take the
medicine. In fact, *praedixit* is always used by Curtius to mean 'foretell' (see
Thérasse's *Index Verborum*): the doctor is said to have warned Alexander that it
would be three days before he could take it. It has been suggested to me that finding
and mixing the ingredients might take as long as that. This seems to me going too
far in defence of Curtius' dramatic invention. Purges were not difficult to come by,
and since they have a clearly defined effect, one would be as good as another if
effective. Pliny, that repository of medical lore, mentions quite a number of them.
As it happens, he nowhere mentions a purge for use against fever or a chill. The
nearest I have found is in the uses of dried figs (23. 121 f.), which *aluum molliunt*
and a decoction of which with fenugreek (again a simple mixture!) will treat
pleurisy and pneumonia, which were probably diagnosed even by Greek physicians
as being what Alexander had contracted. *De Morbis* 44 ff., a discussion of pleurisy
and pneumonia, does not mention purges as treatment. The 'purge', I think, helps
to give the story away as fiction: it is just what a layman, familiar with physicians'
common practices, would make up, even though it was unsuitable in this case. Nor
can I believe that a physician would spend three days on finding and preparing the
'purge'. Only very few infusions have to be left to 'draw' as long as that and I have
found none at all appropriate here. We must also bear in mind that court physicians
would hardly rely on finding familiar plants in the unknown lands to which they
were being taken, or on taking the word of potentially hostile natives for the effects
of the plants they would find there. Philip, obviously one of the court physicians,
must have carried a 'medicine chest' with basic remedies and (e.g.) dried herbs with
him, to last at least for some time. (The physicians were no doubt used to the
duration of Philip's campaigns and had no idea of how long Alexander's would turn
out to be.) Most ancient remedies were simple enough.

Arrian's account, almost certainly from Ptolemy, and his refusal to vouch for the story. Nor will it do to call the Greek phrase a 'weak transitional phrase' (Bosworth 1980*a*: ad loc.): even when he uses it as a transitional phrase, Arrian always uses it of temporal sequence.[21] It means, quite simply, that Parmenio, who (at least as Arrian, following Ptolemy, saw it) had been with Alexander throughout this incident, was then sent off on his mission. Arrian's narrative is consistent and based on his main sources (in fact, presumably Ptolemy). Parmenio's presence, as Berve saw, deprives the Philip story of any claim to authenticity: there can have been no letter from Parmenio to Alexander, dramatically handed to the physician to read. Moreover: why, in this story, is the informant anonymous; and why did he not take his story straight to Alexander?

Bosworth rightly noted that Arrian's indirect narration shows (as occasionally elsewhere) that he refused to take responsibility for the tale. As often, he could not resist the temptation of inserting a good anecdote from the vulgate tradition into his basic narrative—especially an anecdote with such a eulogistic conclusion. What is striking, however, is that Arrian retains indirect speech in the conclusion: he would not subscribe even to this in his own person. He has in fact warned the sophisticated reader that he himself did not believe any of it. Possibly Philip did save Alexander's life, perhaps when the other physicians did not dare to try. The rest is fiction, and marked as such.

Coming not long after the story of the Lyncestian and sharing some features with it,[22] it was later completely amalgamated with it.[23] By the time it reached Seneca (*De Ira* 2.

---

[21] See, e.g., 2. 1. 1, where there is no doubt that the actions described in that chapter (starting with Memnon's capture of Chios) belong to 333, long after Alexander's arrival at Gordium.

[22] But Sisines, whatever he had to say, clearly did come across Parmenio first and said it to him.

[23] See Berve 1926: no. 788, concluding that it was 'deutlich eine Dublette'. Diodorus' displacement of the incident, which (as we saw) was concordantly and correctly placed earlier by the other sources, is puzzling. Perhaps he remembered the association of the incidents of an Alexander and a Philip (is the name 'Philip' significant? perhaps, if the story was spun out of whole cloth) and tried to associate them more closely than his source. However, the solution to this puzzle is hardly worth a great deal of effort and ingenuity.

23. 2), a letter from Olympias had been substituted for the letter from Parmenio. The original point was presumably to serve as a counterweight to the story of the Lyncestian. If we ignore embellishments added by the vulgate in telling of Alexander's hearing of Philotas' 'treason' or of Harpalus' escape, it is the only story on record that shows Alexander as loyal to his friends under suspicion. I have often argued that the court version of Ptolemy and (in part) Aristobulus should not be regarded as the whole truth and that the vulgate tradition, especially as found in Curtius, offers much to correct or supplement it. But at some point one must draw the line. A story that, on the face of it, does not make sense even as told in Arrian, and that Arrian refused to authenticate, is perhaps hardly even worth the long treatment I have given it, were there not a tendency to defend it. It is about as authentic as the supposed conspiracy of Parmenio confessed to under torture by Philotas (Curt. 6. 11. 22), which has also recently acquired a defender. Essentially, Berve was right in his judgement.

One lesson, hinted at above, is that Curtius is given to making up not only speeches (as we all know) but exciting dramatic details, even where, as here, they make no sense. Fortunately, we do not have to believe the story of Alexander's waiting at death's door for three days before receiving his medicine. But I have perhaps been too ready to follow Curtius on other occasions where there is no other source and his dramatic details do not produce obvious nonsense. I am not now as certain as I was that we should fully accept his dramatic account of the arrest of Philotas (6. 8. 16 ff.). Although it is only distantly related to Tiberius' plots as told by Tacitus (see Atkinson 1994: ad loc.), those well-known incidents may have provided points of departure for Curtius' dramatic imagination, elaborating his information (which I think was essentially correct) on relations at the Macedonian court.[24]

---

[24] That the speeches at Philotas' trial are not authentic does not need to be argued. Even speeches in Arrian should not be lightly regarded as such. But the strand of personal relations among the men around Alexander that Curtius found in one of his sources and that is not reproduced in any other of our surviving sources, except occasionally by Plutarch, does seem to add valuable and acceptable information to the court historiographers and the gossips.

But these details are perhaps not important. What really matters about the next conspiracy we must treat, the 'Philotas affair', is whether there was indeed a plot by Dimnus (whoever he was).

In my treatment of the affair in *TAPhA* 91 (1960), 324–38, I implied, without adequate discussion, that there was no such plot: that there was only a conspiracy *against* Philotas, hatched in his absence from the camp and maturing straight after his return. Perhaps I went too far in my implication. Hamilton's suggestion (1969: 134 f.) that there was a plot by Dimnus (though Philotas was not involved in it and merely did not think it important enough to be worth reporting) and that Alexander, already suspicious of Philotas ever since Egypt, was now persuaded by Philotas' many enemies at the court that Philotas must be its prime mover, does not seem an acceptable alternative.[25] It is not, in fact, 'more in accord with the sources', as he writes, except in so far as most of them report that Dimnus was guilty. The sources show a great deal of variation. In Arrian (from Ptolemy) Dimnus is not mentioned: Philotas admits that he heard of 'some plot being hatched' against Alexander and did not report it. In Diodorus (17. 79. 5–6) Dimnus is arrested and kills himself in the course of the investigation.[26] In Curtius (6. 7) we have the usual dramatic elaboration: Dimnus' death is almost worthy of opera. He tries to kill himself, does not quite succeed, is carried into Alexander's presence, and there lives just long enough to hear Alexander's rhetorical (and quite irrelevant) question whether he thought Philotas more fit to be king than Alexander. The only other account is in Plutarch (*Alex.* 49. 7). There Dimnus is said to have been killed while resisting arrest. Plutarch adds that Alexander

[25] I am reluctant to accept it (as well as another scholar's theory that the plot against Philotas was hatched by some of his courtiers and that Alexander himself was entirely innocent) because of what we know about Alexander's personality: he is never demonstrably a simple-minded victim of court intrigue, but (on the contrary) seems to be given to stimulating mutual jealousies (e.g. between Hephaestion and Craterus). In the case of Philotas, Plutarch makes it clear that Alexander, once he had been informed of Philotas' remarks in Egypt, personally took charge of what Plutarch calls the 'plot against Philotas'.

[26] That he confessed before doing so, thus giving Alexander the full information (as Hamilton believes), is not a legitimate deduction from the source, where the page (Metron) informed Alexander 'of everything'. (In Curtius the information comes from Cebalinus: 6. 7. 25.)

now thought the explanation had escaped him. It is this that makes him inclined to listen to the charges advanced by Philotas' enemies, especially since he had already been feeling hostile towards him. Inevitably, Plutarch shies away from directly accusing Alexander.

As far as Philotas in concerned, Plutarch knows only of a plot against him, initiated by Craterus in Egypt and taken over by Alexander. Abandoning temporal sequence by a wide margin, he relates the events leading to Philotas' execution in immediate sequence. Plutarch surely knew all the earlier sources we know and many more. He must certainly have known the vulgate account, as we find it in Diodorus and Curtius: that Philotas was told of a plot against Alexander and at the least evaded his duty of passing the information on to the king or allowing the informants do so. In Plutarch, Philotas never (until his trial, presumably) hears of any plot against Alexander. Of course, even if he did and failed to pass on the information, his alleged explanation, that he did not attach much importance to the matter, would seem credible: the conspirators were unimportant men, the motive (if one was stated) quite probably trivial and the way the matter was said to have been revealed conventional. However, Plutarch did not accept this story at all. He followed a source (we cannot specify it) that reported Cebalinus and Nicomachus as telling Philotas that they had 'very important business' to discuss with Alexander; it was only when they got to see Alexander that they revealed the plot of Dimnus (in Plutarch Limnus), and they did not even then imply that Philotas had known of it.

It is hard to understand why scholars have unanimously (as far as I know) chosen to follow the version found in the vulgate and to ignore the one followed (no doubt deliberately) by Plutarch, without asking why he chose to do so.[27] In Plutarch the 'plot' against Philotas, developed by

---

[27] There is no doubt that Plutarch knew the 'vulgate'; he perhaps assumed that the reader would also know it, so that he needed to state only his divergence from it. The *proskynesis* affair would provide a parallel. There Plutarch omitted the common version of the banquet and opted to tell a (presumably) less known one by Chares; but his allusion to Callisthenes' heroism shows that he both knew the standard version and expected the reader to know it. Here he must surely have seen the implication of the version he followed, that Philotas was innocent and that Alexander knew it.

Alexander in Egypt, turns into what he saw was the plot
against Philotas at Phrada. Plutarch never questions the
existence of a plot by Dimnus and its effect on Alexander.
But, being a better historian than he likes to admit (as is
indeed clear from other instances, both in this *Life* and in
others), he leaves no doubt that he saw that there was no
reason why his source should invent a version that made
Philotas innocent, while there was every reason why the
version officially propounded at the trial and after should
insist that Philotas deliberately suppressed (at least) knowledge of the plot, hence was quite likely a participant in it.
However, he could not pursue his case to its obvious conclusion and accuse Alexander of arranging the judicial
murder of Philotas as well as the undeniable murder of
Parmenio: that would have destroyed the image of
Alexander that he tried to convey and made him out to be a
despicable tyrant. He therefore links Philotas with the plot
of Dimnus by making Philotas' enemies, when poisoning the
king's mind against Philotas, imply among 'ten thousand
other charges' against Philotas that he had indeed known of
the conspiracy by Dimnus and had preferred not to reveal it
(*Alex.* 49. 8–10). (On this, see further n. 25 with text.)

In view of the (apparently) brief treatment of the affair by
Ptolemy, who merely asserted that there was proof of
Philotas' guilt and gave no details (which Arrian would not
have suppressed), and the chain of events that I sketched
forty years ago, I now think it is advisable for the scholar
seeking the truth to follow Plutarch and make the choice that
he made among the sources: it follows that the 'conspiracy of
Dimnus' offered an opportunity to rid Alexander of the
house of Parmenio (what remained of it), which he eagerly
seized. With Dimnus dead, he no doubt had full control over
what Cebalinus and Nicomachus would state at Philotas'
trial, and that would be the only information heard by the
army. The case, in fact, shows the full development of the
method used in the 'discovery' of the 'conspiracy of
Alexander son of Aëropus'.

We are now ready to consider what I described as the
most important question: whether there really was a plot by
Dimnus—or merely one by Alexander and some of his

courtiers against Philotas. In the light of the fuller discussion of the background, and of Plutarch's testimony, this
question requires more careful consideration than I devoted
to it forty years ago.

The Philotas affair, as I insisted at the time, comes sus-
piciously soon after Philotas had been left as the only one of
Parmenio's sons still alive and after he had joined the camp,
having fulfilled his sad duty of burying his brother. There
was now an opportunity for decisive action against Philotas
and Parmenio. Alexander had a long memory: he will not
have forgotten Parmenio's at the least eager embrace of the
new order at Philip's court by a marriage alliance with
Cleopatra's uncle, clearly directed against the interests of
Olympias and Alexander; nor the traumatic incident of
Philotas accompanying Philip when the latter exploded in
anger at Alexander's undercutting his plans for a marriage
alliance with Pixodarus. Plutarch's ἐπετίμησεν ἰσχυρῶς καὶ
πικρῶς ἐλοιδόρησεν ('forcefully rebuked and bitterly abused
him': *Alex.* 10. 3) vividly paints the atmosphere at that inter-
view, which preceded Philip's exiling Alexander's friends
and demanding the arrest and extradition of Thessalus; even
though Plutarch accepts what is clearly Alexander's later
version of the cause for Philip's incommensurate fury, that
he merely thought the match was not good enough for
Alexander. Philotas was obviously not one of the 'friends
and close companions' of Alexander (thus Plutarch, again no
doubt following the later expurgated version): as Hamilton
(1969: 26) rightly points out, he was not exiled when Alexander's friends were (indeed, we find him at Philip's side,
and Hamilton suggests that he may have alerted Philip to
Alexander's treasonable action); and Philotas' father was the
father-in-law (Hamilton mistakenly writes 'son-in-law') of
Alexander's most dangerous enemy.

At the time of his accession Alexander had had to pay Parmenio's price for his and his family's support. Antagonizing
him might have been fatal, but the family's loyal and distinguished service fully justified the forced decision. However,
that memory would be stored alongside the earlier ones.
Even at the time of the action against Philotas and Parmenio,
Plutarch notes that the action was not without danger (*Alex.*

49. 2), and Curtius' account of the *coup d'état*, rhetorically enhanced though it may be, proves him right (Curt. 6. 8. 9 ff.). But by now he felt strong enough to indulge his stored-up resentment by swift action. The question is, I now think, whether the plot by Dimnus provided a lucky opportunity that Alexander eagerly seized (we might compare the action against the Lyncestian Alexander) or whether Dimnus' plot was manufactured in order to entrap Philotas. I would not now exclude the former possibility: the parallel, both for Alexander's luck and for his seizing the opportunity to exploit it, is striking. But the timing, and the care taken in setting the trap, on the whole still makes me incline to the more sinister interpretation. On this reading, Dimnus was suborned to be the tool: his telling his young lover of a conspiracy and warning him not to reveal it would almost ensure that he did so. Everything then went according to plan: Dimnus, when he saw Alexander's soldiers approaching, knew he was being sacrificed and either killed himself or was killed before he could reveal the real plot, and Alexander was safe.

In the light of Alexander's pattern of behaviour, it does not seem impossible, or even improbable, that he would not hesitate to sacrifice an obscure man like Dimnus for the sake of a great prize, and that, as I suggested in my earlier discussion, the whole plot was hatched during Philotas' fortunate absence. As Bosworth has recently demonstrated, Alexander was soon to show mastery on a more massive scale in making 'the victims . . . become the culprits'.[28] How and by what promises Dimnus may have been persuaded to become the key figure in the plot, we can of course never know. I have merely been concerned to point out that the

---

[28] Bosworth 1996*a*: 165. Atkinson 1994: 224 notes Tiberian parallels to Curtius' narrative and suggests they may have influenced Curtius' presentation. If Curtius wrote later than Atkinson believes, Domitian would also have to be considered (Suet. *Dom.* 11). Curtius may have accentuated some of the resemblances (see my comments p. 63 above), but this is no reason to believe (with, e.g., Berve 1926: 395, citing Schwartz) that Alexander was incapable of deviousness towards his enemies. I should perhaps add to my account of Plutarch that his total rejection of the official version (which, I repeat, he must have known) is shown by his statement (49. 7) that Philotas' motive for not taking Cebalinus to see the king remains unknown. For deviousness, see further on Astaspes in the Appendix to this chapter.

fact of his death and the fact that most of our sources (we cannot be sure in Arrian's case) believe in his guilt do not exclude the possibility that he was originally a willing participant.

In any case, an express messenger was now sent to organize the assassination of Parmenio, which I still think was, on either interpretation, the ultimate aim. It was entrusted to Cleander, linked to Parmenio by a brother's marriage and promoted by him. Parmenio, clearly, had never thought of the precedent he was setting when he sacrificed his son-in-law Attalus to Alexander for the sake of his family's power under the new king. We cannot here discuss the trials that followed the death of Philotas. (I discussed them in my earlier article.) But it is worth mentioning that the Lyncestian Alexander was now produced in front of the army and 'tried' for the crime he had been charged with in Asia Minor (Curt. 7. 1. 5 ff.). His execution could be taken for granted and Alexander no longer had to fear that Antipater might stir up Macedonia against him (cf. Just. 11. 7. 2).[29]

The next event that deserves a brief mention is Alexander's suspicion of a conspiracy against him in the scene that led to the death of Cleitus.[30] It was clear even to Alexander, once he was sober, that there had been no conspiracy. But he genuinely suspected (it seems) a conspiracy by his *hetairoi* and perhaps even his guard when they tried to prevent him from killing Cleitus in a drunken fit of rage. This gives us a foretaste of what was to come years later. But what is important about the Cleitus affair is what followed *post Cliti caedem* (as Curtius put it: 8. 4. 30). When Alexander continued to sulk in his tent, in spite of various efforts to 'console' him, the army finally passed a resolution posthumously convicting Cleitus of treason (Curt. 8. 2. 12)—hardly a spontaneous action, one would think. It is

---

[29] Habicht 1977: 514–15 has shown that a son of this Alexander, called Arrhabaeus, survived (no doubt protected by Antipater in Macedonia) to be a 'friend' of Alexander's successors.

[30] The fear of conspiracy: Arr. 4. 8. 8, Curt. 8. 1. 47, Plut. *Alex.* 51. 6—which incidentally shows to most (unfortunately not to all) scholars that the Macedonian dialect was the language of command among Alexander's (and no doubt among Philip's) Macedonian forces.

only Curtius who alerts us to it, and to its effect: *libertas* was now *sublata*. Both Alexander and his officers now knew that the army would support him, no matter what.

There is no more talk of conspiracies for about a year, when we reach a very peculiar plot—the conspiracy of the pages, perhaps the first genuine conspiracy of the reign, certainly the first where the sources allow no doubt as to its real existence. The story is told in all the standard works and need not be set out here.[31] It is also often pointed out that the pages involved (only a handful of the corps) did not belong to the nobles most active and eminent at Alexander's court. The death of Cleitus and its aftermath, as Curtius pointed out, had suppressed opposition. It seems that the sons of those who had gained real prominence had been taught to share their fathers' caution.[32] One cannot help wondering whether the reaction of precisely these boys was perhaps due to dissatisfaction with the lack of rewards and advancement their fathers had received (no one above ilarch, it seems)— and perhaps talked about in the safety of their tents or lodgings. Jealousy felt for those who had made names and fortunes for themselves would not be unexpected. For what it is worth, Hermolaus' speech in Curtius blames Alexander for acquiring riches while his soldiers had nothing but their scars to show. This may well in part represent talk picked up among the lower officer ranks, if it is entitled to any belief.

A detail arousing some interest in the story of this conspiracy is the warning by the Syrian prophetess that, according to Aristobulus, persuaded Alexander to go back to his all-night drinking-bout until the pages' guard was changed. Curtius (8. 6. 14), like Arrian (4. 13. 6), knows both a version

---

[31] Arr. 4. 13, Curt. 8. 6 (the speeches in 7 and most of 8), Plut. *Alex.* 55. Diodorus reported the fate of Callisthenes (hence presumably the pages' conspiracy), but his narrative is not in our text (see Diod. *Per.* 17. 2). Arrian picked up Hermolaus' speech from a vulgate source; indeed, his whole narrative is a *logos*, hence probably composed from various sources in the form in which he tells it. It differs in significant respects from Curtius' elaborate version: each presents one or two items the other lacks. However, the general topic is no doubt based on Cleitarchus, whose assessment of Alexander's deterioration is echoed in Cic. *Att.* 13. 28. 3. (See my analysis in Badian 1996: 20.)

[32] For the story as a whole see, e.g., Bosworth 1988*b*: 117 ff. For the interesting prosopographical item of Philotas son of Carsis, a Thracian, among the conspirators, see Berve 1926: no. 801 and Bosworth 1995: ad loc.

that apparently ascribed his escape to his *fortuna* and one that credited the Syrian; which shows that Aristobulus, at least, did tell the story of the conspiracy. Now, the theme of a supernatural warning of a conspiracy is not unique in the tale of these plots: we noted it in the 'conspiracy' of the Lyncestian Alexander (see p. 58 and n. 13 above). If Aristobulus correctly represents the official version, the ascription to fortune may be an attempt to substitute that well-known concept (compare Plutarch's essay!) for the less than respectable figure of the barbarian seer. If so, it would follow that Alexander knew about the conspiracy (unless we are willing to believe in the divine warning as such) and decided to let it mature and fail, since that was certain to lead to his being fully informed about it. The problem is that Aristobulus, who was determined to deny that Alexander was given to excessive drinking,[33] may have invented the Syrian to 'explain' why Alexander stayed at the party all night. However, he was also given to stressing the favour of gods and fortune for Alexander[34] and, had this been the official version, should have had no hesitation in reproducing it. I am inclined to believe that Alexander did know about the plans, but had no detailed information, and so had recourse to the one way of making sure he would find out.[35]

The execution of the pages was followed by the judicial murder of Callisthenes, fully comparable in method to the judicial murder of the Lyncestian Alexander after the conviction of the 'conspirators' with Philotas.[36] The official

---

[33] Arr. 7. 29. 4, Plut. *Alex.* 75. 6: enthusiastically welcomed by Tarn 1948: ii. 41. (See 39 ff. for his idealizing portrait of the faithful Aristobulus, closer to Alexander than the Macedonian nobles. In fact there is no evidence for his being at all close to Alexander; much of his work seems to have been secondary interpretation.) Berve 1926: no. 121 also idealizes, but less blatantly. Pédech 1984: 354 f., in a basically favourable discussion of Aristobulus, fully recognizes his tendency to naive apologia.

[34] Passages collected by Berve 1926: 65.

[35] In Curtius the boys are aware of the fact that delay would lead to exposure: they want at all costs to avoid waiting seven days for the next opportunity. Actual failure, of course, was likely to lead to a *sauve qui peut* reaction, since no one would want to be anticipated. We cannot tell what happened to Epimenes, who actually started the unravelling of the plot. His fate is not mentioned in Arrian. In Curtius he shares in the rewards given to the informers, but this may be fictitious elaboration.

[36] See Diod. 17. 80. 2, Curt. 7. 1. 5–9 (staged by the king, § 5). Arrian suppresses the story.

version stated that he was not only guilty, but had been denounced (under torture, it seems) by the pages (Arr. 4. 14. 1). Ptolemy, at least, must have been present at the trial and must have known better. He chose, not for the only time, to support his king's memory. Arrian's sympathy is, at least to some extent, with Callisthenes. Indeed, it must have been hard for one who was by profession a philosopher and by choice a panegyrist of Alexander to find those two influences in such sharp conflict. As Bosworth put it (1995: 97), 'Arrian is clearly uncomfortable, and rightly so'. He does report that most of his sources deny that the boys implicated Callisthenes. He does not seem to have known (or if he did, he ignored) the decisive testimony to the fact that Alexander knew this, just as he had known that Philotas was innocent: the letter quoted by Plutarch in *Alexander* 55. 5 f.[37] That Callisthenes was at once executed, as Ptolemy reported, cannot be seriously doubted.[38]

[37] See Hamilton 1969: ad loc., with the reference to his detailed proof that the letter must be authentic. Bosworth 1995: 98 entertains the possibility that it might have been written by a well-informed forger. I cannot put a name to such a putative person, who was close to Alexander at the time, hostile to him, and likely years later to remember the precise location of the commanders addressed. Curtius is wrong in stating that the pages and Callisthenes were tortured to make execution more painful (8. 8. 20 f.). He knew quite well that torture was not used for that purpose, but to extract confessions—which he also knew were not at all reliable (6. 11. 21). But his 'confusion' is deliberate, intended to make the story more graphically appalling. Ptolemy, even in Arrian's summary, can be seen to have separated the torture from the death (Arr. 4. 14. 3: στρεβλωθέντα καὶ κρεμασθέντα). Bosworth (loc. cit.) is unclear and seems to be wrong: Philotas was tortured to extract new revelations, not to intensify execution.

[38] Chares, followed in part by Aristobulus (*ap.* Plut. *Alex.* 55. 9—Plutarch apparently thought they were independent accounts), reported that he was made to accompany the expedition as a prisoner, to be tried by the *synhedrion* at Corinth in the presence of Aristotle(!), but died of a disgraceful disease seven months later, 'at the time when Alexander was wounded in India among the Malli Oxydracae'. ἐν Μάλλοις Ὀξυδράκαις is in all the manuscripts, but universally deleted by editors and commentators in order to save Plutarch's (and often Chares') credit. Even Hamilton 1969: 156, argues that Plutarch 'who had made a special study of Alexander's wounds' (no evidence is given for this except for a German dissertation—there is no such claim in Plutarch) would not have made such an error in chronology. (The time between the pages' conspiracy in Bactria (Arr. 4. 22. 2, cf. Strabo 11. 11. 4.C517) and Alexander's attack on the town of the Malli was about two years.) Hamilton 1969: 122 in fact mentions two occasions when Plutarch makes mistakes over Alexander's wounds. Add that *Mor.* 341c, 343d ff. apparently confuses Malli and Oxydracae. This makes it likely that Plutarch added that phrase, to specify the occasion referred to by Chares. But he cannot have made up the 'seven months' and it cannot be held that he misinterpreted Chares: no one

This seems to have been the end of documented conspiracies by Macedonians against Alexander. There were still rebellions by Iranian nobles,[39] but they are not strictly relevant here. The only (probable) Iranian conspiracy I have been able to find is the one we are almost forced to postulate as preventing Alexander from undergoing the ritual initiation as Great King as Pasargadae. I have sufficiently discussed this elsewhere.[40] However, it was by no means the end of Alexander's suspicion of conspiracies, a suspicion fed by the events at the Hyphasis and later by the disastrous march through Gedrosia.

At the Hyphasis, what must have been a nightmare to him came true. Ever since the death of Cleitus had led to the end of freedom (as we have seen), Alexander had been secure against plots by senior officers because of the unquestioning loyalty of the army shown on that occasion. The pages' conspiracy, as we observed, involved no offspring of any senior officer or any man close to Alexander. What happened at the Hyphasis must have been totally unexpected. First, according to the only full and reliable account (Arr. 5. 25 ff., probably from Ptolemy, except for the speeches, which are probably Arrian's own additions based on vulgate material), the soldiers started grumbling among themselves and some of them went so far as to say they would not march any farther. The base of Alexander's support was collapsing. The only possible response was to appeal (this time) to the officers, to gain their support by rhetoric and promises, and to hope that they would be able to persuade the men to follow. This road was blocked when Coenus stood up to speak in support of the men. There was real danger in this. Coenus, 'in seiner männlich-einfachen Art' (Berve 1926: 218), had always known which side his bread was buttered on. A son-in-law of Parmenio, he had been instrumental in the plot against Philotas and, at least according to the vulgate, had demanded that Philotas be tortured and had

referring to Alexander's wounding in India, without specification, as Chares seems to have done, could have meant anything but the famous almost-fatal wound. Chares' story discredits itself in all details. Aristobulus can be more briefly dismissed: he was 'never one to omit an opportunity to whitewash' (Bosworth 1995: 100, which see also for general discussion).

[39] For brief discussion, see Appendix.   [40] See Badian 1996: 22 ff.

even attacked him at the 'trial' (at length in Curt. 6. 8 ff.). His forceful intervention could only be due to his judging that he could attach the army to himself, even against the king—or so it must have seemed to Alexander.[41]

In the end, seeing officers and men united against him, Alexander surrendered and did what he could to fasten the blame on the gods. What he clearly could not do was to treat the affair as a mutiny (which is how historians see it): it was impossible to punish a limited number of men as responsible for it, as could be done, for example, at Opis later. What was urgently necessary was to remove the danger from Coenus without arousing the army's suspicion or resentment. Alexander was fortunate, as usual. Not long after, Coenus died, not honourably in battle, but of disease. Alexander could defuse suspicion (if anyone had dared to voice it) by giving him a splendid funeral (Arr. 6. 2). The immediate danger was past, and the signal to other prominent nobles would be clear.[42]

Next came the shock at the city of the Malli, where Alexander found his soldiers to be 'sluggish' (βλακεύειν: Arr. 6. 9. 3) in their attack, rushed to expose himself to the enemy and ended by receiving his almost fatal wound, which for the moment regained the remorseful loyalty of the army. The effect, however, threatened to be undone by the disaster of the march through Gedrosia. There is no point in trying to quantify losses or to discuss their distribution. What mattered was the effect on morale. There is no reason to disbelieve the vulgate on this (see Diod. 17. 105. 6; with dramatic exaggeration Curt. 9. 10. 11 ff., esp. 15–16). Alexander had lost his aura of invincibility, of being able (as once at the Hindu Kush) to triumph even over the elements.

The overpowering nature of his suspicion was first shown in his order to the satraps to disband their mercenary armies.[43] Diodorus puts it down to his receiving information that rebellions in his absence had relied on mercenaries. But the overreaction documents a fear approaching panic, though we shall see that Alexander indeed had reason to

---

[41] See now Carney 1996: 33–7.
[42] For discussion of this incident see Badian 1961: 20.
[43] Diod. 17. 106. 3, 111. 1. For the interpretation see Badian 1961: 25 ff.

worry about Iranian rebellions. First, we are not told what alternative ways Alexander had found of keeping order in the satrapies and defending them against raiders and guerrillas. Since he could not spare any of his own men for such duties throughout the kingdom, it is difficult to come up with an answer. Had he lived longer, he would certainly have been forced to attend to this aspect of the problem he had created. If he could not ensure peace, rebellions were bound to follow. Another aspect necessitated immediate action. He cannot have been unaware of the dangerous social, and ultimately political, consequences that would follow the dismissal of tens of thousands of professional soldiers, suddenly deprived of the only way of making a living that they knew and sent to find their way home as best they could. Here an instant solution was found: the decree ordering the Greek cities to readmit all their exiles, most of whom had no doubt, in the manner traditional in the fourth century, enlisted as mercenaries. As I have pointed out, Alexander threw the problem he had created to the cities, on which it imposed intolerable burdens, to solve for him. We do not hear of any effort to assist them in doing so, although Alexander could by now well have afforded it. Moreover, he probably no longer cared about the fact that the decree involved a breach of the oaths sworn between him and the cities on his accession—which they would certainly not have been allowed to ignore with impunity. The extent of his fear could not be more strikingly demonstrated.

The reign of terror after his return from India[44] must in part be due to this same fear; though the element of searching for scapegoats for his failure of leadership in Gedrosia is obvious in the sources. It was not by accident, surely, that

[44] See Badian 1961. There can be no doubt that there was a reign of terror: I took care to collect the actual figures and distinguish possible from attested victims. Bosworth 1971a: 123 charges me with laying 'excessive stress on the arrival of satraps at court, inferring that a summons to court meant danger to the man invited'. All I argued was that 'such a summons *could* [original emphasis] be the prelude to summary trial and execution' (18) and that those summoned had 'ambiguous prospects'—unless, like Peucestas, they were sure of the king's favour. Bosworth's list of those who suffered no harm can be found on my pp. 18–19. However, I still think that any satrap summoned must have felt twinges of uneasiness, in view of what he had seen and heard about; and that, in view of the king's documented duplicity (Philotas and recently Astaspes!), friendly entertainment after arrival did not offer final reassurance.

the only Macedonian commanders caught up in it were Cleander, brother of Coenus, who had so conveniently died in India, and his no doubt hand-picked officers.[45] Those who had organized the murder of Parmenio could be expected, if a case of conflict arose, to put their own interests above the king's.

This was by no means the end of Alexander's suspicions of conspiracy. He clearly thought that Hephaestion's death had been deliberately brought about by his physician, who was punished with impalement—the traditional Persian punishment for traitors (Plut. *Alex.* 72. 5; Arr. 7. 14. 4),[46] and after this he became obsessed with fear of portents and conspiracies (Plut. 73–5; Arr. 7. 22, 24; note 24. 3, Alexander's suspicion that the simpleton who sat on Alexander's throne had done so ἐξ ἐπιβουλῆς ('with treasonable design')). As I put it long ago,[47] he finally 'found himself . . . on a lonely pinnacle over an abyss, with . . . security unattainable'.

Before we leave this subject, we must briefly mention the ancient conspiracy theory regarding Alexander's death: the supposed plot by the sons of Antipater that succeeded in poisoning him. The evidence was well discussed by Bosworth, though he unfortunately substituted for the ancient, not totally absurd, story a fanciful and indefensible one.[48]

---

[45] See Badian 1961. The fact that Cleander and his subordinates were the *only* Macedonian commanders summoned to the court and (probably all of them) executed can hardly be explained except through the connection with Coenus' outspokenness and death.

[46] One is reminded of the authentic story of the physician called in to attend to Stalin on his deathbed: Beria (who, of course, saw his own future as uncertain) screamed at him: 'If he dies, you'll be shot.' I do not know if the threat was carried out.   [47] Badian 1964, 204.

[48] Bosworth 1971a: given up in his more recent work (e.g. 1988b: 171 ff.). O'Brien 1992, 224 showed that it would have been far too dangerous for the generals, if they did intend to kill the king, to use a slowly acting poison: there would surely have been easier and safer ways. A full (and surprisingly extensive) collection of the evidence will be found in O'Brien 1992: 275 n. 7. His chapter 5, despite the idiosyncratic translations from the *Iliad*, gives the best brief survey of Alexander's last months. Attempts to 'diagnose' Alexander's illness (if we believe he died a natural death) are as unprofitable as (e.g.) the similar parlour game of 'diagnosing' Thucydides' plague. The latest I have come across is by Dr David W. Oldach, in the *New England Journal of Medicine* of 11 June 1998. After considering various other possibilities, ranging from (accidental) lead poisoning and (deliberate) poisoning with arsenic (which 'must . . . be given serious consideration') to malaria (which by his own description appears to be a serious possibility), he finally settles for typhoid fever: this, it seems, offers the further advantage that

Much depends on the evidence of the supposed *Ephemerides*: if they are, in any form, accepted as genuine, the theory of the plot is difficult (perhaps not impossible) to maintain. But I do not see how those 'documents', forms of which were known to Arrian and Plutarch, can be contemporary or even near-contemporary.[49] If we reject them, we are left with a situation in which it not only did not pay anyone to tell the truth, unless it coincided with his or his superior's interests, but in which it would have paid practically everyone concerned to lie for political advantage, if the truth was inconvenient. The answer, as most scholars (including now Bosworth) would agree, must be *non liquet*. This is an unsatisfactory conclusion regarding what would be the most important conspiracy against Alexander. But (if I may again quote what I have written),[50] 'there is unfortunately no royal road to *akribeia*, and we may have to live with the possibility that there is no road at all'.

We can now turn to the much shorter topic of Darius III and conspiracies. The first point to make is that only two conspiracies against Darius are in fact attested: one just after his accession, by Bagoas, which he overcame, and one at the end of his reign, to which he succumbed. Yet it seems that the whole of his reign is dominated by fears of conspiracy, which greatly contributed to the disasters he suffered, even though the fears were by no means unreasonable and lack of them might have turned out no better for him.

The starting point must be recognition of the fact that Darius was an interloper, although probably of Achaemenid

ascending paralysis 'may have given the impression of death before it actually occurred' and so account for the report that Alexander's body did not decompose after death. Since he admits that this report is likely to be legend, the suggestion of an 'ascending paralysis' due to illness, easily shown to be untenable, is not worth discussing. As for the rest, his own analysis shows no good reason for preferring typhoid fever to some of the other possibilities he advances. We may note his explanation of why Alexander did not receive better care: 'This patient received little in the way of modern medical care, I believe, because he lived at a time when such care was unavailable.'

Borza adds a long note, essentially undermining the futile attempt by pointing out the unreliability of our information, the influence of propaganda, and the growth of legend. I regret to say that the most prestigious American medical journal has added nothing of value to the parlour game.

[49] My views are argued in Badian 1987 (610 ff. on the *Ephemerides*' reports on Alexander's death).   [50] Ibid. 625.

descent on his father's side, like (by then) hundreds of others.[51] He was 'a certain Codomannus' (Justin 10. 3. 3 ff.) who had been picked up and promoted by Artaxerxes III, for his bravery and no doubt for the very obscurity of his origin, after the latter had exterminated all collateral claimants to the throne. According to Diodorus (17. 5. 5), after Bagoas had killed Arses, Artaxerxes III's son, the royal house was ἔρημος ('destitute') and no one was set κατὰ γένος ('by descent') to succeed him; hence the wicked Bagoas now secured the throne for one of the King's 'friends' named Darius. (The name is proleptic, but the statement must surely be accepted.) We must assume that, among the descendants of (only) Artaxerxes II, said by Justin (10. 1. 1) to have had 115 sons, there must have been others who were the King's 'friends' and who would think themselves no less entitled to succeed. They might now be assumed to be waiting for their chance.

Had Darius been able to distinguish himself by a major military success before he met Alexander, his position would have been immeasurably strengthened. Unfortunately, he had no opportunity for doing so; and indeed, he had never commanded in a battle or a campaign before he came to the throne.[52] There was, fortunately, time enough for him to settle into his position and consolidate his rule, as Philip's death for a while eliminated the Macedonian danger; but he had no good way of using that time to strengthen the Persian

[51] My view of Darius' origin and rise is fully argued in a forthcoming article, 'Darius III', developing views sketched in the *Encyclopaedia Iranica*, s.v. The article is scheduled to appear in *HSPh* 100 (2001). We must assume Achaemenid descent, since no one not of Achaemenid lineage on his father's side had ever, to our knowledge, aspired to the throne and since the supply of Achaemenids was by then plentiful (see below).

[52] That he suppressed a revolt in Egypt, by one Khababash, straight after coming to the throne is a figment due to Kienitz, an Egyptologist without much knowledge of other areas of ancient history and not to be trusted on points of method. The case is described by A. B. Lloyd, a better-informed Egyptologist and better historian, as 'not strong' (*CAH* VI² 345). Although Khababash was certainly at one time recognized as pharaoh, the date is quite uncertain. I think the disturbed time after Ochus' reconquest the most likely setting. None of the Alexander historians tries to build up Darius as a worthy opponent of Alexander. They would hardly have missed the opportunity, if he had indeed won such a major success as the reconquest of Egypt within months, when it had taken his predecessors generations. Their view of him is in fact quite the opposite: see, e.g., Arr. 3. 22. 2 with Bosworth's comment.

position in case Alexander resumed the invasion. He was unlucky in that the Rhodian commander Mentor, architect of the reconquest of Egypt and of Asia Minor, and under Ochus supreme commander in Asia (it seems), had died. However, had he lived, it is doubtful whether Darius could have retained him as such. It certainly seems that he did not fully trust Mentor's brother Memnon, for he, together with Artabazus, had spent many years in exile at the Macedonian court.[53] In fact, Darius' weakness at once appears in Asia Minor. Even when he knew that Alexander was preparing to renew the invasion, he felt unable to appoint a commander-in-chief there. Memnon, as was clear, could not be trusted—and in any case would probably not have been accepted by the noble Persians stationed there, without a strong King like Ochus to impose him. There were indeed eminent nobles, some of them probably Achaemenids, among those commanders, and they might well think their own claims to the throne as good as Darius'. A daughter of his by an earlier marriage had married a noble Mithradates (Berve 1926: no. 525), now one of the commanders in Asia Minor. It is noteworthy that we never find him exercising any authority over the others or transmitting orders from the King.[54] Indeed, we have no evidence for the satraps', before the battle of the Granicus, receiving any orders from the King. He certainly could not trust any of them to hold the supreme command—and win the major victory that was no doubt expected. It was only after the battle and the death and disgrace of the commanders that he appointed Memnon commander-in-chief in Asia; but only after Memnon had sent his wife and son to Darius as hostages—whether, as Diodorus reports, spontaneously, in the hope of thus attaining the

[53] See Berve 1926: nos. 152, p. 83, and 497, p. 251 (*obiter*).

[54] We may safely ignore Mithradates' son Ariobarzanes (no. 116), who is said to have betrayed Darius, and Berve's speculations. Berve, strangely, was taken in by one of the 'Schwindelautoren' (Jacoby, *FGrH* III A, p. 162) cited in Ps.-Plut. *De Fluviis*, who were exposed long ago in the edition of that essay by Rudolf Hercher (1851): Jacoby's comments are based on it. As Professor Bosworth pointed out to me, Berve should at least have known the terse dismissal of 'Aretades' by Georg Knaack in *RE Suppl.* 1 (1903), col. 125. Jacoby justly refers to 'der gelehrte roman Berves'. On the satraps, see (a beginning) Seibert 1987: 442 f. (That essay also has the great merit of trying to overturn the sources', and especially Arrian's, portrait of Darius as a weak coward—a portrait eagerly embraced by most scholars—by rational discussion.)

command, or (as we are entitled to believe) because it had been suggested to him this might be helpful.[55]

Memnon, who planned to carry the war to Greece, died in late spring 333, before the capture of Mytilene, which would have completed the strategic prerequisite to that plan.[56] Darius now had to take the field himself (Diod. 17. 30, Curt. 3. 2. 1).[57] Within six months of hearing of Memnon's death he had collected the forces of the central and western parts of his kingdom (rightly judging that he could not wait for those

[55] Arr. 1. 20. 3; cf. Diod. 17. 23. 5–6. However, Diodorus' phrase ὅπερ καὶ συνέβη γενέσθαι ('and so it actually turned out') raises the suspicion that the whole story of Memnon's initiative and motivation is fiction based on the actual event. It is doubtful whether any of our sources would know them, which they presumably could do only from Memnon himself or a close associate. It is quite *possible*, of course, that he had been told the King suspected him and advised how this could be remedied, but the 'background' to the action must remain suspect.

[56] Alexander, on his way from Gordium (late May 333), had not yet heard of Memnon's death (Curt. 3. 1. 21). See Beloch 1922–27: ii² 2, 312 ff. for the chronology.

[57] I do not see why Atkinson 1980: 100 thinks that Diod. 17. 29. 4 and 31. 1 imply that Darius heard of Memnon's death at Susa. Curt. 3. 2. 2 certainly seems to put the display of the forces of the empire outside Babylon, but does not indicate where Darius received the report. But chronology is not Curtius' strong point, and he does not tell us (or, it seems, care) whether those forces were assembled after news of Memnon's death came in or were already in place. However, since he firmly puts the decision to face Alexander himself after Memnon's death (of which it was the result), we must assume that he thinks of a good deal of time as having elapsed before the spectacle. Diod. 17. 30. 1, 31. 1 is explicit on the sequence, which we have no reason to reject, but does not indicate the King's location. It is a pity that Arrian's frequent lack of interest in chronology, especially in matters away from Alexander, is here at its worst (that he shows little interest in Memnon's operations has often been pointed out). We do not know how much time Memnon had, before his death, to advance the siege of Mytilene; but from what we can gather of his activities before this, probably not very much. We do not know how long Autophradates and Pharnabazus, after his death, τῇ πολιορκίᾳ οὐκ ἀρρώστως προσέκειντο ('vigorously devoted themselves to the siege') before Mytilene surrendered; but to judge by what we know of other attempts, in Classical Greek history, to starve major cities into surrender, it is likely to have been a long process. After this, we do not learn from Arr. 2. 2. 1 whether Pharnabazus, when he took his mercenaries to the mainland, had already received instructions to hand them over to Thymondas, who was to take them to meet the King, or whether he only received those instructions when he arrived in Asia; nor do we know whether he found Thymondas waiting for him or (as the text prima facie implies, for what little this is worth) had to wait for Thymondas' arrival, no matter when he received the instructions from the King. Arrian's regrettable vagueness provides no reason to reject the explicit and detailed account in Curtius and even Diodorus, that it was the news of Memnon's death that made Darius decide he would himself have to march against Alexander. The speed and efficiency he showed on the march only confirm that, whatever his defects as a commander in the field, he was a great organizer.

from the east: see Curt. 3. 2. 9, with an inept comment) and stood at Sochi.[58] His method is shown by his ordering the Greek mercenaries, whom Thymondas was to lead to him, to meet him along the route.[59] We are entitled to deduce that other contingents coming from the west, for example the army of Egypt, received similar instructions. The achievement should be judged by comparison with the length of time it had taken Xerxes and Artaxerxes II to collect a royal army (admittedly including the eastern contingents). It appears all the more admirable in view of the fact that he had to bring the women and children of his immediate family, and those of some other nobles, along with him.[60] That had not been the practice of Persian Kings; and they were bound to delay him. In the circumstances, and even if we discount the lurid picture painted by Curtius and probably not based

[58] The numbers of the Persian forces are, as usual, vastly exaggerated. Diodorus gives 500,000, Arrian surpasses him by giving 600,000 (perhaps from a vulgate source: his main sources may not have estimated the number). Curtius is relatively modest: less than 300,000, plus 30,000 Greek mercenaries (that figure also in Arrian). The true figures are beyond conjecture.

[59] The inclusion of the mercenaries in Curtius' account of Darius' display at Babylon does not mean that Thymondas had in fact arrived there: Curtius almost certainly added them from his own knowledge of the battle of Issus. Even if (as is likely) Darius gave the order to Thymondas as soon as he heard of Memnon's death, they cannot have arrived in Babylon before his departure with the army. Curt. 3. 8. 1 is clear and explicit on where they met it.

[60] Diod. 17. 35. 3 describes the presence of the royal and noble women with the army as κατά τι πάτριον ἦθος τῶν Περσῶν ('in accordance with an ancestral custom of the Persians'). We hear of nothing of the kind in the best-attested Persian armies, those of Darius and Xerxes in Herodotus, and it is unlikely that the 'custom' had developed in Artaxerxes' Egyptian campaign. For the women and children with Darius III, see Curt. 3. 12. 4, 13 ff.: Darius' mother, wife, and daughters (Darius' son: 12. 26); 'the wives and children of Darius' commanders' (13. 6); Ochus' daughters (13. 12, also his wife); Artabazus' wife (sister of Mentor and Memnon, cf. Berve 1926: no. 152) (13. 13), also the daughters of Mentor (i.e. nieces of Artabazus), Memnon's widow and son and the wife of Pharnabazus, nephew of Memnon (see Berve 1926: no. 766) (13. 14). This is the fullest list. Diodorus' pathetic description (17. 35–6) gives no specifics except for the family of Darius (17. 36. 2; 37–8). Arrian also mentions only Darius' family (2. 11. 9, with the vulgate story 12. 6 ff.: we learn that the anecdote of Leonnatus' mission of reassurance is from Ptolemy and Aristobulus: 12. 6). Unnamed Persian ladies are mentioned by all authors, as captured both after the battle and at Damascus. That they included the wives and children of (all of?) Darius' commanders (Curt. 3. 13. 6) is no doubt Curtius' pathetic invention, developed with fine rhetorical phrasing later in that chapter. As we have seen (n. 13 above), this practice by no means guarantees the authenticity of what he reports. For the only ladies actually named, see above.

on any source,[61] the march was a model of organization and speed.

We do not know precisely who Darius' commanders were. The satraps of the western provinces must have led their contingents, as the satrap of Egypt Sabaces did (Arr. 2. 11. 8 and Curt. 3. 11. 10; Diodorus has a different name) and Arsames (Berve 1926: no. 149: perhaps related to Artabazus), satrap of Cilicia, tried to do. Rheomitres (Berve 1926: no. 685) and Atizyes (Berve 1926: no. 179) had lost their satrapies in Asia Minor and perhaps tried to make up for that disgrace by special bravery which led to their deaths. Of those who survived, we know only Nabarzanes (Berve 1926: no. 543), the chiliarch, whom Curtius (3. 9. 1) names as commander of the right wing and Arrian, characteristically, does not name at all, and Darius' brother Ox(y)athres (Berve 1926: no. 586), no doubt commanding the bodyguard. This lack of interest in our sources masks an important question: where was Artabazus (Berve 1926: no. 152), head of the great Pharnacid family and grandson of Artaxerxes II—and brother-in-law of Mentor and Memnon? Berve, arguing from the fact that his wife was captured after Issus, argues that Artabazus must have been in the battle. Unfortunately we do not know his position at this time, but as we have seen, all the noble ladies specifically named as accompanying Darius, apart from those of the royal family, were related to Artabazus. The royal ladies and their children could hardly be left behind: Darius had to guard against their being murdered or (as appropriate) married by some other Achaemenid in his absence, who would thus establish a claim to the throne—especially if Darius failed. The remarkable concentration of Artabazus' relatives (and the

---

[61] It is inconceivable that a large number of noble ladies, who would have to travel in state, were with the expedition. Darius' speed would be inexplicable if he had had to cope with such a major impediment. The 'other Persians' who had sent their women to Damascus along with their possessions (Arr. 2. 11. 9) probably included a fair number of soldiers who had picked up women during the march and in Cilicia itself. That the *graue agmen* of Darius' army (Curt. 3. 7. 1: it could not move fast!) included the traditional 360 concubines, as well as a number of women on horseback, the wives of the *propinqui* and *amici* (Curtius has just specified 15,000 *cognati* alone!), as well as eunuchs and (as in a Roman army) *lixae* and *calones* (all this Curt. 3. 3. 9–25), is undoubtedly a picture due to Curtius' overheated imagination, stimulated by reading about the King's traditional luxury.

families of Mentor and Memnon were, of course, not among the wives of 'all the commanders' allegedly with the expedition!) strongly suggests that Artabazus, one of the most distinguished of the Persian nobles, had been left behind to be in charge of affairs at the centre, and that his loyalty consequently had to be ensured at whatever cost in delay to the expedition. Unfortunately (as we saw) the nature of our Greek sources makes it impossible to prove this. But in view of Darius' insecurity, and remembering that he had received Memnon's family as hostages before entrusting him with an important post, we must surely conclude that Artabazus was in Susa, as someone no doubt had to be, to act practically as vicegerent in the King's and the chiliarch's absence. Darius had acted shrewdly and efficiently.

However, he had in the end been unlucky. The fact was that after his defeat and flight at Issus his family were hostages in Alexander's hands (however generous Alexander's treatment of them, as—no doubt in essence truthfully—depicted by our sources) and he was debarred from any offensive action. His need to guard against conspiracies at home had in the end forced him into assuming the strategic risk of a purely defensive battle against a great tactician. He tried to compensate by making Alexander lavish offers, which Alexander would have been naive to accept, since they would involve garrisoning a stretch of hundreds of miles against an essentially undefeated Persian army.[62] In the end, Darius' unavoidable care to guard against conspiracies led to his being unavoidably forced to give up the initiative. The arrangements he made for Gaugamela were the best any known Persian King had ever made for any recorded battle. He deserved to succeed, and Alexander's victory was nothing less than a military miracle.[63] But the victory

---

[62] We must doubt the vulgate story that Parmenio, that experienced soldier, gave him the stupid advice to accept the main offer, as reported. (Of course, we have no idea of the course of the real negotiations, but major territorial concessions on the part of Darius were obviously unavoidable, and very much in his interest, in case Alexander could be persuaded to accept them.) The military reasons for rejection are so obvious that we need not even consider psychological motivation.

[63] See Diod. 17. 39. 3 f., 53. 1 f.—and the 'Alexander Mosaic', as Nylander has pointed out. The actual course of the battle is beyond recovery, as is true of many ancient battles. No one, least of all Alexander or Darius, can have exercised any real control over the whole battlefield. (See Bosworth 1988*b*: 81 f.).

was decisive, and not least due to Darius' being tactically at the mercy of the attack.

We have a better list of his commanders at Gaugamela than we had at Issus (Arr. 3. 8. 3 ff.: thirteen names of Iranian commanders). There is one noteworthy absence: Nabarzanes the chiliarch, who had been as successful as the fate of battle allowed him to be at Issus (Curt. 3. 9. 1, with 11; cf. Arr. 2. 11. 2). Berve 1926 (p. 268) believes he must have been there. But in fact Mazaeus held the post that he had occupied at Issus, and a man of his eminence could only have been in high command and would have appeared on our list. Did the King no longer trust him? One might be inclined to think so, in the light of later events, but perhaps there is a simpler explanation. This time Darius could not take wives and families with him as hostages. Artabazus (who is also missing in the roll-call) could therefore not have been in charge at home. He was perhaps too old to be given a tactical command. It is likely that the chiliarch was left in that position: he, at least, was not an Achaemenid (had he been of royal blood, the cautious Darius could never have entrusted him with that post), hence could not aspire to the throne. Mazaeus turned out to be a good substitute, as Darius must have known.

However, Darius again had to flee, giving up most of his capitals and taking refuge in remote Ecbatana, where he was safe for the winter (Arr. 3. 16. 1–2; Curt. 5. 1. 9; Diod. 17. 64. 1). In the end he had seven months there. What he did with that dearly bought time, we do not know.[64] No military effect is discernible. In particular, he did not summon or prepare the armies of the east. Nor can we be sure why Darius waited until Alexander was almost upon him before leaving Ecbatana. We are forced to speculate on all this, on the basis of very slight evidence.

Since he had made no effort, in those seven months, to prepare for a continuation of the war, we must assume he intended to give up: to do homage to Alexander, as Alexander

---

[64] He certainly did not expect to fight Alexander with the levy of Scythians and Cadusians that Arrian picked up as a rumour (Arr. 3. 19. 3). The rumour went on to report that in the end they did not turn up! That story can be ignored; but we are no better off than Alexander, who had no idea what Darius was planning (ibid. 1–5).

had at one time demanded, and thus save the rest of his kingdom from devastation—and wait for another chance.[65] For whatever his gesture, he would remain the only legitimately crowned King; and whatever territory Alexander had won, he would have to hold it.[66]

The suggestion covers all the known facts as no other does. But if so, why did he not meet Alexander at Ecbatana and do what he intended to? The answer, as it emerges from subsequent events, must be that there were men around him who had very different ideas: who still hoped to organize resistance in the east round the name of the King.

This means that, when he left Ecbatana, Darius was no longer a free agent. The conspiracy that ultimately cost him his life must have started at Ecbatana. Bessus and Barsaentes (Berve 1926: nos. 212, 205), respectively satraps of Bactria-Sogdiana and of Arachosia-Drangiana, between them a large part of the Upper Provinces, and able to call on Indian tribes as well and (it seems) on Scythian allies (Arr. 3. 8. 3–4), could hope to muster a powerful force. We may well believe, as the vulgate has it,[67] that Bessus, himself no doubt an

---

[65] For this suggestion see especially my articles cited in n. 51.

[66] See n. 62 above with text. If the whole kingdom was handed to him, with Darius alive, this would apply with even greater force.

The eminent Greek epigraphist M. B. Hatzopoulos has recently suggested (1997, esp. 50–1), on the basis of his interpretation of Alexander's letter to Philippi, that Alexander intended to go home with his Macedonians and Greek allies after his stay at Persepolis—thus leaving Darius free to reoccupy all he had lost—and that it was only the reports of Darius' collecting troops and fleeing to the east that made him continue his march. Not to mention the fact that he only received those reports when already on his way to Media (Arr. 3. 19. 1–4), we are left to wonder why, after he had decided to abandon his conquests, they should make him change his mind. Even on Hatzopoulos' interpretation of his text (and despite his pronouncement, p. 50, I still think I proposed a valid alternative: see Badian 1989: 67; and 1993: 136) there are more plausible suggestions. Thus, the ambassadors may have reached Alexander early in 333, during his long stay at Gordium. Whether Leonnatus and Philotas (if the famous *hetairoi*) were among the *neogamoi* sent home for the winter, we cannot guess. (No offspring are attested, but that is not significant.) But in any case they would have had plenty of time to accompany the ambassadors, adjudicate as Hatzopoulos prescribes for them, and return to Gordium before Alexander resumed his march in May. I doubt that historians will find Hatzopoulos' hypothesis appealing.

[67] See esp. Curt. 5. 9–10 (note 9. 2–3: absurd speculation), 10. 1. The idea that anyone would, at this point in Persian fortunes, want to usurp the throne for the sake of being King is quite possibly Curtius' own. Diod. 17. 73–4 does not report Bessus' motives.

Achaemenid, who no doubt thought himself as well qualified
for the upright tiara as Darius, had his own ambitions. But
that would have to wait, in the interests of the kingdom. In
the near future, it was obviously best to keep the King as a
unifying force, with men more eager to fight than he in de
facto control. The two satraps seem to have won the powerful support of Nabarzanes, the chiliarch, whom it seems the
King had trusted before Gaugamela. The three clearly
formed a powerful cabal. They must have mounted their
coup when they saw the King's inactivity at Ecbatana (and,
quite probably, were consulted about his defeatist plans). By
the time the royal train moved east, the King seems to have
been their prisoner.

The position of an unsuccessful King was always unenvi-
able,[68] as Xerxes had known long ago.[69] Darius' unprece-
dentedly disastrous leadership ensured that he could at most
survive as a figure-head. That, as such, he was still important is clear from the actions of the conspirators.

On the final stage of the conspiracy we have at least some
information, though not much that can be trusted. Curtius
gives a detailed and dramatic account, but it consists chiefly
of speeches perfused by his own invention, as is shown
by *sententiae* and commonplaces that would have been
applauded by Seneca, as well as by demonstrably Roman
concepts.[70] In any case, no Greek ever knew more than we

[68] See Calmeyer 1981 (to be read with caution), citing A. Sh. Shahbazi's earlier
studies (nn. 1 and 12).

[69] See Hdt. 8. 100 ff. Modern scholars generally recognize that Xerxes crossed to
Asia at once, not through cowardice but to prevent rebellion. Diodorus reports (we
do not know on what authority) that from Ecbatana Darius sent messengers to the
commanders in the Upper Satrapies, 'exhorting them to preserve their good will
towards him' (17. 64. 2). That may be a Greek guess, but it would be important for
him to do it, no matter what his future intentions. Nothing can be got out of the
romance, characterized by speeches, in Curt. 5. 8 ff. See Atkinson 1994: 138 (on 8.
6–17) for the quality of Curtius' speeches: 'The speech is lacking in material substance.'

[70] See Atkinson's treatment (1994), especially 133. Note such gems as *idemque
erit regni quam spiritus finis*; the good king's maxim, *difficilius sibi esse damnare quam
decipi*; or, perhaps best of all, Nabarzanes' pronouncement: *ultimum omnium mors
est*. For Roman material, see the request that Darius transfer his *imperium* and
auspicium to another (5. 9. 4). These and similar items are obviously Curtius' own,
decorating the basic account derived from Patron. He and his mercenaries would
not only have had no idea of what Persian nobles had been discussing among themselves, but would have had to find an explanation for their final desertion of Darius
and the lateness of their surrender (see text above).

know, and few Persians did. Our information comes mainly, as has often been conjectured, from the Greek mercenaries and their leader Patron (Berve 1926: no. 612). They, by the time they surrendered to Alexander, had much to explain in their conduct, both just before Darius' death and since, and much that needed to be forgiven. This information is certainly no better than our information about conspiracies against Alexander. But the facts have their own logic. As Alexander approached, open confinement was no longer enough to ensure the conspirators' control over the King. To prevent his escaping, perhaps with some loyal troops, and actually succeeding in meeting Alexander, they now had to bind him—with golden fetters, still showing him all due respect (Curt. 5. 12. 20): the fact would later be well remembered. In any case, they still hoped to keep him alive as a figure-head and centre for the resistance they expected to organize. However, slowed down as they were by their captive and their impedimenta,[71] they could not evade Alexander's frantic pursuit; for Alexander had by now been informed of the full situation by Persians who had succeeded in linking up with him before it was too late.[72] He knew that

---

[71] We may ignore the elaborations of the vulgate sources on the details of the march and especially on the size of Darius' forces: Diod. 17. 73. 2 = Curt. 5. 8. 3 (30,000 infantry and, in Curtius 4,000, Greeks; Curtius also adds cavalry and light-armed). Had Darius had anything like this number with him, Alexander with his (ultimately, we are told: Plut. *Alex.* 43. 1) sixty men would have been caught in an inescapable trap. Arrian (3. 19. 5) lists 3,000 cavalry (close to Curtius' 3,300) and only 6,000 infantry, apparently including the Greeks. Even this is, if anything, exaggerated (but see below), as must be the 7,000 talents supposedly taken with him: the number of mules or donkeys needed to transport such a sum in bullion or coin would have reduced the speed of the column to a crawl and ensured that Alexander would have no difficulty in overtaking it. Diodorus found two sources on the final encounter: he prefers the one that stated Darius was dead when Alexander reached him, but notes one that reports they still met and Darius urged Alexander to avenge him on Bessus. Curtius has the story of Polystratus' finding Darius before his death (cf. Plut. *Alex.* 43), presumably therefore did not report a meeting between Alexander and Darius. (A lacuna intervenes.) Arrian briefly states that Darius was dead when Alexander arrived (3. 21. 10). What inspires some confidence is his reporting that many in Darius' force either went home or surrendered to Alexander and that the Greek mercenaries deserted some time before Darius' death (ibid. 2. 4): the account is not infected by Patron's apologia, and the final numbers with Darius may have been quite small.

[72] Bagistanes, accompanied by one of Mazaeus' sons (Arr. 3. 21. 1, Curt. 5. 13. 3, 11, with a different version of the name; Curtius adds a Greek and two Persians, ibid. 7–9, in principle credibly, though the Persian names are garbled). Bagistanes,

it was vital for him to reach Darius still alive—just as the conspirators knew (as their actions show) that it was vital for them not to let him do so. In the end they saw no alternative to killing him. Even our defective tradition shows how reluctantly they did so, barely in time. Bessus, no doubt the only Achaemenid among them, would have to assume the upright tiara and a royal name (Artaxerxes: Arr. 3. 21. 10, 25. 3), hoping that, at least in his own province and among the Indians associated with it, he might command the loyalty that would certainly have gone to the duly consecrated King, had Bessus succeeded in keeping him alive as the nominal centre for resistance.

As I noted at the beginning, the war between Alexander III of Macedon and Darius III of Persia is marked by conspiracies and anticipation and suspicion of conspiracies that form a major motif on both sides and a decisive one on the Persian side. Alexander, a master plotter from the plot that led to his accession, skilfully uses charges of conspiracy to strengthen his position and rid himself of possible centres of rivalry, secure in the allegiance of the Macedonian soldiers, whose unquestioning support helps him in disposing of Philotas and Parmenio. But the master plotter is an easy victim to fear of conspiracy. A trace of it appears in the scene of Cleitus' death, and the confidence apparently fully justified by the outcome of that incident is shattered at the Hyphasis, where an ambitious and unscrupulous senior officer appears to be supporting the army against its king. The disaster in the desert destroyed the myth of Alexander's all-conquering power, and his attempt to claim the rightful succession to the Achaemenids proved unacceptable both to his soldiers and to many of the very Iranians whom it had been intended to attract. The resulting reign of terror on his return from India led to far-reaching decisions, which, had he lived longer, were bound to present him with major political and military problems. When at the end even the gods seemed to turn against him, he became obsessed with fears of conspiracy, from the death of Hephaestion to the

described as a Babylonian, has a purely Persian name. He was no doubt one of the numerous Persians who had colonized Babylonia and, following Persian custom, described himself by his residence, not his descent.

final events round Babylon. It would be a fitting conclusion to this cycle if he had died as a result of a conspiracy. But our sources are unaccommodating, and we simply do not know.

Darius, on the other hand, grew up surrounded by conspiracies, but never (as far as we know) himself engaged in any. Yet, understandably, he was constantly aware of the threat of conspiracies, and the caution this inspired governed the major actions of his reign and (perhaps unavoidably) led to disastrous decisions: the decision to take the women of his household and of another major noble family with him on his march to the west ended by giving Alexander unhoped-for hostages and debarring Darius from taking the military initiative; and this, despite all his careful preparations, was a major factor in his loss of the decisive battle. That defeat ultimately led to the conspiracy of his nobles against him, which, much against their intention, culminated in his death. Its result was to plunge the country that they had all tried to save into devastation and ultimate chaos.

APPENDIX
Some Iranian Rebels

As I pointed out in my text, rebels are not identical with conspirators, though they may of course incidentally conspire. But they are close enough to our topic to deserve a mention, especially as the importance of rebellions led by Iranian nobles while Alexander was in India and perhaps continued after his return (it is only those that will concern me here) has usually been grossly underestimated, not least by me. The sources report them briefly, take them lightly, and never depict them as dangerous: it would not do to show Iranians posing a serious threat to Alexander after the completion of the conquest of their country. I shall here try to make amends, as far as one can do so.

It is a symptom of the way in which this topic has been downplayed, with modern scholars following the ancient sources, that, as far as I can see, no list of these rebels has ever been collected. I hope no important Iranian rebel, or Iranian suspected of rebellion, during that period has been omitted, no matter what the evidence allows us to say.[1] The rebellions seem to have begun when they appeared to have a chance of success: when Alexander was in India, and almost certainly after he was wounded at the city of the Malli, which led to rumours that he had actually died (cf. Diod. 17. 99. 5). Once committed, rebel leaders could not pull back.

1. ASTASPES (Berve 1926: no. 173). Justi takes the name to mean 'owning eight horses, i.e. two quadrigae'—a rather fanciful interpretation, though accepted by Hinz 1975: 48. I suggest that the name is a compound of (av.) *asti* (= friend) and (Med.) *āspa* (= horse); i.e. it means precisely 'Philippos'. Cf. Mayrhofer 1973: 8. 144, p. 131. The name is found in Aeschylus, *Persae* 22, and that man must be an ancestor of the rebel, who obviously belonged to one of the oldest aristocratic families in the Greek record. He was confirmed in his satrapy by Alexander (see Berve), who clearly wanted to avoid unnecessary conflict with Iranian nobles who surrendered.

The interesting fact is that he was not one of those scapegoats blamed for the Gedrosian disaster, as I once thought. It is clear from Curtius' detailed account that Alexander, when he first met him on his return, made no charges against him but treated him in a friendly manner (9. 10. 21: *dissimulata ira comiter allocutus*), even though it was reported to him that the satrap had planned rebellion. After the Bacchic procession, related at great length, Curtius briefly describes what followed, leading up to it with a Tacitean phrase: *hunc apparatum carnifex sequebatur, quippe satrapes Astaspes . . . interfici iussus est* (ibid. 29). Alexander's deceitful friendliness while he prepared his blow recalls the action against Philotas (cf. Curt. 6. 7. 35, 8. 15–16)—and there is no doubt that he realized the danger that he was facing on that occasion. We must conclude that he found it equally dangerous to deal with a member of the oldest Iranian aristocracy, who had had ample time to consolidate his position, without thorough preparation, and that the time gained by the harmless-looking distraction of the games and the procession (whatever precisely the details of that celebration) was used for thorough military preparation of the arrest.[2] Indeed, in the circumstances we should probably believe

[1] Professor Bosworth has reminded me of Orontes (Berve 1926: no. 593) who, although nominally superseded by Mithrenes (Berve 1926: no. 524), may in fact have maintained his independence beyond Alexander's reign. If he did nominally submit and then rebel, that act is undatable, but it is almost certainly not as late as this. At one point (undated, but presumably before the Indian campaign) Alexander sent a force under a Menon (Berve 1926: no. 516) to seize some gold mines in Armenia. We do not know its fate (the text at Strabo 11. 14. 9.C529 is open to debate), but it looks like a raiding party, not a plan to garrison an organized province.

that the celebration, whatever its religious and social purposes, had a serious political–military function.

Curtius is not interested in the end: Astaspes was no Greek or Macedonian, and the operation no doubt went smoothly. He therefore did not see the connection of the events he reports, and we moderns have followed him in this. Characteristically, Arrian does not mention him at all: we may compare the cases of Cleander and his officers. Arrian does mention Heracon (6. 27. 3), but not his fate; Agathon, who had probably been left at Ecbatana to command the Thracian cavalry under Parmenio, is not mentioned at all. (On him see Berve 1926: no. 8.) He was summoned and appeared along with Cleander and Sitalces (Curt. 10. 1. 1) and presumably shared their fate. Curtius, unlike Arrian, does not mention the execution of any of them (10. 1. 8). Arrian's lack of interest in a Persian grandee is only to be expected. (The attempt to charge Arrian with confusing Astaspes with Apollophanes is not worth serious consideration: their fate was not even the same, and the action against Apollophanes can find an easy explanation. Berve's endorsement of the suggestion that Apollophanes' fate was excogitated as a 'parallel' to Astaspes' (1926, p. 57) is simply absurd: no source draws this 'parallel'.)

2. AUTOPHRADATES, in Curtius PHRADATES (Berve 1926: no. 189). Justi, 'das Verständnis (für die Religion) fördernd' is again fanciful, though the second part of the name presumably is *frādat* (increase, promote); the first part, turned into a Greek prefix, is irrecoverable. Probably both he and the homonymous commander of the Persian fleet (Berve 1926: no. 188) are related to the satrap of Lydia who played a mysterious part in the Satraps' Revolt (see *RE Suppl.* 3 (1918), col. 190: they could be nephews). At Nautaca, according to Arrian, Phrataphernes was sent to 'bring back' Autophradates, who had ignored Alexander's orders to join him (Arr. 4. 18. 2). That was in 328/7. Arrian again loses interest in his fate. Fortunately Curtius (10. 1. 39) tells us a little more: at Pasargadae Alexander ordered his execution, because 'he was suspected of aiming at the throne'. We may conclude that he was of Achaemenid descent. Whether Phrataphernes (perhaps also an Achaemenid) had already captured him by the time he briefly

---

[2] Professor Bosworth has pointed out to me the relevance of Arr. *Ind.* 36. 8 f.: when Tlepolemus tried to take over the province after Astaspes' death, he found the natives in control of τὰ ἐρυμνὰ τῆς χώρης ('the strong places of the region'); they severely harassed Nearchus and his no doubt small escort (36. 7) on his return to the coast. This point is actually of some importance for chronology. Astaspes' death must be put while Nearchus was with Alexander, for he had had no trouble going up to meet Alexander with only a few of his men (33. 6). I cannot develop this further here.

joined Alexander at the Hydaspes (Arr. 5. 20. 7—so Berve 1926: no. 814) we cannot tell. It is perhaps more likely that he had not, for otherwise Alexander would presumably have entrusted Phrataphernes with his execution. As Berve sees, he probably only sent the rebel to Alexander after the latter's return from India; he will have ended the war with him only shortly before, some time after his return to his satrapy. That Autophradates could even be suspected of wanting to make himself King shows his importance, and the lateness of his execution shows the seriousness of the resistance he could put up. Our sources are essentially uninterested.

3. BARYAXES (Berve 1926: no. 207: just over five lines). Cf. *bārya* = 'edel, superfein' (Hinz 1975: 64). A Mede, 'certainly of aristocratic descent' (Berve), had 'worn the tiara upright and called himself king of the Persians and Medes' (Arr. 6. 29. 3), but was captured by Atropates and brought to Alexander and executed at Pasargadae. A Mede claiming the throne of (more probably) Medes and Persians must have claimed descent from the old kings of Media, and presumably expected his followers to believe him. That the Persian Atropates would have no sympathy with this arrogation is obvious. (On Atropates see Berve 1926: no. 180. His Persian name was Ātarepāta (Justi), presumably = Protector of the Fire.) We cannot guess how long or difficult their conflict was, but Baryaxes clearly did not succeed in wresting the satrapy from Atropates or in rousing Median nationalism against the Persian satrap.

ORDANES: see no. 5.

4. ORXINES, in Curtius ORSINES (Berve 1926: no. 592). (Curtius' form seems to give an easier Persian original, for which see R. Schmitt in Mayrhofer 1973: 11. 1. 8. 4, p. 291.) Self-appointed satrap of Persis, which he presumably saved from chaos after Phrasaortes' death while Alexander was in India (Arr. 6. 29. 2). He was too proud to pay court to the eunuch Bagoas (cf. Badian 1958*b*), who might have saved him, but instead helped to destroy him. He prided himself on descent from Cyrus (Curt. 10. 1. 23): it is doubtful if Alexander would in any case have let him live, especially since he himself specially honoured Cyrus, at the expense of Darius and Darius' successors. A descendant of Cyrus, ensconced at Pasargadae and of surpassing wealth, would have needed all the patronage he could muster in order to save his life. His arrogation of power, even if a necessary and beneficial act, would not secure him any favour.

If we omit the subplot involving Bagoas, inflated into a moral *exemplum* by Curtius when in fact it was a miscalculation by a proud Persian noble, we can see that once more Alexander started by treating this dangerous man, whose rich presents (Curt. ibid. 24 f.) only underlined the danger he presented, without signs of disfavour. Indeed, it was only after he had left Pasargadae and gone on to Persepolis (Arr. 6. 30) that he sent 'messengers' to arrest and impale Orxines. The punishment seems to show that the charge was rebellion. Alexander, as in the case of Astaspes, faced a situation he thought dangerous and used deceit followed by force to rid himself of the danger. The charge that the descendant of Cyrus had desecrated and plundered Cyrus' sacred tomb (Curt. 10. 1. 33 f.; cf. Arr. 6. 30. 2) was no doubt intended to prevent serious dissatisfaction and unrest in Persis; and so, no less clearly, was the appointment of Peucestas, who had learned the Persian language and was ready to adopt Persian customs (Arr. 6. 30. 2–3), as satrap. Alexander's special commendation of the Persians, 'because they were in all things obedient to Peucestas' (Arr. 7. 23. 3; the praise of Peucestas, τῆς ἐν κόσμῳ αὐτῶν ἐξηγήσεως ('for governing them in good order'), in Arrian's obscure wording, seems to be for keeping Persis in order), shows, as far as our sources ever do, the delicacy of the situation created by Orxines' removal. Alexander can be seen to have been seriously worried.

5. ORDANES (Arr. 6. 27. 3, Berve 1926: no. 590). Cf. later rulers called Vardan(es) (Justi).

6. OZINES (Curt. 9. 10. 19, cf. 10. 1. 9, Berve 1926: no. 579); from (av.) *huzaēna*, 'having good weapons' (Justi, accepted Hinz 1975: 130).

7. ZARIASPES (Curt. ibid., Berve 1926: no. 335); 'having gold-coloured horses' (Mayrhofer 1973: 8. 1833, p. 254: *zariašba*; Hinz 1975: 278: *zaryāspa*).

These must be treated together. Arrian reports only that in (the capital of) Carmania Craterus rejoined Alexander and brought with him Ordanes, whom he had captured after Ordanes had led a revolt. Arrian seems entirely uninterested in the affair. As in some similar cases, he does not bother to inform us of Ordanes' fate (Berve's statement that he was executed is a guess, although no doubt correct). Nor does he mention Zariaspes—which, of course, is no argument against the latter's real existence. As we have seen, Arrian can be singularly uninterested in persons, even in prominent Macedonians whom Alexander punished.

Curtius reports that when Alexander had reached Pura (not named), he received a dispatch from Craterus reporting that he had defeated and arrested two noble Persians, Ozines and Zariaspes, who were 'planning revolt'. At the Carmanian capital, after the trial of Cleander and his associates (whose execution

Curtius fails to report), we are told that those whom Craterus had brought with him as instigators of a Persian revolt were executed. Curtius does not mention Craterus' arrival and does not name his prisoners.

It will be seen that up to a point the reports are complementary. Neither of these authors was greatly interested in Iranian rebellions or discontent and their references even to striking events are likely to be casual. Here Curtius mentions a dispatch from Craterus, received at Pura, which Arrian does not mention; on the other hand, Curtius does not tell us where Craterus actually rejoined Alexander; but since he is with him in the Carmanian capital and was not with him at Pura, it must have been (whether or not Curtius had thought about it) at the Carmanian capital, where Arrian relates it. What we do not know is precisely whom Craterus brought to Carmania, to be executed there. Are there three rebels, two of them mentioned by Curtius and another defeated just before Craterus joined Alexander—all of them executed in Carmania? Again, the fact that Arrian mentions only one is not significant; and one could argue that Curtius did not know about (or did not bother to mention) another defeated rebellion at a later time. On the whole, I am inclined to accept three rebels and explain the fact that we hear only of two in Curtius by name and only of one in Arrian (at a later date) by their obvious lack of interest (especially in Arrian's case) and careless-ness. Note that all three have names that are easily recognized as Greek renderings of Iranian names.

Berve rejects the identification of Ordanes and Ozines (1926: 282), but is willing to consider an identification of Ozines with Orxines, which, on the facts that we know, is easily seen to be absurd. He rightly rejects the identification of Baryaxes with Zariaspes (p. 163): no less absurd, since Atropates did not join forces with Craterus! Curtius cannot be trusted on names, and it is just possible that his Ozines is indeed Arrian's Ordanes; but, to use Berve's term, there is 'kein zwingender Grund' for thinking so. In this case manuscript corruption cannot easily be posited. None of our manuscripts, although often corrupt on names, as even in the section immediately preceding, shows any sign of corruption here. Moreover, as we have seen, Curtius' form can easily be given a plausible Persian etymology. It seems methodo-logically preferable to accept both names.

Whatever the number of rebels, there is every good reason to think that there were serious rebellions going on somewhere along Craterus' route and (I suggest) that Alexander knew about it. Not only would that explain Craterus' dispatch, sent to the first place where he could be sure Alexander could be reached. Above all, it explains the fact that, in addition to the men unfit for service and the elephants, who could not be expected to share the march through the Makran desert, Alexander gave Craterus half the Macedonian infantry—clearly not because he wanted to spare them the hardship of the march, for he even took the whole of the Macedonian cavalry except for the unfit with him. The obvious explanation is that he had heard of the unrest that Craterus was expected to quell. (Thus Berve 1926: 224, s.v. Κράτερος: a good conjecture, but the references are irrelevant.) Once more, we find our sources suppressing reports of Iranian unrest and rebellion, which Alexander seems to have taken very seriously.

The picture is consistent, once disengaged. If we want to get at true Alexander history, we must no longer ignore it. Alexander's conquest was not acceptable to all the Iranian aristocracy, in spite of his efforts to depict himself as the true successor to the Achaemenids—as far as his Macedonians would let him. It has often been observed that after the great purge Alexander did not appoint any Iranian satraps. The facts here set out provide an explanation.

4

Alexander the Great and Panhellenism

MICHAEL FLOWER

In 335 BC Alexander laid siege to the city of Thebes, which was in revolt. Before he began battle, he announced that 'any of the Thebans who wished might come to him and join in the Peace which was common for the Greeks'. The Thebans retorted that 'anyone who wished to join the Great King and the Thebans in freeing the Greeks and destroying the tyrant of Greece should come over to them' (Diod. 17. 9). Needless to say, Alexander was enraged; for, in the words of Demosthenes (14. 3), the Great King was 'the common enemy of all the Greeks'. Thebes was then razed to the ground. That decision, we are told, was not made by Alexander himself, but by the council of his allies. They felt that the punishment was appropriate because the Thebans had fought on the side of Xerxes during the Persian Wars,[1] and because all of the Greeks had taken a solemn oath to destroy the city once the Persians had been defeated.[2]

Contrast the treatment of Thebes with that of Plataea. After his victory at Gaugamela in 331, Alexander ordered the rebuilding of Plataea, which had been destroyed by Thebes in 373, because of her services to Greece in 479 BC.[3]

I would like to thank the following for their suggestions on various aspects of this paper: Ernst Badian, Elizabeth Baynham, Richard Billows, Brian Bosworth, Elizabeth Carney, Harriet Flower, Lara O'Sullivan, Olga Palagia, Ann Steiner, and Ian Worthington.

[1] Diod. 17. 14; Arr. 1. 9. 6–9: Just. 11. 3. 6–9, with Yardley and Heckel 1997: 92–5.

[2] Just. 11. 3. 10. Herodotus (9. 86 ff.) only mentions that the Thebans were given an ultimatum either to surrender their Medizers or to have Thebes captured by siege. Thus Justin's 'solemn oath' probably refers to the so-called Oath of Plataea which is only known from 4th-cent. sources and may be propaganda created during that century: see Yardley and Heckel 1997: 95–6.

[3] Plut. *Arist.* 11. 9; *Alex.* 34. In the former passage, Alexander is said to have ordered this to be proclaimed at the Olympic Games (of 328?); but the chronology is problematic. At Arrian 1. 9. 10 we are told that Alexander's allies decided both to

And so Alexander destroyed one famous Greek city and rebuilt another. Was this just a matter of the carrot and the stick, or were both actions part of the same policy? How did Alexander, on the eve of his invasion of Asia, think that he could get away with destroying one of the most famous cities in Hellas, and yet still retain the goodwill of the Greeks? Our sources tell us that Alexander's motive in destroying Thebes was to deter future revolts.[4] Modern scholars speak of 'shock-waves throughout the Greek world', and of a 'litany of shock and horror'.[5] But there must have been some Greeks, apart from Thebes' immediate neighbours, who believed that each city got exactly what it deserved.[6] The Spartans could only have been delighted.[7] And Aeschines could declare to an Athenian jury in 330 that Thebes' punishment was just.[8] The razing of Thebes and the restoration of Plataea were part and parcel of the same policy, and that policy was panhellenic.

I. PANHELLENISM AS A POPULAR IDEOLOGY

The political programme which we moderns have termed 'panhellenism' was the belief that the various Greek cities could solve their endemic political, social, and economic

---

destroy Thebes and to rebuild Plataea. According to Pausanias (4. 27. 10; 9. 1. 8), Philip had already 'restored the Plataeans'. See Hamilton 1969: 91.

[4] Polyb. 38. 2. 13; Plutarch, *Alex.* 11. 10–11; Diodorus 17. 9. 4.

[5] Worthington 1994: 308; Bosworth 1988*b*: 196. Diod. 19. 54. 2 relates that many Greek cities, even some in Italy and Sicily, participated in the rebuilding of Thebes sponsored by Cassander in 316, but that was much later and under a very different political climate.

[6] Our sources mention some of the Greeks who were fighting with Alexander and who demonstrated their hatred of Thebes: Phocians, Plataeans, Thespians, and Orchomenians. Cf. Diod. 17. 13. 5; Just. 11. 3. 8; Plut. *Alex.* 11. 11; Arr. 1. 8. 8. All of these had been the victims of Theban imperialism: Plataea, Thespiae, and Orchomenus had been destroyed by Thebes in the 370s and 360s; the Phocian cities in 346.

[7] As recently as 367 Pelopidas had trumped a Spartan embassy at Susa by reminding the King that his countrymen were the only ones in Greece who had fought on the King's side at Plataea. See Xen. *Hell.* 7. 1. 34.

[8] *Against Ctesiphon* 133. According to Plutarch (*Alex.* 13) and Justin (11. 4. 9), however, the Athenians were greatly grieved by the destruction of Thebes and Alexander later regretted his action.

problems by uniting in common cause and conquering all or part of the Persian Empire.[9] It was an idea at once appealing to Greek patriotic sentiment, and yet, given the fierce parochialism of the Greek city-states, impossible to effect without external compulsion. Yet in spite of its impracticality, panhellenism was a widespread and broadly 'popular' ideology. Although the origins of panhellenism lie in the fifth century, it was during the fourth century BC that it reached the high-water mark of its appeal, beginning with the *Olympic Oration* of Gorgias (408 or 392) and of Lysias (388 or 384) and culminating in the tracts of Isocrates. In his *Panegyricus*, Isocrates argued that Athens and Sparta together should share the hegemony; he later hoped that a single leader, such as Philip of Macedon, could first reconcile and then lead the united Greeks in the great crusade.[10]

Soon after his decisive victory at Chaeronea in August of 338, Philip began to deftly and carefully exploit panhellenic propaganda in preparation for an invasion of Asia. In the summer of 337 he summoned delegates from various Greek states to Corinth. He there established a permanent seat for what we moderns have termed 'The League of Corinth', an organization which was surely meant both to recall and to be the successor of the Hellenic League of 480.[11] The delegates, at Philip's suggestion, duly declared war on Persia with Philip himself as supreme commander. It has plausibly been suggested that Euphranor's bronze statue group of Hellas and Arete was commissioned and dedicated by Philip at this time, perhaps at the Isthmus, as propaganda on behalf of the

[9] On panhellenism in general, see Kessler 1911; Mathieu 1925; Dobesch 1968; Perlman 1976; Sakellariou 1980; and Green 1996.

[10] See, in particular, *Paneg.* 17, and *Phil.* 9. An unfortunate trend in modern scholarship on Isocrates is to deny the sincerity of his statements about his panhellenist programme: e.g. Kennedy 1963: 198–203; Markle 1976; and Too 1995: 129–50. This topic is too large to deal with here. Suffice it to say that in the *Panathenaicus* (13–14) of 339 BC Isocrates states unambiguously that the main theme of his career had been to exhort the Greeks to concord among themselves and war against the barbarians. See also *Letter 3, To Philip* 6.

[11] See Bosworth 1988*b*: 189–90. Corinth was undoubtedly chosen as the centre for the Greek council because the Greek councillors (*probouloi*) of the original Hellenic League had met at the Isthmus (Hdt. 7. 172. 1; 175. 1), and perhaps because that was as far as the Persians had penetrated in 480–79. An ancillary consideration may have been that Corinth had recently supported Timoleon in his liberation of the Greek cities in Sicily from the threat of Carthage, as suggested by Lane Fox 1973: 93.

projected war.[12] In 336 Philip sent an expeditionary force under his generals Attalus and Parmenio; but Philip was assassinated before he could join them with the main body of his forces.[13] Alexander, after he had settled affairs in Greece and Macedonia to his liking, undertook in person the expedition which his father had begun by proxy.

In the ancient, as so often in the modern world, wars of aggression are clothed in plausible justifications.[14] When the Spartan king Agesilaus invaded Asia in 396 he was greatly admired, according to Xenophon (*Ages*. 1. 8), because he desired to requite the King of Persia for his ancestor's previous invasion of Greece. He also wished to gain independence for the Greek cities in Asia.[15] When first Philip and then Alexander announced their intention of invading Asia, they employed the very same pretexts as had Agesilaus. These pretexts were to free the Greeks in Asia from Persian rule,[16] and to punish the Persians for their invasion of Greece in 480–79 BC,[17] although only the latter, the war of revenge, was officially sanctioned by the League of Corinth. That these were pretexts, and not their true motives, was asserted by Polybius, who wrote that Philip's real motive was conquest for its own sake. Most modern scholars would agree.[18] But why did Philip and Alexander employ these particular pretexts when they seemingly had failed in the past? Agesilaus was recalled to defend Sparta in 394 because the most powerful of the Greek states (Athens, Argos, Thebes, and Corinth) were quick to fight against Sparta with Persian money and had little sympathy for Agesilaus' panhellenic

[12] See Klein 1905: 322 and Palagia 1980: 6, 43.

[13] Ruzicka 1985 analyses this situation in Asia Minor in 337–5.

[14] Cf. Andocides, *On the Peace* 13: 'I believe that all men would agree that it is necessary to go to war for these reasons, either when being wronged or when assisting those who are suffering wrong.'

[15] Xen. *Ages*. 1. 10 and *Hell*. 3. 4. 5. For the panhellenism of Xenophon, see most recently Dillery 1995: 41–119.

[16] Diod. 16. 91. 2 and 17. 24. 1; Theopompus *FGrH* 115, F 253. See Seager 1981, but he does not know this fragment of Theopompus (discussed below).

[17] Arr. 2. 14; Diod. 16. 89; Just. 11. 5. 6; Polyb. 3. 6. On the theme of revenge see Bellen 1974 and Gehrke 1987.

[18] e.g. Brunt 1976: li–lviii; Austin 1993; Billows 1995: 19–20. As Grote 1883: xi. 377 put it: 'a scheme of Macedonian appetite and for Macedonian aggrandizement'. See now Seibert 1998, who surveys earlier scholarship, for a lengthy treatment of this position.

pretensions. And Jason of Pherae, despite Isocrates' claim (*Phil.* 119–20) that he 'obtained the greatest reputation' by merely proclaiming that he intended to cross over to Asia and make war upon the King, was so dreaded by the Greeks that in 370 his assassins were honoured in most of the cities which they entered; this was a clear proof, in Xenophon's opinion (*Hell.* 6. 4. 32), of how much the Greeks feared that Jason would become their tyrant. So why trouble with Greek complaints, when the Macedonians had their own scores to settle with the Persians?

In his letter to Darius in 332 BC, as reported by Arrian, Alexander subtly weaves together Greek and Macedonian grievances (2. 14. 5–6):[19] 'Your ancestors invaded Macedonia and the rest of Greece and did us great harm, although you had suffered no prior injury; I have been appointed *hegemon* of the Greeks and have invaded Asia in the desire to take vengeance on the Persians for the aggressions which you began.' But then he goes on to mention Persian aid to Perinthus in 340 BC, a force dispatched into Thrace by Artaxerxes Ochus, Darius' alleged complicity in the assassination of Philip, and even the moneys sent to various Greek cities in order to stir up insurrection against Macedon. In other words, Alexander did not need to mention Greek complaints against Persia, since there were plenty of Macedonian ones.

The majority of modern scholars, it would be fair to say, consider the panhellenic war of revenge to have been a specious pretext, which brought Alexander little profit.[20] Some have even asserted that Philip and Alexander had no choice but to employ it because the Athenians had represented their resistance to Macedon as a re-enactment, on behalf of the Greeks, of their role in the Persian Wars, and such claims had to be countered.[21] But that cannot be the

---

[19] I am assuming that Arrian's version of this letter is more accurate than that in Curtius (4. 1. 10–14). Bosworth 1980a: 232–3 suggests that it accurately represents contemporary propaganda.

[20] e.g. Grote 1883: xi. 377–8: 'He was himself aware that the real sympathies of the Greeks were rather adverse than favourable to his success.' Cf. Brunt 1965: 206: 'The Panhellenic crusade was a fiction for everyone but modern scholars who suppose that Isocrates' writings were widely admired for anything but their languid eloquence.'

[21] e.g. Austin 1993: 201. Athenian propaganda is analysed by Habicht 1961; see

sole explanation; for Thebes, which had Medized in 480–479, was also claiming to be fighting against Macedon for 'the freedom of Greece'.[22] Our sources tell a different story: Philip and Alexander not only thought that by espousing panhellenist ideology they could win widespread popularity in the Greek city-states, but they actually achieved the desired results. Philip attempted to avoid the suspicions which the Greeks had felt for Jason of Pherae by stressing that he was not their tyrant, but their leader (*hegemon*) and avenger. Diodorus (16. 89) says that Philip 'spread the word that he wanted to make war on the Persians on behalf of the Greeks and to punish them for the profanation of the temples, and this won for him the personal support of the Greeks (ἰδίους τοὺς Ἕλληνας ταῖς εὐνοίαις ἐποιήσατο)'. Diodorus also claims that the delegates at Corinth were genuinely enthusiastic about the expedition: 'He spoke about the war against the Persians and, having held out great hopes, he won the delegates over to war.'[23] And Polybius (3. 6. 13) asserts that Philip won the avowed goodwill of the Greeks (τὴν ἐκ τῶν Ἑλλήνων εὔνοιαν ὁμολογουμένην) by employing the pretext that he was eager to avenge their unlawful treatment by the Persians. Alexander did not fail to notice the favourable reception of these pretexts and he was quick to adopt them as his own. Even his coinage may have been designed with the war of revenge in mind, if the Nike on the reverse of his gold staters, who holds a ship's standard and a wreath of victory in her hands, indeed refers to the Persian debacle at Salamis.[24]

Now, as I have said, it is generally assumed that the true

---

also Thomas 1989: 84–93. In addition to the 'forged' documents discussed by Habicht and Thomas, see Demosthenes, *On the False Embassy* 303–6. Bosworth (1971b) argues that the so-called Congress Decree found in Plutarch's life of Pericles (*Per.* 17) was a forgery from the period after Chaeronea. It was part of Philip's panhellenic propaganda and was intended to demonstrate that 'the mantle of Pericles and fifth century Athens had fallen on Philip and Macedon' (p. 601).

[22] Diod. 17. 9. 5; Plut. *Alex.* 12. 5.

[23] We may be sceptical, since Philip surely would have stage-managed this crucial meeting. It would be important to know Diodorus' source for this. He may be following Diyllus (*FGrH* 73) here: see Hammond 1937. Or, as S. Hornblower 1994b: 18–19 suggests, Diodorus might have constructed this part of the narrative himself; see also his comments in *CR* (1984), 263.

[24] See Stewart 1993: 159–60 and Price 1991: 29–30.

motive of Philip and Alexander was conquest for its own
sake and the extension of Macedonian power. Yet we cannot
know their true feelings and intentions. Contrary to
Polybius, it is not impossible that they had some personal
commitment to 'the war of liberation and revenge'. For individuals sometimes act out of a combination of motives which
are not necessarily mutually consistent nor even wholly
rational.[25] As kings of Macedon they were concerned to
enlarge and enrich their own realms, but as Heraclids they
simultaneously may have desired to surpass their ancestor
Heracles' benefactions to Greece. That may sound far-
fetched to us, but to Isocrates it was a reasonable, and not
just a rhetorical, presumption of motive that Philip might
wish to imitate the goodwill of Heracles towards the
Greeks.[26] What could a Macedonian king offer the Greek
cities in exchange for their co-operation? Ever since the end
of the Persian Wars the Greeks had viewed the Persians with
a complex combination of contempt and fear: contempt for
their alleged servility and effeminacy and fear of the King's
ability to intervene both politically (by subvention of money)
and militarily (by threat of force) in Greek affairs.[27] Philip
and Alexander not only offered the prospect of revenge for
past wrongs but also a psychologically satisfying closure to
Greek fears and apprehensions. There was also the prospect
of enrichment, as the contingent from Thespiae evidently
discovered to their profit (see below).

  Given the pervasiveness of these attitudes towards Persia
in Greek popular thought, panhellenist discourse is unlikely
to have been restricted to Greece's intellectual elite. Nevertheless, Philip and Alexander had extensive contacts with
members of that elite and they were surely influenced by
them. During the fourth century the Athenian rhetorician
Isocrates was the leading exponent of panhellenist ideology.
Yet it has been claimed that the concepts of the war of
revenge and the liberation of the Asian Greeks were foreign
to Isocrates' thought, and thus Philip either conceived of
these slogans on his own or was influenced by someone

---

[25] A similar observation is made by Green 1996: 7.

[26] *Phil.* 113–14; 127.

[27] For feelings of superiority, see Hall 1989; for fear, see Cawkwell 1978: 121–2.

else.[28] This is not true. Revenge is a theme both in Isocrates' *Panegyricus* of 380 BC and in his *Philippus* of 346 BC.[29] The liberation of the Asian Greeks figures both in the *Panegyricus* and elsewhere.[30]

Beginning in the 360s at the latest, Isocrates began to send letters to many of the most powerful kings and dynasts in the Greek world, exhorting them to champion the panhellenist cause.[31] The *Philippus* of 346 BC was the most important of these 'letters'.[32] Isocrates advises Philip (16) 'to take the lead of both the concord of the Hellenes and the campaign against the barbarians'. Two short letters to Philip followed the *Philippus*, one in 344 and another in 338.[33] That final letter, written when Isocrates was 98, is easily the most surprising of all of his compositions; so surprising, in fact, that many scholars feel compelled to deny its authenticity.[34] For what could Philip have thought when he received a letter from a distinguished Athenian which all but congratulated him on winning the battle of Chaeronea? How else might Philip have taken these words: 'On account of the

---

[28] Wilcken 1932: 47–8 asserts that the 'war of revenge' was Philip's idea, not Isocrates', and that it was foreign to Isocrates' thought. Brunt 1965: 207 claims that Isocrates was not interested in revenge and showed little concern for the 'enslaved' Greeks in Asia. Hornblower 1994a: 878 claims that the motif of revenge is all but invisible in the pre-350 BC writings of Isocrates, and proposes (1994a: 878–9; 1994b: 40) that Callisthenes may have recommended this motif to Philip; cf. Momigliano 1934: 165, 195–7. Bosworth 1996a: 148–9 suggests that their reading of Herodotus may have inspired Philip and Alexander to adopt the war of revenge as a pretext.

[29] *Paneg.* 155, 183, 185. *Phil.* 124–6.

[30] *Paneg.* 181; *Phil.* 124; *Panathenaicus* 103; *Letter 9, To Archidamus* 8–10. In the letter to Archidamus he discusses the plight of the Asian Greeks at length and in vivid detail.

[31] We have the introductions to letters which he wrote to Dionysius I, tyrant of Syracuse, perhaps in 368, and to King Archidamus of Sparta in 356 (*Letter 1, To Dionysius* and *Letter 9, To Archidamus* respectively). Speusippus (*Letter to Philip* 13) claims that Isocrates sent virtually the same letter to Agesilaus, Dionysius of Syracuse, Alexander of Pherae, and then to Philip. Too 1995: 199 argues that the letters to Dionysius and Archidamus were deliberately left unfinished due to a calculated strategy of silence, but she is unaware of Speusippus, who claims that Isocrates' other letters were on a par with the *Philippus*.

[32] On this work, see Perlman 1957 and 1969; Dobesch 1968; Markle 1976; and Walser 1984: 115–22.

[33] *Letter 2, To Philip* and *Letter 3, To Philip* respectively.

[34] Perlman 1957: 316 n. 65 considers it spurious on chronological grounds, but its contents clearly do not suit his interpretation of Isocrates' views. In any case, there is no chronological difficulty: see Cawkwell 1982: 316–17.

battle which has taken place, all have been compelled to be
prudent' (2) or 'I am grateful to my old age for this reason
alone, because it has prolonged my life to this moment' (6).

Did Philip think that this was a bad joke? On the contrary,
he must have taken Isocrates seriously. For Isocrates
apparently was on intimate terms with Antipater, and after
the Athenian defeat at Chaeronea the two of them had discussed 'what was advantageous both for Athens and for you
[i.e. Philip]'.[35] None the less, Isocrates and Philip had never
met, and even Isocrates did not know whether he had first
planted the idea in Philip's mind to attack Asia or whether
Philip had conceived the plan on his own.[36] Neither Isocrates, nor perhaps any of his Greek contemporaries, knew
precisely when Philip had made that decision.[37] However
that might be, it is clear that Philip is likely to have valued
Isocrates, not so much as a political theorist, but as a gauge
of popular opinion (not least in the sense of what some,
or even many, Athenians were willing to accept). If Philip
viewed Isocrates in that way in 346, the events of the next
few years can only have confirmed his impression. In 344 the
Athenians refused to give Artaxerxes Ochus assistance in his
effort to recover Egypt,[38] and as late as 341 Demosthenes
(*Fourth Philippic* 33–4) was still trying to convince the
Athenians that they had more to fear from Philip than from
the King of Persia.

Isocrates also sought, and perhaps attained, the attention
of Philip's son. Isocrates wrote the young Alexander a letter

[35] Their conversation is referred to in *Letter 3, To Philip* 1. *Letter 4, To
Antipater* (written in *c*.340) reveals their intimacy. Perhaps they had first met when
Antipater was a Macedonian envoy to Athens for the Peace of Philocrates in 346.

[36] *Letter 3, To Philip* 3.

[37] For recent modern views, see Errington 1981 and Borza 1992: 229–30.

[38] Markle 1976: 89–92 argues that the *Philippus* and the subsequent letter to
Philip of 344 'contributed to hardening Athenian attitudes against Persia and promoting favour towards Philip' and that Isocrates' views influenced the Athenian
Assembly when they contemptuously rebuffed an embassy from Artaxerxes Ochus
in 344, who was seeking Athenian military assistance in his campaign to recover
Egypt (cf. Diod. 16. 44; *FGrH* 324 F 53; Dem. 10. 31–4; and [Dem.] 12. 6–7). But
this theory is refuted by Harding 1994: 178–9, who points out that it is based on a
far from certain restoration in the papyrus text of Didymus' *Commentary on
Demosthenes*, where Androtion (allegedly a pupil of Isocrates) is made the proposer
of the motion which rebuffed the king. In my view the panhellenist writings of
Isocrates reflect popular sentiments to a far greater degree than they helped to form
them.

in *c*.342 which was intended to interest him in Isocrates' own brand of rhetorical education and to undercut the instruction offered by Aristotle.[39] Alexander, however, continued to be tutored by Aristotle and made Aristotle's nephew, Callisthenes of Olynthus, the official historian of his expedition. Both of them were advocates of war against Persia. Callisthenes' biases are well known; he seems to have written up Alexander's campaign as a great panhellenic crusade, surely with his patron's approval.[40] Arrian even has him utter a sentiment which sounds utterly Isocratean. During the *proskynesis* debate, Callisthenes allegedly said (4. 11. 7): 'I deem it worthy of you, Alexander, to remember Greece, for whose sake this entire expedition has taken place, to add Asia to Greece.' As for Aristotle, a peculiar statement in the *Politics* suggests that he too had been affected by panhellenism (1327b29–33): 'The Greek race is both spirited and intelligent; and this is why it continues to be free, to be governed in the best way, and to be capable of ruling all others if it attains a single constitution.'[41] The interest of Aristotle and of Callisthenes in panhellenism, can also be found in Plato. In the *Republic* (470b–471b), which was probably published in the same year as Isocrates' *Panegyricus*, Plato makes essentially the same point that Isocrates does. Greeks should be doing to barbarians, their natural enemies, what they are currently doing to each other, their natural friends, that is, ravaging the countryside and burning their homes.[42]

Indeed, the fact that so many Greek intellectuals advocated war between Greeks and Persians as the solution to Greece's problems indicates that this was a commonly held sentiment. This impression is only strengthened by the fact that all of these men were at odds with each other. Plato and Isocrates were rivals; Isocrates and Aristotle, it is no

[39] *Letter 5, To Alexander*. For an analysis of its contents, see Merlan 1954.

[40] See Pearson 1960: 33–8, 48; Hamilton 1969: liii–liv; Pédech 1984: 51–65; Prandi 1985; Bosworth 1990; and Devine 1994: esp. 97–8.

[41] A late source (*Vita Marc.* 23) claims that Aristotle advised Alexander not to attack Persia, but this is to be rejected as later invention: see Brunt 1993a: 298 and n. 47.

[42] Plato further asserts that enmity between Greeks should be called civil strife (*stasis*), while that between Greeks and barbarians should be called war (*polemos*).

exaggeration to say, despised each other; Aristotle may have left Athens in a pique when Speusippus became Plato's successor as head of the Academy; and Speusippus sent to Philip a pretty nasty critique of Isocrates' *Philippus*.[43] It is significant, however, that Speusippus does not criticize the theme of that work, that Philip should lead the Greeks in a war against barbarians; rather, he thinks that Isocrates did not praise Philip fully enough.[44] We should not be too cynical about the motives of these intellectuals and dismiss panhellenism (like 'toy' Marxism) merely as a fashionable sentiment, devoid of any real commitment, or as a ploy to gain the patronage of dynasts.[45] The fact that Isocrates sent a similar plea to so many powerful individuals shows that he at least was not principally seeking Philip's patronage for himself or his students; for it is difficult to imagine how he could have profited personally from the patronage of Spartan kings.[46] After nearly a century of internecine war which had left mainland Greece impoverished, it is no wonder that many thinking Greeks came to believe that fighting barbarians would be more profitable and more natural than fighting each other.[47]

Lastly, we have a more direct confirmation that panhellenist sentiment was not the preserve of the intellectual elite, but was popular among the average Greek, or at least Athenian, citizen. In 354/3 Demosthenes gave his speech *On*

[43] The ill-will between Isocrates and Aristotle is proved by Dion. Hal. *Isoc.* 18, who cites contemporary sources. The relationship between Aristotle and Speusippus is controversial. Athen. 279e–f (which may not contain authentic information) claims that Speusippus paid the debts owed by Aristotle's close friend Hermias of Atarneus after the latter's execution by the Persians. Aristotle's motives for leaving Athens have been much debated by modern scholars: see Markle 1976: 97 and n. 52 and the thorough discussion by Owen 1983. I incline to the view of Jaeger 1948: 111 that it was for personal, not political reasons.

[44] The standard text and commentary is Bickermann and Sykutris 1928. The authenticity of the letter has been challenged, wrongly to my mind: see Flower 1997: 52 and 52 n. 37.

[45] The desire to win Philip's patronage is stressed by Markle 1976.

[46] See n. 31 above for his letters to Agesilaus and Achidamus.

[47] Markle 1976: 98–9 argues that their motives were selfish and unpatriotic: 'They were not unwilling that Athens ultimately fall under the control of Philip because they felt that either their philosophic dreams or their gross material interests would best be realized under such conditions.' On the other hand, Schachermeyr 1973: 150–1 argued that Callisthenes was motivated by patriotism and not by self-interest, and hoped for a national regeneration through Alexander.

the *Navy-Boards* in which he restrained the Athenians from declaring war on the King of Persia and from asking the other Greeks to join them.[48] Three years later he claimed that he was the first and perhaps the only speaker on that occasion to advise against provoking the King.[49]

In any case, it is a reasonable inference that Alexander, like Philip before him, adopted a panhellenist stance due to the combined influence of Greek intellectuals and of Greek popular opinion. His panhellenist inclinations can only have been confirmed by the following incident. In a highly rhetorical passage of the *Moralia*, Plutarch asserts that Delius of Ephesus, a pupil of Plato, was sent by the Greeks of Asia to ask Alexander to invade Asia.[50] Although Alexander did not need this request, it surely must have verified his decision to employ the liberation of the Asian Greeks as a useful pretext. For it must have seemed that the Greeks who lived under the jurisdiction of the Persian Empire wanted to be liberated and would enthusiastically support him, just as they had supported Agesilaus.[51]

II. PANHELLENISM IN PRACTICE

Against this background, let us now examine some of Alexander's actions which relate to a panhellenist programme. Indeed, the more one looks for signs of panhellenism, the more one finds them. If, however, Callisthenes of Olynthus wrote up the expedition as a panhellenic crusade and if he depicted Alexander as a second Achilles, can we trust what

---

[48] On this speech, see Sealey 1993: 128–9.

[49] *For the Liberty of the Rhodians* 6.

[50] *Mor.* 1126d: 'The one sent to Alexander by the Greeks living in Asia and who most of all incited him and spurred him on to take up the war against the barbarians was Delius of Ephesus, a pupil of Plato.' Brunt 1993a: 291 doubts the authenticity of this report, but without sufficient reason. The Greeks of Asia may have worried that the young Alexander would either cancel or delay the expedition; indeed Antipater and Parmenio are said by Diodorus (17. 16. 2) to have advised Alexander to wait until he had produced an heir.

[51] Xenophon (*Ages.* 1. 38) claims that the Greeks of Asia were bitterly disappointed when Agesilaus was recalled to Greece. It is unclear, however, whether the Asian Greeks were as oppressed as Isocrates claims: Cawkwell 1978: 120–1 thinks that they were actually better off than Greeks living outside of the Persian Empire.

our sources tell us of Alexander's actions? There can be little doubt that Alexander wanted both himself and his expedition to be depicted in those terms, and that his rivalry with and imitation of his ancestors (both Achilles and Heracles) was genuine.[52] Nor was Callisthenes, who died in 327 and whose narrative did not go beyond 329, the only Alexander historian to have depicted that rivalry. Arrian's report (7. 14. 4–5) of Alexander's reputedly excessive mourning for Hephaestion in 324 makes that perfectly clear.[53] And to Alexander's Greek contemporaries, his emulation of Achilles would have appeared inseparable from his panhellenist claims to be avenging Greece, since in the popular imagination the Trojan War had long since become a mythic analogue for the Persian Wars.[54] In fact, we now know that Simonides, in his elegiac poem on the battle of Plataea, had made the comparison between the two wars explicit, and, moreover, gave special emphasis to the death of Achilles.[55] It was natural, therefore, for Herodotus (1. 5) to consider the Trojan War to be the ultimate source of the enmity between the Greeks and the Persians which culminated in the invasions of Darius and Xerxes.

Right from the start of his expedition Alexander cleverly and consciously exploited the assimilation of the Trojan War with the Persian Wars. When he reached the Hellespont he sacrificed at the tomb of Protesilaus at Elaeus, who was the first of the Achaeans to be killed during the Trojan War;[56] and then, in imitation of Protesilaus, he was the first to leap ashore onto Asian soil.[57] Diodorus (17. 17. 2) also

[52] According to Plutarch, *Alex.* 5. 8 (and I see no reason to doubt the historicity of this), Alexander's tutor called himself Phoenix and Alexander Achilles; this conceit almost cost him his life when he actually tried to play the part of Phoenix during a military operation against some Arabs at the time of the siege of Tyre (*Alex.* 24. 10–14). Alexander's emulation of Achilles is discussed by Stewart 1993: 78–86; Ameling 1988; and Cohen 1995. For his emulation of both Achilles and Heracles, see Edmunds 1971.

[53] 'That Alexander cut his hair over the corpse and did the other things, I regard as not unlikely and done in emulation of Achilles, with whom he had a rivalry from boyhood.'

[54] See Hall 1989: 68–9 and Castriota 1992: 1–16. For the conflation of Trojans and Persians in Athenian tragedy, see Hall 1993: 114.

[55] West 1992: fr. 11 and 1993: 4–9; Boedeker and Sider 1996.

[56] Arr. 1. 11. 5.

[57] Arr. 1. 11. 7; Just. 11. 5. 10; Diod. 17. 17. 2. For Alexander's actions at the Hellespont, see Instinsky 1949, with the review by Walbank (*JHS* 70 (1950),

reports that Alexander threw his spear into the beach and declared that he accepted Asia from the gods as spear-won territory.[58] As soon as he crossed he proceeded to Troy, where he sacrificed in the temple of Athena and exchanged his own armour for a set dating from the Trojan War. Those arms were always carried before him in battle.[59] He also crowned the tomb of Achilles and performed other ceremonies there.[60] Xerxes had sacrificed at Troy before invading Greece and so it was only to be expected that Alexander would do likewise before invading Asia.[61] Yet Alexander had familial connections with the Trojan War which rendered his sacrifices particularly symbolic and appropriate. Alexander, like his father, was a descendant of Heracles, who, according to Isocrates (*Phil.* 112), had captured Troy in fewer days than it took Agamemnon years. But unlike his father, he was also a descendant of Andromache and Neoptolemus on his mother's side, and thus of Priam. What significance did this have for him? While at Troy he propitiated the shade of Priam; in the words of Arrian (1. 11. 8), 'he is said to have sacrificed to Priam on the altar of Zeus Herceius, beseeching Priam not to vent his anger on the family of Neoptolemus to which he belonged'. According to Strabo (13. 1. 26–7), Alexander granted Troy special privileges and promised to rebuild the temple of Athena. But this should not be taken to indicate that Alexander was now discarding the traditional assimilation of

79–81); and Zahrnt 1996, who argues that Alexander was simply following Callisthenes' instructions.

[58] Cf. Just. 11. 5. 10, and note Mehl 1980/81 on the concept of 'spear-won territory' in the Hellenistic period. Zahrnt 1996 argues that this detail was a later invention of Cleitarchus since it was incompatible with panhellenist propaganda. Contra Seibert 1998: 56–7, and n. 179, who thinks that the incident, which he takes to be aimed at a Macedonian audience, proves that Alexander was openly planning a war of Macedonian territorial expansion. Whatever Alexander's private intentions, it is far from clear how a contemporary Greek might have interpreted the spear-throw and declaration. I am not convinced by Seibert that a spear-throw is a specifically Persian claim to dominion (cf. Plut. *Mor.* 210e, where Agesilaus boasts that the borders of Sparta extend as far as his spear can reach).

[59] Arr. 1. 11. 7–8; 6. 9. 3.

[60] Arr. 1. 12. 1; Plut. *Alex.* 15. 7–9; Just. 11. 5. 12.

[61] Hdt. 7. 43: 'Xerxes sacrificed a thousand oxen to Athena Ilias and the Magi poured libations to the heroes.' It is controversial which 'heroes' are meant, Trojan or Greek ones, or both. Briant 1996: 565 takes Herodotus to mean 'Priam and his Trojan companions' and that seems reasonable.

Trojans and Persians in Greek thought.[62] Alexander's interconnected imitation and emulation of Achilles overshadowed
and transcended his Trojan ancestry.[63] By sacrificing to
Priam he was doing nothing more than appeasing him for
the sacrilege of Neoptolemus, who had slaughtered him at
the very altar where Alexander made his sacrifice.

After the battle of the Granicus, Alexander sent 300
Persian panoplies to Athens as a dedication to Athena (Arr.
1. 16. 7; Plut. *Alex.* 16. 17–18). The inscription attached to
the dedication was pointed: 'Alexander the son of Philip and
the Greeks except the Lacedaemonians from the barbarians
who dwell in Asia.' Arrian and Plutarch differ as to whether
this inscription was only on the dedications sent to Athens or
was meant for a broader Greek audience. In any case, the
wording was not simply intended to emphasize Sparta's
refusal to join the League of Corinth. It was surely also
meant to recall Sparta's former betrayal of the Greeks in
Asia to Persia first in 412 and then in the infamous King's
Peace of 387/6.

During the battle of the Granicus, Alexander slaughtered
most of the 20,000 Greek mercenaries who fought for the
Persians and dispatched some 2,000 of them as prisoners to
Macedonia, where they would be subject to hard labour.[64]
His justification, as Arrian (1. 16. 6) explains, was because
'though being Greeks, in violation of the common resolu-
tions of the Greeks, they had fought against Greece for
barbarians'.[65] Alexander then proceeded, although with
some flexibility on his part,[66] to keep his word and liberate
the Greek cities of Asia. While en route from Miletus to

---

[62] Bosworth 1988*b*: 281 claims that 'for Alexander the Trojans were not
barbarians but Hellenes on Asian soil', and that 'the descendants of Achilles and
Priam would now fight together against the common enemy'. A different interpretation is given by Georges 1994: 64–5: 'At Troy, therefore, Alexander advertised
the coming end of the millennial conflict between Asia and Greece in his own
person, in a reconciliation and assimilation between Hellas and Troy . . .'. Badian
1996: 17 considers the whole incident a fiction and suggests that it was introduced
by Aristobulus, but he does not know the Strabo passage.

[63] The difference between imitation and emulation is well analysed by Green
1978.

[64] Arr. 1. 14. 4; 1. 16. 2; 1. 16. 6.

[65] Cf. Arr. 3. 23. 8. So too the Hellenic League of 480 had forbidden Medism
(Hdt. 7. 132).

[66] See Badian 1966.

Caria he proclaimed that 'he had undertaken the war against the Persians for the sake of the freedom of the Greeks' (Diod. 17. 24. 1: cf. Arr. 1. 18. 1–2). Later, in Lycia near the city of Xanthus, Alexander was encouraged by the discovery of a bronze tablet which allegedly predicted the destruction of the Persian Empire by Greeks.[67]

After his conquest of Egypt, Alexander consulted the oracle of Zeus Ammon. Did this also have a panhellenist twist to it? Before the expedition of Alexander, there was only one person whose policy was unequivocally panhellenic in the sense of waging incessant war on the possessions of the King of Persia, and that was Cimon, the son of Miltiades.[68] Indeed, Plutarch's account of Cimon's last expedition against Egypt and Cyprus in c.450 BC foreshadows the later expedition of Alexander the Great. Plutarch (*Cimon* 18. 1; 18. 6) claims that Cimon's purpose was 'to get profit from Greece's natural enemies' and that 'he had in mind nothing less than the total destruction of the King's power'.[69] Plutarch (*Cimon* 18. 7) then adds an intriguing detail: 'Cimon himself, about to set mighty conflicts in motion and keeping his fleet together off Cyprus, sent messengers to the shrine of Ammon to put some question to the god. No one knows the purpose of their visit nor did the god deliver an oracle to them, but as soon as the messengers approached he ordered them to leave; for Cimon, he told them, was already with him.' The god did not give a response, knowing that Cimon had already died. If Cimon's operations were preliminary to a land invasion of Asia, for which he would need Spartan aid, perhaps that was the subject of his attempted consultation of the oracle of Zeus Ammon at Siwah Oasis.[70]

It would be naive not to question Plutarch's source for all of this. It has been suggested, not unreasonably, that Cimon's plan to destroy the Persian Empire and his

[67] Plut. *Alex.* 17. 4.

[68] Cf. Plut. *Cimon* 19. Much more could be said about Cimon's panhellenism, but this I must do elsewhere (*Classical Antiquity* 19, 2000).

[69] This assessment of Cimon's plans was accepted by Wade-Gery 1945: 219–22.

[70] An eagerness to co-operate with Sparta is indicated by Cimon's famous dictum (Plut. *Cimon* 16. 8–10); when urging the Athenians in c.462 to help the Spartans put down a helot revolt, he exhorted them 'not to allow Greece to become lame or Athens to be deprived of her yoke-fellow'.

attempted consultation of the oracle of Zeus Ammon at Siwah Oasis, possibly about that very topic, were invented by Callisthenes of Olynthus in order to make Cimon a precursor to Alexander the Great.[71] The reverse, however, may rather be true. Alexander may have been consciously evoking the example of Cimon, whom Plutarch (*Cimon* 19. 5) calls 'the Greek *hegemon*', by consulting Ammon. Alexander may have wanted the Athenians and other Greeks to see him as completing the task which Cimon had begun more than a century earlier.

Before the battle of Issus, Alexander encouraged his Greek forces with the appropriate panhellenic themes. Curtius (3. 10) and Justin (11. 9. 3–6) claim that Alexander said what was appropriate to each of the nationalities in his army (Macedonians, Greeks, Illyrians, and Thracians) and give a similar account of what he said to the Greeks. To quote Justin: 'he rode round his troops addressing remarks tailored to each nationality among them' and he 'inspired the Greeks by reminding them of past wars and of their deadly hatred for the Persians'.[72] The battle of Gaugamela was nothing short of a panhellenist set piece. As Plutarch describes it (*Alex.* 33. 1), before the battle 'Alexander made a very long speech to the Thessalians and the other Greeks and when they encouraged him with shouts to lead them against the barbarians, he shifted his spear into his left hand and with his right he called upon the gods, as Callisthenes says, praying to them, if indeed he was truly sprung from Zeus, to defend and strengthen the Greeks.'[73] Following

---

[71] Schreiner 1977: 21–9. Even if this is correct, Callisthenes attributed to Cimon an undertaking which he must have assumed would have been believable to his contemporary Greek audience. Parke 1967: 215 suggests that Cimon may have tried to consult Zeus Ammon in an attempt to get oracular support for his aid to Egyptian insurgents against Persia (Thuc. 1. 112. 3), but that the story, as Plutarch tells it, is a later invention. Thomas 1989: 203–5 points out that Cimon was little remembered in 4th-cent. Athenian oral tradition and I suppose that might have made it easier for Callisthenes (or indeed someone else) to elaborate the details of his attempted consultation.

[72] Arrian (2. 7. 3–7) has Alexander address his various commanders as a group, but this is not necessarily incompatible with additional pre-battle harangues to his troops: see Bosworth 1980a: 204.

[73] The propagandistic intent of this passage is revealed by the fact that no mention is made of the Macedonians. Callisthenes obviously meant it for Greek consumption. But perhaps Alexander gave separate speeches to the Greek and

the battle Alexander took steps 'seeking', as Plutarch (*Alex.* 34) says, 'to win the favour of the Greeks'.[74] He wrote to them that the tyrannies had been abolished (meaning those in Asia) and that the Greeks were autonomous. He wrote separately to the Plataeans that he would rebuild Plataea because their ancestors had furnished territory to the Greeks for the struggle on behalf of their freedom. He also sent a portion of the spoils to the people of Croton because the athlete Phayllus had fitted out a ship at his own expense with which he fought at Salamis in 480 (Plut. *Alex.* 34).[75] In this way Alexander, always mindful of the significant gesture, linked his victory at Gaugamela with the Greek victories at both Plataea and Salamis.[76]

As Alexander proceeded eastwards, more gestures followed. After the capture of Susa in 331 he sent (or promised to send) back to Athens the bronze statues of Harmodius and Aristogeiton and the seated figure of Artemis Celcaea which Xerxes had removed (Arr. 3. 16. 7–8); something which he may actually have done in 324 (Arr. 7. 19. 2).[77] Finally, we have the burning of Persepolis. When Alexander first arrived he handed over the city proper, apart from the palace complex, to be sacked by his troops. According to the vulgate tradition, Alexander proclaimed that Persepolis was the 'most hostile' city in Asia and should be destroyed in retaliation for the invasions of

Macedonian parts of his line (as at Issus) and he was shrewd enough to say what was appropriate to each group (although not necessarily what Callisthenes reported).

[74] For the translation, see Hamilton 1969: 91. Hammond 1993: 66–7 n. 22 claims that the phrase is misunderstood by Hamilton and translates: 'Seeking honour for himself A wrote to the Greeks.' But Plut. *Flam.* 9. 5 and *Cim.* 4. 7 decisively show that Hamilton is correct.

[75] Herodotus (8. 47) implies, probably wrongly, that the Crotoniates had sent him out officially. See Hamilton 1969: 92.

[76] Hamilton 1969: 91 comments: 'Alexander ostentatiously marked his position as *Hegemon* of the Corinthian League, and, by connecting his victory with the ancient victories of Salamis and Plataea, emphasized the Pan-Hellenic character of the war.'

[77] It is possible that Alexander merely promised to return these statues and that the restoration actually took place during the joint reign of Seleucus I and Antiochus (292–281 BC), as suggested by Bosworth 1980a: 317, who accepts the testimony of Pausanias (1. 8. 5) and Valerius Maximus (2. 10, ext. 1) over that of Arrian.

Xerxes and Darius.[78] Alexander then wintered at the palace complex and Plutarch claims that when Demaratus the Corinthian, who had been a friend of Philip's, saw Alexander seated on the throne of Darius, he said that 'those Greeks were deprived of great pleasure who had died before seeing Alexander seated on that throne'.[79] None the less, at the end of his sojourn, the palace was destroyed. The official explanation for this act of terrorism is provided by Arrian (3. 18. 12; cf. Strabo 15. 3. 6): that Alexander wished to punish the Persians for their invasion of Greece, the destruction of Athens, the burning of the temples, and for all their other crimes against the Greeks. Whether this truly was a pre-meditated act or whether an intoxicated Alexander was spontaneously induced to torch the palace by a precocious Athenian whore, was controversial in antiquity and is still so today.[80] Nevertheless, there is no good reason to doubt Arrian's explanation (which is not at all irreconcilable with the vulgate tradition).[81] Whether or not Alexander had yet heard the outcome of the war against Agis, he had no choice but to select one of the Persian cities for destruction if he was to fulfil the promises which both he and his father had made to the Greek members of the Corinthian League. The palace complex at Persepolis, associated as it was with Darius and Xerxes, was the perfect offering to Hellenic sensibilities.

On the level, however, of popular sentiment it is irrele-vant what motivated Alexander or which version of the inci-

[78] Diod. 17. 70. 1–6; and more fully, Curt. 5. 6. 1–8. Cf. Plut. *Alex.* 37. 3–5. Contra Hammond 1992, who argues that the vulgate version was an invention of Cleitarchus with no basis in historical fact. He concludes (p. 364): 'The city of Persepolis was not damaged.'

[79] Plut. *Alex.* 37. 7, reported again at 56. Plutarch also claims (37. 5) that Alexander debated whether to set up a statue of Xerxes which had been knocked over, but decided not to because of his expedition against the Greeks.

[80] Badian 1994 revives the argument that Alexander deliberately burned Persepolis because he had not yet heard the outcome of Agis' war. Bloedow 1995 attempts to refute Badian's chronology and asserts (unconvincingly to my mind) that Alexander's decision both to ravage the city and to burn the palace was wholly irrational. Chronology aside, Badian correctly points out (p. 284) that the Thais story may report the way in which the destruction, planned in advance, was actually carried out. For this suggestion, see also Connor 1985: 98–9.

[81] See esp. Wilcken 1932: 144–5, although he asserts that the Thais story was invented by Cleitarchus. Bloedow 1995: 29–34 gives a comprehensive survey of modern scholarship on this topic.

dent is the 'true' one. The prostitute Thais, according to the vulgate sources, incited Alexander and his companions by pointing out how fitting it would be for the burning of Athens to be avenged by a Greek woman. Curtius even has her declare that Alexander would then win most favour among all the Greeks.[82] That Alexander did indeed win favour is confirmed by a dedication made by the Thespians which celebrates the destruction of Persepolis as an act of ancestral revenge (*Palatine Anthology* 6. 344): 'The men of spacious Thespiae once sent these hoplites, avengers of their ancestors, into barbarian Asia; they who destroyed Persian cities with Alexander and dedicated a cunningly made tripod to loud-thundering Zeus.'[83] Thus even if Arrian's version is merely an after-the-fact justification, it was a justification which at least some (and probably many) Greeks took seriously and sympathized with. Modern scholarship tends to concentrate on the differences between Arrian's version and the vulgate tradition; but what they have in common is actually more important. The justification is the same in each: ancestral revenge. The Thais story, in the words of one modern scholar, 'was just what Greeks at home longed to hear'.[84]

III. PANHELLENISM AFTER THE BURNING OF PERSEPOLIS

Did Alexander's panhellenism end with the burning of Persepolis? Had it outlived its usefulness as political propaganda? Because Alexander soon disbanded his allied contingents at Ecbatana in 330 (Arr. 3. 19. 5–6; cf. Diod. 17. 74. 3; Curt. 6. 2. 15–17), it is generally asserted that the panhellenic

---

[82] Plut. *Alex.* 38; Diod. 17. 72; Curt. 5. 7. 3, 'Thais, herself also drunk, declared that he would win most favour among all the Greeks, if he should order the palace of the Persians to be set on fire; and she said that this was expected by those whose cities the barbarians had destroyed'. On the portrayal of Thais, see especially Baynham 1998a: 95–9.

[83] Θεσπιαὶ εὐρύχοροι πέμψαν ποτὲ τούσδε συνόπλους | τιμωροὺς προγόνων βάρβαρον εἰς Ἀσίην, | οἳ μετ᾽ Ἀλεξάνδρου Περσῶν ἄστη καθελόντες | στῆσαν Ἐριβρεμέτῃ δαιδάλεον τρίποδα. The text is that of Page 1975, lines 5881–4. See Bellen 1974: 60–4 and Lane Fox 1973: 93.

[84] Hammond 1992: 363.

part of the expedition was over.[85] But this was not true for several reasons and it should be emphasized that no ancient source marks this as a turning point.[86] This is yet another invention of modern scholars. First of all, to Alexander's panhellenic audience in Greece the burning indeed would have signalled that the destruction of Athens had been avenged, but it would not obviously have signalled the end of the panhellenic campaign. Isocrates had urged Philip (*Phil.* 154) 'to rule as many of the barbarians as possible' and Alexander still had a long way to go in order to fulfil that recommendation. Secondly, Arrian says that 'not a few' of the Greek troops stayed on as mercenaries; and this may have been Alexander's way of transferring the cost of their maintenance from their home cities to himself in the wake of his seizure of the Persian royal treasuries.[87] In any case, given that Isocrates had contemplated that Philip might use no Greek troops other than mercenaries (*Phil.* 86, 96), the dismissal of allied forces was not in itself significant.[88]

[85] Brunt 1965: 203 is typical: 'The Panhellenic war was then over, and Alexander sent the Greek contingents home (Arr. 3. 19. 5)'. Note also Hamilton 1973: 90 and Bosworth 1988*b*: 96–7. Hatzopoulos 1997 argues that it had been Alexander's original intention to return to Macedonia after the burning of Persepolis. Arrian, however, only says that Alexander sent the Thessalian cavalry and the other allies back to the sea; he gives no explanation.

[86] The fact that Alexander's Macedonian troops mistakenly took the death of Darius and the dismissal of the Greek allies as a sign that the expedition was over, in no way indicates a change in Alexander's intentions or propaganda; they wanted to return home and Alexander produced arguments suitable for persuading them to stay. See Diod. 17. 74. 3; Curt. 6. 2. 15–6. 3. 18; Just. 12. 3. 2–3; and Plut. *Alex.* 47.

[87] According to Diodorus (17. 74. 3–4) and Curtius (6. 2. 17), Alexander paid a bonus of 1 talent to each of the cavalry and of 1,000 drachmae to each of the infantry whom he dismissed. As Bosworth (1980*a*: 336) suggests, the 2,000 talents specified by Arrian (3. 19. 5) and Plutarch (*Alex.* 42. 5) covers only payments made to the allied cavalry. Diodorus further mentions that he gave the incredible sum of 3 talents to each of the Greeks who chose to remain in 'the king's army'. Even if this latter figure is an exaggeration, it shows that Alexander was both willing and able to retain his allied Greek forces at his own expense. Less than a year later, however, when Alexander was about to cross the Oxus river, he sent home those of the Thessalian cavalry who had volunteered to remain (Arr. 3. 29. 5); perhaps they had been disaffected by the execution of their former commander Parmenio (cf. Arr. 5. 27. 5).

[88] At *Phil.* 86 Isocrates points out that the approval of the Greeks, even without their actual participation in the expedition, would be sufficient to secure Philip's success. At *Phil.* 96, he writes: 'As for soldiers, you will immediately have as many as you want; for the present condition of Greece is such that it is easier to assemble a larger and stronger army from vagabonds than from active citizens'. Two years

Thirdly, even after the burning, Alexander still invoked a resolution of the League of Corinth in dealing with Greek mercenaries in Persian service. According to Arrian (3. 23. 8), while in Hyrcania he replied to the envoys of some 1,500 mercenaries who were seeking terms of surrender, 'that those who fought with the barbarians against Greece contrary to the decrees of the Greeks were guilty of grave wrongs'. When after an interlude in which he campaigned against the Mardians, the full body came to his camp, Arrian (3. 24. 5) says that 'he also dismissed those of the other Greeks who had been serving with the Persians as mercenaries since before the peace and the alliance which had been made with the Macedonians (i.e. by the Greeks in 337 BC); the rest he ordered to serve under him at the same rate of pay'. Since Alexander gave the 'guilty' ones a full pardon and enlisted them in his own army,[89] there was no need to mention the 'decrees' of the Greeks unless panhellenic propaganda still mattered. Alexander may well have been manipulating these mercenaries psychologically by holding out the threat of punishment, but that is not incompatible with his constant references to what was expected of Greeks nor does it explain his panhellenic justification for dismissing a part of them.

Fourth, an incident took place in the summer of 329 that unequivocally demonstrates that the war of revenge was still being employed as propaganda. Curtius narrates in vivid detail how Alexander, after he had crossed the Oxus river, came upon a small town in Bactria, inhabited by the Branchidae.[90] These Branchidae, Curtius tells us, were the descendants of the priests who had violated the temple of Apollo at Didyma and betrayed it to Xerxes in 479. Alexander took a terrible revenge upon them for their

later, however, in *Letter 2, To Philip* 17–21, he suggests that Philip could more quickly and more safely conquer the barbarians and add to his empire if Athens were actively to assist him.

[89] Cf. also Diod. 17. 76. 1–2 (who alone mentions the pardon) and Curt. 6. 5. 6–10.

[90] 7. 5. 28–35. Cf. Diod. 17, table of contents κά; Plut. *Mor.* 557b; Strabo 11. 11. 4 and 14. 1. 5. Curtius and Diodorus derive from Cleitarchus; Strabo from another source, most probably Callisthenes (see below). For discussion see Pearson 1960: 240; Bellen 1974: 63–5; Bigwood 1978: 36–9; Parke 1985; and Bosworth 1988b: 108–9.

ancestors' treachery: the Branchidae were massacred as traitors and their town was destroyed root and branch. One might be tempted to dismiss the explanation, if not the entire story, as a fiction of Cleitarchus if it were not for an important piece of circumstantial evidence. Strabo (17. 1. 43) tells us that Callisthenes referred to the temple at Didyma as 'plundered by the Branchidae who sided with the Persians in the time of Xerxes'. Callisthenes was the first historian to date the plundering of the temple to 479, as opposed to Herodotus (6. 19) who says that it happened in 494. This makes it highly probable that Callisthenes also reported Alexander's justification for the massacre of the Branchidae in 329 and that he depicted it as yet another example of revenge taken for Xerxes' desecration of Greek temples.[91]

Fifth, for what it is worth, Onesicritus thought that pan-hellenism still mattered for Alexander as late as 326; for when he was crossing the river Hydaspes in a storm just before his battle with Porus, according to Onesicritus, Alexander cried out 'Oh Athenians, could you possibly believe what sort of dangers I am undergoing in order to win a good reputation in your eyes.'[92] Perhaps Alexander was here using panhellenic propaganda as a justification for the annexation of territory beyond the limits of Persian suzerainty.

Sixth, what about the liberation of the Greeks of Asia? Was that theme also dropped when it was no longer useful or convenient? During the winter of 325/4 BC the historian Theopompus of Chios wrote a letter to Alexander in which he laments that although Harpalus had spent more than two hundred talents on memorials for his deceased mistress, no one had yet adorned the grave of those who died in Cilicia 'on behalf of your kingship and the freedom of the Greeks'.[93] This does not demonstrate that Theopompus was himself a panhellenist;[94] rather, it indicates that a Greek on the island

---

[91] See Tarn 1948: ii. 272–5, who astutely makes the attribution to Callisthenes, but less plausibly argues that the massacre never took place. Parke 1985 expands Tarn's argument that Callisthenes was Strabo's source, while accepting that the massacre actually occurred.

[92] Plut. *Alex.* 60. 5–6 (= *FGrH* 134 F 19).

[93] *FGrH* 115 F 253.

[94] See Flower 1997: 89.

of Chios, who was trying to ingratiate himself, thought that 'the freedom of the Greeks' of Asia was still an important slogan to Alexander. Many of those cities must have felt that Alexander was sincere enough, since they not only granted him divine honours, but maintained his cult for centuries after his death.[95]

Seventh and last, we have Diodorus' description of the funeral pyre of Hephaestion, which was no doubt designed by Alexander himself.[96] Hephaestion died in the autumn of 324, after the marriages at Susa and the banquet of reconciliation at Opis. Diodorus (17. 115. 4) says of the pyre, which must have looked like a ziggurat, that the first level was decorated with the prows of 240 quinqueremes, each bearing two kneeling archers and armed male figures; this, we can infer, alluded to the battle of Salamis.[97] The fourth level, he tells us, carried a centauromachy rendered in gold and the sixth level was covered with Macedonian and Persian arms, 'signifying the bravery of the one people and the defeats of the other'.[98] The centauromachy, in particular, was surely meant to evoke the Greek–barbarian antithesis of fifth-century Athenian public monuments.[99]

I am not suggesting that revenge on Persia on behalf of Greece and the liberation of the Asian Greeks were Alexander's primary motives for invading Asia. Indeed, our sources claim that he later regretted the destruction both of

[95] Habicht 1970: 17–25, 245–6; Badian 1981: 59–63; Flower 1997: 258–61.

[96] According to Plut. *Alex.* 72. 5, Alexander wished that Stasicrates were alive to design it. At 72. 8 Alexander is described as 'devising and contriving with his artists'. On this monument, see Schachermeyr 1954: 118–40. For a more recent discussion with earlier bibliography, see McKechnie 1995, although his thesis is untenable that the description in Diodorus comes from a literary *ekphrasis* composed by Ephippus of Olynthus and as such bears no relation to anything planned by Alexander. The pyre has, in fact, been excavated and the remains conform to Diodorus' description; see Olga Palagia's chapter 'Hephaestion's Pyre and the Royal Hunt of Alexander' in this volume.

[97] The connection between the battle of Salamis and the representation of a ship would have been obvious to a Greek spectator. On one of the painted screens which decorated the throne of the statue of Zeus at Olympia, there were personifications of 'Greece and Salamis, who holds in her hand the ornament made for the top of a ship's bow' (Paus. 5. 11. 5).

[98] Colledge 1987: 140 suggests that the monument may have been a physical expression of Alexander's public prayer for 'harmony and partnership in rule between Greeks and Persians'; but this ignores Diodorus' interpretation. I assume that Diodorus was not merely guessing.

[99] See Castriota 1992: 34–43, 152–65.

Thebes and of Persepolis.[100] I am merely suggesting that panhellenism and political self-interest were neither incompatible nor mutually exclusive. No one would deny that Alexander adjusted his policies to suit his needs. For instance, when Alexander was at Gordium in 333 an embassy arrived from Athens asking for the release of the Athenian mercenaries who had been captured at the Granicus. Alexander refused 'because', as Arrian explains, 'he did not think it safe, with the Persian war still in progress, to dismiss the fear of those Greeks who were willing to fight on behalf of the barbarians against Greece'.[101] But later, when he reached Tyre in 331, he gave back the Athenian prisoners. Not coincidentally, this was just when he learned that a revolt was brewing in the Peloponnese.[102] Likewise, although Alexander claimed to be liberating the Greek cities of Asia, he was ready enough to exact contributions when he needed money. This may seem cynical, but Alexander, even if he believed in his pretexts on one level, could not afford to be sentimental.

Granted that Alexander was willing enough to manipulate panhellenism in order to suit his immediate political and financial needs, in what respects could he be said to have actually deviated from panhellenist principles? Was it when after the battle of Gaugamela, as Plutarch records (*Alex.* 34. 1), he was proclaimed 'King of Asia'? If this report is accurate, it surely would not have troubled the likes of Isocrates, who had recommended to Philip (*Phil.* 154) that he 'be a benefactor to the Greeks, a king to the Macedonians, and rule over as many of the barbarians as possible'.[103] In other words, Isocrates, in my view, was giving carte blanche to Philip to establish an empire in Asia.

Or was it when Alexander received *proskynesis* from barbarians? Xenophon implies that Agesilaus had compelled barbarians to do *proskynesis* to Greeks.[104] But what pan-

[100] Thebes: Arr. 2. 15. 2. Persepolis: Arr. 6. 30. 1; Plut. *Alex.* 38. 8; Curt. 5. 7. 11.
[101] Arr. 1. 29. 5–6. Cf. Curt. 3. 1. 9.
[102] Arr. 3. 6. 2. Cf. Curt. 4. 8. 12–13.
[103] Cf. also 120, 139, 141. I agree with Ellis (1976: 227–9) that in 346 Isocrates might have been satisfied had Philip only conquered Asia Minor; but that does not entail that he would have either desired or expected Philip to stop there. When he wrote to Philip in 338 he foresaw nothing less than the conquest of the Persian Empire (*Letter 3, To Philip* 5). Cf. also *Letter 2, To Philip* 11.
[104] *Ages.* 1. 34.

hellenist, one may ask, would have requested *proskynesis* from Greeks, with its implication of the divinity of the recipient? Here it is relevant that Isocrates had written to Philip in 338 (*Letter 3, To Philip* 5) that after he had conquered the Persian Empire 'there shall be nothing still left but to become a god'. Isocrates was surely speaking figuratively (or perhaps 'rhetorically') and was not predicting the establishment of a ruler cult. But Alexander, or even Philip for that matter, might have taken him literally.[105] In that case, even the foremost proponent of panhellenism might have seemed to sanction Alexander's assumption of divine honours. And Callisthenes of Olynthus was willing enough to promote Alexander's divine sonship, and probably his posthumous deification (if the *proskynesis* debate in Arrian is historical); problems only arose when Alexander was unwilling to wait for the latter.[106]

Did Alexander betray the Greek race when he married a Bactrian princess and two Persian royal ladies? Had not Cimon, the first true champion of panhellenism, been the son of a Thracian king's daughter? Did Alexander abandon the panhellenic cause when he befriended Persian nobles and employed them in the administration of the empire and army? Aristotle allegedly had advised Alexander 'to be a leader to Greeks and a despot to the barbarians, to look after the former as after friends and relatives, and to deal with the latter as with animals or plants'.[107] Alexander did not follow

[105] See Fredricksmeyer 1979: 58 (and n. 54 for earlier bibliography): contra Badian 1981: 31 n. 9.

[106] It is beyond reasonable doubt that Callisthenes depicted Alexander as the son of Zeus/Ammon: cf. Polybius 12. 12b. 2–3 and 12. 23. 4 = Timaeus, *FGrH* 566 F 155 and F119a respectively; Arr. 4. 10. 1–2; Plut. *Alex.* 33. 1 = Callisthenes, *FGrH* 124 F 36; with Bosworth 1996a: 109–14. If the *proskynesis* debate, as recorded by Arrian, preserves the main lines of Callisthenes' speech (see Bosworth 1995: 77–86), then he was willing to cede posthumous deification to Alexander. Contrary to Bosworth 1988a: 116–17 and 1996a: 111, it seems to me likely that Callisthenes mentioned the posthumous deification of Heracles as a hint to Alexander that he too might be granted divine honours after death. The deification of Heracles is mentioned in both versions of Callisthenes' speech: Arr. 4. 11. 7 and Curt. 8. 5. 17.

[107] Plutarch, *On the Fortune of Alexander* 329b (= Rose F 658); rejected as apocryphal by Brunt 1993a: 297 n. 44, on the grounds that it is incompatible with Aristotle's philosophy to classify barbarians with plants. But Aristotle is speaking rhetorically and he is only saying that they should be treated as animals and plants, not that they were categorically the same. Moreover, in the *Politics* (1333^{b}39–1334^{a}3) he asserts that it is a proper object of military training to hold despotic

Aristotle's advice and he had a good precedent for acting
otherwise. When Agesilaus was in Asia he was joined by the
Persian Spithridates, whom Lysander had persuaded to
revolt (Xen. *Hell.* 3. 4. 10), and fell in love with Spithridates'
son Megabates (Xen. *Ages.* 5. 4–5; *Hell. Oxy.* 21. 4). Agesilaus
then attempted to make an alliance with Pharnabazus, the
satrap of Hellespontine Phrygia (Xen. *Hell.* 4. 1. 36), and
he established guest-friendship with his son (4. 1. 39–40).
Isocrates had predicted to Philip in 346 that many of the
King's satraps were ready to revolt and would fight on his
side, and he encouraged him to proclaim freedom throughout Asia.[108] This was precisely the policy of Agesilaus, who
not only tried to make an alliance with Pharnabazus, but
even offered to increase the number of his subjects.[109] Indeed, Agesilaus' offer to Pharnabazus prefigures the prayer
of Alexander at Opis that Persians and Macedonians might
rule together in concord and partnership.[110] One might object, of course, that Agesilaus was merely attempting to
establish a buffer zone between the territory of the King and
the Greek cities on the coast, and thus was not offering
partnership with Pharnabazus.[111] But by sacrificing at Aulis he
portrayed himself, and he was portrayed by Xenophon, as
intending, in Plutarch's words, 'to fight for the person of the
King and the wealth of Ecbatana and Susa'.[112] So whatever

power over those who deserve to be slaves. According to Aristotle, barbarians were
'natural slaves' in that they were by nature more servile than Greeks. This was
because they were deficient in reason (*logos*): see *Politics* $1252^b5–9$, 1255^a, 1260^a12,
$1285^a20–4$; Brunt 1993*b*: 343–88 and Garnsey 1996: esp. 107–27. Later on in Book
7 of the *Politics* ($1327^b23–36$) he also gives a climatic explanation, similar to that
found in Hippocrates, *Airs, Waters, Places*. Badian 1958*a*: 440–4 argues that this
later passage represents a revised view of barbarians; but Kraut 1997: 94 thinks that
there is no conflict with earlier statements.

[108] *Phil.* 104: 'If, however, you cross over into Asia, he (Idrieus, satrap of Caria)
will be pleased to see it, thinking that you have come to assist him. You also will
cause many of the other satraps to revolt, if you promise them freedom and proclaim this word throughout Asia.' Cf. *Letter 3, To Philip* 5.

[109] Xen. *Hell.* 4. 1. 34–6.

[110] Arr. 7. 11. 9. It makes little difference whether Xenophon is citing what
Agesilaus had actually said. From the point of view of cultural stereotypes, it is
significant that Xenophon, writing for a panhellenic audience, would represent
Agesilaus as making such an offer. As Lewis 1977: 152 points out, Xenophon's attitude to collaboration with the upper classes of Iran foreshadows that of Alexander.
See Hornblower 1994*a*: 69–70 for guest-friendships between Greeks and Persians
in the early 4th cent.   [111] See Cartledge 1987: 193 and 213.

[112] For talk of the conquest of the Persian Empire, see Xen. *Hell.* 4. 1. 41; Xen.

Agesilaus' real or secret intentions, Alexander might easily have taken his dealings with Pharnabazus and other local elites as a model of what might be done.

Alexander, therefore, had the example of Agesilaus before him. Closer to home, his father Philip had been willing to forge a marriage alliance with Pixodarus, satrap of Caria.[113] And it also could be argued that when it came to the treatment of non-Greeks, he rejected the view of Aristotle that barbarians were slaves by nature in favour of the attitude of Xenophon and Isocrates. In the *Cyropaedia* Xenophon depicts Cyrus the Great as a paradigm of the good leader and he seemingly came under the spell of Cyrus the Younger, to whom he gives a lengthy eulogy in the *Anabasis* (1. 9). In his *Hellenica* (4. 1. 29–38) he portrays Pharnabazus as a man of virtue fully equal to Agesilaus. Although Xenophon ends his *Cyropaedia* by contrasting the impiety, greed, effeminacy, and cowardice of the contemporary Persians with their former excellence in those very respects, he clearly believed that some Persians, like Pharnabazus and the younger Cyrus, exemplified the old virtues.[114] More generally, he praised the 'discipline' of those Persian nobles who, without removing their embroidered clothing and gold jewellery, leapt into the mud to extricate some wagons when Cyrus gave them the order (*Anabasis* 1. 5. 7–8). Alexander, like Xenophon, would discover Persians whom he could admire and employ.[115]

Isocrates, for his part, believed that Greeks were culturally superior to non-Greeks, but he based that superiority not on

Ages. 1. 8, 1. 36, and 7. 5–7; Plut. *Ages.* 15. On the other hand, *Hell. Oxy.*, col. 21. 4 (Chambers) implies that Agesilaus merely envisioned the annexation of Asia Minor west of Cilicia.

[113] Plut. *Alex.* 10. The initiative, we are told, came from Pixodarus, who proposed to marry his eldest daughter to Philip's son Arrhidaeus.

[114] Xenophon's favourable treatment of some Persians is well discussed by Georges 1994: 207–43. Note also Hirsch 1985.

[115] And even before his expedition Alexander surely must have known Artabazus, whom he later appointed satrap of Bactria, when Artabazus and his family were exiles at Philip's court in the 340s (Diod. 16. 52. 3; Curt. 6. 5. 2–3). Schachermeyr 1973: 133 wonders whether Alexander was influenced by his early acquaintance with the children of Artabazus by a Rhodian woman (the sister of Mentor and Memnon) when he arranged the marriages at Susa between the Macedonian and Iranian nobility. For Alexander's eventual use of Iranians in both army and administration, see, in particular, Bosworth 1980*b*.

nature but on education and form of government. At
Panegyricus 150 he writes that it is not possible for men
brought up and governed as were the Persians either to have
a share in any other virtue or to be successful in war.[116]
Nevertheless, he must have allowed the possibility that
barbarians could be raised to the level of Greeks, since he
said of King Evagoras of Cyprian Salamis (*Evag.* 66) that he
'converted the citizens of Cyprus from barbarians into
Greeks'.[117] In the anti-Spartan section of the *Panathenaicus*
(209) he asserts that the Lacedaemonians are more backward
than the barbarians in terms of education (*paideia*), since
whereas the latter have made many discoveries, the
Lacedaemonians cannot even read or write. But Isocrates'
statements as to what should be done with barbarians who
resist conquest are not consistent, probably because the
spread of Hellenic culture to non-Greeks was not of particular interest to him.[118] He did not rule it out on theoretical
grounds, but he did not promote it either.

Thus panhellenism as represented by Xenophon and
Isocrates was not incompatible with the belief that non-
Greeks were potentially the equal of Greeks. Isocrates
admitted the possibility that they could be Hellenized,
whereas Xenophon admired some of them in terms of their
own culture. That Alexander believed that non-Greeks
could be Hellenized is indicated by his arranging for the
30,000 Iranian youths, the so-called Epigoni, to be taught
Greek and trained in Macedonian arms and tactics.[119] It is
also significant that, apart from Alexander's partial use of

[116] See de Romilly 1993: 289.

[117] See Usher 1994: 142–5. Cartledge 1994: 150 misinterprets the passage
because it does not fit in with his preconceptions. *Panegyricus* 50, a famous passage
in which Isocrates claims that Greekness was defined by attainment of Athenian
culture and not by blood, is probably not relevant to this question: *pace* de Romilly
1993: 291 and Usher 1994: 142–3. Cartledge 1994: 149–50 is correct on this point.

[118] In the *Panegyricus* (132) he says they should be treated as perioeci, in the last
letter to Philip as helots (3. 5), and in the *Philippus* he claims that Philip will win the
goodwill of the non-Greek peoples 'if it is through your efforts that they are set free
from barbarian despotism and obtain the protection of Greece' (155). The word I
have translated as 'protection' is *epimeleia*, and it has the connotation of 'benign
oversight'. In other words, it is protection for the benefit of the protected: see
Perlman 1967, who refutes Baldry 1965: 66–72.

[119] Arr. 7. 6. 1; Diod. 17. 108. 1–3; Curt. 8. 5. 1; Plut. *Alex.* 71. 7; with Briant
1982a: 30–9.

Persian apparel in his court, the only Macedonian or Greek whom we know (in Alexander's lifetime) to have 'gone native' by adopting Persian language and dress on a daily basis was Peucestas, the satrap of Persis.[120] Otherwise, it was always Persians in our sources who undertook to dress like Greeks or to learn the Greek language, but never vice versa.[121]

There were other ways too in which Alexander seems to have followed an Isocratean programme. Isocrates had warned that the poor and destitute, who wandered as exiles or sought employment as mercenaries, were a growing and imminent danger.[122] This concern of his has won him the label 'crypto-oligarch' by some modern scholars,[123] but the problem was real enough. The solution which he proposed to Philip was to plant them in colonies on the fringes of the Greek world where they would form a buffer zone.[124] It is somewhat unclear whether Isocrates was only thinking of colonies in western Asia Minor or in whatever region Philip happened to reach the limit of his conquest (although we can well imagine that he would have liked to place such undesirables as far away as possible). In any case, this is exactly what Alexander attempted to do with the Greek mercenaries in his service when he used them to garrison the cities which he founded.[125] That those who had been placed in Bactria and Sogdiana balked at this treatment and rebelled is irrelevant.[126]

[120] For Alexander's dress, see Brunt 1976: 533 and Bosworth 1980*b*: 4–8. His court dress combined the traditional Macedonian hat and cloak with the Persian diadem, tunic, and girdle. For Peucestas, see Arr. 6. 30. 2 and 7. 6. 3; Diod. 19. 14. 5. Does Plut. *Alex.* 47. 9 imply that Hephaestion also adopted some Persian customs in his daily life?

[121] Bosworth 1980*b*. Hamilton 1988 attempts to modify some of Bosworth's arguments. Compare their interpretations of Peucestas on pages 12 and 475–6 respectively.

[122] *Letter 9, To Archidamus*; *Paneg.* 168; *On the Peace* 24; *Phil.* 120–2.

[123] Cartledge 1993: 43, following the lead of Baynes 1955: 144–67.

[124] *Phil.* 120–2.

[125] For a sceptical account of the number of cities actually founded by Alexander, see Fraser 1996, who limits Alexander's genuine foundations to eight (excluding Alexandria in Egypt). For Alexander's motives in founding cities, see Arr. 4. 1. 3–4; and Fraser 1996: 171–90. Later Macedonian settlements in Asia (particularly in Asia Minor) are discussed by Billows 1995: 146–82.

[126] Curt. 9. 7. 1–11; Diod. 17. 99. 5–6 and 18. 7. 1. On their revolt, see Holt 1988: esp. 80–6.

To be sure, an older generation of scholars, mostly in Germany, made unreal claims both for the influence and the insight of Isocrates; specifically that his recommendations prefigured the League of Corinth.[127] The truth is that Isocrates gave no thought to how his plans might be institutionalized.[128] He assumed that Philip would become the acknowledged leader of Greece by virtue of his prestige and accomplishments. Alexander too had no interest in the working of institutions and he had no time for constitutional niceties. Greeks should obey him by virtue of his preeminent prestige (and perhaps his divinity). None the less, he had not completely forgotten the original nature of his relationship to the Greek cities; for in 324 he dispatched Craterus to take charge of Macedonia, Thrace, Thessaly, and 'the freedom of the Greeks', which here means the Greeks of the mainland.[129]

Although Alexander did not hesitate to infringe upon the autonomy of the Greek cities when he issued the Exiles' Decree in 324,[130] he was still concerned to maintain their goodwill and win their approbation; if they had become insignificant in his eyes, he would not have sought their recognition of his divinity. To be sure, Isocrates and other wealthy conservative Greeks would not have been pleased with that Decree, but, as we shall see, Alexander had no choice in practical terms.[131] Diodorus (18. 8. 2) gives Alexander's motives as 'partly for the sake of fame, and partly wishing to have many devoted personal followers in each city to counter the revolutionary movements and defections

[127] Wendland 1910: 123–82, esp. 134 and Kessler 1911; they are refuted by Wilcken 1929.

[128] He never advanced any concrete political or constitutional proposals in his writings to various dynasts, including Philip. See Dobesch 1968: 89 ff. and 213 ff.

[129] Arr. 7. 12. 4.

[130] Diod. 18. 8. According to [Dem.] 17 (*On the Treaty with Alexander*): 16, it was a provision of the League of Corinth that one member city could not support the restoration of exiles by force into another member city. Perhaps Alexander did not see himself as being covered by this provision, if the Exiles' Decree was indeed issued with the sanction of the Corinthian League. For the view that Alexander was acting in blatant violation of Greek autonomy, see Bosworth 1988*b*: 220–8 and 1996*a*: 130–2.

[131] As late as 339 Isocrates was still arguing that colonization in Asia could easily accommodate all of Greece's destitute (*Panath.* 13–14).

of the Greeks'. Can this be right? Alexander was always interested in 'fame', but was he so perverse as to plunge a now quiet and acquiescent Greece into turmoil in pursuit of a far from predictable political advantage? Once we recognize that Diodorus' source, Hieronymus of Cardia, was no great admirer of Alexander,[132] then his explanation need no longer be accepted at face value. In fact, the self-interested motives which Hieronymus attributed to Alexander are essentially the same as those which he credited to Polyperchon, who re-enacted the Exiles' Decree in 319 as part of his effort to consolidate his hold over Greece against Cassander and Antigonus.[133] Why then did Alexander issue so extraordinary an order, if not for his own personal advantage? It was because a general restoration was the only possible solution to what was rapidly becoming a dangerous situation both politically and militarily, since neither his own employment of Greek mercenaries nor his planting of garrison colonies in the far east were sufficient to absorb the vast numbers of unemployed exiles.[134] And given that our sources for activities in Greece during this period are so meagre, we cannot exclude the possibility that the Exiles' Decree was formally ratified by the League of Corinth. The *synhedrion* of the League should have been holding one of its regular meetings at the Olympic Festival of 324 and thus it had the opportunity to give the Decree official sanction.[135] In as much as Diodorus (18 . 8. 6) claims that 'the majority (of the Greeks) accepted the restoration of the exiles as a good

---

[132] See Richard Billows, 'Polybios, Alexander the Great, and Hieronymos of Cardia' in this volume.

[133] Diod. 18. 55–6 with Heckel 1992: 193–5, and n. 118 (for additional bibliography). According to Diod. (18. 55. 2–4), 'it seemed best to them [i.e. to Polyperchon and his advisers] to free the cities throughout Greece and to dissolve the oligarchies established in them by Antipater; for in this way they would most of all humble Cassander and also win great fame for themselves and many important allies'. The ensuing edict (or *diagramma*) of 319 mandated the restoration of those who had been exiled after Alexander had crossed into Asia.

[134] On the purpose of the Decree, see the excellent discussion by Green 1991: 449–51. Note also Hammond and Walbank 1988: 81, where Hammond stresses Alexander's sincerity in attempting to establish more settled conditions in the Greek world of city-states.

[135] This is suggested by Cawkwell 1978: 175. The *synhedrion* of the Hellenic League created by Antigonus and Demetrius in 302 (*ISE* no. 44, lines 65–74) regularly met at the national festivals during peacetime, and it is a reasonable inference that the same was true under Philip and Alexander.

thing', and only mentions the Aetolians and Athenians as 'taking it badly', there is no reason why the *synhedrion* would not have given its validation.

In sum, Alexander had come as close to fulfilling the recommendations of Isocrates as the master himself could reasonably have expected any dynast to do (which is not at all to speculate that Isocrates would have been satisfied). Although Alexander had not peacefully 'reconciled' the leading Greek states (Argos, Sparta, Thebes, and Athens) in the way that Isocrates had recommended to Philip in 346, he had brought it about (to again quote Isocrates' words to Philip in his letter of 338) that 'all were compelled to be prudent (εὖ φρονεῖν)'. That letter, the last thing which Isocrates wrote, also makes it clear that for him reconciliation was but a means to an end and that the use of force was acceptable as a last resort. Isocrates' lifelong dream, the Greek conquest of Asia, had been fulfilled by no one less than a descendant of Heracles and Achilles.

IV. PANHELLENISM AND CONQUEST IN THE WEST

Now if panhellenism was as broadly popular as I have argued, and if Alexander never wholly abandoned it, why did it fail to be an effective ideology? Or did it fail? If looked at superficially, Alexander's panhellenic acts and words might seem to have had little impact on popular opinion. Despite the fact that he claimed to be fighting 'on behalf of Greece',[136] nearly a third more Greeks fought as Persian mercenaries at the Granicus than were in his own army.[137] The leading states of mainland Greece (Athens, Thebes, and Sparta) accepted Persian money and openly rebelled when they felt ready. After the battle of Issus, Parmenio captured Athenian, Spartan, and Theban ambassadors who had been sent to Darius.[138] More Spartan ambassadors were captured

[136] Diod. 1. 16. 6; 1. 29. 5.

[137] There were about 20,000 Greek mercenaries on the Persian side (Arr. 1. 14. 4); at that time Alexander's army contained 7,000 Greek allied infantry, 5,000 Greek mercenary infantry, 1,800 Thessalian cavalry, and 600 other Greek cavalry, for a total of 14,400 (Diod. 17. 17).

[138] See Arr. 2. 15 and Curt. 3. 13. 15 for the ambassadors. The expectation to

in Hyrcania in 330.[139] Alexander himself was well aware at the start of his expedition that if he suffered a major defeat it would prompt a revolt in Greece.[140]

Such matters, however, are not always what they seem. Mercenaries fight for whoever will pay them and their employer is no indication of political loyalties; and once the war began, given the harsh treatment which befell those defeated at the Granicus, they may well have feared to change sides. Nor is it surprising that envoys should have been sent to Darius before Issus; for despite the fact that most Greeks considered barbarians to be inferior to themselves, many still considered the military power of the King to be irresistible and there was an expectation that Alexander would be crushed in Cilicia.[141] Even so, Athens was the only member of the Corinthian League to send an embassy. What else would one expect of Theban exiles and a disaffected Sparta?

Rebellions, to be sure, are more serious than diplomatic overtures. Are they so easily explained? The revolt of Thebes in 335 and of Athens in 323–2 both occurred after the death of the Macedonian king, which traditionally was a time of dynastic turmoil. There was unrest in Greece after Philip's death because no one could have guessed that the young king would liquidate his many rivals so effectively and so quickly. As it was, the Thebans only took up arms when a rumour came that Alexander himself had died in Illyria (Arr. 1. 17. 2–3).

In 323 the situation was more complex. There was no obvious successor to the Macedonian throne (cf. Diod. 18. 9.

receive Persian money is mentioned by Demosthenes, *Fourth Philippic* 31–4 and Diod. 17. 62. 1–3. Demosthenes is said to have received Persian gold in 336: see Aeschines, *Against Ctesiphon* 239; Dinarchus, *Against Demosthenes* 10, 18; Diod. 17. 4. 7–9; Plut. *Demosth.* 20. 4–5.

[139] Arr. 3. 24. 5; Curt. 6. 5. 6–8.

[140] Cf. Arr. 1. 18. 8; 2. 17. 1–4.

[141] Isocrates, *Paneg.* 138: 'And yet there are some who marvel at the magnitude of the King's affairs and say that he is difficult to make war against.' *Phil.* 139: 'I am not unaware that many Greeks believe that the power of the King is invincible.' Plato states in a matter of fact way (*Laws* 685c) that the Greeks of his time were afraid of the Great King; and Demosthenes makes the same claim a few years later (*Fourth Phil.* 33–4 of 341 BC), arguing that the Athenians should rather be afraid of Philip. According to Aeschines (*Against Ctesiphon* 164), Demosthenes openly predicted that Alexander would be 'trampled under the hoofs of the Persian horse'.

1) and it was a reasonable conjecture that the empire would split apart. Diodorus gives two specific causes for the outbreak of the Lamian War: the large gathering of mercenaries at Taenarum in Laconia as a result of Alexander's order that his satraps dismiss their mercenary forces (17. 111. 1–3), and the discontent of the Athenians and Aetolians with the Exiles' Decree (18. 8. 6–7). Both of these inducements to rebellion had been needlessly caused by Alexander himself. In fact, without the 8,000 battle-hardened mercenaries who formed the core of Leosthenes' army, Athens might not even have declared war at all. Nor was Athens actively preparing for rebellion before news came of Alexander's death.[142] Alexander, had he lived, could certainly have dealt with this situation diplomatically (e.g. by recognizing the Athenian claim to Samos).

So the disaffection in mainland Greece in 336–5 and 323–2 says nothing about the popularity either of Philip's or of Alexander's panhellenist programme; for the Greeks had no reason to believe that the next king would continue his predecessor's policies. Ironically, the continuing potency of panhellenic propaganda was to be exploited not by Alexander, but by Athens. At the outbreak of the Lamian War, the Athenians proclaimed that, just as in 480, they considered Greece to be the common fatherland of the Greeks and were risking everything on behalf of their common safety and freedom (Diod. 18. 10. 1–3).

Only one revolt actually took place during Alexander's expedition and that was led by a state which was not a member of the League of Corinth. This was the uprising instigated by Sparta in 331 under her king Agis III. Athens did not join Sparta, in part because the Athenians must have realized that Sparta was fighting, not for the freedom of Greece, but in order to restore her own hegemony in the Peloponnese.[143] That was a goal hardly worth fighting for

---

[142] This is convincingly demonstrated by Worthington 1994.

[143] de Ste Croix 1972: 378, however, points out that Alexander held as virtual hostages the crews of 20 Athenian triremes (Diod. 17. 22. 5). But Badian 1994: 259–60 rightly counters that we cannot be sure that the crews were up to their full complement (a maximum of 4,000 men) and that in any case it is most unlikely that all of them were Athenian citizens. Furthermore, de Ste Croix's assumption that the Athenians would have feared lest Alexander do to their city what he

and some Greeks preferred to support Macedon against Sparta.[144] Greece on the whole was quiet and submissive during Alexander's reign.

It is, of course, difficult for us to discern to what extent this quiet was simply due to the fact that the Greek cities had been completely cowed into military submission. In practical terms Alexander succeeded where Agesilaus had failed because he, unlike Agesilaus' Sparta, had the human and material resources to simultaneously fight wars on two fronts. None the less, it is unlikely that Alexander's panhellenism had no effect whatsoever on popular opinion. For even if it often seems hollow in retrospect, propaganda does make a difference and is important in the waging of wars and in the creation of empires. From Alexander's point of view panhellenism may have seemed very effective indeed. The forces of Agis had been thoroughly crushed and the Athenian response to the Exiles' Decree of 324 was not rebellion but diplomacy. It is plausible to suppose that Alexander, under the influence of these successes, would have re-employed panhellenic propaganda had he lived to carry out his programme of conquests in the western Mediterranean.[145] It suited Alexander to pose as an Achaemenid when exercising direct control over lands once ruled by Persia, but what advantage would Persian royal dress and court protocol gain him in the west? We tend to think in terms of how Alexander would have acted as the 'King of Asia', forgetting that he was about to leave the east and may not have intended to return any time soon.[146]

had done to Thebes, seems to me to be doubtful, since Alexander's panhellenic propaganda made it clear that Thebes was being punished for her Medism in 480–79.

[144] Badian 1994: 258–68 demonstrates that we cannot extract from our sources the numbers of Greeks who fought on each side; he refutes the claim of de Ste Croix 1972: 165 that 'Sparta's revolt was crushed by an army which is likely to have contained roughly twice as many Greek citizen soldiers as the 12,000 or so who fought for and with Sparta.'

[145] Contra Wilcken 1932: 226, who asserts: 'Certainly nothing now was further from Alexander's thoughts than a Panhellenic policy like that of his early years . . .'.

[146] Whether Alexander technically became Darius' successor as the King of Persia or created a new position for himself as the 'King of Asia', is controversial. The former, as Hammond 1986: 79 points out, would have been unpalatable to Greeks and Macedonians alike, for whom 'the Great King, the King of Kings, was the symbol of oriental despotism and tyrannical oppression'. The latter alternative,

Although his exact plan of conquest cannot be recovered, our sources (apart from Arrian) are unanimous that Alexander intended to campaign in the west,[147] and in dealing with the Greek cities of Sicily and south Italy a panhellenist stance would again be useful. That may partly explain his honouring of Croton for the services of Phayllus at Salamis and his eagerness to read the Syracusan historian Philistus, whose history was sent inland to him by Harpalus, the only prose work amidst a shipment of tragedies and dithyrambic poems.[148] In the name of Greek liberty he could have waged war against the Carthaginians in Sicily, against the Bruttians and Lucanians in Italy, and even against the Romans and Etruscans.[149] In Sicily, Alexander would have been following the example of Dionysius I of Syracuse, whose pretext for declaring war on Carthage was the liberation of the Greek cities under Carthaginian control.[150] He may also have been aware of the posthumous heroic honours which recently (mid to late 330s) had been paid to Timoleon at Syracuse for his achievements in liberating the Greeks of Sicily and defeating the Carthaginians in battle.[151] And yet Timoleon, despite his success in driving out tyrants, had not ejected the Carthaginians from the western part of the island; that would have to wait for the Romans.[152] Given what we think

which seems to me the more likely of the two, was not at all incompatible with Isocratean panhellenism. See now the thorough study by E. A. Fredricksmeyer in this volume, 'Alexander the Great and the Kingship of Asia'.

[147] Plut. *Alex.* 68. 1–2; Curt. 10. 1. 17–19; Diod. 18. 4. 4. Although Arrian (7. 1. 3–4) reports that some of his sources claimed that Alexander intended to attack Sicily and Italy, he is himself uncertain as to Alexander's intentions. A full recent discussion of Alexander's future plans is in Bosworth 1988a: 185–211.

[148] An interest in the career of Dionysius perhaps lies behind Alexander's request that Harpalus send him the books of the historian Philistus (Plut. *Alex.* 8. 3); Philistus was a contemporary of Dionysius and depicted him favourably. See Brown 1967: 366–7.

[149] Delegations from all of these peoples were sent to Alexander at Babylon in 323 (Arr. 7. 15. 4–6; cf. Diod. 17. 113. 1–2 and Just. 12. 13. 1–2), perhaps because they realized that Alexander was planning to attack them. See Bosworth 1988b: 166. Curtius (4. 4. 18) claims that Alexander actually declared war on Carthage after the capture of Tyre in 332, but that is unlikely.

[150] Diod. 14. 46. 5; 14. 47. 2; 15. 15. 14.

[151] See Diod. 16. 90. 1; Nepos, *Timoleon* 5. 4; Plut. *Timoleon* 39; and Habicht 1970: 150.

[152] Diod. 16. 82. 3 gives the details of Timoleon's treaty with the Carthaginians in *c.*338 BC, which specified that the river Halycus would be the boundary of the Greek and Carthaginian spheres of control.

we know of Alexander's character, he should have felt compelled to surpass Timoleon's accomplishments and fame. Alternatively, if Alexander preferred to attack Carthage before dealing with the Sicilian Greeks, it lay open to him to renew the war of revenge by exploiting Ephorus' claim that the Carthaginians were co-operating with Xerxes when they invaded Sicily in 480 BC.[153]

In Italy Alexander could have represented himself as completing the work of his uncle Alexander, king of Epirus, who in late 331 had perished in the defence of Tarentum against the Lucanians and Bruttians.[154] Just as the Tarentines had previously called in Archidamus of Sparta and Alexander of Epirus, and would later summon another Spartan and another Epirote, Acrotatus and Pyrrhus respectively, so surely they would have invited Alexander to champion their cause. Indeed, three Apulian vases, painted around 330 and attributed to the so-called Darius Painter, show Hellas tying a victor's fillet around her own head while being crowned by Nike. Beneath her is a depiction of Darius in a chariot fleeing Alexander who pursues him on horseback. This demonstrates that in the west Alexander's victory at Gaugamela (or perhaps Issus) was not being perceived as a strictly Macedonian affair, but as the triumph of Greece over Asia.[155] If in their view Alexander, acting as the commander of all

---

[153] Diod. 11. 1. 4–5 and Ephorus, *FGrH* 70 F 186.

[154] For his campaigns in Italy, see Just. 12. 2. 1–5; Livy 8. 3. 6–7; Strabo 6. 1. 5; and Werner 1988. According to Justin (12. 3. 1), when Alexander heard of his death, he prescribed for his army a three-day period of mourning. Justin further claims (12. 1. 5 and 12. 3. 1) that Alexander only feigned sorrow, but was secretly pleased by the death of a rival. That is hardly likely: *pace* Yardley and Heckel 1997: 198. It is possible that the two Alexanders may have been acting in concert (as asserted by Lane Fox 1973: 90), but this cannot be proved.

[155] See Stewart 1993: 150–7, 431–2, with figs. 25–8 and Cohen 1997: 64–8, 214 nn. 50–1 for discussion and full bibliography. These are: a volute krater, Naples 3256, from Ruvo (Trendall and Cambitoglou 1982: 18/40, figs. 25–6, text fig. 4); an amphora fragment, Copenhagen Nationalmuseet 13. 320 (Trendall and Cambitoglou 1982: 18/88, fig. 28); and the engraving of a lost vase, ex-Hamilton collection. An intact amphora from Ruvo (Naples 3220, Trendall and Cambitoglou 1982: 18/47, fig. 27) also shows Alexander pursing Darius, but there are no gods or personifications above. The most striking of these is the fragment from Copenhagen which shows Hellas (with her name inscribed) being crowned by Nikai from both sides. The suggestion that these images reflect pro-Macedonian propaganda and perhaps should be connected with the exploits of Alexander of Epirus in Italy, is disputed by Stewart 1993: 150–7: for the other view, see

the Greeks, had triumphed over the barbarians of Asia on behalf of Hellas, the south Italian Greeks might well have expected him also to conquer the barbarians in the west, especially since both Sicily and south Italy were considered to be within the boundaries of Hellas.[156] And in Etruria too Alexander could have posed as the champion of Greek interests, since Etruscan piracy was interfering with Athenian commerce.[157] Moreover, Strabo (5. 3. 5) claims that Alexander sent a complaint to the Romans about their sponsoring of piracy. At that time Rome was already the most powerful state in central Italy and it is conceivable that he may have been looking for an excuse to attack her.[158]

It might be objected that Alexander, *hegemon* of the Greeks, king of the Macedonians, and now king of Asia as well, no longer needed to worry about propaganda: he would merely attack whomever he liked without justification or explanation in his drive for universal dominion. That seems unlikely. The Sicilian and Italian Greeks had substantial resources at their disposal and Alexander would have needed their co-operation, no matter the size of the army which he brought with him. If he had actually read his Philistus, he would have known that the Italian Greeks had thwarted Dionysius I by allying themselves with the Carthaginians.[159] He surely knew that Alexander of Epirus had fallen out with the Tarentines by threatening their sovereignty and autonomy.[160] As his interests shifted from the Persian east to the Greek west, Alexander would have had to be very careful in

Schmidt, Trendall, and Cambitoglou 1976: 107–8; Moreno 1979: 515–18; and Geyer 1993.

[156] At least by the Greek doctor Democedes of Croton and his Persian escort (Hdt. 3. 130. 1; 3. 137. 4) and by the chorus of Trojan women in Euripides' *Troiades*, lines 220–9. According to Isocrates (*Phil.* 112), Heracles set up the so-called pillars of Heracles to be the boundaries of Hellenic territory. Note also Pindar, *Pythian 1*, lines 71–5 with Ephorus, *FGrH* 70 F 186.

[157] Harassment by Etruscan pirates prompted the Athenians to establish a colony on the Adriatic coast in 324 (Tod 1948: no. 200, esp. lines 221–32). Both Hyperides and Dinarchus gave speeches, now lost, dealing with the problem of Etruscan piracy (see Tod 1948: 288).

[158] The Romans, in turn, sent an embassy to Alexander in 323, perhaps in reply to his complaint. See Arr. 7. 15. 4–6 and Pliny, *NH* 3. 57–8; with Bosworth 1988a: 83–93.

[159] Diod. 15. 15.

[160] Strabo 6. 3. 4.

the way he presented both himself and his aims. Panhellenist discourse, with its emphasis on revenge for past wrongs, freedom of Greek cities, liberation from barbarians, and Hellenic territorial expansion, was especially well suited to the concerns and aspirations of the western Greeks.

5

Alexander the Great and the Kingship of Asia

ERNST FREDRICKSMEYER

For Gloria, *uxori carissimae*

In this contribution I will try to show, first, that Alexander's kingship of Asia, as proclaimed in 331 BC, did not mean, as is often thought, the Persian kingship, but was a unique creation of Alexander himself, and, second, that Alexander's Persian innovations after the death of Darius in 330 were not primarily designed, as is commonly thought, to establish Alexander as Great King, but rather were meant to reform Alexander's kingship by addition of the Persian component, and to establish Alexander, ultimately, as an absolute monarch.

This is the extensively revised version of a paper first presented at an Alexander-conference at the University of Wisconsin in Madison on 3 Nov. 1977. I benefited from the comments made on that occasion by my colleagues, and especially Prof. Charles Edson and Prof. Nicholas Hammond, who expressed themselves in substantial agreement with my thesis. Since then, Prof. Hammond has published his own view of Alexander's kingship in Asia, in *Antichthon* 20 (1986). We agree, most importantly, that the designation 'King of Asia' at Plut. *Alex.* 34 does not mean 'King of Persia', but our views differ in other respects. I would like to think, however, that our interpretations, in the balance, are complementary rather than contradictory.

I wish to thank the conveners of the Alexander conference at the University of Newcastle, Prof. Brian Bosworth and Dr Elizabeth Baynham, for their invitation to present this paper, even though, I think, they have not been entirely convinced by it. On the other hand, it is gratifying to note that my view of the predominance of the Macedonian component over the Persian in Alexander's kingship is in accord with the conclusions reached by Prof. Bosworth (1980*a*), that far from Alexander attempting a fusion between Macedonians and Persians in the military organization and the administration of the empire, the Macedonians remained dominant. I also wish to thank my colleagues at the conference for their comments and criticisms, especially Prof. Ernst Badian for his observations, as well as Dr Pat Wheatley, the designated respondent, for his commentary, and for graciously giving me a written version of it. Most importantly, I wish to thank Prof. Bosworth for his incisive and valuable critique of the paper. I have taken account of all criticisms even though not agreeing in every instance. Still, all in all, the paper has been greatly improved as a result. Any remaining faults are my own.

I   Intro

According to Plutarch, *Alex.* 34. 1, by Alexander's conquest of Darius at Gaugamela on 1 October 331, the empire of the Persians was thought to be completely destroyed, and a few days later, at the nearby village of Arbela, Alexander was proclaimed 'King of Asia'. Although Plutarch is the only source to provide this information, it is accepted by virtually all historians as historical.[1] To my knowledge, only Franz Altheim and Paul Goukowsky have rejected it. Their reasons are not persuasive. Altheim claims that 'King of Asia' would have identified Alexander as successor of the Achaemenid kings, but that 'King of Asia' was not a Persian title, and that Alexander's actions until after the death of Darius in 330 were incompatible with the position of Great King.[2] It is true that 'King of Asia' was not an Achaemenid title. But neither did it designate Alexander, as Altheim thinks, as Darius' successor, and hence it did not oblige him to act as such. Whatever 'King of Asia' meant, Alexander had claimed possession of 'Asia' already in 334 at the Hellespont, and he claimed the designation 'King of Asia' two years later in a letter to Darius (see below). There is no reason to doubt, therefore, that after the decisive victory at Gaugamela Alexander was proclaimed 'King of Asia'.

Goukowsky, unlike Altheim, accepts the proclamation as historical, but he believes that it took place in 324, not in 331. He notes that at *Alex.* 34, Plutarch reports two things in addition to the proclamation, one, Alexander's letter to the Plataeans promising to rebuild their city, and second, his order for the abolition of tyrannies in Greece, but that at *Arist.* 11. 9 he assigns the announcement of Alexander's munificence to the Plataeans to the Olympic Games of 324, when Alexander ordered the return of the exiles (Diod. 17. 109. 1; 18. 8. 2–5). Goukowsky thinks that Plutarch is mistaken in assigning Alexander's munificence to the Plataeans to two separate occasions, in 331 and in 324, and that

---

[1] e.g. Hamilton 1969: 90; Hammond 1980: 148; 1986: 76; Bosworth 1980*b*: 5; 1988*b*: 85; Badian 1985: 437; Wirth 1973: 29; Dobesch 1975: 105; Lock 1977: 100; Will 1986: 94; Berve 1938: 145; Schachermeyr 1973: 277; Bengtson 1977: 346; Green 1991: 297.

[2] Altheim 1947: 177–84, 202; 1953: 66, 104; 1970: 195–7.

Alexander's order for the abolition of tyrannies makes better sense in 324 than in 331. Therefore, Goukowsky believes, this order, and along with it Alexander's benefaction to the Plataeans, as well as the proclamation of Alexander as King of Asia, at Plut. *Alex.* 34, are to be assigned to 324. Goukowsky:

Puis, en 324, reconsidérant sa politique grecque d'un point de vue qui n'était plus celui du 'roi des Macédoniens' avec lequel les cités avaient conclu la *symmachie* de Corinthe dirigée contre les Perses, il fit proclamer par le héraut, en termes officiels, son accession à la *'basileia tês Asias'*.[3]

Goukowsky's case depends on the assumption that Plutarch's two reports on Alexander's dealings with the Plataeans must apply to one occasion only, the Olympic Games of 324. The texts suggest otherwise. At *Alex.* 34. 2, with reference to 331, Plutarch writes: 'He wrote to the Plataeans in particular that he would rebuild (ἀνοικοδομεῖν) their city because their forefathers had furnished their land to the Hellenes for the struggle on behalf of their freedom.' At *Arist.* 11. 9 he writes that the generosity of the Plataeans to the Hellenic cause became so famous that 'many years afterwards, when Alexander was already King of Asia, he built the walls of Plataea and had a proclamation made by the herald at the Olympic Games that the King bestowed (ἀποδίδωσι) this favour on the Plataeans for their bravery and generosity, because they gave their land to the Hellenes in the Median war . . .'. In short, in 331 at Arbela, Alexander promised the Plataeans to rebuild their city, and in 324 at Olympia he announced that he had done so (at any rate, rebuilt their walls), or was in the process of doing so.[4] It appears, then, that Alexander's letter to the Plataeans promising his benefaction should be left where it stands in Plutarch's text, after the victory at Gaugamela, and so should therefore Alexander's proclamation as King of Asia.

[3] Goukowsky 1978: 175.
[4] We should note that actually 'nothing connects the rebuilding of Plataea with the Exiles' Decree [of 324]. The year could be 328.' That is, Alexander after announcing at Arbela in 331 his intention to rebuild Plataea (Plut. *Alex.* 34) may have given instructions (to Antipater?) 'to rebuild the walls of Plataea and have the completion announced at the next Olympics' (Plut. *Arist.* 11. 9), that is, in 328. Prof. Bosworth, *per litt.*

If we do accept the report of Alexander's proclamation, it should be worth while to consider a bit more closely what it meant. It is usually assumed that 'King of Asia' here meant King of Persia, and of the Persian Empire. But there are difficulties with this view.

1. Alexander had undertaken the war to punish the Persians for their outrages against the Macedonians and the Greeks and their gods in 480–479, not to take on the Persian throne as Darius' successor, with the ritual and other obligations which this succession would have entailed. Such an act would have been considered by them a betrayal of the panhellenic cause, and an abomination. The anti-Persian animus pervading the proceedings at Arbela (Plut. *Alex.* 34. 2–4) speaks a clear and different language. The official objective of the campaign imposed on Alexander a religious obligation to the Greek gods which was incompatible with the Persian succession, and which we may believe he took seriously. In his letter to Darius after the battle at Issus he appealed to Persian outrages against the Macedonians and Greeks (Arr. 2. 14. 5–6). Macedonian hostility toward the Persians persisted throughout the campaign.

2. In the same letter to Darius after Issus, Alexander called himself not only 'King of Asia' but also, proleptically, 'Lord of all Asia' (τῆς Ἀσίας ἁπάσης κυρίου), and claimed to be Darius' absolute master (Arr. 2. 14. 8–9; Curt. 4. 1. 13–14; cf. Justin 11. 12. 2). This suggests a distinction between 'King of Persia' and 'King of Asia', one is Darius, the other Alexander. Thus it appears that at this point Alexander saw himself as the King of Persia's overlord with his own title encompassing the latter. As for the Persian kings' claims (albeit formulaic) to universal rule ('King in all the earth', 'King of Kings', etc.), Arrian says that Alexander (in 324?) thought (*expressis verbis?*) that 'the kings of the Persians and Medes had not ruled even a fraction (οὐδὲ τοῦ πολλοστοῦ μέρους) of Asia and so had no right to call themselves "Great Kings" ' (Arr. 7. 1. 2–3).

3. The precise meaning of Plutarch's statement at *Alex.* 34. 1 is difficult to pin down, but I think there is a good

possibility that he means to distinguish between the 'Persian Empire' and 'Asia'. The 'Persian Empire' is now dead (παντάπασιν . . . ἐδόκει καταλελύσθαι), and Alexander was proclaimed king over the lands, and potentially beyond, which formerly the Persians ruled, that is, Asia. Thus Plutarch seems to imply that Alexander did not take over the Persian Empire (it no longer existed), but replaced it.

4. This interpretation is supported by the fact that the Greeks in Alexander's time (and Alexander must have had at least one eye on his Greek audience) used the term 'Asia' usually not as denoting the Persian Empire, but in a geographic sense which, depending on the context, could mean less, but also more, than the present Persian Empire.[5] Since, however, 'Asia' was often considered the domain of the Persian kings,[6] Alexander's claim to 'Asia' suggested a claim, as well, to the (former) Persian Empire. Alexander himself seems never to have used the term 'Asia' for the Persian Empire, but only for his own empire, or as a geographic entity.[7]

5. The Greeks very rarely called the Persian king 'King of Asia', but 'King' or 'Great King' or 'King of Persia' or 'the Persians'.[8] We should expect, therefore, that if at Arbela

[5] See Oost 1981: 265–82 for a collection of the evidence.

[6] e.g. Aesch. *Pers.* 73–4, 548–50, 584–90, 762–4, 929–31; Hdt. 1. 130, 192; 5. 49; 9. 116; Xen. *Mem.* 3. 5. 11; Isoc. *Evag.* 65, 68; *Paneg.* 178, 179; *Phil.* 66.

[7] At the Hellespont (334), Alexander hurls his spear into the soil of Asia to signify that he 'received Asia from the gods as won by the spear': Diod. 17. 17. 2. After the battle at the Granicus (334), Alexander sends votive gifts of spoils, with an inscription, to Athena at Athens, 'from the barbarians dwelling in Asia': Arr. 1. 16. 7 = Plut. *Alex.* 16. 18. Alexander says (331) that by the battle at Gaugamela there is to be decided the sovereignty of 'all Asia': Arr. 3. 9. 6. In an inscription on a votive offering to Athena Lindia after the battle at Gaugamela Alexander calls himself 'Lord (κύριος) of Asia': *FGrH* 532 F 1, 38. Alexander speaks to Pharasmanes of his intention to be 'in possession of all Asia' (329/8): Arr. 4. 15. 6. Alexander speaks of taking Asia in its entirety (326): Arr. 5. 26. 2, 6, 8. Alexander boasts of having conquered 'all Asia' (326): Arr. *Ind.* 35. 8. Alexander expresses the ambition (324/3?) to be called 'King of all Asia': Arr. 7. 1. 2. Near Babylon Libyan ambassadors congratulate Alexander on his 'kingship of Asia' (323): Arr. 7. 15. 4.

[8] In Greek literature up to and including the time of Alexander I have counted only five references to 'King of Asia', but forty-five to 'Great King'. *Great King*: Aesch. *Pers.* 24; Hdt. 1. 188, 192; 5. 49; 8. 140; Aristoph. *Acharn.* 65, 113; *Av.* 486; *Plut.* 170; Xen. *Anab.* 1. 2. 8; 1. 4. 11; 1. 7. 2, 13, 16; 2. 3. 17; 2. 4. 3; Plato, *Apol.* 40d8; *Soph.* 230e1; *Alc.* 120a3; *Chrm.* 158a4; *Ly.* 209d6; *Euthd.* 274a7; *Grg.* 470e4; 524e4; *Men.* 78d3; *R.* 553c6; *Leg.* 658c6; 694e5; *Ep.* 363c1; *Erx.* 393d1; *Lys.* 2. 56; 19. 25; And. *De Pac.* 29; Arist. *Mu.* 398ᵃ12; 398ᵃ30; 398ᵇ1; Isoc. *Paneg.* 121; *Evag.* 20, 64; *Phil.* 132; *Arch.* 84; *De Pac.* 47, 68; *Epist.* 2. 11; 3. 5. Of the five references to

Alexander meant his army, and the Greek world, to understand that he took over the Persian kingship as Darius' successor, he would have assumed one of his titles, but he did not.

6. There is no trustworthy evidence that the Persian kings ever called themselves 'King of Asia', even in correspondence with Greeks. Cyrus' title 'Asia's King' in his epitaph cited by Aristobulus, as quoted by Strabo (*FGrH* 139 F 51b = Strabo 15. 3. 7), is almost certainly incorrect, written down years later under the influence of Alexander's empire. It is not meant to quote Cyrus' title but uses 'Asia' in a geographic sense, as is also suggested by Aristobulus' version of the quote, at F 51a, cited by Arrian 6. 29. 8, which uses the verb βασιλεύω rather than the noun βασιλεύς: τῆς Ἀσίας βασιλεύσας 'having ruled (as king) over'. In the version given by Onesicritus (*FGrH* 134 F 34 = Strabo 15. 3. 7) Cyrus calls himself more plausibly (than 'King of Asia') 'King of Kings'. It is unlikely that the Persian kings would have used the title 'King of Asia' inasmuch as it would have placed a limitation on their claims to universal dominion ('King in all the earth', etc.).[9]

In the well-known story of Darius' reaction to the report of Alexander's chivalrous treatment of his family (after Issus), Darius is said in the version given by Arrian (4. 20. 3) and Curtius (4. 10. 34) to have prayed the god to give his power to none other than Alexander, if he were to be no longer 'King of Asia'. This expression probably reflects a time when it had become familiar through Alexander's kingship. In any case, the expression is Greek, not Persian. So in Arrian's version Darius invokes 'Zeus Basileus', which is Greek for Ahuramazda.[10] If Darius referred to himself by title, we don't know which one he would have used. In the version given by Plutarch (*Alex.* 30. 13 and *Mor.* 338f)

'King of Asia', four apply to 'Asia' in a geographic sense, with reference to Europe or Hellas (or the Hellenes): Lys. 2. 21. 2; 2. 27. 1; 2. 60. 5; Isoc. *Phil.* 76. 5. In the remaining reference, Xen. *Hell.* 3. 5. 13, the context does not allow a determination. But note that Xenophon has seven references to 'Great King'. If at *Hell.* 3. 5. 13 he uses 'King of Asia' as a title for the Persian king, this may be the only such usage in Greek literature up to the time of Alexander.

[9] Heinrichs 1987: 487–540. Some scholars believe there was no inscription at all on Cyrus' tomb, e.g. Stronach 1978: 26.

[10] Bosworth 1995: 134.

he speaks of himself as holding 'the throne of Cyrus'. So possibly Darius said 'King of Persia'.

In Arrian (3. 25. 3), in the autumn of 330, 'some Persians' informed Alexander that Bessus had assumed the upright tiara and called himself 'King of Asia'. Diodorus (17. 74. 2 and 83. 7) has, more accurately, 'King'. If the Persian informers told Alexander (in Greek) 'King of Asia', it may have been to present Bessus as Alexander's challenger. The information in Arrian (6. 29. 3) that at some time during Alexander's Indian campaign, a certain Baryaxes, a Mede, had assumed the upright tiara and proclaimed himself 'King of the Persians and Medes' is more accurate.

7. Alexander's assumption of a diadem as his royal insignia in Asia, probably at Arbela, suggests that 'King of Asia' here did not mean King of Persia, since the Persian royal insignia was not the diadem but the upright tiara. Alexander's diadem probably was not even Persian.[11]

8. Alexander's actions at least until the death of Darius, most significantly the destruction of Persepolis, are incompatible with the status of Great King.

Now, if the term 'King of Asia' did not mean King of Persia or the Persian Empire, what did it mean? Let us ask, first, who made the proclamation? The passive voice of ἀνηγορευμένος shows that it was not Alexander himself but someone else, and under the circumstances this was almost certainly Alexander's army.[12] If it was the army, was the *anagoreusis* an informal, spontaneous acclamation by the troops flush with victory, of no lasting significance,[13] or was it a formal act bestowing an official title?[14] It is to be

[11] Fredricksmeyer 1997: 97–109.

[12] Since Plutarch does not actually state that the proclamation was made by the Macedonian army, one might speculate that it was made by the Persians in Alexander's entourage and the local Assyrian dignitaries. I consider this extremely unlikely. Such an act would have been so remarkable that it almost certainly would have been mentioned by Plutarch's source. Alexander had claimed the kingship of Asia already in his letter to Darius after Issus, and we may take it that the Macedonians now formalized the claim by their proclamation. At *Demetr.* 37. 2 and *Pyrrh.* 7. 2 and 11. 6, Plutarch also uses the verb ἀναγορεύω for the proclamation of a king by the Macedonian army.

[13] So e.g. Berve 1938: 145; Ritter 1965: 52; Hamilton 1969: 90; Lock 1977: 100; Andreotti 1957: 125.

[14] So e.g. Wilcken 1932: 137, 149, 245; 1970: 139 and n. 5; Schachermeyr 1973: 276–85; Granier 1931: 31–2; Dobesch 1975: 105–6; Hammond 1980: 148.

expected that at some time Alexander would adopt a formal title for his Asiatic kingship (in Macedonia he was 'King of the Macedonians'), and as there is no evidence that he adopted a Persian title, or any other title, and since Alexander had already previously, in his letter to Darius after Issus, called himself 'King of Asia', it is very probable indeed that now at Arbela, when the Persian Empire was considered dead, Alexander would adopt 'King of Asia' as an official title. This is corroborated by the fact that the proclamation apparently was made in the course of a formal ceremony. Plutarch says (loc. cit.) that Alexander now made a number of important transactions, awards of gifts and estates, assignments of provinces, orders for the abolition of tyrannies in Greece, awards to Croton in Italy for her aid to the Greek cause in the Persian invasion, and a promise of benefactions to Plataea for her sacrifices for the Greeks in the Persian invasion. These measures were probably not taken in secret but were, if only for their propaganda value at the time, publicly announced, and since Alexander stayed at Arbela only a few days, we should infer that the announcements, and Alexander's proclamation as King, were made on the same occasion. This would suggest that there was a formal ceremony, and that the term 'King of Asia' proclaimed at this ceremony was a formal title.

But is it likely that by accepting the title 'King of Asia' from his Macedonians, even if at his initiative, Alexander would have wished to be indebted to them for his new kingship? He had claimed 'Asia' from the outset solely on his own authority by virtue of his conquest and the grace of the gods, and thus was not indebted for it to anyone else (Diod. 17. 17. 2; Justin 11. 5. 11; Arr. 2. 14. 7).[15] As noted, it was probably on this occasion that Alexander assumed a diadem as the insignia of his new kingship. If this is correct, it is reasonable to speculate that he himself donned this diadem rather than having it placed on him by someone else—to show that he owed this kingship to no human authority, that the army confirmed this constituent act by their proclamation, and that the whole transaction then was ratified by the gods (ἔθυε τοῖς θεοῖς μεγαλοπρεπῶς, Plut. loc. cit.).

[15] Schmitthenner 1968: 31–46; Mehl 1980/81: 183–6; Instinsky 1949: 29–40.

These gods were the Graeco-Macedonian gods to whom it was Alexander's, and ancestral, custom to sacrifice,[16] whom he invoked at the Hellespont for his 'conquest' of Asia (Diod. 17. 17. 2), whom he invoked again for his claim to the kingship of Asia in his letter to Darius after Issus (Arr. 2. 14. 7–9), and on whose behalf he had officially undertaken the war in the first place, to punish the Persians for the outrages committed by them in their invasion of 480–479 (Diod. 16. 89. 2; cf. 11. 29. 3; Arr. 2. 14. 4; 3. 18. 12; Polyb. 3. 16. 13; 5. 10. 8; Justin 11. 5. 6).[17] Probably before his departure for Asia in 334, Alexander issued his new 'imperial' coinage, on which he featured Zeus, Athena, and Heracles apparently as patron gods of the war.[18] At the Hellespont he inaugurated the war by dedicating on both sides of the strait altars to these same gods (Arr. 1. 11. 7).[19] There is reason to believe, as well, that Alexander also considered from the beginning Dionysus as his tutelary deity, as the divine-heroic model (the only one available) in the conquest of the east.[20] At Gordium (333), Zeus Basileus identified Alexander as the destined ruler of Asia (Arr. 2. 3. 2–8), and at Siwah (331), Zeus Ammon confirmed the promise.[21] No doubt, then, Alexander attributed his victory at Gaugamela, and his kingship of Asia, to these and the other Graeco-Macedonian gods to whom he regularly sacrificed, not, as has been said,

---

[16] e.g. Arr. 3. 16. 9; 3. 25. 1; 3. 28. 4; 5. 3. 6; 5. 8. 2–3; 5. 20. 1; 6. 3. 2; 7. 11. 8; 7. 14. 1; 7. 24. 4; 7. 25. 2–6; *Ind.* 18. 11; Plut. *Alex.* 76. 1–5; Curt. 4. 6. 10.

[17] For a list of the gods worshipped by Alexander, all Greek (or considered as such), with the sole exception of Apis and (?) Isis in Egypt (Arr. 3. 1. 4–5), Bel-Marduk and other (?) gods in Babylon (Arr. 3. 16. 5), and (according to ancestral custom) 'gods of the locale' (Curt. 3. 8. 22; 9. 9. 27), see, conveniently, Berve 1926: i. 85–90; Samuel 1985: 77–82. Alexander's dedication to 'the Samothracian Cabiri' at the Hyphasis (Philostr. *Vit. Apoll.* 2. 43. 94), if historical, may have been influenced by the precedent of Philip and Olympias, who in their early years had been initiated into their Mysteries (Plut. *Alex.* 2. 1–2).

[18] Price 1991: 29–31; 1974: 24–5, with pls. 11. 60 and 63; Mørkholm 1991: 42, with pls. 1. 7–10. For the early date of these coins, see Price 1991: 27–9. Some scholars believe they were not inaugurated before the year 333/2. See Le Rider 1995–96: esp. 831–3, 842–6, 857–60.

[19] Fredricksmeyer 1991: 204. Note also Alexander's altars to Zeus, Heracles, and Athena after the victory at Issus. Curt. 3. 12. 27.

[20] Fredricksmeyer 1997: 97–109.

[21] On Zeus Basileus at Gordium, see Fredricksmeyer 1961: 160–8; on Zeus Ammon at Siwah, see Fredricksmeyer 1991: 199–214.

to Ahuramazda, 'the tutelary deities of the Persian empire and the Achaemenid family', or 'the gods of Asia'.[22]

Alexander made this very clear soon afterwards by his treatment of Persepolis. Among the Persian capitals, Persepolis was uniquely the holy city of Ahuramazda as the supreme deity of the Persian Empire and the Achaemenid dynasty. It was the seat of the New Year's Festival (in March) in celebration of Ahuramazda and his deputy on earth, the Great King, when the god consecrated and each year reconfirmed him as the ruler of the empire.[23] During his four months' (intermittent) stay in the city (January to May) Alexander had the opportunity to stage, even if on a reduced scale, the New Year's Festival and to obtain his own consecration as legitimate successor of Darius, who by his disgraceful flight at Issus and Gaugamela appeared to have forfeited all moral right to the throne.[24] That this measure was a realistic option for Alexander is suggested by his actions in Egypt and in Babylon.

In both Egypt and Babylon, it is not unlikely that Alexander had himself enthroned as legitimate successor of the native kings by performing the required rituals, or at least he did everything just short of it to demonstrate his piety to the native gods. A formal enthronement, in the temple of Ptah in Memphis, is mentioned only by Ps.-Callisthenes 1. 34. 4. But we know that Alexander sacrificed to the sacred bull Apis, who was the soul and incarnation of Ptah (Arr. 3. 1. 4); assumed the official titles of the Pharaoh; and performed the royal duty of caring for the Egyptian temples. The sacrifice to Apis may have been part of the ritual of the enthronement and coronation ceremony.[25] Of the five Pharaonic titles,

[22] e.g. Lenschau 1932: 368 and Miltner 1954: 296 (Ahuramazda); Briant 1982a: 379 (Persian tutelary deities); Dascalakis 1966: 84 (gods of Asia).

[23] We have no literary information on the function of Persepolis, but what is here stated, based on the archaeological evidence, represents the scholarly consensus. See Pope 1957: 123–30; Ghirshman 1957: 265; Krefter 1971: 13 and 96; Erdmann 1960: 38–47; Widengren 1959: 252–5; Nylander 1974: 137–50.

[24] On personal courage and victory in war as qualification for the Achaemenid kingship, see Wiesehöfer 1994: 24–30. Apart from the initial sack and the final conflagration, Alexander's stay at Persepolis is very thinly documented. But if he had done anything comparable to what he is reported to have done in Egypt and in Babylon, this would hardly have gone unnoted by our sources, if only because it would have been totally at odds with the initial sack and final conflagration.

[25] Koenen 1977: 31 and 53.

three are attested on inscriptions: as Horus (I) he was 'the
strong prince', with the additions 'who attacked the foreign
lands' (sc. probably Persia) and 'the protector of Egypt'. As
'King of Upper-Egypt and King of Lower-Egypt' (IV) he
was 'beloved of Amun and chosen of Ra', and as 'Son of Ra'
(V) he was 'Alexandros'. The bestowal of this titulary probably was part of the accession ceremony.[26] I agree with
Wilcken that 'the adoption of the royal state must have
found expression in some official act'.[27]

One should think also that only as the rightfully
enthroned Pharaoh could Alexander have ordered restoration and repair of temples, as he did of the temple of
Amenhotep III at Luxor, and of Thutmosis III and of
Khonsu at Karnak, and have given instructions for safe-
guarding the sanctity of temple precincts.[28] These measures
set Alexander off against Xerxes and Artaxerxes Ochus, who
in the Egyptian tradition defiled the sacred bull Apis and
also otherwise outraged Egyptian religious sensibilities.[29]

It is not unlikely that, as in Egypt, so also in Babylon
Alexander had himself formally consecrated as king. There
may have been two such ceremonies for the Babylonian
kings. One, at the New Year's Festival (Akîtu) when Bel-
Marduk confirmed, or reconfirmed, the candidate in the
kingship.[30] The festival took place in the spring (March),
while Alexander left Babylon no later than early December
(331). Perhaps Marduk's priests arranged a substitute
ceremony for Alexander.[31] As the New Year's Festival legitimated the kingship on an annual basis, there may have been
another ceremony for the initial inauguration of the king.[32]
Alexander's sacrifice to Bel-Marduk, reported by Arrian (3.
16. 5), may have been part of this inauguration ceremony.

[26] Sethe 1904: 116–19 (nos. 2–5); Gauthier 1916: 199–203; Wilcken 1932: 113–
16; 1970: 261–2; Fairman 1988: 74–81; Koenen 1977: 31 and 53; Milns 1969: 101.

[27] Wilcken 1932: 114. Cf. 1970: 261 n. 5.

[28] Gauthier 1916: 199–203; Wilcken 1970: 263. The recent attempt by Burstein
1991: 139–45 to show that Alexander was not enthroned as Pharaoh does not carry
conviction. But note that Badian also doubts a coronation: 1996: 14; 1985: 433 n. 1.

[29] Kienitz 1953: 55–60, 107–8.

[30] Kuhrt 1987: 30–40; Dombart 1924: 114–18; Meissner 1925: 97. Cf. Hartmann
1937: 145–60; Erich Ebeling, *RE* 14 (1930), s.v. Marduk, cols. 1658–70, 1670.

[31] Bosworth 1980*a*: 316; Kuhrt 1987: 52; Schachermeyr 1973: 282 and n. 326.

[32] Pallis 1926: 174–83.

Arrian says that Alexander did everything else as well in compliance with the instructions of the Babylonian priests (Arr. 3. 16. 5). In particular he also fulfilled the royal duty of caring for the temple of Bel-Marduk by ordering the reconstruction of his massive temple complex Esagila which allegedly had been ruined by Xerxes, who as justification for this had appealed to the will of Ahuramazda (Arr. 3. 16. 4–5; 7. 17. 1–3; Strabo 16. 1. 5; Joseph. *C. Ap.* 1. 192).[33] In these ways Alexander acted like the first Achaemenid rulers who, unlike their successors, presented themselves in Egypt and Babylon as devotees of the native gods and legitimate successors of the native kings. What F. K. Kienitz has said about Egypt applies in principle as well to Babylon:

[The native priests hated] Kambyses, Xerxes und Ochos nicht als Eroberer und Fremdherrscher, sondern als Misachter des heiligen Gesetzes der Götter. Umgekehrt war Dareios nichts anderes als der gute und fromme Pharao, der Liebling und Schützer der Götter. Dass er aus der Persis und nicht aus Ägypten stammte, war für diese Auffassung gleichgültig.[34]

Alexander's actions in Egypt and Babylon leave little doubt that he meant to give these countries a special status in his kingdom of Asia; they stand in the sharpest possible contrast with what he did in Persepolis.

Like the other Persian capitals, Persepolis fell to Alexander without resistance. But while he spared the others, on his arrival at Persepolis he handed the city over to his troops, all but the palace complex to be used as headquarters and garrison, for unrestricted plunder, rampage,

---

[33] On Alexander's benefaction to Esagila, cf. Sachs 1977: 146–7. On Xerxes' appeal to Ahuramazda, see Hartmann 1937: 159; Widengren 1965: 138. On the care for Marduk's temple as a royal obligation, see Saggs 1969: 363–70; Kuhrt 1987: 49; Dombart 1924: 115; Zimmern 1926: 12.

[34] Kienitz 1953: 63. Cf. Dandamaev 1976: 99: 'Die Herrschaft des Kyros in Babylonien wurde nicht als Fremdherrschaft empfunden, weil er ja die Herrschaft formell aus Marduks Händen erhalten hatte, indem er alte religiöse Zeremonien durchführte.' See further Kuhrt 1987: 48–52; Widengren 1965: 137. Cf. Wiesehöfer 1994: 34. In Babylonian cuneiform documents Alexander is called 'King of Lands', an ancient Babylonian title which had not been used by the Persian kings since Xerxes. Bosworth 1980a: 316; Wilcken 1932: 139–40; Lane Fox 1973: 249. The reference in Babylonian astronomical diaries to Alexander as 'king of the world' as well as 'king of all countries' seems to be descriptive rather than titular. Sachs and Hunger 1988: p. 179, no. 330, rev. l. 11 and p. 181, no. 329, obv. l. 1. On Alexander in Babylon, see also Geller 1990: 5–6.

and slaughter, with frightful excesses, and then ordered the removal of the huge treasury hoard of the Persian kings, up to some 120,000 talents in gold and silver bullion, to Susa and perhaps other places, some 400 miles (to Susa) over rough terrain in wintertime, although its continued safety could easily have been insured where it was (Diod. 17. 70. 1–71. 3; Curt. 5. 5. 2; 5. 6. 1–9; Plut. *Alex.* 37. 3–4; Arr. 3. 19. 7; Strabo 15. 3. 9). These two measures, the initial sack of the city and the removal of the treasure, a gigantic logistical project, indicate that Alexander had decided on the destruction of the city from the beginning.[35]

Four months later, before his departure, Alexander put the remaining palace complex to the torch (Arr. 3. 18. 11–12; Strabo 15. 3. 6; cf. Diod. 17. 72. 2–6; Curt. 5. 7. 3–11; Plut. *Alex.* 38; Cleitarchus, *FGrH* 137 F 11 = Athen. 13. 576d–e). The alleged purpose, according to our sources, was to punish the Persians for their offences against the Greeks. This was the official *Parole* of the campaign under Alexander's leadership as *hegemon* of the Hellenic League. It presented a commitment which, no doubt reiterated in vows to the gods at numerous sacrifices in the presence of the army, needed to be fulfilled by some dramatic act. This we can understand. But the appropriate choice for the revenge was not Persepolis, but Susa. Susa was the centre and symbol for the Greeks of Persian power, aggression, and arrogance. From Susa had been launched the invasions of Greece, from Susa had been dictated the humiliating King's Peace, in Susa Greek emissaries had been forced again and again to debase themselves in homage to the Great King. Yet Alexander spared Susa. Persepolis, on the other hand, at this time was little known and meant little to the Greeks.[36] It

---

[35] The initial sack of the city was no doubt also a palliative to Alexander's troops after their recent setback at the Persian Gates, but it was surely not the only, or decisive, motive. It accorded with Alexander's policy. Otherwise, how to account for the final firing of the palaces? The removal of the treasury cannot be explained entirely as a security measure. The process of removing it posed, we should think, a greater security risk than its continued presence under strong guard would have done, unless Alexander meant to abandon the city. Nor is it likely that Alexander meant to insure the safety of the treasure by diversifying it. In that case one should expect that he would remove part, but not all, of it. At Susa there was already a deposit of some 50,000 talents (Arr. 3. 16. 7; Curt. 5. 2. 11).

[36] Pope 1957: 129: 'The Greeks seem never to have heard of [Persepolis] until the time of Alexander.' Cf. Erdmann 1960: 46.

has been suggested that by the time of his departure from the city, Alexander had not yet learned of the defeat of Agis' 'revolt', and that he meant to curry favour with the Greeks by this dramatic act of vengeance. But it is hard to believe that Alexander would commit an act of such signal import for his rule in Asia for the sake of the ever-elusive goodwill of the Greeks, especially since report of the event could hardly be expected to reach Greece in time to affect the outcome of the war.

It is reasonable to think, therefore, that one reason, and, I would suggest the decisive reason, why Alexander destroyed Persepolis was its status in Asia as the religious centre of the Persian Empire. By this view, the destruction of Persepolis not only enacted the long-awaited vengeance against the Persians, but it was also in accord with Alexander's proclamation as King of Asia at Arbela, as a clear signal that his own kingship was not a continuation or renewal of the Persian kingship, but superseded it, not by grace of Ahuramazda, but by his own prowess, and the grace of the Graeco-Macedonian gods.

By this interpretation, Alexander's destruction of Persepolis was a calculated act of policy, as Arrian and others believe (Arr. 3. 18. 11–12; Strabo 15. 3. 6; Plut. *Alex.* 38. 8). According to the vulgate account, probably derived from Cleitarchus (*FGrH* 137 F 11 = Athen. 13. 576d–e), Alexander ordered the destruction on the spur of the moment at a drinking party on the urging of the Athenian courtesan Thais (Diod. 17. 72. 2–6; Curt. 5. 7. 3–7; Plut. *Alex.* 38).[37] The role of Thais in the affair is probably fictional (as a Persian king had destroyed Athenian temples, so now an Athenian girl, and a courtesan at that, destroyed the sacred capital of the Persians), but the vulgate account may well be true in that Alexander had decided to mark the destruction of the citadel with grand sacrifices both to his other gods, and especially also to Dionysus with a *Komos* (Diod. 17. 72. 1 and 4: Alexander θυσίας τε μεγαλοπρεπεῖς τοῖς θεοῖς συνετέλεσεν καὶ τῶν φίλων λαμπρὰς ἑστιάσεις ἐποιήσατο

[37] Most scholars today believe that the deed was an act of policy. See esp. Wiesehöfer 1994: 37–9, with n. 92; Lauffer 1981: 105, with n. 14; and Borza 1995: 217–38. But see also Bloedow 1995: 23–41, who reverts to the opinion that Alexander acted on impulse.

. . . πάντες . . . τὸν ἐπινίκιον ἄγειν Διονύσῳ παρήγγειλαν). This scenario is the more plausible if it is correct, as I believe, that Alexander regarded Dionysus as one of his champions in his conquest of Asia.

In the Persian tradition Alexander was execrated as the destructive, godless foreign invader, who among other misdeeds ordered the destruction of one of the two existing copies of the Avesta which had fallen into his hands, while ordering the other copy taken to Alexandria for trans-literation into the Greek script of everything in it dealing with philosophy, astronomy, medicine, and agriculture.[38] If indeed Alexander found these copies (at Persepolis?) and ordered one of them to be destroyed (while preserving the other for the benefit of Greek science), it would be clear evidence that he meant to suppress the Achaemenid religious tradition. Our information derives from late Iranian sources (9th–10th cent. AD), but it may have at least some truth in it, as it accords with Alexander's known scientific curiosity and his wilful destruction of Persepolis. As S. K. Eddy has observed,

All the Persian propaganda says that Alexander . . . was a man without true religious ideas . . . the true religion [of Ahuramazda] that he had undone was the theology of Achaemenid kingship.[39]

II

At Persepolis Alexander could not have foreseen the radical change in the situation effected soon afterwards, in the late summer of 330, by the death of Darius at the hands of his own men, and the usurpation of his throne by his murderer and kinsman, Bessus. Alexander recognized quickly that it

[38] Altheim 1953: 86–8. Cf. Frye 1984: 139 n. 2.

[39] Eddy 1961: 59. Cf. Boyce 1979: 78. Alexander's employment of Persian magians for his Persian followers at the reconciliation banquet at Opis in 324, how-ever, suggests that in contrast to the religious ideology of the Achaemenid dynasty he meant to respect the religious traditions of the Persian people (Arr. 7. 11. 8). On the distinction between the religion of the Achaemenids and that of the people, see von der Osten 1956: 82–99. We may also note a later, favourable tradition of Alexander in Iran which, influenced by the Alexander Romance, presented him as a Persian prince and mighty king, a Muslim, wise man, and even prophet. See Wiesehöfer 1994: 19.

now became imperative for him to present himself to the Persians as more qualified to rule, by virtue both of his victories and of his magnanimity toward them, than the regicide Bessus. To this end, he now began to introduce a series of innovations in his kingship which have been, or might be, seen as evidence for Alexander's accession as Great King of the Persian Empire.[40] They raise two major questions. One, do they in fact provide this evidence, and two, what bearing did they have on Alexander's status as King of Asia as proclaimed at Arbela? I will first identify the innovations as far as possible in chronological order.

1. Treatment of Darius' body with royal honours; torture and execution of Bessus in the Persian mode; and royal treatment of Darius' family.[41]
2. Adoption of articles of the Persian royal dress.[42]
3. (Alleged) adoption of Darius' signet ring.[43]
4. (Alleged) adoption of Darius' diadem.[44]
5. Adoption of Persian traditions and institutions: a bodyguard of distinguished Persians including Darius' brother Oxyathres; Asian court ushers (ῥαβδοῦχοι Ἀσιαγενεῖς, Diod. 17. 77. 4); the office of court chamberlain; Darius' harem, including eunuchs; distributing coins to women in Persis; distributing cloaks with purple borders, as worn by Persian

[40] e.g. Ritter 1965: 52 n. 3: 'Von der Ausrufung [at Arbela] wird deshalb kein Gebrauch gemacht, um die Königswürde nicht auf sie begründen zu müssen, sondern ihr eine andere Rechtsgrundlage geben zu können', to wit, the Persian kingship. Berve 1938: 150: 'Dass Alexander das persische Königtun übernahm . . . wird, abgesehen von der Bestellung persischer Satrapen, an einer Anzahl von Massnahmen oder Handlungen deutlich.' Schachermeyr 1973: 321: 'Alexander wollte [jetzt] zum legitimen Rechtsnachfolger des letzten Dareios werden.'

[41] *Darius' corpse*: Arr. 3. 22. 1, 6; cf. 3. 23. 7; 3. 25. 8; Diod. 17. 73. 3; Just. 11. 15. 15; Plut. *Alex.* 43. 5–7; Pliny, *NH* 36. 132. *Bessus*: Arr. 3. 30. 3–5; 4. 7. 3; Curt. 7. 5. 38–40; 7. 10. 10; Diod. 17. 83. 9; Plut. *Alex.* 43. 6; Just. 12. 5. 10–11. *Darius' family*: Diod. 17. 37. 6; 38. 1; 54. 2, 7; 67. 1; 77. 4; Plut. *Alex.* 21; 22. 5; 30; 43; *Mor.* 338e; Curt. 3. 12. 17–26; 4. 10. 18–34; 5. 2. 18–22; 6. 2. 9, 11; Arr. 2. 12. 3–5; 4. 20. 1–3.

[42] Eratosthenes, *FGrH* 241 F 30 = Plut. *Mor* 329f–330a; Plut. *Alex* 45. 1–4, with the emendation of Μηδικῆς to Μακεδονικῆς as proposed by Coraes and Schmieder; Ephippus, *FGrH* 126 F 5 = Athen. 12. 537e; Diod. 17. 77. 5; Curt. 6. 6. 4; Plut. *Alex.* 51. 5. Cf. Curt. 3. 3. 17–19.

[43] Curt. 6. 6. 6.

[44] Diod. 17. 77. 5; Curt. 6. 6. 4; Just. 12. 3. 8.

courtiers, to the *hetairoi* for (at least some) ceremonial functions.[45]

6. Recruitment of Iranians and other natives into the army.[46]

7. Appointment of Persian satraps.[47]

8. Attempt to introduce among the Macedonians the obeisance (*proskynesis*) to the king (327).[48]

9. The office of grand vizier (*hazârapati*) as the most powerful official in the realm (324).[49]

10. (Possible) adoption of the Persian royal fire cult (324?).[50]

11. Marriage, in the Persian mode, to a daughter of Darius and perhaps also a daughter of Artaxerxes Ochus (324).[51]

12. Use of a golden throne, with Persian eunuchs in attendance, and consultation of Persian seers (324).[52]

On examination, it appears that none of these innovations, as far as they are historical, individually or in aggregate, prove Alexander's assumption of the Persian kingship. All of them allow of different explanations as well.

1. The treatment of Darius' body and of his family can be seen as the victor's magnanimity, as the generosity of one king to another. As for Alexander addressing Sisygambis as 'mother' (Diod. 17. 37. 6; Curt. 3. 12. 17, 25), I don't think that he meant to take over, in supersession of Darius, the role of the head of the Achaemenid house. The explanation

---

[45] *Bodyguard*: Diod. 17. 77. 4; 18. 27. 1. *Court constables*: Diod. 17. 77. 4; Plut. *Alex.* 51. 2. *Court chamberlain*: Diod. 16. 47. 3; Hdt. 3. 84; Plut. *Alex.* 46. 2. *Harem*: Diod. 17. 77. 6–7; Curt. 3. 3. 24; 6. 6. 8; Just. 12. 3. 10. *Coins*: Plut. *Alex.* 69. 1. *Purple garments*: Diod. 17. 77. 5; cf. Curt. 6. 6. 7; Just. 12. 3. 9; Xen. *Anab.* 1. 2. 20; 1. 5. 7–8; Curt. 3. 2. 10; 3. 8. 15; 3. 13. 13.

[46] See Bosworth 1980b: 15–21 for references and discussion.

[47] Berve 1926: ii. s.vv. Sabictas, Abistamenes, Mazaeus, Mithrenes, Abulites, Phrasaortes, Astaspes, Oxydates, Ammianapes, Satibarzanes. See also Seibert 1985: 206–17.

[48] Plut. *Alex.* 54. 3–55. 1; Arr. 4. 10. 5–12. 5; Curt. 8. 5. 5–24. Cf. Hdt. 1. 134; 7. 136; Xen. *Anab.* 3. 2. 13; Plut. *Art.* 22. 4; *Alex.* 74. 2–3; Curt. 8. 5. 22.

[49] Schachermeyr 1970: 31–7; Berve 1926: ii. 173; Frye 1963: 93; Heckel 1992: 366; Badian 1985: 485.   [50] Diod. 17. 114. 4. Cf. Plut. *Alex.* 54. 4 (*hestia*).

[51] Chares, *FGrH* 125 F 4 = Athen. 12. 538b–539a; Phylarchus, *FGrH* 81 F 41 = Athen. 12. 539b–540a; Arr. 7. 4. 4–8; Diod. 17. 107. 6; Curt. 10. 3. 12; Plut. *Alex.* 70. 3; *Mor.* 329d–e; Just. 12. 10. 9–10.

[52] Aristobulus, *FGrH* 139 F58 = Arr. 7. 24. 1–3; Diod. 17. 116. 2–4; Plut. *Alex.* 73. 7–74. 1; Ephippus, *FGrH* 126 F 4 = Athen. 12. 537d.

rather is his chivalry which he accorded also to other royal and aristocratic women.[53] As for Bessus, he had not only murdered Darius, but claimed the Persian kingship as his successor. But Alexander punished him as a regicide (on principle hated by all kings), not as rebel against himself as Great King.

2. Alexander adopted from the Persian royal attire only the robe with the golden sash, and rejected the other items, most importantly the key royal insignia of the upright tiara. The occasional claim that Alexander adopted the upright tiara (Arr. 4. 7. 4; Lucian. *Dial. Mort.* 12. 4; *Itin. Alex.* 89) is almost certainly in error.[54]

We should note, however, some alleged numismatic evidence for Alexander's upright tiara. There are preserved several specimens of what appears to be a commemorative coin (decadrachm) issued by Alexander shortly after his return from India.[55] It shows on one side a full-length portrait of Alexander in full Graeco-Macedonian armour wielding the thunderbolt of Zeus. The headgear has a high upward-curling point or peak and is surmounted by a crest, with a tall plume rising above the line of the crest.[56] The first specimen found, struck off centre, does not show the crest and plume, and the headpiece was thought to represent the Persian upright tiara.[57] But since the discovery of additional specimens, most scholars today identify the headpiece as a Macedonian infantry helmet of the Phrygian-Thracian type.[58] Even so, if the piece suggests, as well, the upright tiara (the ambiguity could be intentional), it would present Alexander as conqueror of Darius rather than as Great King, as is indicated by the remainder of Alexander's attire, the Graeco-Macedonian armour, and especially the crest and plume surmounting the piece, which the tiara did not have. As tiara, the piece therefore would be purely symbolic

[53] Fredricksmeyer 1998: 178–80, with references.

[54] See Heckel in Yardley and Heckel 1997: 203–4; Bosworth 1980*b*: 5 and n. 30; 1995: 50; Brunt 1976: 533; Ritter 1965: 41–7.

[55] Hill 1927: 205: 'It is not easy to find an occasion for such an issue except [by Alexander] just after the Indian expedition.'

[56] Price 1991: 33, 452–3, pls. 1–3; Bosworth 1994*b*: 831, fig. 39.

[57] So e.g. Hill 1922: 191.

[58] e.g. Price 1982: 76: 'There is no reason to suppose that there is anything oriental about this headdress.'

of Alexander's conquest of Darius and the Persian Empire.
It does not constitute evidence that Alexander adopted the
Persian royal tiara as emblem of his own kingship.

3. According to Curtius (6. 6. 6.), at some time after
Darius' death, Alexander adopted Darius' signet ring for
dispatches in Asia, while retaining his own ring for dispatches to Europe. Berve opined: 'Deutlicher konnte die
Nachfolge der Achämeniden schwerlich dokumentiert
werden.'[59] However, even if Curtius' information is correct
(which it probably is not), Alexander's adoption of Darius'
ring could well have signified not, as Berve thought,
Alexander's succession of Darius, but rather his conquest.
That is, the victor takes over the property of the vanquished.
Curtius in the same passage (6. 6. 5) says that Alexander
explained these adoptions as war trophies (*spolia*). But in any
case, Curtius' claim about the two rings is almost certainly
wrong. It is at odds with all other information about
Alexander's ring and, significantly, with Curtius himself.[60]
It has recently been argued, to my mind convincingly, that
Curtius' statement at 6. 6. 6 is to be rejected, and that
Alexander used from beginning to end only one ring, his
own.[61]

4. If the information at Diodorus 17. 77. 5, Curtius 6. 6.
4, and Justin 12. 3. 8 is correct that at some time after
Darius' death, Alexander adopted Darius' diadem to make it
the key emblem of his own kingship, it does not provide
support for Alexander's Achaemenid succession, since the
diadem in Darius' dress was not exclusively royal but worn
also by members of the high nobility (Xen. *Cyrop.* 8. 3. 13).
The insignia of the Persian kings was the upright tiara, and
if Alexander had wished to signify his succession of Darius,
he would have done this by assuming the upright tiara.[62] It is

[59] Berve 1938: 151.
[60] Curt. 3. 6. 7; 3. 7. 14; 10. 5. 4; 10. 6. 4–5; 10. 6. 16; Arr. 6. 23. 4; 6. 29. 10; Plut.
Alex. 39. 8; *Mor.* 333a; Diod. 17. 117. 3; 18. 2. 4; Just. 12. 15. 12; Nep. *Eum.* 2. 1.
[61] Hammond 1995: 199–203.
[62] Cf. Gschnitzer 1968: 168: It is to be doubted that the diadem, 'das bei den
Persern nicht dem König allein gebührte, gerade die Rechtsnachfolge der
Achämeniden ausdrücken sollte'. Contra, Ritter 1965: 50: 'Wenn [Alexander] als
Kopfschmuck nur das Diadem, nicht die aufrechte Tiara übernahm, so ersetzte
dieses . . . jene Kopfbedeckung der Grosskönige *und sollte ihn als deren Nachfolger
kennzeichnen*' (my emphasis).

fairly certain that he did not. But Alexander's diadem as insignia of his kingship, as noted, probably was not even Persian, but rather taken from the iconography of Dionysus as Alexander's predecessor in the conquest of the east.[63]

5. The bodyguard of distinguished Persians was a political desideratum with the growing presence of Persians at court and in the army, and as a means to tie the Persian nobility more closely to Alexander on a personal basis. Even so, it was kept separate from, and subsidiary to, Alexander's Macedonian Guard. The Asian court ushers could be regarded as lowly menials comparable to the Scythian slave constables at Athens. The office of court chamberlain, or master of ceremony (εἰσαγγελεύς), went not to a Persian, but to the Greek Chares. The royal harem was a time-honoured Oriental institution, and showed Alexander as a potentate in this tradition. It is doubtful that Alexander made much, if any, use of it. The gift of coins to Persian women in the tradition of the Persian kings showed Alexander's own generosity as the new king. The distribution of purple garments to the *hetairoi* in the manner of the Persian kings served Alexander's policy of rapprochement and fusion which required the adoption by the Macedonians of at least some Persian customs, and it shows his desire to emulate the pomp of the Persian kings. It does not show his accession to the Persian throne as Darius' successor.

6. Alexander's extensive recruitment of Persians and other natives into the army became a practical necessity as he faced a growing manpower shortage with the fighting in Bactria and Sogdiana, increased difficulties of reinforcements from the west, the campaign in India, and the incipient disaffection of the Macedonians. The Persian forces provided a counterweight to the Macedonians (ἀντίταγμα, Diod. 17. 108. 3) and reduced Alexander's dependence on them, while the native troops, under firm control in the command structure of the army, served as hostages for the good behaviour of their compatriots at home. And of course, as their new king, Alexander had employed native troops from the beginning, or at least since his defeat of Darius at Issus (Arrian. 2. 14. 7; Justin 11. 5. 11).

[63] Fredricksmeyer 1997: 97–109.

7. Alexander appointed Persian satraps even before the death of Darius (Cappadocia, Babylonia, Armenia, Susiana, Persis, Carmania, Media, Parthia, and Hyrcania), and after Darius' death he appointed two Persians who submitted to him but who had betrayed Darius, while one of them was one of his murderers (Satibarzanes).[64] It is clear that Alexander appointed Persian satraps for their competence and usefulness to him.

8. *Proskynesis.* It was customary in the Near East to perform some sort of salaam (*proskynesis*) before social superiors, and obligatory for all to perform the act before the King in the form of a deep bow, genuflexion, or (depending on circumstances) even prostration on the ground. The Orientals performed it for Alexander from the beginning, as a matter of course, not as the King of Persia, but as king, and now their king. The Macedonians and Greeks, on the other hand, did not perform the act, considering it appropriate only for gods and, when performed for the Great King (who was not a god, though everything just short of it) as a mark of Oriental servility.[65] When after Darius' death Alexander embarked on his strategy of collaboration between Macedonians and Persians, he obviously could not, and would not wish to, discontinue the practice among the Orientals, which means that he would expect it from the Macedonians and Greeks along with the Orientals. In 327, Alexander arranged for the introduction of the practice among the Macedonians and Greeks. It would mean their acknowledgement, on par with the Orientals, of Alexander as an absolute potentate, and in addition it held for them the implication of acknowledging Alexander, at least potentially, as divine. Many of the Macedonians resented it, and Callisthenes openly refused. Alexander decided to drop the matter, for the time being. Callisthenes of course was a marked man. I do not think the matter had anything to do with Alexander's succession of Darius as Great King.

A word should be said about the role of the 'kiss' in the affair. According to Chares (*FGrH* 125 F 14a = Plut. *Alex.* 54. 4–6), the plan was that at a banquet, when the rite was to be introduced (for the Macedonians and Greeks), Alexander

---

[64] Above, n. 47.   [65] Above, n. 48.

would, after drinking from his cup, hand it to the person next to him, that he was to rise so as to face the *hestia*, drink from the cup and then do *proskynesis* to Alexander, after that to kiss him and resume his place on the couch, and so on with each guest in turn. The privilege of kissing the king was Persian. But among the Persians, it was restricted to the King's immediate family and 'kinsmen' (Arr. 7. 11. 1 and 6–7; Hdt. 1. 134). Apparently, Alexander meant, at least on this occasion, to make *proskynesis* more palatable to the Macedonians and Greeks by extending to all who performed it the privilege of the kiss. So while they would do obeisance to Alexander as their absolute lord, as the Orientals did, Alexander in turn would honour them as near-equals (according to Hdt. 1. 134, among the Persians the kiss was restricted to equals or near-equals). Apparently the kiss as *quid pro quo* was abandoned along with the *proskynesis*.

The privilege of kissing Alexander had not accompanied *proskynesis* for the Persians. We learn from Arrian (7. 11. 1) that it was not until the Macedonian mutiny at Opis in 324 that Alexander adopted (in a fit of pique) the Persian royal custom of appointing distinguished Persians as 'kinsmen' with the privilege of kissing him. But when the Macedonians quickly submitted, and one of the officers told him that what grieved the Macedonians was that he had now made some of the Persians his 'kinsmen' with the permission to kiss him, while none of the Macedonians had yet enjoyed this privilege, Alexander broke in: 'But I regard all of you as my kinsmen, and from now on that is what I will call you' (Arr. 7. 11. 6–7). This free-wheeling use by Alexander of Persian royal tradition, both with respect to the King's 'kinsmen' and the kiss, shows that Alexander adopted Persian customs for practical purposes as it suited him. It does not show that he meant to present himself as Great King.[66]

9. Alexander's creation of the position of grand vizier (chiliarch) was in the tradition of Philip in that he also introduced into his kingship a number of Persian institutions in his drive for greater autocracy.[67] As Alexander had

---

[66] On the *proskynesis* affair, cf., most recently, Badian 1985: 457–60; 1996: 21–2; Bosworth 1995: 77–90; Atkinson 1994: 201. See also Brunt 1976: 535–43 and (still valuable) Balsdon 1950: 371–6. Cf. Frye 1972: 102–7.

[67] Kienast 1973: *passim*.

appointed as court chamberlain the Greek Chares, so he
appointed as chiliarch not a Persian but Hephaestion, and
after Hephaestion's death, Perdiccas.[68]

10. There is evidence for the practice by the magians in
the Achaemenid period of an empire-wide royal fire cult.
This fire was considered sacred, in some sense divine, and
represented the King's life and charisma. The central fire,
the royal fire proper, was maintained for the King at his
court, and accompanied him everywhere.[69] It is possible that
at some time after Darius' death, perhaps not until after his
return from India, Alexander adopted this cult. Diodorus
says that at Hephaestion's death in October 324, Alexander

ordered all inhabitants of Asia to make sure to extinguish what is
called among the Persians 'the sacred fire' (τὸ ἱερὸν πῦρ) until he
had concluded the obsequies. This the Persians used to do at the
death of their kings. And people considered the order a bad omen
and thought that heaven was foretelling the death of the king.
(17. 114. 4–5)

If this information is correct, it shows that the magians had
applied to Alexander the royal fire cult. It does not prove
that Alexander himself adopted and practised the cult. If he
did adopt it, it is not clear whether he did so as Darius'
successor and Great King, or as King of Asia who adopted
some Persian institutions. Certainly the order to extinguish
the fire, which, after all, was thought to symbolize and safe-
guard Alexander's own life and royal power, even when full
allowance is made for the intensity of his grief over
Hephaestion's death, shows that he did not take this cult
very seriously.[70]

11. In 324, at Susa, Alexander celebrated, with great
pomp and splendour, a mass wedding, in the Persian mode,

[68] Berve 1926: ii. s.vv. Badian 1985: 485 n. 1 doubts that Hephaestion and
Perdiccas held all the traditional powers of a Persian grand vizier.

[69] Xen. *Cyrop.* 8. 3. 12; Curt. 3. 3. 8–9; 4. 13. 12; 4. 14. 24; 5. 1. 20; Diod. 17.
114. 4–5; Amm. 23. 6. 34. Schachermeyr's discussion of the Persian fire cult and
Alexander's adoption of it is highly speculative and must be used with caution
(1970: 38–48; 1973: 380–3, 682–5). On the scanty and controversial archaeological
evidence for the Achaemenid fire cult (temples/altars), see Schippmann 1971:
473–86, 514–15.

[70] Badian 1985: 486 n. 1 suggests that Diodorus' information may be 'anachronistic fiction by a later source'. In the Iranian tradition, far from adopting the fire
cult, Alexander 'killed magi', and 'quenched many fires'. Boyce 1979: 78.

at which some 10,000 of the Macedonian rank and file formalized their liaisons with Oriental women, some 80 of Alexander's *hetairoi* married Persian noblewomen, and Alexander himself married Darius' daughter Statira, and perhaps also Parysatis, a daughter of Artaxerxes Ochus. The purpose of these unions clearly was to cement and symbolize Alexander's new programme of solidarity between his western and eastern subjects, and especially between the Macedonians and Persians as the two leading peoples in the empire. If the Macedonian rank and file married any women of their choice and standing, and the *hetairoi* married Persian noblewomen, it was only fitting for Alexander himself to marry the noblest of them all, that is, a daughter, or daughters, of the former Great King(s). Viewed in this light, the weddings are evidence of Alexander's policy of rapprochement with the Persians, not of his succession to the Persian throne. If Alexander had meant his marriage(s) to effect his dynastic succession of Darius as Great King, we would expect that at least some Greek or Macedonian women would be given to Persian men. As it was, the Macedonian dominance over the Persians in these unions was obvious.

12. Alexander's use, after his return from India, of a golden throne on at least some occasions of state business.[71] The royal throne, unknown as such to the Macedonians, in the Near East was a primary symbol of royalty. It was sacrosanct, endowed with royal and divine mana, and for anyone other than the king to sit in it was a capital offence.[72] On one occasion, at Babylon, when an unknown person unaccountably took a seat on Alexander's momentarily empty throne, the seers declared this a bad omen, Alexander followed their advice to have the man interrogated under torture, and, when this proved unsatisfactory, to have him executed.[73]

[71] Above, n. 52. We can infer from the anecdote in Curt. 8. 4. 15–17 (cf. Val. Max. 5. 1 ext. 1; Front. *Strat.* 4. 6. 3) that in 328/7 Alexander had not yet adopted the (Persian) throne with its taboo, but expressed disbelief in it.

[72] Meissner 1925: 63–4; Krefter 1971: 57–9, 96–102; Alföldi 1950: 537–51; Germain 1956: 303–13; Hinz 1979: 63–4.

[73] Above, n. 52. At Alexander's approach to Babylon, the Chaldeans, alleging an oracle from their god Bel-Marduk (Arr.), had warned him not to enter the city, but from a distrust of their motives Alexander did not follow their advice (Arr. 7. 16. 5–17; Diod. 17. 112; Plut. *Alex.* 73. 1–2; Just. 12. 13. 3–6, according to whom the

This incident suggests that in his last period Alexander was becoming increasingly superstitious and paranoid, and influenced by the traditions of eastern despotism. But there is no evidence that the throne belonged to Darius, and if it did, it could have been understood as a war trophy (cf. Curt. 6. 6. 5). That Alexander's throne was not meant to identify him as Great King is suggested by the reverence with which the Macedonians regarded it (and his other insignia) after his death (Curt. 10. 6. 4; Diod. 18. 60. 6–61. 1). Considering that they scrapped his attempts at integration and remained staunchly anti-Persian, it is perhaps unlikely that they would regard Alexander's throne in this way if they considered it as a symbol of his Persian kingship.

So much here for the individual innovations. While none evinces Alexander's Achaemenid kingship, the time of their introduction should also be noted. Alexander introduced the majority of them in the months following Darius' death, during the remainder of 330, but others later, and some as late as 324. This suggests that they were occasioned by practical political and military considerations and needs as they arose in the course of events. Our sources attribute them to Alexander's desire to emulate the extravagance and luxury of the Persian court, to impress the Persians and secure their allegiance, and to gain greater ascendancy over the Macedonians (e.g. Diod. 17. 77. 4–7; Curt. 6. 6. 1–10; Justin 12. 3. 8–12; Plut. *Alex.* 45. 1–4; 47. 5–10; Arr. 4. 7. 4; 7. 6. 5). They do not view them as assumption of the Persian kingship. Considering their unquestionable prejudice against the Orientals, and in light of Alexander's unpopular policy of reconciliation and co-operation, I believe they would not have failed to inform us if they thought that Alexander's Persian innovations meant his takeover of the Persian kingship.

warning was given by Persian magians). Smelik 1978–9 has argued (not quite convincingly) that the Chaldeans sincerely believed that some disaster threatened Alexander's life in Babylon, and when he entered the city against their advice, they staged an ancient rite of enthroning a substitute king to deflect the evil portended for Alexander to the substitute. This rite, Smelik believes, lies behind our report of the stranger on Alexander's throne (the idea is not new). But, according to Smelik, from a disdain of Babylonian (barbarian) beliefs, Alexander aborted the ritual. He concludes: 'His misunderstanding and distrust toward the Babylonian priesthood show once more his Graeco-Macedonian prejudice against Barbarians and Babylonians in particular' (108).

And finally, we should think that a legitimate and convincing assumption of the Persian kingship entailed a number of conditions; but, as far as we know, Alexander met none of them.

1. The adoption of the upright tiara as the key insignia of the Persian kingship.[74] Instead of the upright tiara, Alexander adopted as the insignia of his own kingship a diadem which, as already noted, probably derived from the iconography of the hero-god Dionysus as his predecessor in the conquest of the east.[75] Such a diadem would accord with Alexander's proclamation as King of Asia after Gaugamela, not with an assumption of the Persian kingship as Darius' successor.

2. The assumption of the Persian kingship probably required an act of enthronement.[76] The Achaemenid palaces contained thrones as permanent fixtures, and a portable throne accompanied the King in transit or in the field. No doubt Alexander came upon Darius' throne after each encounter with him. There is no indication that either then or in any of the great capitals, before or after the invasion of India, Alexander performed an act or ritual of enthronement.[77]

---

[74] On the upright tiara, see Ritter 1965: 6–18, with references.

[75] Above, n. 63.

[76] This may be inferred from the precedent of the Assyrians, for whom a regular enthronement ritual is attested (Meissner 1925: 63–4), from the prominence of the royal throne and the motif of the accession to the throne in Achaemenid iconography and inscriptions (see e.g. Krefter 1971: 57–9, 96–102, with *Beilagen*; Wilber 1989: pl. 12 and figs. 23–5, 60–1; Ghirshman 1957: figs. 6, 8, 10–11; von der Osten 1956: pls. 52–3, 62; Erdmann 1960: 29–47; Hinz 1979: 55, 63–4; Sarre and Herzfeld 1910: *passim*; Herzfeld 1920: *passim*), and from references to the Persian throne, and accession to the throne, in Graeco-Roman literature (Hdt. 3. 61, 64; 7. 15–16; Xen, *Anab.* 2. 1. 4; Pl. *R.* 8. 553C; Curt. 8. 4. 16–17; Plut. *Mor.* 338f; 340b; 488f; Nicolaus of Damascus, *FGrH* 90 F 60. 45; Val. Max. 5. 1; Front. *Strat.* 4. 6. 3. Cf. Germain 1956: 303–13; Alföldi 1950: 537–51).

[77] When he occupied Susa in 331, Alexander came upon Darius' throne during a tour of the royal palace, and on an impulse took a seat in it. Diod. 17. 66. 3–7; Curt. 5. 2. 13–15; Plut. *Alex.* 56. 1; *Mor.* 329d; *Ages.* 15. 4 (at *Alex.* 37. 7, Plutarch places the incident at Persepolis). I do not see how Berve 1938: 150 could take this as a rite of enthronement: 'Dass Alexander das persische Königtum übernahm [wird] an einer Anzahl von Massnahmen oder Handlungen deutlich. Zu Susa hatte er bereits vor aller Augen den Thron der Achämeniden bestiegen.' Correct, Altheim 1947: i. 175: Alexander's act 'war die übermütige Geste des Siegers, Ausfluss seines Temperamentes, nie aber der wohlüberlegte Anspruch auf Rechtsnachfolge'. So also Ritter 1965: 50: 'So ist der Schluss erlaubt, dass Alexander keine feierliche

3. Assumption of the royal titles. In addition to the
ubiquitous 'King', the titles of the Achaemenid kings were
'Great King', 'King of Kings', 'King over Pârsa', 'King of
Countries' (with such variants as 'King of countries containing all kinds of men', and 'King of many countries'), and
'King in this Earth' (with such variants as 'King in this great
earth far and wide' and 'King in all the earth'). They occur
on numerous inscriptions, weights, seals, and vases. In 83
(largely fragmentary) inscriptions published by Ronald
Kent, I have counted 'Great King' 51 times, 'King of Kings'
39 times, 'King of Countries' (with variants) 37 times, and
'King in the Earth' (with variants) 25 times.[78] There is no
evidence that Alexander adopted any of these titles. When
Plutarch in his *Life of Demetrius* (25. 3) says that Alexander
did not call himself 'King of Kings', he may be referring to
the notorious Persian title, and if so, we should infer from
the context (the contrast between Alexander's modesty and
Demetrius' pretentiousness) that he does not mean 'King of
Kings' in distinction to other Persian titles, but as representative of these titles. That is, Alexander did not call himself
what the Persian kings called themselves.

In a list of Achaemenid royal names on Babylonian astronomical texts, Alexander is mentioned as 'the great King' in
connection with his benefaction to the temple of Esagila.[79]
In the list, the names of kings, from Cyrus to Darius III,
appear either without title (20 times) or with 'the King'
following the name (22 times), and once with 'King of
countries' following the name. 'Great King' does not occur.
Is it possible that 'the great King' for Alexander is here
complimentary and descriptive rather than titular, in recognition of his benefactions to the Babylonian priests and his
conquest of Darius? To the Orientals, Alexander was now
naturally the 'great King'. But there is no evidence that
Alexander himself adopted, then or at any time, this (or any
other) Persian title.

Thronbesteigung inszeniert hat. Ein offizieller, öffentlicher Akt, mit dem
Alexander sich offen in die Tradition der Achämeniden gestellt hätte, wäre schwerlich aus der Überlieferung verschwunden.'

[78] Kent 1961: 116–57. Cf. Heinrichs 1987: 523–4; Griffiths 1953: 148.
[79] Sachs 1977: 129–47.

4. The consecration at Pasargadae. The new Great King apparently was required to undergo a 'royal initiation' at the hands of the Persian priests at Pasargadae as successor of the empire's founder Cyrus. Plutarch writes: 'A little while after the death of Darius (II), the [new] king journeyed to Pasargadae, in order to undergo the royal inauguration ceremony (τὴν βασιλικὴν τελετήν) at the hands of the Persian priests. There is here a sanctuary of a warlike goddess [Anahita] whom we might liken to Athena. Into this sanctuary it is necessary for the candidate to pass, and there to take off his own garb and put on that which Cyrus the Elder wore before he became king; and (then) he must consume a cake of figs, eat turpentine, and drink a cup of sour milk. Whatever else they do in addition is unknown to outsiders' (*Artax.* 3. 1–2, from Ctesias).[80]

At his occupation of Pasargadae in 330, Alexander paid his respects to Cyrus, known to the Greeks as a great ruler and a good man (Xen. *Cyrop.*), by ordering the restoration of his tomb (Aristobulus, *FGrH* 139 F 51a and b = Arr. 6. 29. 4–11 and Strabo 15. 3. 7; Plut. *Alex.* 69. 3–5; cf. Diod. 17. 81. 1–2; Curt. 7. 3. 3; Arr. 3. 27. 4–5). But there is no indication that, either then or at his second visit in 324, Alexander underwent the required inauguration ceremony at Pasargadae.

5. A consecration at Persepolis. It is very likely that the Persian kingship required for its legitimacy the performance by the King of the appropriate ritual acts at Persepolis as the servant and vicegerent of Ahuramazda.[81] Alexander could have ordered the reconstruction of the city at any time, as he had ordered repairs on temples in Egypt and the rebuilding of the huge temple tower Esagila in Babylon. On his return to the city in 324, Alexander 'did not approve the destruction' (Arr. 6. 30. 1). This was only politic as it accorded with

[80] On the sanctuary, see Calmeyer 1980: 306–7 (not accessible to me); on the ritual, see Alföldi 1951: 11–16; Widengren 1960: 225–37; Junge 1944: 49 and 169 n. 16; von der Osten 1956: 75; Cook 1983: 137. Cf. Badian 1996: 20: 'Pasargadae was the sacred capital, the place where the "mysteries" of the King's coronation took place.'

[81] Krefter 1971: 13: Persepolis 'war die Krönungs-, Huldigungs- und Begräbnisstätte aller Achämeniden Könige von Darius dem Grossen bis zu Dareios III. Kodomannos.' Pope 1957: 125: 'Persepolis was a ritual city . . . imbued with the peculiar virtue of royal authority, conferred by the power of Ahura Mazda.'

his new relationship with the Persians. But if Alexander had taken the much more noteworthy step of ordering the city's reconstruction, or at least made some amends, and if he had made some arrangement to secure his consecration by Ahuramazda as Darius' legitimate successor, this would probably not have gone unnoted.

6. Placing an Achaemenid emblem on his coins (?). As we have noted, probably before the start of the invasion in 334, Alexander issued his new imperial coinage, featuring his ancestor Heracles and Zeus the King on his silver tetradrachms, and Athena in Corinthian helmet and Nike on his gold staters.[82] These coins accorded well with Alexander's imperial ambitions. On crossing the Hellespont (334) to begin the campaign, he placed it under the special aegis of these same gods, Zeus, Athena, and Heracles, by dedicating altars to them on both sides of the strait (Arr. 1. 11. 7). At about the time of Gaugamela (331), Alexander ordered his eastern mints (Cilicia and Phoenicia) to replace on some of his gold staters the serpent on Athena's helmet with a lion griffin.[83] As G. F. Hill noted long ago, the Greeks traditionally regarded the lion griffin as 'the enemy par excellence of the Persians'.[84] Conversely, at no time subsequently did Alexander introduce on any of these coins an emblem of the Persian kingship, such as, perhaps, the archer or bow, the dentate crown, or the upright tiara.[85] On the contrary, as we have already noted, after his return from India, in 324, Alexander issued a commemorative decadrachm which featured on the obverse a full-length portrait of Alexander in full armour wielding a thunderbolt, with a winged Nike above him about to place a victory wreath on his head. The thunderbolt identified Alexander as son of Zeus, in accord with the revelation of Zeus Ammon in 331. While Zeus himself was featured as the King on Alexander's imperial tetradrachms, the Nike on the decadrachm recalls the Nike of Alexander's gold staters. There, Nike was anticipatory, now she crowns Alexander for his final conquest of

[82] Above, n. 18.
[83] Price 1991: 29.
[84] Hill 1923: 156–61.
[85] For Achaemenid royal coinage, see e.g. Root 1979: 116–18; Jenkins 1972: figs. 121, 116, 117, 122.

Asia. Thus on the decadrachm of 324 Alexander presented himself as the Hellenic/Macedonian warrior and conqueror of Asia, not as Great King of the Persian Empire.[86]

7. And, finally, beyond the Persian innovations I have cited, we know that the Persian kingship was circumscribed by a mass of rituals, taboos, and prohibitions.[87] Was Alexander, notoriously impatient of any restraints on the untrammelled exercise of his power, willing to assume such a burden? Not very likely.

CONCLUSION

There is little in our knowledge of Alexander's career that is certain, and the thesis I have presented here is no exception. But I hope to have shown that there is a very real possibility, if not a probability, that Alexander's kingship, as proclaimed at Arbela in 331, did not mean the Persian kingship, and that Alexander assumed the Persian kingship at no time subsequently. Instead, Alexander's kingship in Asia was a unique creation of Alexander himself. Subsequently to the death of Darius in 330, and significantly also after his return from India in 324, Alexander introduced into his kingship a series of innovations which were prompted by practical political and military considerations. The Persians could view these innovations as effecting the Persian kingship, and thus could more readily give their allegiance to Alexander as their rightful king and, if they wished, as 'Great King'. The Macedonians, on the other hand, at Arbela no doubt expected, with their traditional prejudice against barbarians and in reference to the war of revenge, that Alexander's new kingship would mean his despotic rule, with their support, over the Orientals. Alexander's innovations after Darius' death signalled, rather, his autocracy over the Macedonians as well as the Orientals. They did not, however, bring about, or constitute, the Persian kingship. That is, after Darius' death Alexander did not

---

[86] Above, n. 56.
[87] See e.g. Hinz 1979: 55–79, and *passim*; Widengren 1959: 242–57; Frye 1963: 90–107.

replace the constitutional basis of his kingship of Asia, as proclaimed at Arbela, by the Persian kingship in succession of Darius, but he developed, or reformed, his kingship by grafting onto it innovations that were designed, ultimately, to establish it as an absolute monarchy. Within this monarchy, legitimated by conquest and the will of the gods, the Macedonians were to be the leading component, but all subjects were to be equal with respect to Alexander as their absolute master. This, we may believe, was the true import of Alexander's prayer at Opis in 324, that 'the Macedonians and Persians should enjoy harmony as partners in the government' (ὁμόνοιάν τε καὶ κοινωνίαν τῆς ἀρχῆς Μακεδόσι καὶ Πέρσαις) (Arr. 7. 11. 9, trans. Brunt). The absolute master, however, was the King of Asia, not Great King of Persia.

6

Hephaestion's Pyre and the Royal Hunt of Alexander

OLGA PALAGIA

After Alexander's death, a series of monuments depicting him hunting a lion along with one or more Companions began to appear on the Greek mainland. Lion hunts thus re-entered the repertory of mainstream Greek art. They marked a new wave of Orientalism, introduced in Greek art in the wake of Alexander's conquests. They were short-lived, however, as they did not outlast Alexander's marshals. I would like to discuss here their history, meaning, and purpose in relation to the Successors' power struggles in the last decades of the fourth century. It will be argued that the lion-hunt iconography was borrowed from the east to emphasize the participants' intimacy with the king and that it was used by the Successors in their propaganda war to confer legitimacy on their aspirations to rule Alexander's empire. In this as in so many other things, they may have simply followed their leader.

The lion-hunt motif was first employed by Alexander to honour an intended successor. Hephaestion died at Ecbatana in autumn 324 and his body was conveyed by Perdiccas and the army to Babylon for burial some time in the next few months.[1] Alexander's choice of Babylon as Hephaestion's burial site must reflect his intention to move his capital there. A Greek lion excavated at Ecbatana

This chapter would not have been written but for the generous historical advice and encouragement of Brian Bosworth, who kindly provided a platform for it. I am grateful to Alain Pasquier for providing every facility for the study of the Messene relief, Louvre MA 858, and to Jean-Luc Martinez for his assistance. The photo Fig. 14 is reproduced by kind permission of Maria Lilimbaki-Akamati. I also gratefully acknowledge help from Ernst Badian, Richard Billows, John Boardman, Eugene Borza, Susan Rotroff, and Alan Shapiro. The drawing of the Mausoleum is reproduced courtesy of Geoffrey Waywell and the Trustees of the British Museum.

[1] Arr. 7. 14. 1–10; Diod. 17. 110. 7–8; Plut. *Alex.* 72; Just. 12. 12. 12. See also Heckel 1992: 65 and 88–9.

(Hamadan) probably commemorates Hephaestion's death.[2] There is no doubt that the funeral prepared by Alexander in spring 323 was fit for royalty or at least a king's heir.[3] The sacred fires of the Persians were extinguished throughout the Asian Empire as was customary at a Persian king's demise.[4] No wonder this was taken as an omen for Alexander's own death. Alone among the Companions who died during the campaign, Hephaestion received heroic cult, as attested by the ancient sources[5] and by a relief from Pella, Hephaestion's home town, dedicated by a certain Diogenes to the hero Hephaestion.[6] The cult at Pella was presumably founded by Antipater on Alexander's order.[7]

Hephaestion's funeral pyre, described by Diodorus, has been the subject of controversy on account of its vast scale and expense, as well as the limited amount of time allocated to its construction.[8] Alexander died barely eight months

---

[2] Lane Fox 1980: 384–5; Heckel 1992: 90 n. 150.

[3] e.g. Arr. 7. 16. 8.

[4] Diod. 17. 114. 4–5. See also Arr. 7. 14. 9; Heckel 1992: 89. On the sacred fire of the Persians see Briant 1996: 260–2.

[5] Hephaestion's heroization was authorized by the oracle of Ammon. Arr. 7. 14. 7; 7. 23. 6; Plut. *Alex.* 72. 3; Just. 12. 12. 12 (erroneously described as deification); Hyp. *Epitaph.* 21 (cult of Hephaestion in Athens). Diod. 17. 115. 6 erroneously states that Ammon approved of Hephaestion's deification: Alexander had requested it but Ammon only approved of heroic cult. Diodorus also says that Alexander had sacrifices performed to his friend as πάρεδρος θεός, presumably in relation to his own godhead. See also Habicht 1970: 30–5; Goukowski 1976: 274–5; Bosworth 1988b: 171, 288; Heckel 1992: 90 n. 150; Cawkwell 1994: 300; Badian 1996: 25. On the divinity of Alexander see Habicht 1970: 17–36; Badian 1981; Bosworth 1988b: 278–90; Badian 1996; Bosworth 1996b. Cults of Alexander: Stewart 1993: 419–20.

[6] Thessaloniki Museum 1084. Despinis *et al.*, 1997: no. 23, fig. 44 (Voutiras). Hephaestion's hairstyle (hair parted in the middle, sideburns) recalls Alexander's on the Alexander mosaic (Cohen 1997: pl. II) and must be a deliberate *imitatio Alexandri.*

[7] Compare Alexander's letter requesting Cleomenes to start a cult of Hephaestion in Alexandria : below, n. 44.

[8] On Hephaestion's pyre see Völcker-Janssen 1993: 100–16. Alexander ordered a pyre to be prepared in Babylon : Arr. 7. 14. 8. Description of the pyre: Diod. 17. 115. 1–5: αὐτὸς δὲ τοὺς ἀρχιτέκτονας ἀθροίσας καὶ λεπτουργῶν πλῆθος τοῦ μὲν τείχους καθεῖλεν ἐπὶ δέκα σταδίους, τὴν δ' ὀπτὴν πλίνθον ἀναλεξάμενος καὶ τὸν δεχόμενον τὴν πυρὰν τόπον ὁμαλὸν κατασκευάσας ᾠκοδόμησε τετράπλευρον πυράν, σταδιαίας οὔσης ἑκάστης πλευρᾶς. εἰς τριάκοντα δὲ δόμους διελόμενος τὸν τόπον καὶ καταστρώσας τὰς ὀροφὰς φοινίκων στελέχεσι τετράγωνον ἐποίησε πᾶν τὸ κατασκεύασμα. μετὰ δὲ ταῦτα περιετίθει τῷ περιβόλῳ παντὶ κόσμον, οὗ τὴν μὲν κρηπῖδα χρυσαῖ πεντηρικαὶ πρῷραι συνεπλήρουν, οὖσαι τὸν ἀριθμὸν διακόσιαι τεσσαράκοντα, ἐπὶ δὲ τῶν ἐπωτίδων ἔχουσαι δύο μὲν τοξότας εἰς γόνυ κεκαθικότας τετραπήχεις, ἀνδριάντας δὲ πενταπήχεις καθωπλισμένους, τοὺς δὲ μεταξὺ τόπους φοινικίδες ἀνεπλήρουν πιληταί. ὑπεράνω δὲ τούτων τὴν

after his friend and soon after the extravagant state funeral.[9] Diodorus' description seems to reflect a real monument. The actual pyre where the body was burnt should not be confused with the project for Hephaestion's tomb, misleadingly called a pyre by Diodorus, which was found among Alexander's last plans and quashed by Perdiccas and the army.[10]

Alexander had part of the city walls of Babylon demolished so that the bricks could be reused to form a huge platform on which to set up the pyre. The pyre itself was a hollow construction, consisting entirely of piles of palm trunks, abundant in Babylon. As it was all destined to the torch, it was presumably built of perishable, preferably combustible material and need not have taken too long to make, given a large workforce. Its exterior was decorated with five friezes. Diodorus does not specify their material but clay seems very likely;[11] in some cases this was gilded. The iconography must have been approved by Alexander since it seems to reflect his preoccupations during the last years of his life. It betrays an uneasy blend of religious and political symbolism of mixed Oriental and Macedonian origin. The pyre also took the form of a victory monument on account of the large number of military symbols. Several iconographic motifs are familiar from Attic grave monu-

δευτέραν ἐπανεῖχον χώραν δᾷδες πεντεκαιδεκαπήχεις, κατὰ μὲν τὴν λαβὴν ἔχουσαι χρυσοῦς στεφάνους, κατὰ δὲ τὴν ἐκφλόγωσιν ἀετοὺς διαπεπετακότας τὰς πτέρυγας καὶ κάτω νεύοντας, παρὰ δὲ τὰς βάσεις δράκοντας ἀφορῶντας τοὺς ἀετούς. κατὰ δὲ τὴν τρίτην περιφορὰν κατεσκεύαστο ζῴων παντοδαπῶν πλῆθος κυνηγουμένων. ἔπειτα ἡ μὲν τετάρτη χώρα κενταυρομαχίαν χρυσῆν εἶχεν, ἡ δὲ πέμπτη λέοντας καὶ ταύρους ἐναλλὰξ χρυσοῦς. τὸ δ' ἀνώτερον μέρος ἐπεπλήρωτο Μακεδονικῶν καὶ βαρβαρικῶν ὅπλων, ὧν μὲν τὰς ἀνδραγαθίας, ὧν δὲ τὰς ἥττας σημαινόντων. ἐπὶ πᾶσι δὲ ἐφειστήκεισαν Σειρῆνες διάκοιλοι καὶ δυνάμεναι λεληθότως δέξασθαι τοὺς ἐν αὐταῖς ὄντας καὶ ᾄδοντας ἐπικήδιον θρῆνον τῷ τετελευτηκότι. τὸ δ' ὕψος ἦν ὅλου τοῦ κατασκευάσματος πήχεις πλείους τῶν ἑκατὸν τριάκοντα.

[9] The funeral took place after the departure of the second lot of ambassadors from the Greek cities: Arr. 7. 23. 2; Diod. 17. 114. 1.

[10] Diod. 18. 4. 2. McKechnie 1995 argued that the pyre described by Diodorus was purely a rhetorical exercise. Bosworth 1988b: 164 questioned the existence of the pyre. For the actual pyre excavated in Babylon see below, p. 173.

[11] Clay capitals were used in the pyre of Derveni Tomb I, dating from c.320–290: Themelis and Touratsoglou 1997: 153, figs. 41–3. On the date of the Derveni tombs: Themelis and Touratsoglou 1997: 183–5. For the use of unbaked clay plaques in Athenian funerary monuments of the Hellenistic period see Grandjouan 1989: 42. Even their iconography is akin to some motifs of Hephaestion's pyre, for example wild animals and ships: Grandjouan 1989: 34.

ments of the fourth century, others will later occur in Macedonian tombs of the late fourth and third centuries.

The bottom course comprised gilded prows of quinqueremes carrying statues of kneeling archers and standing warriors, interspersed with palm columns.[12] Ships were again used in the decoration of Alexander's funeral cart.[13] The ships in the pyre are best interpreted as an allusion to Hephaestion's military command. Hephaestion is not known to have commanded a fleet except during the Tyrian campaign in 332,[14] but Alexander's last plans included the building of an enormous fleet and the transformation of Babylon into a grand naval base.[15]

Second from the bottom came a frieze of flaming torches resting on snakes. The handguards of the torches were decorated with gilded wreaths. Eagles flew off the top of the flames. The eagle carrying a snake in its claws is a well-known omen of victory.[16] In the time of the Successors an eagle carrying a snake was used as a heraldic device on the tomb of Alcetas at Termessus.[17] When not shown together, the eagle and snake belong to various manifestations of Zeus, the great god of the Macedonians. Whereas the eagle is the symbol of Zeus Olympius, both Zeus Ammon and Zeus Meilichius are sometimes represented in snake form. Given Alexander's association with Ammon,[18] the snakes in the pyre can more readily be attributed to him.[19] The funerary

[12] A marble pair of kneeling Scythian archers was used in a funerary monument from the Athenian Kerameikos: Athens, National Museum 823 and 824. Clairmont 1993: i, nos. 20a–b. Palm columns: I follow Miller's interpretation of φοινικίς (Miller 1986: 410–11).

[13] Diod. 18. 27. 1. Miller 1986.

[14] Curt. 4. 5. 10. Heckel 1992: 69–70.

[15] Arr. 7. 19. 4–6; Diod. 18. 4. 4; Curt. 10. 1. 19. Quinqueremes in Alexander's fleet: Arr. 7. 19. 3; 7. 23. 5. Bosworth 1988b: 170. Goukowski 1976: 273 also associates the pyre's ships with Alexander's last plans.

[16] Hom. *Iliad* 12. 200–7; Plut. *Timol.* 26. 6.

[17] Pekridou 1986: 88–100, pl. 10 with full discussion of the iconography of the motif.

[18] Bosworth 1988b: 282–3.

[19] Zeus Olympius holds an eagle on the coins of Alexander: Price 1991: pls. 18–141. Eagle holding Zeus' thunderbolt as a coin type of Alexander: Price 1991: pls. 143–4. Zeus Meilichius represented in snake form: Nilsson 1976: 411–16; Burkert 1985: 200–1. He was a deity of vegetation, also associated with the Underworld. Zeus Ammon in snake form as Alexander's real father: Plut. *Alex.* 3. 2. Zeus Ammon's snakes pointing the way to Siwah: Arr. 3. 3. 5. A colossal cult statue of a snake, probably Zeus Ammon, was excavated in the temple near the

symbolism of the torch is well attested in the Hellenistic period.[20] Torches are also associated with mystery cults, particularly those of Dionysus and Demeter and Kore, which held great promise for the afterlife.[21] The frequent appearance of Dionysus and the two goddesses in the iconography of Macedonian tombs and the inclusion of banqueting vessels and dining couches or thrones in virtually every tomb betray the popularity of their cults, especially Dionysus', in Macedonia.[22] The torches must belong to Dionysus judging by Alexander's intimate association with him.[23] This level is therefore of a religious character and seems to denote Hephaestion's regeneration and immortality: in other words, apotheosis. Alexander had hoped to achieve this through the divine agency of Ammon but the oracle only authorized the heroization of Hephaestion.[24] By the time Ammon's answer reached Babylon, however, the pyre was near completion transmitting the wrong message.

The third frieze is of great interest to our quest: it was decorated with a hunt involving a great variety of wild beasts. This level emphasized Hephaestion's intimacy with the king through his participation in a royal hunt. The fourth frieze was gilded, showing a centauromachy, which is also found in the Judgement Tomb at Leucadia at the end of the century.[25] The battle of Greeks and centaurs had served as an allegory of the fight against Persia since the Persian invasions of Greece in 490 and 480.[26] This level may be

theatre of Vergina in 1991: Saatsoglou-Paliadeli 1994: 12–16, pl. 21; ead. 1995: 53–5. Its date is unknown. This is so far the only cult statue of a snake from the Greek world. Snakes decorating Macedonian tombs: Miller 1993: 40 with n. 35.

[20] Palagia 1997: 71.

[21] Palagia 1997: 71 with nn. 53–4.

[22] Rape of Persephone fresco, Vergina Tomb I: Andronikos 1994. Vergina throne with painting of Pluto and Persephone: Ginouvès 1993: 160, fig. 137. Leucadia, Palmette Tomb with Pluto and Persephone fresco in lunette: Rhomiopoulou 1997: 31, 33, fig. 26. *Kline* from Potidaea with Dionysus: Sismanidis 1997: 63, pl. 4b. Bronze krater from Derveni with Dionysus and thiasos: Giouri 1978; Themelis and Touratsoglou 1997: 70–2, B 1, pls. 14–17. A banqueting frieze and a torch procession decorate the newly discovered Macedonian tomb of *c.*300 at Agios Athanasios near Thessaloniki: Tsimbidou-Avloniti 1997.

[23] Goukowski 1981; Bosworth 1996b.

[24] Above, n. 5.

[25] Petsas 1966: 100–7, colour plates 1; 3–4; 10. 1.

[26] Castriota 1992: 40–2.

interpreted as an allusion to Hephaestion's contribution to Alexander's panhellenic campaign against Persia. Finally, the top frieze, also gilded, had a series of alternate lions and bulls, symbols of the gods of Babylon, Ishtar and Adad respectively.[27] These animals functioned as guardians of the pyre.[28] The door to Alexander's funeral cart was equally guarded by lions (Diod. 18. 27. 1).

Macedonian and barbarian arms, no doubt real ones, were piled on top of the pyre, intended to burn with the corpse. Such a scene, with armour piled on top of a pyre, is depicted on an Apulian volute-krater of the 330s showing the funeral of Patroclus.[29] The arms bring to mind Arrian's (7. 14. 9) statement that the Companions dedicated their weapons to the dead Hephaestion. Aelian (*VH* 7. 8) says that Alexander burnt his own arms along with him. The dedication of barbarian and Macedonian arms is described by Diodorus as a symbol of conquest and defeat but it may have also symbolized universal mourning for Hephaestion in Alexander's Asian empire.

According to Aelian (*VH* 7. 8), gold and silver objects were thrown into the fire,[30] and Diodorus (17. 115. 1) mentions gold and ivory figurines of Hephaestion commissioned by the Companions in order to please Alexander. Arrian's statement (7. 14. 9) that the Companions dedicated themselves to Hephaestion probably alludes to the dedication of miniature ivory portraits. Among the small ivories excavated in the tombs of Macedonia some are taken for portraits, though most formed part of the decoration of wooden funerary couches. The burnt ivory eyes found in Derveni Tomb I indicate the inclusion of statues of perishable material in Macedonian pyres.[31] Finally, around or on top of the pyre were set up hollow statues of sirens, capable

---

[27] Roux 1992: 391–3.

[28] Compare the pairs of lions on top of the Mausoleum (Fig. 1) (Waywell 1978: 27–34) and of griffins on the Belevi tomb (Ridgway 1990: 188; Webb 1996: 78, figs. 32 and 37). For these monuments see below, n. 33.

[29] Naples, Museo Nazionale 81954. *LIMC* i (1981), s.v. Achilleus, no. 487 (A. Kossatz-Deissmann).

[30] Compare the gold and silver cups given by Alexander to Calanus for burning on his funeral pyre: Arr. 7. 3. 2.

[31] The couches are now collectively discussed by Sismanidis 1997, 134–53. Ivory eyes from Derveni: Themelis and Touratsoglou 1997: 57, pl. 59.

of accommodating real singers, who sang laments at the funeral. Their performance at any rate would have preceded the cremation. The introduction of real-life laments indicates that the pyre described by Diodorus served for the cremation of Hephaestion's body and was not a permanent memorial. Laments played on the flute also accompanied the conveyance of the remains of Demetrius Poliorcetes from Corinth to Demetrias (Plut. *Demetr.* 53. 2–3). Representations of sirens are familiar from Attic funerary iconography of the fourth century[32] and recur in the funerary couch of the third-century Belevi tomb, which seems to have been built for Lysimachus but was possibly used for Antiochus II.[33]

Archaeology has confirmed the accuracy of Diodorus' account. The remnants of Hephaestion's pyre were identified by Koldewey while he was excavating Babylon in 1904.[34] He found a huge brick platform, surviving to a height of about 7.5 metres. The bricks had been piled up and then burnt in an intense fire which preserved on them the imprints of burnt palm trunks. This platform is just inside the city walls, east of the palace and north of the Greek theatre built by Alexander. The fact that it stands within the city walls suggests a heroon rather than a simple funerary monument. In addition, Manolis Andronikos' excavation of Tomb II at Vergina uncovered, above the tomb, the remnants of a pyre, built on a brick platform. The pyre had the form of a building with a door (including a door knocker) and contained burnt arms and armour, animal bones, the trappings of four horses (presumably sacrificed), clay and bronze pots, a gold wreath and small ivories from a wooden couch.[35] The pyre of Derveni Tomb I had the form

[32] e.g. Athens, National Museum 774 and 775. Clairmont 1993: i, no. 2a–b.

[33] Ridgway 1990: 194, pl. 88. On the Belevi tomb see now Webb 1996: 76–9, fig. 32. This tomb, remarkable for its blend of Greek and Persian iconography, has parallels with Hephaestion's pyre. The centauromachy is another common motif.

[34] Koldewey 1914: 310–11; Wetzel, Schmidt, Mallwitz 1957: 3, pls. 2 and 19b; Oates 1986: 159.

[35] Andronikos 1984: 69; Phaklaris 1986; Themelis and Touratsoglou 1997: 166. The contents of this pyre are now on display in the Great Tumulus Museum at Vergina. Other remnants of pyres adjacent to Macedonian tombs are discussed in Miller 1993: 62–4; Themelis and Touratsoglou 1997: 146–8. The pyres were supported by bricks and contained wooden couches with ivory and glass orna-

of a Doric building with clay column capitals.[36] Better still, a monument similar to Hephaestion's pyre from the late fourth century was excavated at Salamis, Cyprus.[37] As it resembles no other funerary monument on the island, its origin is almost certainly Macedonian. Originally dubbed Nicocreon's pyre, it could be more readily associated with the fateful naval battle at Salamis between Ptolemy and Demetrius Poliorcetes in 306.[38] Plutarch (*Demetr.* 17. 1) records a magnificent burial generously provided by Demetrius for his dead opponents. An even more magnificent burial for his own people may be postulated.

The Salamis pyre rests on a brick platform, about a metre high. Its remains contained burnt arms and armour, gilded clay objects as well as real gold wreaths, and, most important of all, the fragments of sixteen large statues of men and women of unbaked clay which were burnt by the fire. The surviving five heads are thought to be portraits. Life-size clay heads of men and women, belonging to two distinct types, were also found by Andronikos over an early fifth-century tomb in the cemetery of Vergina. These were interpreted as chthonic deities.[39] On top of the Salamis pyre a stone pyramid was erected as a permanent memorial. The addition of a stone monument to the remnants of the pyre may serve as an explanation of Diodorus' enigmatic phrase about Alexander's unrealized plans for the completion of Hephaestion's pyre.[40] Diodorus in fact refers to the tomb,

ments, gilded clay and wooden objects, arms and armour, animal bones, silver vessels, and a single example of an Orphic text on papyrus.

[36] Themelis and Touratsoglou 1997: 150–4.

[37] Karageorghis 1969: 171–99, pls. 152–8 and 171; Karageorghis 1992. The tumulus was 10m. high, with a 50m. diameter at the base. No human remains were found inside.

[38] On the battle and its consequences: Plut. *Demetr.* 15–17; Diod. 20. 47–53. Gruen 1985; Billows 1990: 152–5. Karageorghis 1992 identified the Salamis pyre as the cenotaph of King Nicocreon of Salamis and his family, who were once thought to have committed mass suicide in 311, and attributed it to Demetrius Poliorcetes, who would have built it in 306. Diod. 20. 21. 1–3, however, makes it clear that the mass suicide was committed by the family of King Nicocles of Paphos: see also Billows 1990: 143.

[39] Kottaridou 1989; Ginouvès 1993: 32–5; Themelis and Touratsoglou 1997: 155. For a free-standing clay hunting group of small size found in the pyre of Tomb IV at Vergina see Drougou *et al.* 1996: 47.

[40] Diod. 18. 4. 2: ὁ γὰρ Περδίκκας παραλαβὼν ἐν τοῖς ὑπομνήμασι τοῦ βασιλέως τὴν

which he misleadingly calls a pyre. In the light of the
Salamis pyre we can visualize Hephaestion's tomb as a stone
building erected on the brick platform of the original pyre,
and taking a form not dissimilar to it: a high podium
decorated with friezes and topped by a pyramid. The tomb
was of course never built. Petrified pyres like the one at
Salamis were already in existence by 323, erected by fourth-
century satraps with dynastic ambitions, like the Mausoleum at Halicarnassus (Fig. 1)[41] and the Nereid Monument
at Xanthus.[42] They too contained friezes around the podium
with statues all over, and the Mausoleum was topped by a
stepped pyramid. In sum, Hephaestion's pyre entailed the
deification of its owner. His permanent tomb, on the other
hand, would have denoted a founder hero by analogy with
the Mausoleum (Mausolus as the second founder of Halicarnassus), which Alexander had surely visited.[43] Alexander
instructed Cleomenes to erect two *heroa* of Hephaestion in
Alexandria, where Hephaestion's name was to be invoked in
all commercial contracts.[44] The iconography of the pyre
suggests that Alexander acknowledged Hephaestion's share
in his own power and glory not only on a mundane but also
on a celestial level.[45]

The important point about Hephaestion's pyre is the
introduction of an animal hunt frieze, presumably at the
instigation of Alexander. This motif comes at the end of a
long Oriental tradition. Though hunters are sometimes
shown in Greek grave monuments of the Classical period,

τε συντέλειαν τῆς Ἡφαιστίωνος πυρᾶς, πολλῶν δεομένην χρημάτων . . . ἔκρινε συμφέρειν
ἀκύρους ποιῆσαι.

[41] Mausoleum: Waywell 1978; Hornblower 1982: 223–74; Clayton and Price
1988: 100–23 (G. B. Waywell); Jeppesen 1992; Jeppesen 1998.

[42] Childs and Demargne 1989.

[43] Hornblower 1982: 258–61.

[44] Arr. 7. 23. 7: ἔλεγε γὰρ ἡ ἐπιστολὴ κατασκευασθῆναι Ἡφαιστίωνι ἡρῷον ἐν
Ἀλεξανδρείᾳ τῇ Αἰγυπτίᾳ, ἔν τε τῇ πόλει αὐτῇ καὶ ἐν τῇ νήσῳ τῇ Φάρῳ, ἵνα ὁ πύργος
ἐστὶν ὁ ἐν τῇ νήσῳ, μεγέθει τε μέγιστον καὶ πολυτελείᾳ ἐκπρεπέστατον, καὶ ὅπως
ἐπικρατήσῃ ἐπικαλεῖσθαι ἀπὸ Ἡφαιστίωνος, καὶ τοῖς συμβολαίοις καθ' ὅσα οἱ ἔμποροι
ἀλλήλοις ξυμβάλλουσιν ἐγγράφεσθαι τὸ ὄνομα Ἡφαιστίωνος. Hephaestion's name on
contracts would have been appended to the king's name and regnal year as an additional honour or it may even have provided the chief means of dating.

[45] Alexander had offered Hephaestion a share of the empire by marrying him to
his wife's sister, Drypetis, at Susa in 324: Arr. 7. 4. 5. Heckel 1992: 86–7. Above, n.
5, for a possible association of the cults of Hephaestion and Alexander.

FIG. 1. The Mausoleum at Halicarnassus. Drawing by Susan Bird. After P. A. Clayton and M. J. Price, *The Seven Wonders of the Ancient World* (London 1988) fig. 61 on p. 119.

they only hunt hares and do not ride. The quarry is rarely, if ever, shown.[46] Mounted hunters in pursuit of wild animals, common in funerary monuments of the Persian Empire in the fourth century, are completely unknown on the other side of the Aegean before Alexander's conquest of Asia.[47] Panthers, boars, bears, stags are hunted in close proximity indicating that the hunt takes place in a game preserve. There is no evidence that such parks existed in Macedonia before the death of Alexander. After the battle of Pydna in 168 BC the Romans found game parks in Macedonia (Polyb. 31. 29. 3–4) but these may well have been introduced after the conquest of Asia. The game parks (*paradeisoi*) of the Persian Empire are described by Xenophon (*Cyrop.* 1.4. 5–11; 6. 28–9) as exercise grounds, where the hunt of wild animals forms part of an aristocrat's military training, sometimes even a substitute for war. Hunters may come across boars, bears, panthers and all manner of wild beasts in one day. Such parks were artificial not only as regards the animals reared in them but also the trees and plants they contained, which were often imported at great expense. Game parks in the age of Alexander are certainly attested in Syria, Persia, Babylon, and Sogdiana.[48]

Persian mounted hunters are illustrated on Graeco-Persian gems of the fifth and fourth centuries.[49] A grave relief of the early fourth century from Çavuşköyü (Daskyleion) shows a Persian nobleman hunting a boar.[50] The dead tree tends to be a stock motif, indicative of the countryside, and we often see it in friezes.[51] There are hunting friezes in three monumental tombs created by Greek artists for Persian satraps in Caria and Lycia in the first half of the fourth century. A panther and boar hunt appears on

[46] e.g. Attic grave relief, Basle, Antikenmuseum BS 233/5 175 + Brauron Museum BE 812. Clairmont 1993: i, no. 1. 289.

[47] Except for the lekythos of Xenophantus, showing a Persian royal hunt in a Babylonian setting: below, n. 117.

[48] Achaemenid *paradeisoi*: Tuplin 1996: 88–131. Arr. *Ind.* 40. 4; Arr. 7. 25. 3; Plut. *Demetr.* 50. 5–6; Diod. 16. 41. 5; 19. 21. 3; Curt. 8. 1. 11–19. See also below, nn. 70–1.

[49] Boardman 1970: 314–16, pls. 886; 888–9; 904–5; Anderson 1985: 67–8, fig. 25.

[50] Istanbul Archaeological Museum 1502. Pfuhl and Möbius 1977: i, 30, no. 73, pl. 19; Anderson 1985: fig. 26. For a list of representations of hunts from Asia Minor see Kleemann 1958: 132–3.

[51] Dead tree as a stock motif: Carroll-Spillecke 1985: 153.

the north frieze of the heroon of Trysa.[52] The mounted
hunters on the east frieze of the temple of the Nereid
Monument from Xanthus hunt a boar, panther, and bear.[53]
The Mausoleum of Halicarnassus had a free-standing hunting group, which included a boar and panther.[54] A fragment
of a mounted Persian hunter in the British Museum is
among the finest sculptures of the Mausoleum.[55]

Further hunting scenes were created by Greek artists for
royal patrons in Phoenicia under Persian rule. The royal
cemetery of Sidon, excavated in 1887, contained eighteen
sarcophagi, two of which are Phoenician anthropoid, two are
Egyptian, and the rest Greek.[56] King Tabnit's name, inscribed on one of the anthropoid sarcophagi, shows that the
burial ground was reserved for royals.[57] Four of the sarcophagi in pure Greek style carry scenes relating to the lives of
Phoenician dynasts. They include hunting episodes. We
begin with the three that pre-date Alexander. The so-called
Satrap Sarcophagus, dating from the last quarter of the fifth
century, shows mounted Persians hunting a panther and stag
(Fig. 2).[58] The so-called Mourning Women Sarcophagus,
attributed to Strato I and dated to the 350s, has a hunting
scene running round the bottom ledge. Persians on foot and
horseback hunt a boar, bear, panther, and deer in a landscape interspersed with dead trees (Figs. 3–5).[59] The so-
called Lycian Sarcophagus of the first quarter of the fourth
century has hunting scenes on each of the long sides: a
mounted boar hunt (Fig. 6) and a lion, hunted from a pair of
four-horse chariots (Fig. 7)—which brings us to the lion-
hunt motif.[60]

Lion hunts in Archaic and Classical Greek art are confined

---

[52] Vienna, Kunsthistorisches Museum. Oberleitner 1994: 46, figs. 99–100.
[53] London, British Museum. Childs and Demargne 1989: 279–83, pls. 115–19.
[54] London, British Museum. Waywell 1978: 172–5.
[55] London, British Museum 1045. Waywell 1978: 110–12, fig. 34.
[56] Gabelmann 1979; Hitzl 1991: 73–9.
[57] Istanbul Archaeological Museum 78. Tabnit died c.520. Hitzl 1991: 74–5.
[58] Istanbul Archaeological Museum 367. Kleemann 1958: 125–39, pls. 2b and
8–11; Hitzl 1991: cat. 16.
[59] Istanbul Archaeological Museum 368. Fleischer 1983: 30–5, pls. 12–17; Hitzl
1991: cat. 18.
[60] Istanbul Archaeological Museum 369. Schmidt-Dounas 1985: 61–70, pls. 2; 6;
Hitzl 1991: cat. 17.

FIG. 2. Satrap Sarcophagus. Istanbul Archaeological Museum 367.
Photo DAI Istanbul 70/42.

FIG. 3. Mourning Women Sarcophagus. Istanbul Archaeological
Museum 368. Photo DAI Istanbul R 1771.

FIG. 4. Mourning Women Sarcophagus. Istanbul Archaeological
Museum 368. Photo DAI Istanbul R 19. 737.

FIG. 5. Mourning Women Sarcophagus. Istanbul Archaeological
Museum 368. Photo DAI Istanbul R 19. 738.

FIG. 6. Lycian Sarcophagus. Istanbul Archaeological Museum 369.
Photo DAI Istanbul 71/59.

FIG. 7. Lycian Sarcophagus. Istanbul Archaeological Museum 369.
Photo DAI Istanbul 71/58.

to the mythological episode of Heracles killing the Nemean
lion.[61] No lions were to be found south of Thrace (Hdt. 7.
125) and Greek artists had no first-hand knowledge of them.
The exception that proves the rule is the statue base of the
pancratiast Pulydamas of Scotussa. Even though he won an
Olympic victory in 408, his statue was only set up in
Olympia in the fourth century, created by the sculptor
Lysippus as a posthumous, imaginary portrait.[62] Pulydamas

---

[61] *LIMC* v (1990), s.v. Herakles, pp. 16–34 (W. Felten).
[62] Paus. 6. 5. 1–7. Paus. 6. 5. 4 echoes Hdt. 7. 125. Base: Olympia Museum L 45.
Moreno 1987: 43–55; 1995: 91–3.

had acquired quasi-heroic stature since his exploits went beyond the Olympic stadium. He was reputed to have killed two lions with his bare hands, which placed him on a par with Heracles. The first lion he encountered had strayed from Thrace onto Mt. Olympus; the second was in Asia, where he travelled at the invitation of Darius II. The reliefs on the base record the two historic encounters with the lions. It is interesting that the association with the lion carries heroic connotations and nothing else.

Not so in Asia, where lions were symbols of kingship.[63] Assyrian palace reliefs of the eighth and seventh centuries illustrate ceremonial hunts by the Assyrian kings, taking place in the game parks of Babylonia, as indicated by the palm trees and the lush vegetation.[64] The royal hunts were carefully controlled affairs. On the reliefs the king hunts on foot, from a chariot, or on horseback, using bow and arrow, javelin and sword, while the lions are released from cages. At the end of the day the king offers libations over the dead lions. Lion hunting is clearly interpreted as a ritual act, one of the duties of kingship.

The hieratic lion hunts were taken up by the Achaemenid successors of the Assyrian Empire and reflected in their minor arts.[65] According to Herodotus (3. 129), Polybius (frg. 133), and Diodorus (15. 10. 3), the Persian king always hunted on horseback or riding a chariot. Among the earliest representations is a gold scabbard cover of the sixth or fifth century from the Oxus Treasure in the British Museum.[66] A cylinder seal of Darius I shows him shooting lions from a chariot in a Babylonian landscape of palm trees.[67] Graeco-Persian gems may bear the only images of non-royal Persians hunting lions, but these were private documents of limited circulation.[68] In the context of the art of Asia, the Lycian sarcophagus from Sidon showing a lion hunt

[63] Royal hunts of the Assyrians and Persians: Briant 1996: 242–4.
[64] Reade 1983: 53–60; Anderson 1985: 63–7; Briant 1991: 219; Collon 1995: 152–6.
[65] Kleemann 1958: 127–8; Briant 1991: 217–22.
[66] Curtis 1989: 52, fig. 60.
[67] London, British Museum 89337, Collon 1995: fig. 146a; *Alessandro Magno* 1995: 261, cat. 57.
[68] Boardman 1970: pl. 889. Graeco-Persian gem with the Great King hunting a lion on horseback: Boardman 1970, fig. 293.

FIG. 8. Floor mosaic from Pella. Pella Archaeological Museum. Photo T.A.P.

FIG. 9. Alexander Sarcophagus. Istanbul Archaeological Museum 370. Photo DAI Istanbul 8111.

conducted from chariots (Fig. 7) must be attributed to one of the kings of the city.

Participation in a royal hunt had its hazards. The king would not tolerate anyone striking at the quarry before him (Plut. *Mor.* 173d). Not only does Xenophon (*Cyrop.* 4. 6. 3–4) relate such a story about the king of Assyria, but closer to home, Alexander had the royal page Hermolaus flogged for anticipating his strike at a boar (Arr. 4. 13. 2). On the other hand, Tiribazus was known to have enjoyed the favour of Darius II for saving his life when a pair of lions attacked him (Diod. 15. 10. 3). The records of Alexander's campaign mention three lion hunts. They are all associated with one or other of the Companions who either came to the king's rescue or distinguished himself by killing a particularly ferocious beast. Clearly the Companions had an interest in keeping such memories alive in their later years. So long as Alexander was alive, they enjoyed his gratitude and special favour. After his death, however, when every man was out for himself, the lion imagery acquired a deeper significance.

The earliest known episode is a lion hunt in Syria in 332, before the death of Darius, where Alexander's life was preserved thanks to the intervention of Craterus. The story is recounted in the dedicatory inscription of Craterus' Monument at Delphi, on which more below.[69] It is also known to Plutarch (*Alex.* 40. 4–5), who was aware of the significance of the lion hunt as a quest for supreme power. He has a Laconian ambassador describe that particular hunt as Alexander's struggle for the kingship. In another lion hunt in Syria, Lysimachus distinguished himself by killing a ferocious lion of exceptional size; in later years he would boast of the scars made by the animal's claws. When Lysimachus attempted to spear a lion before Alexander, however, in the game park of Bazeira (Sogdiana) in 328, he was rebuked and reminded of his misadventure in Syria.[70] We have seen that Hermolaus the page had been flogged for

[69] Below, nn. 71 and 73.

[70] Lysimachus and the lions: Curt. 8. 1. 14–17; Plut. *Demetr.* 27. 3; Paus. 1. 9. 5; Just. 15. 3. See also Briant 1991, 215–16; 222; Heckel 1992: 268–69; Lund 1992: 6–8. Justin's story that Alexander threw Lysimachus into a lion's cage is surely apocryphal.

a similar offence. Was Alexander's more tactful treatment of
Lysimachus due to his higher status as a Bodyguard? In any
event, Alexander succeeded in killing the lion at Bazeira
with no help from his friends. Curtius (8. 1. 18) relates that
Alexander in fact took so many risks during that hunt, that
afterwards the Macedonians voted that he should never
again risk his life by hunting on foot or without company.
Arrian (4. 13. 1), however, says that the Macedonian king
always hunted on horseback in the Persian manner, in the
company of his pages, and that Philip II introduced this
practice. Lacking a similar hunting episode in relation to
Alexander, Perdiccas had to make up his own: Aelian (*VH*
12. 39) preserves a story of the marshal entering a lion's den
and stealing its cubs.

We do not know whether Alexander treated such royal
hunts as anything more than sport. In retrospect they
acquired a symbolic significance: those who had hunted
with him were entitled to a share of his rule. The trend
was set by 321, when Craterus commissioned a bronze
group to be erected at Delphi in commemoration of the lion
hunt in Syria, and had himself represented as coming to
Alexander's rescue.[71] Craterus chose Alexander's own
favourite sculptors: Lysippus was his best portrait maker,[72]
and Leochares had made the gold and ivory Argead family
group at Olympia (Paus. 5. 20. 9–10). The Delphi group of
the two hunters, the quarry, and the dogs must have been
colossal, judging by the size of its niche. No horses are
described by the ancient sources and the mention of man-to-
lion combat (εἰς χέρας ἀντιάσαντα) in the inscription suggests
that the two hunters faced the lion on foot. The dedicatory
inscription credits the monument to Craterus' son, Craterus
the Younger, but he would have been barely one year old at
his father's death.[73] Craterus' widow, Phila, would have set

---

[71] Pliny, *NH* 34. 64; Plut. *Alex.* 40. 5; *FdD* III. 4. 2 (Paris, 1954), no. 137, pl. 23
(inscription: below, n. 73); Hölscher 1973: 181–4; Saatsoglou-Paliadeli 1989;
Völcker-Janssen 1993: 117–32; Stewart 1993: 270–7; 390–1; Moreno 1995: 35. The
'high' chronology adopted in this article follows Bosworth 1992.

[72] Plut. *Alex.* 4. 1; Pliny, *NH* 7. 125. Further sources: Stewart 1993: 360–2.

[73] Υἱὸς Ἀλεξάνδρου Κράτερος τάδε τὠπόλλων[ι] | ηὔξατο τιμάεις καὶ πολύδοξος ἀνήρ·
| στᾶσε, τὸν ἐν μεγάροις ἐτεκνώσατο καὶ λίπε παῖδα, | πᾶσαν ὑποσχεσίαν πατρὶ τελῶν,
Κράτερος, | ὄφρα οἱ ἀΐδιόν τε καὶ ἁρπαλέον κλέος ἄγραι, | ὦ ξένε, ταυροφόνου τοῦδε
λέοντος ἔχοι· | ὅμ ποτε, Ἀλ[εξά]νδρωι τότε ὅθ' εἵπετο καὶ συνεπόρθει | τῶι

up the group soon after his death. Lysippus' last recorded activity is the design of an amphora for the foundation of Cassandreia in 316 and he would have been an old man by then (Athen. 11. 784c), so the completion of the monument probably pre-dates 316.

Craterus' intention transpires from the inscription: he had saved the life of the king of Asia from a bull-killing lion. The Oriental lion-versus-bull imagery recalls the reliefs on the Apadana staircase in the royal palace at Persepolis.[74] It is implicitly royal. According to Arrian (*Succ.* F 19), Craterus dressed and behaved like a king and imitated Alexander in all but the royal diadem. The Delphi Monument was a political statement: he was about to cross the Aegean with Antipater, regent of Macedon and his own father-in-law, claiming the rule of Asia from Perdiccas.[75] His stature and popularity in the Macedonian army was so great, that Eumenes was only able to defeat him by concealing his identity from the rank and file (Plut. *Eum.* 6. 7). The colossal scale of the bronze group was worthy of a Successor. Years later, when Craterus was long dead, Cassander visited Delphi and was overwhelmed by the impact of the monument even though he was already master of Greece (Plut. *Alex.* 74. 6).

A floor mosaic of the late fourth century, excavated in one of the dining rooms of the 'House of Dionysus', a palatial mansion at Pella, shows two Macedonians hunting a lion on foot, using spear and sword (Fig. 8).[76] They are both heroically nude but for a billowing chlamys, and shown as equals, with the king on the left being differentiated by his kausia. The egalitarian spirit of the mosaic reflects the mores of the Macedonian nobles: not for them the mounted king in mixed Oriental dress (see below). This mosaic has long been thought to represent Craterus coming to Alexander's res-

πολυαιν[ήτωι τ]ῶιδε Ἀσίας βασιλεῖ, | ὧδε συνεξαλάπαξε, καὶ εἰς χέρας ἀντιάσαντα | ἔκτανεν οἰονόμων ἐν περάτεσσι Σύρων.

[74] *Alessandro Magno* 1995: 244.

[75] Voutiras 1984.

[76] Pella Museum. The 'House of Dionysus' is dated to the last quarter of the 4th cent. and is the largest private house found at Pella: Makaronas and Giouri 1989: 160–8. On the mosaic: Robertson 1982: 246; Stamatiou 1988: 214–15, pl. 39, 2; Makaronas and Giouri 1989: 167–8, pl. 25b; Ginouvès 1993: 121, 126, fig. 112; *Alessandro Magno* 1995: 221–2.

cue.[77] It is a very attractive interpretation, which fits both Craterus' high standing in Alexander's court and his distaste of Alexander's Orientalism, and entails ownership of the house by Craterus' family.[78] Since no dogs are involved, however, it need not be a direct reflection of the Delphi group.

Another sculptured lion hunt involving Alexander is the relief frieze on the so-called Alexander Sarcophagus from Sidon (Figs. 9–11).[79] It was excavated in the royal necropolis of Sidon and is stylistically the latest of the relief sarcophagi from the cemetery. By general consensus, it is attributed to Abdalonymus, the last Phoenician king of Sidon, who owed his appointment to Alexander after the battle of Issus.[80] Hephaestion had acted as the king-maker.[81] Abdalonymus is mentioned in the ancient sources only in connection with his rather unorthodox rise to power.[82] He is also epigraphically attested by a bilingual dedication to Aphrodite by his son, found on Cos.[83] The end of his rule is unknown. It has been suggested that it came to an end after the battle of Gaza in 312 or that it went down to 306/5 to coincide with the end of the mint of Sidon.[84]

In addition to a number of battles between Macedonians and Persians, the sarcophagus carries two hunting scenes. Although the iconography follows the usual pattern of battles and hunts of the satrapal funerary monuments, it probably commemorates historic events. Persians hunt a panther on one of the narrow sides (Fig. 9), [85] while Macedonians and Persians hunt a lion and stag on one of the long

[77] For an alternative interpretation as Hephaestion: Moreno 1993: 103–4, figs. 6–7, 9, 11.

[78] The mosaic of Dionysus riding a panther (Robertson 1982: 243, fig. 1; Makaronas and Giouri 1989: 167, pl. 24) from the same house may be taken as an allusion to Alexander's conquest of India. On Alexander/Dionysus, conqueror of India, see Bosworth 1996b.

[79] Istanbul Archaeological Museum 370. Von Graeve 1970; Hölscher 1973: 189–96; Stamatiou 1988: 211–12, pl. 39,1; Messerschmidt 1989; Billows 1990: 8 with n. 19; Hitzl 1991: cat. 19; Stewart 1993: 422–3, figs. 101–6.

[80] On Abdalonymus see Messerschmidt 1989; Billows 1990: 444–5; Grainger 1991: 34–5, 61–2.

[81] Heckel 1992: 69.

[82] Diod. 17. 47. 1–6; Curt. 4. 1. 16–26; Just. 11. 10. 9.

[83] Kantzia 1980: 1–16; Sznycer 1980: 17–30.

[84] Mint of Sidon: Price 1991: 435–6.

[85] Von Graeve 1970: pls. 42–5.

FIG. 10. Alexander Sarcophagus. Istanbul Archaeological Museum 370.
Photo DAI Istanbul 8120.

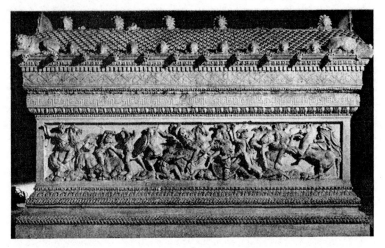

FIG. 11. Alexander Sarcophagus. Istanbul Archaeological Museum 370.
Photo DAI Istanbul 8122.

sides (Fig. 10). Alexander has been recognized near the left edge of the principal battle scene on account of his lion-scalp helmet (Fig. 11).[86] He spears a Persian rider whose horse is collapsing under him. This may be a stock motif, as it is repeated in the Alexander mosaic. But whereas the Alexander Sarcophagus almost certainly represents the battle of Issus,[87] which had special significance for Abdalonymus, the Alexander mosaic may be a depiction of the battle of Gaugamela.[88]

Alexander is placed in a corresponding position in the lion hunt and his regal status is implied by the depression for the addition of a royal diadem (Fig. 10). An alternative identification as Demetrius Poliorcetes is less likely, unless the sarcophagus was made after his adoption of the royal title in 306/5. But we have no reason to believe that he also adopted Alexander's unorthodox attire.[89] On both sides of the sarcophagus Alexander wears an Oriental-style chiton with tight-fitting sleeves and an overfall, similar to those worn by the Persians. He omits, however, other paraphernalia of Persian dress like the trousers and tiara. His attire must be retrospective, for it was only after Darius' death in 330 that Alexander adopted a mixed Persian and Macedonian dress, his purple chiton with white central stripe being Persian, whereas his chlamys and shoes were Macedonian.[90] Alexander's dress is adopted by another Macedonian on the sarcophagus, also wearing a Boeotian helmet, in the centre of the battle scene. He is generally recognized as Hephaestion, Abdalonymus' patron:[91] his wholesale adoption of Alexander's Oriental policies could easily have extended to matters sartorial.

---

[86] Von Graeve 1970: 133–6, pls. 24,1; 25,1; 26; 49.

[87] Von Graeve 1970: 133.

[88] Hölscher 1973: 145–51. On the mosaic see now Cohen 1997.

[89] The identification with Demetrius was suggested by Charbonneaux 1952 (*non vidi*). Contra Hölscher 1973: 189 n. 1183; Briant 1991: 216 n. 8. On the coronation of Demetrius in 306/5 cf. the sources cited above, n. 38. There is no suggestion that Demetrius' clothes were other than Macedonian: Plut. *Demetr.* 41. 4–5; 44. 6; Athen. 12. 535f–536a.

[90] Arr. 4. 7. 4; 4. 9. 9; Diod. 17. 77. 5; Athen. 12. 537e = Ephippus, *FGrH* 126 F 5; Athen. 12. 535f = Duris, *FGrH* 76 F 14; Curt. 6. 6. 4; Plut. *Alex.* 45. 2; Plut. *Mor.* 329f–330a = Eratosthenes, *FGrH* 241 F 30; Just. 12. 3. 8. Further references in Stewart 1993: 352–7. See also von Graeve 1970: 85–6; Badian 1996: 21 with n. 48.

[91] Von Graeve 1970: 151, pls. 28–9; 53,1; 55,1; Dintsis 1986: 3, pl. 2,6.

In the hunting scene Alexander rides behind a horseman in full Persian dress, almost certainly Abdalonymus, whose horse is being attacked by a ferocious lion.[92] Another Persian on foot is about to strike the lion with an axe, while a third horseman in Macedonian chlamys and short chiton, usually identified with Hephaestion, attacks from the right.[93] The fact that Hephaestion hunts the lion on horseback as an equal of the two kings accords well with his quasi-royal appearance before the mother of Darius after the battle of Issus.[94] He was perhaps the only Companion who had assumed regal airs with Alexander's full approval. If the lion hunt is a historic event, it could be a memorial to one of Alexander's famous hunting expeditions in the game parks of Syria. Abdalonymus, being his appointee, would have had every reason to commemorate his participation in such an expedition. His appearance alongside Alexander certainly enhanced his claim to the throne of Sidon even though he came from a lateral branch of the royal house. Since we do not know what became of him during the wars of the Successors, he may well have had a reason to press his claim not recorded in our sources.

We now come to the most intriguing of Alexander's hunts, the fresco on the façade of Tomb II at Vergina (Fig. 12). This tomb was excavated by Manolis Andronikos in 1977 and still awaits full publication.[95] It housed the cremated remains of a mature man and a young woman, buried in pomp with a glittering array of gold and silver objects. This is not the place to discuss the complex problems of the tomb's date but I agree with the majority of scholars that it is a royal burial.[96] This is suggested not only by the richness of the funerary paraphernalia but also by the iconography of the lion-hunt fresco, a motif suitable for royalty, and by the gold diadem which was worn over a cloth or skin hat (presumably a *kausia diadematophoros*, a Macedonian

[92] Von Graeve 1970: 136–8, pls. 24,1; 25,1; 38 (Abdalonymus); 48; 51, 1.
[93] Von Graeve 1970: pl. 53,2.
[94] Arr. 2. 12. 7; Diod. 17. 37. 5–6; Curt. 3. 12. 17. Heckel 1992: 69. For Hephaestion's imitation of Alexander's hairstyle see above, n. 6.
[95] Preliminary report: Andronikos 1984: 97–197.
[96] For doubts that the Great Tumulus of Vergina contains royal tombs see Faklaris 1994; Themelis and Touratsoglou 1997: 143 with n. 51.

Olga Palagia

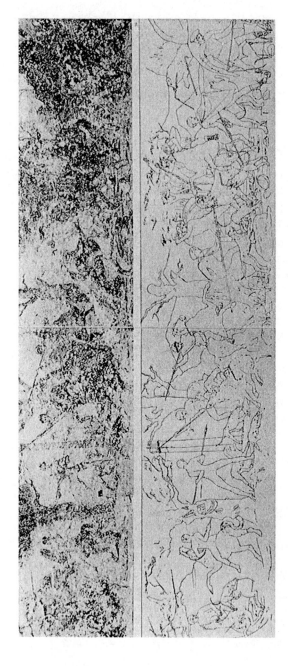

Fig. 12. Hunting frieze from Tomb II at Vergina. Drawing by G. Miltsakakis. After M. Andronikos, *Vergina* (Athens 1984), fig. 59.

king's hat introduced by Alexander himself according to Athen. 12. 537e).[97] The excavator's belief that it covered the remains of Philip II and his wife Cleopatra has not been universally accepted.[98] The alternative identification of the tomb's owners as Philip III Arrhidaeus and his wife Adea Eurydice, originally proposed by Phyllis Lehmann and endorsed by Eugene Borza, is more in accord with the situation in Macedonia after Alexander's death which seems to be reflected in the tomb.[99] Not only was the later royal couple of approximately the same age group as the earlier one,[100] but also no such quantities of gold and silver were available to the Macedonians before Alexander's conquests.[101] The gilded arms and armour deposited near the queen in the antechamber suggest a royal archer and invoke the royal insignia of the Achaemenids: a *gorytos* filled with arrows, greaves of uneven height (presumably to facilitate kneeling) and a spear.[102] Adea Eurydice, who had an additional claim to kingship as the daughter of Amyntas IV, had a military upbringing thanks to her mother, Cynnane, daughter of Philip II and the Illyrian Audata.[103] Borza has suggested that the tomb contained some of Alexander's paraphernalia.[104]

[97] On the gold diadem and kausia see Andronikos 1984: 171–5.

[98] Andronikos 1984: 226–33. Followed, among others, by Prag 1990; Hammond 1991: 73–82; Briant 1991: 242–3; Hatzopoulos 1994: 92–111; Prag and Neave 1997: 53–84. For a discussion of the various possibilities see Miller 1993: 3.

[99] Lehmann 1980 and 1982; Borza 1987; 1992: 261–2. See also Adams 1980 and 1991; Robertson 1982: 246; Tripodi 1991; Baumer and Weber 1991; Stewart 1993: 274, fig. 11.

[100] In their forties and late teens–early twenties respectively. For the ages of Philip III Arrhidaeus (born *c*.358) and Adea Eurydice (born *c*.338–336) see Berve 1926: 11, nos. 781 and 23. For the ages of the tomb's occupants (35–55 for the man and 19–28 for the woman) see Xirotiris and Langenscheidt 1981: 153; 155; Musgrave 1991, 3–4. According to Xirotiris and Langenscheidt 1981, the man's bones show no eye or leg injuries. This conflicts with the interpretation of Musgrave, Prag and Neave, recently again summarized in Prag and Neave 1997: 53–84.

[101] Cf. Alexander's speech at Opis: Arr. 7. 9. 6. Despite the exaggeration of Alexander's rhetoric, the archaeological record confirms that the amount of gold and silver found in Tomb II is unparalleled in Macedonia. On the riches amassed as a result of the Macedonian conquest of Persia see now Themelis and Touratsoglou 1997: 186.

[102] Compare the Great King represented as an archer carrying a spear on golden darics: Briant 1996: 227–8, fig. 11.

[103] Athen. 13. 560f = Duris, *FGrH* 76 F 52; Polyaen. 8. 60. See also above, n. 100.

[104] Borza 1987. See also below, n. 159.

The iconography of the gold and ivory shield,[105] depicting Achilles and Penthesilea, is particularly apt for Alexander, who claimed Achilles as an ancestor and used him as a role model. A shield with a similar Achilles and Penthesilea device is associated with Alexander in Roman medallions of the third and fourth centuries AD. On one of the Aboukir medallions of the third century AD Alexander receives the shield from Nike;[106] a number of brass contorniates minted in Rome in the second half of the fourth century AD show Alexander as the new Achilles holding the same shield on his lap, the rest of his armour on the ground.[107] The Aboukir medallions are attributed to Caracalla or to one of his immediate successors.[108] Caracalla had visited Alexander's mausoleum in Alexandria and presumably removed Alexander's arms and drinking cups which he is known to have used in Rome afterwards.[109] Alexander's shield would have thus ended up in Rome and it may well have carried an Achilles and Penthesilea device similar to the Vergina shield. Finally, the only datable objects found inside Tomb II, four clay spool salt cellars of the Attic variety, are confined to the last quarter of the fourth century according to the publication of comparable examples from the Athenian Agora.[110]

The iconography of the hunting fresco may also support the attribution of Tomb II to Arrhidaeus, who was a non-combatant in Alexander's campaign and therefore we should not expect any battle scenes to have adorned his tomb.[111]

---

[105] Illustrated in Andronikos 1984: fig. 93.

[106] Alföldi and Alföldi 1990: 111, pl. 245,3. Legend: *ΑΛΕΞΑΝΔΡΟΣ ΒΑΣΙΛΕΥΣ*.

[107] Alföldi 1943: 103, no. 7, pl. III 6–7; Alföldi and Alföldi 1990: 111–12, pls. 22,7–12; 23,1. Legend: *ΑΛΕΞΑΝΔΡΟΣ ΒΑΣΙΛΕΥΣ*; Berger 1994: no. 56L.

[108] *The Search for Alexander* 1980: 103–4, nos. 10–11; 115, no. 33; Stewart 1993: 50–1.

[109] On Caracalla see Dio 78. 7. 1; Herodian 4. 8. 9. The sources do not explicitly say that Caracalla removed anything from Alexander's *sema*, but considering Macedonian burial practices of placing arms and drinking vessels in tombs, the implication is that this is where Caracalla acquired them. Alexander's arms were placed in the funeral cart (and conveyed to Alexandria): Diod. 18. 26. 4.

[110] Rotroff 1997: 166 with n. 71 dates the Agora examples to 325–295. Two clay spool salt cellars were also found in the Derveni tombs, dated by their excavators to 320–290: Themelis and Touratsoglou 1997: 184. Abundant pottery was recovered from the pyre of Vergina Tomb II, but it is still unpublished: above, n. 35.

[111] The newly reconstructed frieze on one side of the king's funerary couch, found in the main burial chamber and now in the Great Tumulus Museum at

The fresco is damaged in places and not always easy to 'read'. It is a frieze-like compendium of hunting scenes in a wooded, rocky setting with a plain in the middle and mountain ridges looming on the horizon. There are eight dogs,[112] three hunters on horseback and seven on foot. All but one is youthful and beardless. Only a drawing prepared for Andronikos' original report has ever been published (Fig. 12), and it attempts to interpret rather than represent.[113]

The abrupt transitions of the terrain, the different varieties of trees, including two dead ones, and the incongruous cohabitation of disparate animals such as a bear,[114] a lion, a boar, and two deer suggest that the hunting campaign is taking place in a large game park, perhaps over several days. The composition is divided into groups around each animal, with a distinct concentration of figures on the right side, which is clearly open-ended, as the last hunter has no quarry (Fig. 13). If we assume that the fresco derives from a panel painting in one of the Macedonian palaces at Pella or Aegae,[115] the hunter at the extreme right may be an excerpt of a scene of hunters with nets, omitted from the fresco. This might explain why the lion episode is slightly off-centre. It might also help shift the emphasis from the young horseman wreathed with leaves to the bearded one spearing the lion. The trappings of a rural sanctuary indicate that the scene is set in a sacred grove. A votive tablet and a ribbon hang from a tree;[116] a tall pillar topped by three posts stands

Vergina, is also thought to show a mounted hunt though no trace of wild beasts is evident. Previous restoration: Andronikos 1984: fig. 75. A second funerary couch, perhaps with battle scenes between Greeks and Persians on both sides, accompanied the queen's burial in the antechamber.

[112] On the dogs see Reilly 1993.

[113] Drawing: Andronikos 1984: fig. 59; Miltsakakis 1987. Andronikos 1984: 106–19, figs. 58–69 on the hunting fresco.

[114] The bear bites a broken javelin. This hunting motif is more common with lions and appears on the coins of Amyntas III, Perdiccas III and Cassander: Miller 1991: 54–5; Tripodi 1991: 148; Briant 1991: 238–40; Greenwalt 1993: 515–19. The projecting parts of the axles of the wheels of Alexander's funeral cart were decorated with gilded lion heads gnawing a javelin: Diod. 18. 27. 3.

[115] Frescoes in Macedonian tombs could have had contemporary variants more accessible elsewhere, as attested by the Rape of Persephone in Vergina Tomb I, known from two Roman versions: Oakley 1986; Andronikos 1994: 105–6; 127–130. Borza 1987 attributed Tomb I to Philip II, his last wife, Cleopatra, and their infant daughter. See also Adams 1991.

[116] Tree with votive tablets: compare the red-figure calyx-krater in Berlin,

FIG. 13. Hunting frieze from Tomb II at Vergina, detail. After M.
Andronikos, *Vergina* (Athens 1984) fig. 63.

nearby, and these may be the legs of a tripod stand rather
than the aniconic statuettes implied by the restoration.[117]
Tripods are sacred to both Apollo and Dionysus; the present
one could indicate that the game park is sacred either to
Apollo, one of the patron gods of hunting, or to Dionysus,
the most popular god of the Macedonians.

The lion hunt is based on stock motifs familiar from the
Alexander Sarcophagus, only more spread out, with a
hunter on foot replacing the mounted Abdalonymus and
equally interposing himself between the king and his quarry.
A young horseman, set apart and framed by two dead trees,
dominates the centre. His isolation may denote heroization
and the dead trees may for once be meaningful, indicating
that he is no longer among the living. He is wreathed with

Staatliche Museen v. 1. 3974, *LIMC* vii (1994), s.v. Telephos, no. 55 (M. Strauss).
Tree with ribbons: compare the votive relief in Munich, Glyptothek 206, Smith
1991: fig. 214.

[117] Compare a royal hunt of Darius and Cyrus (named) in a game park with
tripods and palm trees on the late 5th-cent. Attic relief lekythos signed by
Xenophantus, from Kerch, now in St Petersburg, Hermitage *Π* 1837. 2. Tripodi
1991: 163–5; Tiverios 1997.

laurel and has big, fierce eyes. He wears an Oriental-style purple chiton with an overfall, similar, but for the lack of sleeves, to Alexander's chiton on the Alexander Sarcophagus. He also wears a bracelet and shoes. His pose is very similar to the fighting Alexander on the Alexander Sarcophagus, and Andronikos had no difficulty identifying him with Alexander.[118] The purple chiton must be a sign of royalty. There is no evidence that Macedonian royalty used it before Alexander.[119] Alexander's wreath may be an allusion to heroic status as witness the heroes of the Calydonian boar hunt on an Apulian calyx-krater of the fourth century.[120] Under normal circumstances, the central position in the frieze would be reserved for the owner of the tomb,[121] but this is no ordinary burial and the fresco was not painted under normal circumstances.

The bearded horseman about to spear the lion from the right towers above everyone else and is the only one who has eye contact with the animal. The prey is almost certainly his. He may well be the tomb's owner. Andronikos had arrived at the same conclusion and identified him with Philip II on account of his beard, which he thought indicated an older person.[122] He interpreted all beardless figures except Alexander as royal pages in Philip's court.[123] The hunters wearing kausias and chlamydes, however, are obviously adult men, not adolescents.[124] If we place the hunters in Alexander's court, however, bearing in mind that Alexander had introduced the fashion of shaving one's chin (Athen. 13. 565a), we are obliged to stand the question on its head. The

---

[118] Andronikos 1984: 116. He was alternatively identified with Alexander IV (though he is a mature man, not a boy) by Tripodi 1991: 147.

[119] Royal purple: e.g. Curt. 4. 1. 23; Plut. *Pyrrh*. 8. 1. No sign of royal purple in Macedonia before Alexander: Reinhold 1970: 29.

[120] Berlin, Staatliche Museen 3258. Anderson 1985: fig. 19. *LIMC* vi (1992), s.v. Meleagros, no. 27 (S. Woodford). That Alexander's wreath implies posthumous heroization was also suggested by Baumer and Weber 1991: 34.

[121] So Stewart 1993: 276. See also above, n. 118.

[122] Andronikos 1984: 116. See also Baumer and Weber 1991: 34.

[123] Andronikos 1984: 117. On the institution of royal pages introduced by Philip II in imitation of Persian practice: Arr. 4. 13. 1; Curt. 5. 1. 42; 8. 6. 2–6; Aelian, *VH* 14. 48; Kienast 1973: 28–32.

[124] As pointed out by Prestianni Giallombardo 1991. Hatzopoulos 1994: 92–111 attempted to categorize them as royal youths (νεανίσκοι) but there is no evidence of such a group in the courts of Philip II or Alexander.

bearded rider is the odd man out, perhaps older, but also defying court fashion. Despite the poor preservation, we can still see that he is dressed in purple.[125] The analogy with Alexander on the Alexander Sarcophagus is evident. In terms of the composition, however, this figure occupies Hephaestion's place in the hunt, a position analogous to royalty. Philip III Arrhidaeus is perhaps the best candidate for this figure.[126] He was barely two years older than Alexander[127] but the beard may be explained in various ways. Either he was not allowed to use razors being half-witted,[128] or his appearance in the fresco reflects his actual appearance at the time of his death. We should expect him to have cultivated a public image close to Philip II, whose name he adopted upon his accession.[129] Arrhidaeus has been tentatively recognized as the bearded man wearing a royal diadem in the pediment of the Alexander Sarcophagus which represents the murder of Perdiccas.[130] It is perhaps no accident that he is the only bearded figure in the entire sarcophagus. His royal dress in the hunting frieze may be retrospective.[131] Or it may be accurate. Brian Bosworth has argued that in 324 Alexander proclaimed his half-brother king of Babylon, a ceremonial title given to a close relative of the Great King.[132]

Alexander and Arrhidaeus apart, only the hunter with the net at the extreme right wears a chiton (Fig. 13). Andronikos restored him as a Macedonian wearing a kausia, a chiton with short sleeves, and an animal-skin cape. His tall hat, however, is far more exotic than a kausia; moreover, his skin

[125] His headdress was thought to be a lion-skin cap by Tripodi 1991: 191 n. 104.

[126] Also suggested by Tripodi 1991: 147.

[127] Berve 1926: 11, no. 781: above, n. 100.

[128] Arrhidaeus' mental condition: Diod. 18. 2. 2; Plut. *Alex.* 10. 2; 77. 7–8; Just. 13. 2. 11; 14. 5. 2. See Heckel 1992: 144–5 with n. 434.

[129] He was named Philip by the army: Curt. 10. 7. 7; Diod. 18. 2. 4.

[130] Von Graeve 1970: 138–42, pls. 67; 68,1; Stewart 1993: 301–2. Perhaps the little ivory head from the king's funerary couch in Vergina Tomb II identified by Andronikos (1984, figs. 79–81) with Philip II, could be Philip III Arrhidaeus instead. An identical head, probably showing the same man, must come from the other side of the couch (Andronikos 1984: fig. 86). All other heads are beardless. One may draw parallels with the hunting fresco on the tomb façade. In fact, at least one side of the couch may show a royal hunt: above, n. 111.

[131] Like Alexander's dress in the Alexander Sarcophagus.

[132] Bosworth 1992: 75–9. The physical presence of the king in Babylon was essential for the annual celebration of the New Year festival: Oates 1986: 108.

is darker than that of the other hunters. Alone among the hunters he uses a safe weapon, the net, and is denied their heroic nudity. His distinctly Oriental air suggests that he may be one of the Oriental noblemen, including the brothers of Rhoxane and Barsine, recruited by Alexander into the royal squadron in 324 and issued with Macedonian equipment (which would explain the Greek chiton and boots) (Arr. 7. 6. 4–5).

The hunter who stands between Alexander and the lion is a magnificent figure, iconographically related to representations of Meleager in the Calydonian boar hunt.[133] He proudly displays a purple kausia and chlamys, royal gifts that Alexander, after his return from India,[134] and later Eumenes,[135] were in the habit of distributing. Even though the figure is highly idealized, perhaps a certain individual is meant.[136] One cannot help thinking of Cassander, who presented himself as King Philip Arrhidaeus' champion in 317[137] and commissioned his and Adea Eurydice's tomb in 316, celebrating their burial with funeral games,[138] several months after their assassination by Olympias.[139] Even if Alexander had not presented Cassander with purple garments, Cassander could easily have pretended that he did receive them. Alternatively, the garments may symbolize his closeness to Arrhidaeus, whose successor he aimed to be. It may be no accident that Cassander's eldest son was named Philip, emphasizing the ties with his grandfather Philip II and his uncle Philip III.[140]

---

[133] e.g. gilded relief hydria of the third quarter of the 4th cent., Istanbul Archaeological Museum 2922. *LIMC* vi (1992), s.v. Meleagros, no. 32 (S. Woodford).

[134] Plut. *Mor.* 11a; Athen. 12. 537e=Ephippus, *FGrH* 126 F 5; 12. 539e; 12. 540a. Fredricksmeyer 1994: 154–5.   [135] Plut. *Eum.* 8.

[136] Moreno in *Alessandro Magno* 1995: 142 identified him with Ptolemy and the hunter with the axe with Hephaestion.

[137] Diod. 19. 11. 1; 19. 35. 1; Just. 14. 5. 2–3. Adams 1974: 89; Hammond and Walbank 1988: 139–40; Carney 1994: 367–8. The hunter in purple kausia and chlamys was also identified with Cassander by Baumer and Weber 1991: 37.

[138] Diod. 19. 52. 5; Athen. 4. 155a. Cassander also gave a royal burial to Adea Eurydice's mother, Cynnane, killed by Alcetas in 321. On her murder see Arr. *Succ.* F 1. 22–3; Polyaenus 8. 60.

[139] Diod. 19. 11. 4–7; Just. 14. 5. 10; Paus. 1. 11. 3–4; 1. 25. 6; 8. 7. 7; Aelian, *VH* 13. 36. See also Adams 1974: 91; Carney 1994: 368–70.

[140] Philip IV: Plut. *Demetr.* 36. 1; Just. 15. 4–16. 1. 1; Paus. 9. 7. 3. Hammond and Walbank 1988: 210.

In 316 Cassander made a number of moves calculated to bring him closer to the throne of Macedon.[141] Not only did he bury Arrhidaeus with a pomp that was a successor's duty, he also married Alexander's half-sister, Thessalonice, and founded Cassandreia, calling it after his own name, a king's prerogative.[142] One of the demes of Thessalonice, which he also founded, was named after Alexander's famous horse, Bucephalas.[143] His refoundation of Thebes in 316 increased his standing with the Greeks.[144] More pertinent to our theme is Cassander's patronage of the arts.[145] In 316 he hired Lysippus, Alexander's sculptor, to design an amphora for Cassandreia (Athen. 11. 784c).[146] The mutual antipathy between Alexander and himself notwithstanding,[147] he did not hesitate to glorify his wife's half-brother and sons' uncle: not only did he name his youngest son Alexander,[148] he also commissioned a painting of the battle of Alexander and Darius from Philoxenus of Eretria (Pliny *NH* 35. 110). Vergina Tomb III, containing the remains of an adolescent boy now generally thought to belong to Alexander IV, must have been built at Cassander's instigation.[149] Last but not least, Cassander was responsible for the royal palace at Vergina (Aegae).[150]

[141] Diod. 19. 52. 1–6. For an assessment of Cassander's actions in 316 see Adams 1974: 97–103; Goukowski 1978: 105–11; Hammond and Walbank 1988: 145–6; Miller 1991; Carney 1994: 376–7.

[142] Billows 1995: 90 on the founding of cities as a royal act. Marriage to Thessalonice: Diod. 19. 52. 1; Paus. 9. 7. 3; Just. 14. 6. 13. Foundation of Cassandreia: Diod. 19. 52. 2; Strabo 7 frg. 25.

[143] Steph. Byz. s.v. Boukephaleia. Foundation of Thessalonice: Strabo 7 frgs. 21, 24–5. On the foundations of Cassandreia and Thessalonice see Vokotopoulou 1997.

[144] Diod. 17. 118. 2; 19. 52. 2; Paus. 9. 7. 2; Athen. 1. 19c.

[145] Hammond and Walbank 1988: 209–10. On Cassander's building activity inside Macedonia attested by the archaeological record see Themelis and Touratsoglou 1997: 190; Pandermalis 1997: 42; Stephanidou-Tiveriou 1997: 216–18; Phaklaris 1997: 70.

[146] For a possible portrait of Cassander by Lysippus in Athens see Palagia 1998. Another portrait of Cassander was erected by the Rhodians in the agora of their city for his help against Demetrius' siege in 304: Diod. 20. 100. 2.

[147] Diod. 17. 118. 2; Paus. 9. 7. 2; Plut. *Alex.* 74, *Mor.* 180f. Bosworth 1988*b*: 162.

[148] Alexander V: Plut. *Demetr.* 36. 2–6; Paus. 9. 7. 3; Just. 16. 1. 1. Hammond and Walbank 1988: 210.

[149] Tomb III and Alexander IV: Andronikos 1984: 198–217; Borza 1987; Musgrave 1991: 7–8; Adams 1991; Miller 1993: 4; Drougou *et al.* 1996: 62–7.

[150] Andronikos 1984: 38–46; Ginouvès 1993: 82–8.

Let us now turn to the left half of the composition. It is taken up by four boys, three being naked, the fourth wearing a cloak billowing in the wind over his left arm. They hunt deer and a boar. The pair hunting the boar do so without nets, spearing it head on, in the manner of young Macedonians earning their right to recline at table (Athen. 1. 18a). These boys may well be royal pages, who were known to accompany the king in his hunting expeditions since the days of Philip II.[151] The special emphasis given to the royal pages in such a fresco can be readily explained if we bear in mind that two of Cassander's younger brothers, Iolaus and Philippus, acted as royal pages to Alexander. Iolaus was dead by 316.[152] The year before, Olympias had overturned his grave in revenge for his alleged murder of Alexander and assassinated Cassander's brother Nicanor as a reprisal for the same crime, which she laid at the door of Antipater's family (Diod. 19. 11. 8).

If Cassander deftly manipulated the arts to convey political messages, the hunting fresco may be interpreted in such a light. It could be a memorial to a royal hunt, which took place in a game park in Babylon in spring 323, shortly after Cassander's arrival there.[153] Alexander kept lions in Babylon as attested by Plutarch (*Alex.* 73. 6), where an ass killing the king's biggest lion was taken as a portent of death. The participation of Cassander and his brothers in a royal hunt involving both Alexander and his immediate successor, Philip III, would have served the double purpose of pointing out Cassander's claim to the throne of Macedon and of exonerating himself and his brothers from Alexander's alleged poisoning.[154]

What of the Greek-looking trees, however, and the mountainous ground? Theophrastus says that Alexander ordered Harpalus to introduce Greek trees in the gardens of

[151] Arr. 4. 13. 1. See also above, n. 123.

[152] On Cassander's brothers as royal pages: Arr. 7. 27. 2; Curt. 10. 10. 14; Just. 12. 14. 9; Heckel 1992: 293–5. At the risk of over-interpretation, one might suggest that the dead Iolaus is the nude horseman turning his back to the spectator.

[153] Cassander in Babylon: Arr. 7. 27. 1–2; Diod. 17. 118. 1–2; Curt. 10. 10. 17; Plut. *Alex.* 74. 2. That the Vergina fresco depicts an Oriental lion hunt was first suggested by Robertson 1982: 246.

[154] Alexander's alleged poisoning: Bosworth 1988b: 162; 171–3; Heckel 1992: 293 n. 115.

Babylon, laying emphasis on leafy plants to provide shade in the blazing hot landscape.[155] The mountainous landscape is reminiscent of Macedonia and Andronikos had indeed suggested that the hunting scene is set there. Babylon is situated in a flat area. Perhaps the Greek artist of the Vergina fresco improvised.[156] A good parallel is provided by Italian Renaissance depictions of the Holy Land, all based on the Italian countryside. Finally, the sacredness of the game park brings us back to the motif of the ceremonial lion hunts of the Assyrians and the Achaemenids. It is the only evidence so far that some of Alexander's royal hunts may have involved a ritual element.

In conclusion, we shall discuss briefly a number of monuments in Macedonia and mainland Greece from the period of the Successors. A life-size horseman in Pentelic marble from Pella (Fig. 14), with rough-picked back for attachment to a wall, may have belonged to a funerary hunting or fighting group by comparison to a boar hunt group in Pentelic marble from the cemetery of Vergina (Veroia Museum).[157] The Pella horseman wears an Oriental chiton, albeit sleeveless, and a chlamys. His dress is reminiscent of that worn by Alexander in the Vergina hunting fresco (Fig. 12). His lowered right arm, possibly once holding a spear, and the striding horse find their closest parallels in the horseman on the now lost fresco of the Kinch Tomb at Leucadia.[158] He too wears an Oriental chiton with sleeves and a Persian tiara under a Macedonian helmet of a type similar to that found in Vergina Tomb II. It is remarkable that his headdress is identical to Alexander's on the so-called Porus medallions.[159] These two figures, along with Alexander on the Alexander Sarcophagus and the Vergina hunting frieze are, apart from the putative Hephaestion on the

---

[155] *History of Plants* 4. 4. 1; Plut. *Mor.* 648c.

[156] Carroll-Spillecke 1985: 182–4: the artist replaced the Persian *paradeisos* with a Greek sacred grove. Briant 1993: 272–3 postulates the introduction of Persian *paradeisoi* in Macedonia after Alexander's death: cf. Polybius 31. 29. 3–4.

[157] Both monuments are unpublished.

[158] Miller 1993: 109–10, pl. 8a.

[159] Vergina iron helmet: Andronikos 1984, 140–1, figs. 97–8. Borza 1987 suggests that this helmet belonged to Alexander. 'Porus medallions': Price 1991, 51; 452; 456–7, pl. 159G–H; Stewart 1993: 201–7, fig. 69; *Alessandro Magno* 1995: 241, no. 33; Lane Fox 1996.

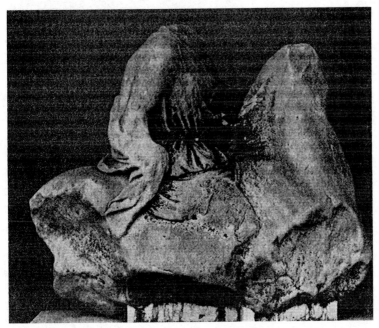

FIG. 14. Marble horseman in Oriental chiton. From Pella. Pella Archaeological Museum. Photo author.

Alexander Sarcophagus, the only Macedonians in Oriental chiton known so far. Could they all be representations of Alexander? Only the discovery of further monuments can shed light on this question.

Cassander must have been responsible for a group of portraits viewed by Pyrrhus in Larissa: Philip, Alexander, Perdiccas, Cassander, and 'the other kings' (Lucian, *Adv. Ind. et Libr. Mult. Em.* 21). Lucian may be accused of two faux pas: he uses the singular εἰκών for portrait, instead of the plural, εἰκόνες, and counts Perdiccas among the kings. The mythical founder of the Argeads has been postulated,[160] but even this would not explain Cassander's presence in an Argead group portrait. Perdiccas III, Philip II's predecessor and brother, or even Perdiccas the Bodyguard should not be ruled out. After Alexander's death and until his own, Perdiccas the Bodyguard was king in all but name (Diod. 18.

[160] Stewart 1993: 411–12.

36. 7). If we take Philip to mean Philip III Arrhidaeus rather than Philip II, a historic occasion might be found for a grouping of these figures. They could all have met in Babylon in the last months of Alexander's life. The use of the singular εἰκών could signify not an array of single portraits but an action group. Perhaps Lucian describes a hunting group consisting of Alexander, Arrhidaeus, Cassander, Perdiccas, and possibly other Companions who later attained kingship, Lysimachus for example. The fresco of Vergina Tomb II immediately springs to the mind. Considering Cassander's championship of Arrhidaeus, such a monument would have made sense in 317 or 316, when Perdiccas was but a harmless memory and Lysimachus a trusted ally.

Lysippus' son and pupil, Euthycrates, was responsible for a bronze group of Alexander hunting, dedicated at Thespiae.[161] It is not clear whether Alexander was shown alone or with a Companion. As Thespiae was a faithful ally of Macedon, the patronage of this group should be attributed to a master of Macedon who had also hunted with Alexander. Since Euthycrates was a son of Lysippus, his career would have spanned the late fourth and early third centuries. Cassander is perhaps the most obvious candidate but Polyperchon cannot be entirely ruled out.

Polyperchon's patronage could be postulated for an architectural relief frieze from Messene (Figs. 15–18).[162] A single block survives from a slightly curved frieze, dated on stylistic grounds to around the turn of the fourth century or the early years of the third. The block has been ascribed to a round base of colossal dimensions. But round bases are rare at all times and there are no other such bases from the early Hellenistic period.[163] We assume that the block formed part of a hunting frieze, involving more animals and hunters like the Vergina fresco to which it is iconographically related. It may have belonged to a funerary monument (a tholos) rather than a base. Funerary monuments in the form of naiskoi

---

[161] Pliny, *NH* 34. 66; Hölscher 1973: 185–6.

[162] Made of marble, not limestone as usually described. If a base, its estimated diameter would be 1. 50m. Paris, Louvre MA 858, Stewart 1993: 276–7; 427, fig. 89; Moreno 1995: 174.

[163] Jacob-Felsch 1969: 79; Schmidt 1995: 30–8.

have indeed been found inside the walls of Messene. The relief is usually taken to reflect Craterus' Monument at Delphi.[164] The rider on the left is unmistakably Macedonian as witness his kausia, Macedonian chlamys, and belted chiton with short sleeves. The lion hunt would have involved the king, so Alexander must have been represented. He is usually identified with the hunter wielding an axe and wearing a lion-skin, by comparison with Heracles, Alexander's mythical ancestor.[165] But the hunter with the axe, indispensable to all lion hunts, was meant to deal the final blow to the beast. One hardly expects him to be one of the leading players of the drama, as the nobles would have hunted with spears and swords, as on the Pella mosaic (Fig. 8). He is more likely a barbarian by analogy with the Persian wielding an axe on the Alexander Sarcophagus (Fig. 10). His nudity and lion-skin recall the Indian tribe of the Sibi, who claimed descent from Heracles and were dressed in animal skins.[166] Alexander is not likely to be the mounted hunter either, because he lacks the diadem and Oriental chiton. The horseman may well be the Companion who wished to advertise himself through this hunt and may be thought of as royal or aspiring to royalty; in fact, he is usually identified with Craterus. Alexander would have appeared behind him, as on the Alexander Sarcophagus.

But why should the Craterus Monument be reflected in a frieze at Messene? It was Polyperchon who controlled Messene from 316 until the early years of the third century.[167] He was Craterus' deputy even before their departure from Opis in 324,[168] and would have been familiar with Craterus' dedication at Delphi which he may well have wished to emulate. As a sometime regent of Macedon, he had quasi-royal status, which is also implied by the lion-hunt iconography. A memorial of Alexander's last surviving general involved in a hunt with Alexander is an attractive

---

[164] Stamatiou 1988: 213, pl. 39,3; Moreno 1993: 122–4, figs. 23, 25; Stewart 1993: 274 and 427.

[165] Athen. 12. 537e = Ephippus, *FGrH* 126 F 5 records that in the last months of his life Alexander would disguise himself at banquets as Heracles with lion-skin and club.

[166] Arr. *Ind.* 5. 12; Curt. 9. 4. 2–3. Bosworth 1995: 218.

[167] Diod. 20. 28. 1–4; Plut. *Pyrrh.* 8. 3. Billows 1990: 141; Heckel 1992: 201–4.

[168] Arr. 7. 12. 4. Heckel 1992: 125 with n. 338; 141; 190–3.

FIG. 15. Frieze block from Messene. Paris, Louvre MA 858. Photo Museum.

FIG. 16. Frieze block from Messene, detail. Paris, Louvre MA 858. Photo Museum.

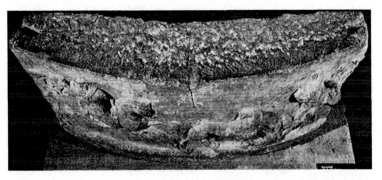

FIG. 17. Frieze block from Messene, top. Paris, Louvre MA 858. Photo Museum.

FIG. 18. Frieze block from Messene, right side. Paris, Louvre MA 858. Photo Museum.

possibility. Polyperchon seems to have particularly distinguished himself in the Indian campaign and may have wished to commemorate one of the hunts in that area. Royal lion hunts in India are attested by Curtius (9. 1. 32): Alexander may well have organized one. The Messene relief frieze may in fact be the last monumental representation of Alexander's royal hunts, commemorating an unrecorded exploit of Polyperchon on his tomb.[169]

Oddly enough, it is in the minor arts of Athens that a record of these hunts survives after the passing away of the Successors. Mould-made bowls of the late third and early second centuries carry hunting scenes in game parks which include the mounted hunt of a lion.[170] A unique painted West Slope kantharos from the Athenian Agora shows the hunt of a variety of wild animals in a sacred grove.[171] It was dedicated to Artemis and Dionysus and both deities seem to be involved in the hunt. The echo of Alexander's royal hunts, especially of the Vergina fresco with shades of Dionysus, lingers in the hunting iconography.

[169] Stewart 1993: 281–2 credits the Messene base to Craterus' son, Craterus the Younger.

[170] Rotroff 1982: 19; cat. nos. 238–72. She dates the bowls to *c*.225–175. An Alexandrian influence cannot be ruled out.

[171] Athens, Agora Museum P 6878. Rotroff 1997: 54–6, cat. no. 271, pls. 26–7.

7

Ptolemy and the Will of Alexander

Brian Bosworth

One of the more enigmatic documents from antiquity is the so-called *Liber de Morte*, the colourful account of Alexander's death and testament which concludes the extant versions of the Alexander Romance.[1] This is a detailed and vibrant story. It develops the ancient rumours that Alexander was poisoned by a conspiracy among his senior marshals, led and orchestrated by Antipater's son, Cassander. Over a dozen supposed conspirators are mentioned by name, and a handful of dignitaries, among them Perdiccas and Ptolemy, are categorically exonerated. The story moves on to the drafting of Alexander's Will over a day and a night, and then the document is quoted in its entirety, complete with a covering letter to the Rhodians, who are entrusted with its preservation. In the Will Alexander makes provision for the succession, in the first place for the son he anticipates from Rhoxane, and he partitions out his empire with appointments strikingly different from the actual satrapal division which took place at Babylon. This is a remarkably detailed document, replete with names—and names of historical individuals, and the context is damningly relevant to historical events. Not only was the great conqueror

---

[1] The chief extant versions are contained in *Metz Epitome* 87–123 and Redaction A of Pseudo-Callisthenes (3. 30. 1–33. 25 Kroll). They are printed in parallel columns in Merkelbach 1977: 253–83 (the standard work). An Armenian translation of the 5th cent. AD provides a valuable control (Wolohojian 1969: 149–59). There are shorter, derivative versions in Julius Valerius (3. 30–5) and the Romance of the Archipresbyter Leo 30–4 (Pfister). The Will alone is reproduced in *Excerpta Latina Barbari* (*Chronica Minora*, ed. C. Frick, i (Leipzig, 1892), 270–4). The principal sources, Greek and Latin, are conveniently printed in sequence by Heckel 1988: 86–107. Unfortunately no apparatus is provided, and for study of these deeply corrupt texts one cannot dispense with the standard editions. The recent discussion of the Alexander Romance by Fraser 1996: 212–14, briefly restates the interpretation of Merkelbach.

murdered by those closest to him; the express provisions of his Will were systematically disregarded by his successors, and the actual dismemberment of the empire was a flouting of his last wishes.

The story that is transmitted is unhistorical. That at least is evident. But it has a clear political animus, as was pointed out over a century ago by Adolf Ausfeld, who noted first that the story of Alexander's death differed in detail and general atmosphere from the rest of the Romance.[2] Secondly, the details of the narrative are pointedly relevant to the political struggle which followed Alexander's death. In particular the accusations of poisoning were current immediately after the king's demise, and they were the matter of political debate at Athens. Hypereides literally lost his tongue for proposing honours for Iolaus, the supposed minister of the poison.[3] That established a prima-facie case that the perpetrator of the fiction came from the camp of Perdiccas, the adversary of Antipater in the first bout of civil wars. Ausfeld's arguments were repeated and strengthened by Reinhold Merkelbach some sixty years later,[4] but even so they fail to hold conviction. Too many of Perdiccas' close associates are indicted by name as parties to the poisoning,[5] and Alexander's Will contains numerous provisions which were blatantly disregarded by the regent, in particular the specific provision that his body should go to Egypt. What is more, Perdiccas' sphere of operation is relatively narrow, restricted

[2] Ausfeld 1895, expanded and modified in Ausfeld 1901. For a useful exposition of the *status quaestionis* see Heckel 1988: 2–5.

[3] [Plut.] *Mor.* 849f; cf. 849c; Plut. *Demosth.* 28. 4. For the early allegations of poisoning see Bosworth 1971a: 113–16; Bosworth 1988a: 175–6, 182–3. For general statements that the rumours were deliberately repressed see Curt. 10. 10. 18; Just. 12. 13. 10; Diod. 17. 118. 2.

[4] Merkelbach 1977: 161–92, esp. 186: 'All dies paßt nur ins Jahr 321.' His position has been recently endorsed (without further arguments) by Fraser 1996: 213–15, 224–6. See, however, the detailed refutation by Seibert 1984. The arguments against a dating to the era of Perdiccas are to my mind irrefutable, but Seibert is too ready to dismiss the hypothesis that the work is the product of propaganda. Why otherwise would a forger concoct such a detailed fabrication in such flagrant contradiction of the historical facts? The object can only be to insinuate that what happened at Babylon (and later) was deliberate flouting of Alexander's dying wishes.

[5] Notably Medeius, Peithon, and Peucestas; cf. Bosworth 1971a: 116 n. 4; Heckel 1988: 37–9.

to the territories east of the Zagros.[6] If the document as it appears in the Romance is the work of Perdiccas' party, it was framed in a remarkably counter-productive fashion. The purported Will of Alexander practically indicted everything Perdiccas planned or achieved after his death.

More recently Waldemar Heckel has attacked the orthodoxy root and branch, and redated the document to the second period of civil war, specifically to the year 317.[7] Then the regent Polyperchon was attempting to combat a challenge to his authority by Antipater's son, Cassander. Cassander's ally, Antigonus, was locked in a struggle with Eumenes, who had a royal commission in the east, and the satrapal forces of the Iranian plateau. Polyperchon was at loggerheads with both Cassander and Antigonus, and, it can be argued, the provisions of the Will were most detrimental to the lieutenants of Antigonus, while Cassander was inextricably damned by the rumours of poisoning. In addition the idiot king, Philip Arrhidaeus, whose cause Cassander had championed in 317, is implicitly disowned. He is only given tenure until the birth of a son by Rhoxane, who is then to become king.[8] In 317 Alexander IV, the infant son of the conqueror, was championed by Polyperchon and the Queen Mother, Olympias, and Arrhidaeus they denounced as a usurper. The purported Will of the Romance, it might be thought, has exactly the perspective one would expect from Polyperchon. His enemies are seen to be frustrating the wishes of the dead king, and his protégés are directly favoured in the provisions of the Will.

The context of 317 is far preferable to that of 321, and Polyperchon is more plausible than Perdiccas as the perpetrator of the document. Even so, there are internal inconsistencies. The position of Seleucus is a particularly

[6] *Metz Epit.* 118; Ps.-Call. 3. 33. 9; Wolohojian 1969: 274, p. 155; *Exc. Barb.* 272. 15–17; on the corruption at Ps.-Call. 3. 33. 15, repeated in Jul. Val. 3. 33 (1397–1401), see below, pp. 224–5.

[7] Heckel 1988, *passim*: The exact dating is conveniently tabulated on p. 86, where the *terminus post quem* is alleged to be Eurydice's alignment with Cassander in summer 317 and the *terminus ante quem* the spring of 316. For sharp criticism see Seibert's review in *Gnomon* (1990), 564–6.

[8] *Metz Epit.* 115; Ps.-Call. 3. 33. 11; Jul. Val. 3. 33 (1378–83): Leo 33; cf. Wolohojian 1969: 273, p. 154; *Exc. Barb.* 270. 24–5. For discussion see below, p. 227 and Heckel 1988: 50–2.

nasty conundrum. In 317 he was allied with Antigonus against Eumenes and the satrapal coalition.[9] Polyperchon could hardly be expected to be friendly or favour him in a spurious will which he was concocting. Yet, when Alexander comes to assign Babylon, he does not give it to Archon, the satrap confirmed at Babylon and who held office down to 321. Seleucus himself is anachronistically given the command, which in fact he only obtained at Triparadeisus in 321 at the behest of Antipater.[10] That is a most surprising distortion to come from the camp of Polyperchon. One can hardly escape the dilemma by chronological manipulation.[11] When Eumenes was facing Seleucus and the Antigonid forces, he concocted a fake letter claiming that Cassander was dead, Olympias was in firm control of Macedon, and Polyperchon had invaded Asia with the royal army.[12] That is the exact juncture at which Heckel claims the Will was forged, and exactly the period when one would least expect Seleucus to receive any favouritism in Polyperchon's propaganda. Yet his control of Babylonia is confirmed and sanctioned by the dying Alexander.

There is a similar problem with Asander, satrap of Caria. He was a relative of Antigonus,[13] and co-operated with him during the invasion of Asia Minor in 321 and later in the

[9] Diod. 19. 12. 1–13. 5, 17. 1, 18. 1 etc. Cf. Billows 1990: 91, 106–7; Grainger 1990.

[10] Seleucus is given Babylonia in all versions of the Romance (*Metz Epit.* 117; Ps.-Call. 3. 33. 15; Jul. Val. 3. 33 (1395–6); Leo 33), as in Dexippus' *History of the Successors* (*FGrH* 100 F 8. 7). Otherwise Archon is unimpeachably attested as holding the satrapy in 323 (Diod. 18. 3. 3; Just. 13. 4. 23) and losing his life in its defence in 321 (Arr. *Succ.* F 25. 5 (Roos)). For Seleucus' appointment at Triparadeisus see Arr. *Succ.* F 1. 35 (Roos); Diod. 18. 39. 6.

[11] Heckel explicitly adopts the fashionable 'low' chronology, and argues that Seleucus' alliance with Antigonus came only in the early part of 316, after the document was forged for Polyperchon.

[12] Diod. 19. 23. 2; Polyaen. 4. 8. 3. The context of the letter was clearly Cassander's first invasion of Macedon, early in 317 and before the news of the schism in Macedonia had reached the east. The forgery strengthened Eumenes' position as the representative of the kings, and the situation as he represented it implied that Philip III was still alive. For discussion see Bosworth 1992: 62–4, 81. Antigonus' alliance with Seleucus clearly came in early summer 317, and it was presumably common knowledge in the west at the time of the dynastic crisis in Macedonia.

[13] Arr. *Succ.* F 25. 1 (Roos): κατὰ γένος ἐπιτήδειος ὤν. I do not see why Heckel 1988: 64 argues that Asander 'made no move to support Antigonus'. Contra Billows 1990: 62–3.

campaign against Eumenes and the Perdiccan faction over the winter of 320/19.[14] His loyalty to his relative was unquestioned in 317, but we do not find the negative bias in the Romance that we would expect. Instead Asander joins the small band of angels who are exculpated by name from the poisoning.[15] He is also confirmed in his satrapy of Caria (to which admittedly he was appointed at Babylon).[16] Such favour is not impossible in a propaganda document directed against the Antigonids, but it reads better after 314, when Asander defected to the camp of Ptolemy.[17] The Will of Alexander could then be mobilized to criticize Antigonus' subsequent invasion of Caria. One may make a similar case from the extraordinarily favourable treatment of Ptolemy,[18] which we shall examine in detail presently. In 318 he opposed Eumenes, who retaliated by challenging his control of Syria,[19] and he maintained friendly relations with Antigonus down to 316.[20] However, practically every policy he adopted is foreshadowed and vindicated in Alexander's Will, and, if the document represents the propaganda of Polyperchon, its purpose can only be to detach him from the Antigonid fold by judicious flattery. But such flattery might well alienate Eumenes, who had quarrelled with Ptolemy the previous year.

[14] Arr. *Succ.* F 1. 41 (Roos). Cf. Varinlioglu *et al.* 1990: 73–6.

[15] *Metz Epit.* 98; Ps.-Call. 3. 31. 9; Wolohojian 1969: 265, p. 150; *Exc. Barb.* 272. 4–5.

[16] *Metz Epit.* 117; Leo 33; Jul. Val. 3. 33 (1393—corrupt). For the historical evidence of Asander's satrapy see Diod. 18. 3. 1; Arr. *Succ.* F 1a. 6 (Roos)); Curt. 10. 10. 2; Just. 13. 4. 15; Dexippus, *FGrH* 100 F 8. 2, and for the numerous inscriptions attesting his tenure see J. and L. Robert 1985. They confirm the evidence of Dexippus against the rest of the tradition (including the Romance) that his name was not Cassander but Asander.

[17] Diod. 19. 61. 2, 4; 75. 1. For details see Billows 1990: 116–21, and on the chronology Wheatley, 1998b is now fundamental.

[18] This is well emphasized by Seibert 1990: 566: 'die Möglichkeit . . . daß der Autor vielleicht im Interesse des Lagiden . . . geschrieben haben könnte'.

[19] Diod. 18. 62. 1, 63. 6, 73. 2.

[20] After his naval victory in the Propontis Antigonus sent his fleet directly to Phoenicia, where he frustrated Eumenes' attempt to win back the territory for the kings (Polyaen. 4. 6. 9; cf. Diod. 18. 73. 2), and though he took no direct part in the campaigns of Paraetacene and Gabiene, Ptolemy remained an ally of Antigonus until the expulsion of Seleucus. Then Antigonus appealed to him διαφυλάσσειν τὴν προϋπάρχουσαν φιλίαν (Diod. 19. 56. 4). For the two years preceding (including the period of dynastic tumult in Macedonia) Ptolemy was firmly aligned with the enemies of Polyperchon.

Finally, the role of the author of the propaganda is extremely curious. Polyperchon himself is never mentioned, an aspect of the document which Heckel finds 'subtle and ingenious'.[21] That would only be the case if his position was implicitly strengthened by the propaganda; readers would come away believing that Polyperchon's regency was inevitable and right. But surely the reverse is true. Polyperchon owed his position to the direct appointment of Antipater,[22] and Antipater is perhaps the chief target of the document. He orchestrated the poisoning of Alexander, and Alexander's Will excludes him from Macedonia, confining him to the general supervision of western Asia Minor.[23] Macedon was not his to dispose of, let alone the regency of the kings. The Will practically invalidates Polyperchon's appointment, when a discreet explicit reference might have strengthened it. He was Craterus' second in command between 324 and 322, regent of Macedon in the absence of Craterus and Antipater in 321/20.[24] It would have been easy to insert his name alongside that of Craterus as regent in Macedonia and to award himself a royal princess alongside Craterus, Lysimachus, and Ptolemy. The failure to mention Polyperchon in effect undermines his legitimacy. It gives the impression that Alexander himself did not consider him worth a command, and his actual friend and patron is the prime villain of the piece. If this is propaganda, then it risked backfiring embarrassingly. On the other hand, if the document was composed after Cassander occupied Macedonia in 316, then Polyperchon's obscurity is just what we would expect. He lingered on as a minor player in the

---

[21] Heckel 1988: 81; cf. 48–53.

[22] Diod. 18. 48. 4–5; Plut. *Phoc*. 31. 1. Although it is sometimes argued (e.g. Hammond and Walbank 1988: 130 with n. 3; Hammond 1989: 255) that Antipater's choice was ratified by an Assembly of arms bearers, there is no reference in the sources to any such acclamation. All Diodorus states is that at the time of Polyperchon's appointment Cassander saw that the inclinations of the Macedonians favoured his rival (18. 54. 2: ὁρῶν δὲ τὴν τῶν Μακεδόνων ὁρμὴν κεκλιμένην πρὸς τὸν Πολυπέρχοντα). In other words, Cassander felt that Polyperchon, temporarily at least, was more popular than he. There is no indication that the popular favour had been evinced in a formal acclamation.

[23] *Metz Epit.* 110, 117; Ps.-Call. 3. 33. 9, 15; Jul. Val. 3. 33 (1394–5); Leo 33; *Exc. Barb.* 276. 7–8; cf. Heckel 1988: 61–3.

[24] For references and discussion see Heckel 1992: 192–4.

dynastic struggle, a pale reflection of his former eminence,[25] and there was no reason for Alexander's Will to earmark him for command.

There is one last problem with existing interpretations. Both Merkelbach and Heckel find it impossible to account for the extraordinary prominence of the Rhodians, who are the guardians of the Will, have their autonomy and dispensation from garrisons explicitly guaranteed, and receive a generous annual subsidy of money, grain, and naval fittings from Egypt.[26] Such prominence makes little sense in the context either of 321 or 317, and it is universally believed that the references to Rhodes are later interpolations, added some time between the Antigonid siege of the city and the Third Macedonian War.[27] Now, it is perfectly possible that we are dealing with an interpolated document. If the purported Will of Alexander were widely read and known,[28] Rhodian patriots might have claimed for themselves a special place in Alexander's affections, and maintained that their welfare was guaranteed and prescribed by the creator of the Hellenistic kingdoms. However, it is not a single interpolation. References to the Rhodians occur throughout the Will as well as in the covering letter, and they do not read as alien implants. It is obviously better if one can find a context for them which is consistent with the rest of the propaganda. A single, coherent document composed at a particular moment for a particular purpose is preferable to a composite production, growing layer by layer according to the interests of different groups at different times.[29] What we

---

[25] After the murder of Heracles he was reduced to the status of a mercenary condottiere in the Peloponnese, operating in loose alliance with Cassander (Diod. 20. 28. 3–4; 100. 6; 103. 5–7). No successful action is recorded (though he was able to garrison Arcadian Orchomenus and other cities in the area), and the date and circumstances of his death are unknown.

[26] *Metz Epit.* 107–9, 116, 118; Ps.-Call. 3. 33. 2–6, 12, 14; Wolohojian 1969: 272, pp. 153–4; Jul. Val. 3. 33 (1385–6); *Exc. Barb.* 272. 1–2.

[27] So Merkelbach 1977: 145–9; Heckel 1988: 12–13, 69–70; Fraser 1996: 213; cf. Fraser 1972: ii. 947–9 n. 16. There is a useful survey by Hauben 1977: esp. 311–15, acknowledging that the *terminus post quem* might be advanced to 309/8 but favouring a date in the late 3rd cent. BC.

[28] It was reported as fact by the source used by Diodorus at 20. 81. 3; Curt. 10. 10. 5 personally disbelieves the existence of a will but claims that it was on attestation (*ab auctoribus tradita*).

[29] This is a point well taken by Seibert 1984: 258–60, who remarks that the sheer

need is a context in which the Rhodians can be wooed and flattered with promises of freedom and subsidies from Egypt, and the Antigonids and the house of Antipater can be simultaneously attacked. In such a context the central player would need to be Ptolemy, who is consistently promoted and eulogized in the document and is strongly associated with Rhodes. Can we provide a context in which all the factors are satisfied?

The period which I consider best fits the political bias of the document is that which followed the Peace of 311. In that year Antigonus had reluctantly come to terms with three of his rivals—Cassander, Lysimachus, and Ptolemy.[30] Like all such compacts it provided simply a breathing space, in which all parties exploited its terms to their own advantage. Antigonus invaded the territories of Seleucus, who had not been included in the peace,[31] while Cassander secretly murdered the titular king, Alexander IV, together with his mother, Rhoxane.[32] There was now no head to the empire, although the enumeration of regnal years continued in Egypt and Babylonia as though the young Alexander were still alive. One last heir to Alexander's blood survived, Heracles, son of Barsine, who had been resident at Pergamum with his mother for the last fifteen years and more.[33] Antigonus was happy to release the boy to the tender

number of hypothesized interpolations weighs seriously against an early date of composition.

[30] Diod. 19. 105. 1. See also Antigonus' detailed and tendentious letter of explanation which survives in a famous inscription of Scepsis (*OGIS* 5 = Welles 1934: no. 1).

[31] This is now generally assumed, and seems incontrovertible. See the literature survey by Seibert 1983: 123–7 with Billows 1990: 132; Grainger 1990; Lund 1992: 61.

[32] Diod. 19. 105. 2. This is a prospective note; the Parian Marble (*FGrH* 239 B 18 dates the murder to the archon year 310/9, immediately before the death of Heracles, son of Barsine. Whatever the precise date of Alexander's murder, it must have pre-dated the elevation of Heracles, who is sent to recover his kingship and is termed 'king' (Diod. 20. 20. 2–3; 28. 1–2); that presupposes that there was no other king in Macedonia. Trogus' *Prologus* 15 lists Alexander's death before that of Heracles, while Justin 15. 2. 1–2 inextricably conflates the two (Schachermeyr 1920, contra Hammond and Walbank 1988: 165–70). Paus. 9. 7. 2 mentions Heracles before Alexander, but they are not explicitly in chronological order, and there is some confusion; both are said to have died by poison.

[33] According to Just. 13. 2. 7 he was already resident in Pergamum by the time of Alexander's death; cf. Diod. 20. 20. 1.

mercies of Polyperchon, who promoted him as an Argead returning to his ancestral kingdom[34] and then cynically murdered him to obtain a favourable accommodation with Cassander. That was in 309.[35] The same year saw Ptolemy take the field and proclaim himself the champion of the Greek communities of Asia Minor and Greece proper, striking both at Antigonus and at Cassander.

The campaign had probably begun in the spring of the year. At that time Antigonus was busy with the invasion of Babylonia, and vulnerable to a challenge in Asia Minor. Accordingly Ptolemy accused him of violating the autonomy clause of the peace by occupying some unnamed cities with garrisons (Diod. 20. 19. 3). He sent his lieutenant Leonides on a mission of liberation into Rough Cilicia, where he subjugated some cities, presumably Celenderis and Nagidus, which were recognized to be colonies of Samos.[36] Simultaneously he appealed to cities under Cassander and Lysimachus, asking for their cooperation against the rising power of Antigonus. That was a general challenge. At first the initiative flagged, when the young Demetrius fought back successfully in Cilicia, but then Ptolemy himself intervened, and sailed to the Lycian coast (Diod. 20. 27. 1). The size of his armament is not given, but it must have been formidable. Ptolemy felt secure enough in his numbers to take with him his pregnant wife, Berenice, who gave birth to his future heir on the island of Cos, tended by the physicians of the guild of Asclepius.[37] His intervention now proved spectacularly successful. Phaselis he besieged and captured; Xanthus he took

---

[34] Diod. 20. 20. 2–3; cf. Lyc. 803–4, where Heracles is represented as pure Argead and there is no allusion to his oriental extraction. For further details of the murder see Plut. *Mor.* 530d.

[35] Diodorus relates the episode over two archon years 310/9 and 309/8. That is consistent with the Parian Marble's dating to 310/9. In Diodorus these events are related concomitantly with Ptolemy's intervention in Asia Minor in summer 309, while in the Parian Marble Heracles' death comes in the archon year immediately preceding Ptolemy's stay on Cos, which is correctly dated to 309/8.

[36] Mela 1. 77; Scymnus *ap.* Hdn. 2. 2, p. 925. 7 (Lentz). Two brothers from Nagidus were honoured at Samos towards the end of the 4th cent. (C. Habicht, *MDAI(A)* 87 (1972), 204–7), and the city was important in the reign of Ptolemy Philadelphus, when it served as a base for the foundation of Arsinoe, a few kilometres to the east (*SEG* 39. 1426; cf. Jones and Habicht 1989: 332–4, 336–8).

[37] Parian Marble, *FGrH* 239 B 19; Theocr. 17. 58–76; cf. Sherwin-White 1978: 83–4, 97–8.

immediately by storm, Caunus after a concerted attack on its
two citadels.[38] He then moved to Cos, where he established
his court, and extended his network of 'liberated' cities. By
the spring of 308 Myndus had come over to him, as had
Iasus and possibly Aspendus.[39] Only Halicarnassus escaped
his grasp. Demetrius was able to occupy it by land and
relieve his garrison, which was under siege from Ptolemy.[40]

In early 308 Ptolemy took his challenge to central Greece.
His armada proceeded through the Cyclades and ejected a
garrison from Andros (whether Antigonid or installed by
Cassander we are not informed). Once at the Isthmus he
occupied the key cities of Corinth and Sicyon, promoting his
crusade of autonomy,[41] and, once master of Corinth, he celebrated his ascendancy by presiding over the Isthmian
Games of summer 308, holding them to commemorate the
cause of freedom.[42] By this time and probably long before
Cassander was in open hostility, in danger of losing his grasp
on southern Greece. Ptolemy was becoming ascendant, and
he had gone as far as to intrigue for the hand of Cleopatra,
the sister of Alexander the Great, who resided in state at
Sardes under the eye of an Antigonid garrison commander.
Cleopatra, long resistant to the overtures of successive
dynasts, now made preparations to cross the Aegean to join
her latest suitor.[43] She was prevented from leaving, and later
murdered, but for a brief period it seemed as though
Ptolemy had brought off the most desirable political union
of the age. That was the high tide of his success. In Greece
his propaganda of liberation did not have its intended fruits,
and the cities of the Peloponnese failed to provide the necessary support for a campaign to eject Cassander's garrisons.
Ptolemy accordingly made peace with the ruler of Macedon,
guaranteeing either side its possessions. Then he took his

---

[38] Diod. 20. 27. 1–2; Polyaen. 3. 16. 1, on which see below, p. 234.

[39] Diod. 20. 37. 1 (Myndus); on Iasus and Aspendus see below, pp. 230–5.

[40] Plut. *Demetr.* 7 fin. The episode is undated, but must surely be associated with
Ptolemy's intervention at Cos.

[41] Diod. 20. 37. 1; cf. Polyaen. 8. 58.

[42] *Suda*, s.v. Δημήτριος: αὐτονόμους τε δὴ τὰς πλείστας τῶν Ἑλληνίδων πόλεων
ἀφίησι καὶ τὰς Ἰσθμιάδας σπονδὰς ἐπήγγελλε κελεύων οἷα ἐπ' ἐλευθερώσει
θαλλοφοροῦντας θεωρεῖν εἰς τὰ Ἴσθμια.

[43] Diod. 20. 37. 3–6; Parian Marble, *FGrH* 239 B 19; cf. Macurdy 1929: 275–7;
Seibert 1967: 19–20, 23–4; Carney 1988: 401–3; Billows 1990: 144–5.

forces from Greece, leaving Leonides as his regent in Corinth.[44]

These were stirring events, which brought Ptolemy into collision with Cassander and the Antigonids. They provide an adequate context for propaganda which elevated Ptolemy at the expense of his rivals. Can we also explain the prominence that Rhodes enjoys in the *Liber de Morte*? Now, there is no doubt that the Rhodian loyalty to the Antigonid cause was shaken during this period. The islanders had assisted Antigonus in 315 when he was building his war fleet, and two years later they made a formal alliance and contributed on a small scale to Polemaeus' invasion of Greece.[45] This commitment was notably lacking in 306, when they refused a contingent to Demetrius' naval force against Ptolemy, claiming that they wanted common peace with everybody.[46] They had moved from alliance and co-operation to an unhelpful neutrality, and the person who gained from it was Ptolemy. The time for that change of attitude was Ptolemy's stay on Cos in 309/8. Then he was practically on the doorstep of Rhodes, and he had operated on both sides of the Rhodian *peraea*, at Myndus and Caunus.[47] But no actions are attested against Rhodes or any Rhodian possession. That might be due to a freakish distribution of evidence, but the likelihood is that Ptolemy used diplomacy rather than force in his dealings with Rhodes. He was championing autonomy, and, if the island had no Antigonid garrison, there was no reason to intervene. What is more, Rhodes boasted a large, seaworthy navy which had humbled Attalus in 320, when he took the remains of Perdiccas' war fleet to the Carian coast and attempted a campaign of conquest there.[48] It was better not to risk losses and win the island's friendship through subsidies and downright flattery. In that context it made sense to suggest that Alexander had

[44] Diod. 20. 37. 2: *Suda*, s.v. Δημήτριος.

[45] Diod. 19. 57. 4, 58. 5, 61. 5, 62. 7, 64. 5, 77. 3. These passages are amassed and discussed by Hauben 1977: 321–8. See also Berthold 1984: 61–6.

[46] Diod. 20. 46. 6, cf. 82. 1; Hauben 1977: 328–9; Billows 1990: 165–6.

[47] In the mid-4th cent. the Rhodian *peraea* seems to have comprised the coastline between Cnidus and Caunus (Ps.-Scylax 99; Fraser and Bean 1954: 51–3).

[48] Arr. *Succ.* F 1. 39 (Roos). This was a formidable force of 10,000 foot and 800 cavalry, directed against Cnidus and Caunus as well as Rhodes, but the Rhodians alone are accredited with repelling it.

envisaged annual subsidies to Rhodes, which Ptolemy, unlike Antigonus, would honour; Alexander had also promised
to withdraw his garrison (which the Rhodians expelled in
323) and guaranteed their freedom in perpetuity.[49] The
Rhodians could even be represented as the guardians of
the Will; and it might have been suggested that the agent
entrusted to deliver it[50] never reached the island. Ptolemy
could then present his own copy of the document, together
with an account of Alexander's death which showed him
poisoned by those closest to him and entrusting his last
dispositions to the Rhodians in his hour of extremity. The
document, then, had a dual purpose. It was designed to win
a powerful ally and at the same time denigrate the two
dynasts whom Ptolemy was challenging for supremacy. As
far as the Rhodians were concerned it was effective, and
from that time onwards their relations with Ptolemy were
cordial.

We have, then, a general context for the propaganda and a
probable author in Ptolemy. The details of the document
afford corroboration to a remarkable degree. One of the
features of the Will is the provision made for the royal
princesses, the sisters of Alexander. The dying king
instructs Craterus to marry Cynnane, Lysimachus to have
Thessalonice—and Ptolemy to take Cleopatra.[51] As we have
seen, Ptolemy attempted to gain Cleopatra's hand early in
308 and was frustrated by Antigonus. The document represents the marriage as the will of Alexander, and makes the
odium of Cleopatra's murder even worse. Ptolemy was the
only dynast who complied with his king's wishes. By contrast, Craterus ignored Cynnane, leaving her to be interned

[49] *Metz Epit.* 107, 118; Ps.-Call. 3. 33. 4–5; Wolohojian 1969: 272, p. 153 (with-
drawal of garrison and freedom). For the actual expulsion of the garrison in 323 see
Diod. 18. 8. 1.

[50] *Metz Epit.* 109 names the agent as Ismenias the Theban; the Armenian
version has Holcias deliver the letter to the Theban 'Asmenos', and it causes rejoic-
ing to Ismenias (Wolohojian 1969: 275, pp. 155–6). This is a rare correspondence
with the earlier body of the Romance, where Ismenias delivers a lament for the
destruction of Thebes (Ps.-Call. 1. 46a. 1–3, 11; Wolohojian 1969: 128–31, pp.
69–73; cf. Berve 1926: ii. 420, no. 33).

[51] Ps.-Call. 3. 33. 13, 15; *Metz Epit.* 117; Wolohojian 1969: 274, pp. 154–5; Jul.
Val. 3. 33 (1388–9, 1398–9); Leo 33; cf. Heckel 1988: 55–9, in whose scheme the
provisions are strangely anachronistic (cf. 59: 'Ironically, the Pamphlet may have
alerted Kassandros to Thessalonike's potential'), and Seibert 1984: 255–6.

by Antipater, until she fled to Asia Minor, where she was murdered by Perdiccas' brother with Perdiccas' connivance.[52] Thessalonice too was married in contravention of the Will. Cassander took her in 316, and was immediately denounced by Antigonus for doing so.[53] The Will confirms that the marriage, if not an act of force, as Antigonus claimed, was a defiance of Alexander's last wishes. The other marriage provision was the transfer of Rhoxane to Perdiccas, which was once again disregarded in the act, as Perdiccas pursued first Antipater's daughter, Nicaea, and then Cleopatra herself,[54] while Rhoxane was left in an unhappy limbo. Ptolemy alone, so the Will implies, attempted to honour Alexander's wishes, but he was prevented by the machinations of his rival.

The king's wishes are equally explicit when it comes to the disposition of his body. It is to be conveyed to Egypt (not, we may note, to Siwah), where the burial is to be performed under the instructions of the Egyptian priesthood.[55] Here again Ptolemy could be seen to have respected the provisions of the Will. He prevented Perdiccas diverting the body to Aegae, the Macedonian capital, and escorted the cortège reverently to Memphis.[56] Thanks to Ptolemy the dead king's provisions were for once respected. There is a somewhat peculiar section dealing with the restoration of

[52] Arr. *Succ.* F 1. 22–3 (Roos); Polyaen. 8. 60; Diod. 19. 52. 5. Arrian confirms that Cynnane's murder was deeply resented by the Macedonian rank and file.

[53] Diod. 19. 52. 1, 61. 2; Just. 14. 6. 13 (where Arrhidaeus strangely appears as the father of Thessalonice—Paus. 8. 7. 7 explains the error).

[54] Diod. 18. 23. 1–3; Arr. *Succ.* F 1. 21, 26 (Roos); Just. 13. 6. 4–7; in the long apocryphal debate between Demades and Deinarchus (*P. Berol.* 13045, lines 190–5 = Kunst 1923: 23) it is claimed that Alexander himself betrothed Perdiccas to Nicaea. Alexander's marital plans for his marshals were clearly the subject of speculation in later times.

[55] *Metz Epit.* 108, 119; Ps.-Call. 3. 33. 6, 10, 16; Wolohojian 1969: 272, pp. 153–4; Leo 33.

[56] The consensus of the historical sources is that Alexander expressed a wish to be buried at Siwah (Diod. 18. 3. 5, 28. 3; Curt. 10. 5. 4; Just. 12. 15. 7; 13. 4. 6; cf. Badian 1967: 185–9). Whether Ptolemy interred the body at Memphis (Parian Marble, *FGrH* 239 B 11; Paus. 1. 7. 1; Curt. 10. 10. 20) or ultimately in Alexandria (Diod. 18. 28. 3–6; Strabo 17. 1. 8 (794); *Heidelberg Epit.*, *FGrH* 155 F 2. 1; Paus. 1. 7. 1 attributes the move to Philadelphus), it was as much a contravention of Alexander's wishes as was Perdiccas' alleged plan to transfer the body to Aegae (Paus. 1. 6. 3). The Will repeatedly vindicates Ptolemy's actions, reporting Alexander's command to be buried *in Egypt*, and the Romance cites an oracle of Zeus which specifically prescribes *Memphis* (Ps.-Call. 3. 34. 1). Cf. Fraser 1972: ii. 31–3 n. 79.

Thebes, in which the king states that the city has suffered
enough and would be restored with a grant of some 300
talents from the royal treasury.[57] For standard views of the
document, which assume a dating before the restoration,
this is a vexing problem. Merkelbach thought the passage
interpolated, while Heckel supposed that Cassander might
actually have been inspired by the hostile propaganda.[58] In
effect Cassander solemnly refounded Thebes in 316, as a
grand gesture to gain popularity in the Greek world.[59] It was
promptly condemned by Antigonus,[60] but the refoundation
enjoyed international support and was clearly welcomed
widely. However, it was Cassander's idea and the credit was
primarily his; its commemoration is hardly consistent with
the general tenor of the document. But this is the exception.
Ptolemy himself championed the cause of the Thebans
when he was in Greece. A famous document, brilliantly
edited by Maurice Holleaux, records contributions to the
Theban regeneration.[61] Immediately before a dedication by
Demetrius from spoils from the siege of Rhodes (304), there
are two contributions by a Philocles spaced around other
donations, from Eretria, Melos, and—significantly—Cos.

[57] *Metz Epit.* 120; Ps.-Call. 3. 33. 7–8. In the Romance (Ps.-Call. 1. 47)
Alexander orders the rebuilding of the city soon after its destruction, as a tribute to
the athletic feats of 'Cleitomachus'.

[58] Merkelbach 1977: 190; Heckel 1988: 70: 'it is not impossible that Kassandros'
decisions to rebuild Thebes and to marry Thessalonike were both influenced by a
Pamphlet that was hostile to him'.

[59] Diod. 19. 53. 1–2, 54. 1; cf. Paus. 9. 7. 1–2; Parian Marble, *FGrH* 239 B 14.
All sources stress the popularity of the refoundation (Merkelbach 1977, 190–1 n.
89), and it is not surprising that the Antigonids withdrew their initial opposition.

[60] Diod. 19. 61. 2–3: καὶ Θήβας ἀνέστησε τὰς ὑπὸ Μακεδόνων κατασκαφείσας.

[61] *SIG*³ 337; cf. 24–35. Holleaux' identification of Philocles as the lieutenant
of Ptolemy has not gone unchallenged; Seibert 1970: 344, suggests, rather
implausibly, that he was a rich Athenian, the son of Phormion. It seems unlikely
that any Athenian private citizen was in a position to disburse multiple donations
amounting to hundreds of talents. On the contrary, Philocles moves in the
company of kings and cities, and must have been a personage of international distinction. Why Ptolemy is not recorded as the donor proper remains a problem, and
the incongruity has been often noted (Merker 1970: 144–5; Seibert 1970: 343). It is
possible that Philocles held a local command comparable to that of Leonides at
Corinth or Aristobulus near Iasus (see below, p. 231) and made the dedication from
his own resources with the approval and blessing of Ptolemy but in his own name.
Hauben 1987a: 416–18 n. 18, argues that Philocles was already king of Sidon at the
time of the dedication, and 'Philocles' lavish gifts can be explained by the mythical
bonds that existed between Sidon and Thebes', adding (n. 22) that the inscription
'*may* have mentioned Philocles' regnal title'.

What is more, Philocles in all probability is the lieutenant of Ptolemy who captured Caunus in 309, and is attested acting in concert with Leonides, Ptolemy's viceroy in Corinth.[62] It is practically incontestable that Ptolemy championed the cause of the resurgent Thebes, encouraged his allies to give contributions, and supplied funds through one of his chief lieutenants. And the funds are very large. The second donation amounted to no less than 100 talents, and, if the first was comparable in size, we are approaching the 300 talents which the Will earmarks for the restoration of Thebes. Once more Ptolemy could be seen as promoting the purported wishes of his king.

Other detailed provisions have a direct relevance to the political context of 309/8. The donations to the great Hellenic centres of Athens, Delphi, and Miletus are only to be expected, and could be made at any period. Cnidus, however, appears a little incongruous with its large donation of 150 talents, the same sum that Miletus received.[63] But Cnidus lay at the tip of the peninsula directly facing Cos,[64] and it was one of the communities Ptolemy would have wooed at the same time as Rhodes. If it had no Antigonid garrison, it might be won by diplomacy and the provision of a donation, which Alexander had allegedly promised.[65] Cnidus shows the positive side of the propaganda. The negative comes with the 150 gold talents promised to Argos.[66] This was natural enough from a king who had boasted of his Argive ancestry, but the provision had a sting in its tail. Of all the Greek cities which had suffered at the hands of Cassander Argos had probably been worst treated. In 316 he had forced the city to renounce its ties with Polyperchon and left a garrison there under the command of

[62] See below, pp. 233–4.

[63] *Metz Epit.* 120; Ps.-Call. 3. 33. 18 (corrupt).

[64] On the site see Bean and Cook 1952: 202–4, 210–12. The neighbouring site of Triopium had been occupied by the Persians in 334/3, when they (like Ptolemy) were operating from a base on Cos (Arr. 2. 5. 7).

[65] At any event the city was neutral in 305/4, and sent envoys to broker a peace between Demetrius and the Rhodians (Diod. 20. 95. 4). They may even have acted upon the initiative of Ptolemy (Diod. 20. 99. 2).

[66] *Metz Epit.* 120; Ps.-Call. 3. 33.17. There is slight variation of detail. In the *Metz Epitome* the king's panoply is earmarked for the temple of Hera, while in Ps.-Call. it is part of the first fruits intended for Heracles. The difference is slight, perhaps due to corruption in one of the traditions.

Apollonides. The following year there was an attempt to shake off the occupation, which ended, it is alleged, in some five hundred citizens being shut in the prytaneum during debate and burnt alive.[67] To add insult to injury Cassander then presided over the Nemean Games of summer 315. There is little wonder that when Ptolemy attended the Isthmia in 308, he held the games in the name of freedom,[68] and in the propaganda that he concocted Argos enjoyed a high place in the list of Greek beneficiaries. Alexander's expressed wish to promote and honour the city of Heracles would have heaped even more odium upon Cassander.

The disposition of the provinces also promotes Ptolemy's interests. In the first place, Egypt is explicitly and consistently marked out for him. Alexander orders him there before he dies; and he is granted the realm of Egypt in the Will and instructed to bring the king's body there.[69] Similarly, in the covering letter to the Rhodians he is explicitly designated satrap of Egypt, and named as an executor along with Craterus, Perdiccas, and Antipater,[70] the only satrap to be associated with that elect company. But far more controversial was Syria, which Ptolemy had annexed from Laomedon in 320 and never ceased to claim as his own. He demanded its recognition early in 316 and attempted to regain it from the Antigonids in 312/11.[71] On the other hand, his enemies from Eumenes onwards denounced his designs on Syria as improper.[72] Now, in the Will Ptolemy's regime is not extended to Syria, but on the other hand Laomedon is not named as the intended satrap. All versions claim that role for Meleager.[73] For Ptolemy the fabrication was highly convenient. Meleager died at Babylon, executed at the be-

[67] Diod. 19. 54. 3, 63. 2.

[68] Diod. 19. 64. 1 (Cassander at the Nemea). On Ptolemy at the Isthmia see n. 42 above.

[69] *Metz Epit.* 111; Wolohojian 1969: 274, p. 115; *Metz Epit.* 119; Wolohojian 1969: 274, p. 115; Leo 33; *Exc. Barb.* 272. 13–14. On the textual corruption in Ps.-Call. and Julius Valerius see below, pp. 224–5.

[70] Ps.-Call. 3. 33. 9: Κρατέρῳ ἐντετάλμεθα καὶ τῷ Αἰγύπτου σατράπῃ Πτολεμαίῳ καὶ τοῖς κατὰ τὴν Ἀσίαν Περδίκκᾳ καὶ Ἀντιπάτρῳ.

[71] For the annexation in 320 see Diod. 18. 43. 1–2; App. *Syr.* 52. 263–5; Parian Marble, *FGrH* 239 B12 (misdated); Wheatley 1995. For his later claims to recognition see Diod. 19. 57. 1.   [72] Diod. 18. 63. 6, 73. 2.

[73] *Metz Epit.* 117; Ps.-Call. 3. 33. 15; Jul. Val. 3. 33 (1396–7); Leo 33; *Exc. Barb.* 272. 10–11.

hest of Perdiccas,[74] and could never have taken his satrapy. Laomedon, then, did not have Alexander's mandate, and Ptolemy could claim some justification in attacking him. As for Cilicia there is no reference either to Philotas, the friend of Craterus, whom Perdiccas expelled in 321, or to his replacement, Philoxenus, who was confirmed at Triparadeisus.[75] The *Metz Epitome*, the only text to give a coherent reading, gives the name of the intended satrap as Nicanor.[76] It is too common a nomenclature for a confident identification, but it may be relevant that the lieutenant of Ptolemy who expelled Laomedon from Syria was a Nicanor.[77] The propaganda possibly insinuated that it was he, Ptolemy's friend, and not Philotas who was intended for Cilicia. In that case Ptolemy might have claimed that the whole of the Levant from the borders of Egypt to the Cilician Gates was in the hands of usurpers, and his actions against Syria were not unjustified aggression.

In the context of Ptolemaic propaganda the assignment of Babylonia to Seleucus also makes excellent sense. It was Ptolemy who supported Seleucus during his years of exile, and he provided the little army which won Babylon for Seleucus in 312/11.[78] On the other hand, Ptolemy cannot have been happy with the spectacular expansion of territory which his former protégé rapidly achieved. Within a year, according to Diodorus (19. 92. 1), he had easily acquired Media and Susiana, and boasted of his conquests to Ptolemy and others, 'already possessing royal majesty'. That in part explains his omission from the Peace of 311.[79] The Will

[74] Curt. 10. 9. 20–1; Diod. 18. 4. 7; Arr. *Succ.* F 1a. 4 (Roos). For his role at Babylon see Errington 1970: 51–7; Billows 1990: 53–5; Heckel 1992: 168–70. Meleager's actual position, as defined in the settlement, was subordinate to Perdiccas (Arr. *Succ.* F 1a. 3 (Roos)). He received no satrapy.

[75] For Philotas and Philoxenus see Heckel 1988: 63, 108.

[76] *Metz Epit.* 117: *Ciliciae imperatorem facio Nicanorem.* Ps.-Call. 3. 33. 14 fuses the provisions for Cilicia with Antigonus' satrapal assignment, while Leo 33 conflates Antipater's supervisory role in Asia Minor with the satrapy of Cilicia. *Exc. Barb.* 272. 6–7 makes a certain 'Filon' governor of Isauria and Cilicia.

[77] Diod. 18. 43. 2; cf. Peremans and van 't Dack ii, no. 2169.

[78] Diod. 19. 90. 1–91. 5; App. *Syr.* 54. 273–4; Parian Marble, *FGrH* 239 B 16. Cf. Schober 1981: 94–7; Grainger 1990: 72–5; Winnicki 1989: 69–72, 76–82.

[79] Diod. 19. 105. 1 names only Cassander, Lysimachus, Ptolemy, and Antigonus as parties to the peace; so too Antigonus' letter to the Scepsians (Welles 1934: no. 1). It is now generally agreed that Seleucus was not included (cf. Seibert 1983: 123–7 with bibliography; Billows 1990: 132–3; Grainger 1990: 86–7).

accordingly limits him to Babylon and the land around.[80] Neighbouring provinces are explicitly assigned to others. Mesopotamia to the north is allocated to Peithon, presumably Peithon the Bodyguard, who was given Media in the Babylon distribution.[81] For Media itself and Susa the provisions of the Will are desperately corrupt in all versions,[82] and little can be made of them. What is certain, however, is that Seleucus had no part in them. Ptolemy's actions are once more vindicated. In supporting Seleucus he was honouring Alexander's wishes, and by attacking him, as he did in 310,[83] Antigonus was violating them. On the other hand, Seleucus was given no authority outside Babylonia. In fact the supervision of the eastern satrapies between Babylon and Susa is explicitly delegated to Perdiccas,[84] and the extension of Seleucus' regime is implicitly precluded.

So far the provisions of the Will, and the document as a whole, serve the purposes of Ptolemy surpassingly well. There is almost nothing which tells against its interpretation as Ptolemaic propaganda. In some versions of the Will it seems to be Perdiccas who is given Egypt, with Ptolemy apparently confined to Libya.[85] This is superficially impres-

---

[80] *Metz Epit.* 117: *Babylonem et agrum Babyloniacum, qui postea adiunctus est Seleuco, qui mihi armiger fuit, sub imperium do.* Ps.-Call. 3. 33. 15; Jul. Val. 3. 33 (1395–6); Leo 33; *Exc. Barb.* 272. 12.

[81] *Metz Epit.* 117; Jul. Val. 3. 33 (1395—'Uton'); *Exc. Barb.* 272. 8–9 ('Tapithon'). For Peithon's actual assignment to Media see Diod. 18. 3. 1; Arr. *Succ.* F 1a. 5 (Roos); Dexippus, *FGrH* 100 F 9. 2; Curt. 10. 10. 4; Just. 13. 4. 13.

[82] *Metz Epit.* 121; Ps.-Call. 3. 33. 22. The texts suggest that Alexander envisaged a change of satrap in both regions. The chosen incumbent in Media is variously given as 'Craterus' (*Metz Epit.*) or 'Oxyntes' (Ps.-Call.). The original reading lies beyond conjecture, and it seems most unlikely that Πείθων Κρατεύα underlies the corruption (Heckel 1988: 61, 67); that fails to account for the distortion in Ps.-Call. and the fact that Peithon figures in the Will as the intended satrap of Mesopotamia.

[83] The campaign is attested mainly in the Babylonian Chronicle of the Successors. For text and discussion see Schober 1981: 105–31; see also Grainger 1990, 87–94. I cannot accept the reconstruction proposed by Billows 1990: 141–3.

[84] *Metz Epit.* 118: *hisque omnibus summum imperatorem Perdiccam facio*; cf. Ps.-Call. 3. 33. 9, 15; Wolohojian 1969: 274, p. 155; Jul. Val. 3. 33 (1400—see n. below); *Exc. Barb.* 272. 13–17.

[85] Ps.-Call. 3. 33. 15, as it is preserved, reads as though Alexander assigned Egypt to Perdiccas and 'Libyke' to Ptolemy (Αἴγυπτον δὲ Περδίκκᾳ καὶ Λιβυκὴν [καὶ] Πτολεμαίῳ), and the text is so understood by Julius Valerius. In two other passages Perdiccas also appears to have authority in Egypt (Ps.-Call. 3. 33. 19, 24). The anomaly is Merkelbach's strongest argument that the Will was originally a figment of Perdiccan propaganda, worked up in successive redactions. After 321 the docu-

sive, but other versions are categorical that Ptolemy alone was given Egypt,[86] and Heckel is certainly correct to argue that the text of Pseudo-Callisthenes was corrupted at an early stage.[87] I cannot argue the case fully here, but it seems to me that Heckel is right that the name of Perdiccas is an error of anticipation, and that the text originally stated that 'Egypt and Arabike and Libyke I assign to Ptolemy'.[88] The two annexes of Egypt, as marked out by Alexander in 331, were included in Ptolemy's domains in the Peace of 311. It is perfectly possible that a scribe's eye jumped ahead from Ἀραβικήν, or the like, to read Περδίκκαν. Then Perdiccas could be understood to have been the recipient of Egypt. Other passages are similarly corrupt,[89] and give no support to Merkelbach's thesis that Perdiccas was originally the ruler of Egypt named in Alexander's Will.

There is, however, one anomaly. In the famous list of guests at Medius' party six only are cleared of the allegation

ment acknowledged Ptolemy as ruler of Egypt, but in some branches of the tradition the earlier references to Perdiccas escaped the revision (Merkelbach 1977: 184–5).

[86] Ptolemy is unequivocally assigned Egypt in the parallel passages of *Metz Epit.* 117; Leo 33; *Exc. Barb.* 272. 13–14; and in the initial letter to the Rhodians *all* versions, including Ps.-Call. 3. 33. 9, refer to Ptolemy as satrap of Egypt.

[87] Heckel 1988: 32–3, contra Merkelbach 1977: 69. Ausfeld 1901: 523 n. 4 had already argued for corruption; cf. Seibert 1984: 257.

[88] Αἴγυπτον δὲ ⟨καὶ⟩ Ἀραβικήν καὶ Λιβυκήν [καί] Πτολεμαίῳ. There is some warrant for this in *Exc. Barb.* 272. 13–14, which assigns to Ptolemy 'Egypt and the lands around it as far as Upper Libya'. For Alexander's settlement in 331 with separate commands in Libya to the west and Arabia around Heroonpolis see Arr. 3. 5. 4; Curt. 4. 8. 5. On the settlement of 311 see Diod. 19. 105. 1: Πτολεμαῖον δὲ τῆς Αἰγύπτου καὶ τῶν συνοριζουσῶν ταύτῃ πόλεων κατά τε τὴν Λιβύην καὶ τὴν Ἀραβίαν.

[89] At Ps.-Call. 3. 33. 24 Perdiccas is delegated to set up bronze statues of Alexander and his parents, divine and human (so Jul. Val. 3. 33 (1434–7)). *Metz Epit.* 121 claims that Ptolemy received the commission, while the Armenian version instructs Holcias to erect statues in Olympia, as well as Ptolemy in Egypt (Wolohojian 1969: 274, p. 155). It looks as though the original version provided for all the major protagonists erecting statues at different venues, Holcias in Greece, Ptolemy in Egypt, and presumably Perdiccas in the far east (compare the round robin to senior officers for the protection of Rhodes: Ps.-Call. 3. 33. 9). A similar conflation may underlie the error common to Ps.-Call., the Armenian version and Julius Valerius, which has Perdiccas as ruler of Egypt establish a priesthood to Alexander; the original might have conflated Ptolemy's brief to establish the priesthood in Alexandria with a comparable commission to Perdiccas in the east of the empire. This type of contraction is more credible than the theory of a partial and incompetent redaction, which attempted but failed to excise references to an unhistorical regime of Perdiccas in Egypt.

of poisoning. Those six include Perdiccas,[90] the enemy of
Ptolemy, who attacked him in 321 and who, it seems, was
depicted in an invidious light in Ptolemy's History of
Alexander's reign.[91] Why should Ptolemy's propaganda have
cleared Perdiccas of poisoning, when it was possible to leave
him among the alleged culprits? One way out might be to
detach the Will from the romantic story of poisoning. The
Will might be the original corpus onto which the sensational
story of poisoning was grafted, and so, one might argue, the
allegations come not from Ptolemy but from a later compiler. That is a possible explanation, but not particularly
satisfactory. A better approach is to focus on a remarkable
aspect of the tradition which is only found in Pseudo-
Callisthenes and (in an abbreviated form) in the version of
the Archipresbyter Leo.[92] According to this story Perdiccas
suspected that Alexander had chosen Ptolemy as his successor, and made an informal compact with him whereby
they would co-operate in the administration of the empire.[93]
This has been long recognized as a piece of Ptolemaic propaganda, which states as fact not merely that he was the son of
Philip II but also that his origins were recognized by both
Alexander and Olympias. Ptolemy was the natural successor,
according to the propaganda, with credentials at least equal
to those of Philip Arrhidaeus. The story also denigrates
Perdiccas, whose invasion of Egypt could be seen as a violation of the compact with Ptolemy. But the whole episode
presupposes that Perdiccas was ignorant of the plot against
Alexander. If he believed that Ptolemy was the designated
successor, his interests were clearly to keep Alexander alive

[90] *Metz Epit.* 98; Wolohojian 1969: 265: p. 150; Ps.-Call. 3. 31. 8. The texts are
corrupt, but Perdiccas' name is clear in all.

[91] This seems generally agreed; cf. Errington 1969: 236–40; Bosworth 1980*a*: 26,
80–1, 311–12; 1996*a*: 140; contra Roisman 1984.

[92] Ps.-Call. 3. 32. 9–10; Wolohojian 1969: 269, p. 152; Leo 32. 3.

[93] Ps.-Call. 3. 32. 9: ἔτι δὲ καὶ τὴν Ὀλυμπιάδα πεποιηκέναι φανερόν, ὡς ἦν ἐκ
Φιλίππου. Cf. Merkelbach 1977: 33–4: 'Hier hat sich eine Tendenzerfindung der
frühesten Diadochenzeit erhalten.' Following Pfister 1946: 48, Merkelbach claimed
that the passage was interpolated; it interrupts the story of the composition of the
Will and has no part in any tradition but Leo. If so, the interpolation is nearly as
old as the text into which it is inserted. What is more, *Exc. Barb.* 272. 13, 276. 4–6
claims that Ptolemy had the *cognomen* Philippus. That can only be a confused
reference to the tradition that he was son of Philip II, in which case the propaganda
is integral to the Will.

until the situation was rectified. He could not be inculpated in the plot if he were to be represented as pre-empting Ptolemy's succession to the kingship. In this context Perdiccas had to be exonerated from the suspicion of poisoning. That did not, however, mean that he was placed in a good light. His interests were simply to prevent others replacing Alexander.

We may now move to the most important part of the Will, the provision for the succession. Arrhidaeus is designated king, but only as a temporary measure until Rhoxane's child is born. If the child is male, it is to take over the kingship; if female, the Macedonians are themselves to choose a king, who may or may not be Philip Arrhidaeus.[94] The text is categorical. Alexander's unborn son was his preferred heir. In the context of 309 this was charged with significance. Alexander IV and his mother had recently perished at the hands of Cassander. The odium of the murder was accordingly underlined in every way. Rhoxane is portrayed in the document as a devoted and exemplary wife, easing her husband in his last agonies. She is carefully provided for in the Will, given as wife to Perdiccas, and her son is Alexander's preferred heir.[95] In actuality she was defrauded by Perdiccas, and she and her son were kept in sordid captivity by Cassander until their murders. The propaganda ensured that the horrid deed would continue to blow in every eye. But there was a positive side. The Will states that in the absence of a son by Rhoxane the Macedonians should choose their own monarch.[96] That is remarkably similar to one of the proposals attributed to Ptolemy at Babylon,[97] and it

---

[94] *Metz Epit.* 115; Ps.-Call. 3. 33. 11; Wolohojian 1969: 273, p. 154; Jul. Val. 3. 33 (1380–1); Leo 33; cf. Heckel 1988: 50–1.

[95] Note the impressive and sentimental scene where Rhoxane collapses at the feet of her dying husband, who embraces her and places her hand in Perdiccas' (*Metz Epit.* 112; Wolohojian 1969: 279, pp. 154–5). Heckel 1988: 52–3 draws attention to the tendentious nature of the description, but has difficulty relating the propaganda to 317. It gained force once Rhoxane was in Cassander's power and interned at Amphipolis (Diod. 19. 52. 4). Antigonus had denounced her treatment as shameful (Diod. 19. 61. 1, 3; Just. 15. 1. 3), and after her murder it made sense for Cassander's enemies to represent her as the loving and cherished wife of Alexander.

[96] *Metz Epit.* 115: *ipsique regem, quem videbitur, cooptent.* See the rest of the evidence cited at n. 94 above.

[97] Just. 13. 2. 11–12: *melius esse ex his legi, qui pro virtute regi suo proximi*

suited his actions in 309/8. In that year he emerged as the champion of liberty, the preferred husband of Cleopatra, and his propaganda emphasized that he was duly carrying out the wishes of Alexander which had been consistently flouted, first by Perdiccas and Antipater and now by Antigonus and Cassander. Ptolemy by contrast was the ideal heir to Alexander, and it would be appropriate for him to assume the kingship.

It can hardly be denied that the kingship was very much in the air after the murder of the young Alexander. There were centripetal and separatist ambitions. The great dynasts could establish themselves as self-declared kings, with absolute powers in the territories under their sway, or they might compete for supremacy to succeed to Alexander's position as paramount ruler in both Europe and Asia. Those were arguably the ambitions of Perdiccas and Antigonus, and it is usually argued that Ptolemy and Seleucus advocated a different monarchy, based on the independence of their territorial units.[98] From 305 onwards Ptolemy probably was a separatist, but he may not have been consistent in his ambitions. Indeed there is evidence that he encouraged his subjects to term him king even before he adopted the title for dating purposes in Egypt. In 309 he may well have been intriguing for international recognition as the proper successor to Alexander. As we have seen, the propaganda of the *Liber de Morte* suits such pretensions admirably. Is there other, more explicit evidence of Ptolemy's regal ambitions?

As it happens, Diodorus has a rogue reference to Ptolemy as king. When he begins the narrative of 309, he describes

fuerint. Curt. 10. 6. 15 reflects a different tradition in which Ptolemy proposes a scheme for collective leadership around the empty throne of Alexander. Errington 1970: 50–1, 74–5 prefers Curtius to Justin, as does Schachermeyr, 1970: 136, 156. Schur 1934: 132 apparently opted for Justin, 'aus Hieronymos die sehr glaubhafte Notiz'.

[98] The fullest exposition is that of Müller 1973. For a bibliographical *mise au point* see Seibert 1983: 136–40. A more radical interpretation is advanced by Gruen 1985, who argues that Antigonus' claims were not essentially different from those of his competitors; all were aiming for absolute authority within their respective spheres of interest on the basis of 'personal achievement and dynastic promise'. For recent succinct expositions of the problem see Lund 1992: 155–61 and Sherwin-White and Kuhrt 1993: 118–20.

Ptolemy's intervention in Asia Minor, and all but one of the manuscripts term him 'Ptolemy the king' (Πτολεμαῖος ὁ βασιλεύων).[99] The passage could be erroneous, the work of an incompetent glossator, but there is corroboration elsewhere.

A famous and rhetorical passage of Plutarch describes the announcement of Demetrius' victory at Salamis, the announcement which triggered Antigonus' assumption of the diadem and its conferment upon Demetrius. That announcement, made in highly theatrical style by the courtier Aristodemus of Miletus, addressed Antigonus as king. As it is usually represented, his message reads: 'Hail, King Antigonus; we are victorious over Ptolemy.'[100] As such, it is traditionally taken to be the first explicit regal acclamation addressed to any of the Successors; Antigonus had proved himself king by military victory over a lesser mortal. The text, however, states something rather different. The manuscript reading, apparently unanimous, is: 'Hail, King Antigonus; we are victorious over *King* Ptolemy.'[101] Long ago J. J. Reiske deleted Ptolemy's title, which he saw as a gloss.[102] Successive editors were content to place it in square brackets, with a simple reference to Reiske's edition. *Delevit Reiske* was the universal chorus, and the Loeb editor omitted Ptolemy's regal appellation without a hint of the true manuscript reading.[103] In fact Reiske's hypothesized gloss is somewhat difficult to explain. If Plutarch's text read simply 'we are victorious over Ptolemy', then there would be no need to add the epithet 'king', for Plutarch himself notes a few lines later that Ptolemy received his formal acclamation as king only after Aristodemus' charade. There is nothing in the context to make a scribe think that Ptolemy was already

[99] Diod. 20. 27. 1. One Florentine manuscript (Laur. plut. LXX n. 12) has the reading δυναστεύων, which Wesseling accepted on the analogy of 20. 19. 3 (Πτολεμαῖον τὸν Αἰγύπτου δυνάστην). At 18. 21. 9 Diodorus also refers to Ptolemy as king, in the context of the annexation of Cyrenaica in 321. In the eyes of most scholars that is a blatant anachronism: F. Jacoby, *RE* 8, 2 (1913), s.v. Hieronymos, no. 10, col. 1554; Seibert 1969: 65; J. Hornblower 1981: 52–3.

[100] Plut. *Demetr.* 17. 6; cf. Müller 1973: 80–3; Gruen 1985: 254–7.

[101] χαῖρε, βασιλεῦ Ἀντίγονε, νικῶμεν βασιλέα Πτολεμαῖον ναυμαχίᾳ.

[102] *Plutarchi Chaeronensis quae supersunt omnia*, ed. Io. Iacobus Reiske, v (Leipzig, 1776), 696.

[103] As a result most recent historians fail to note the manuscript reading. Müller 1973: 80 is an exception, but even he is content to refer to Ziegler's bracketing of βασιλέα 'nach Reiskes Vorgang' and does not discuss its justification.

king, and no reason for a gloss. The received text is the *lectio difficilior*.

If, on the contrary, we retain the manuscript reading, the message of Aristodemus becomes pregnant with irony. It lays heavy emphasis on the title of king. Ptolemy had regal pretensions (and had been addressed as king by his courtiers), but Demetrius and Antigonus had shown what real kings should do.[104] Their military victory at Salamis elevated them above their royal rival. Antigonus reacted by having both himself and his son proclaimed kings by the assembled commons, and assumed the diadem. It was a public demonstration of all the attributes of kingship, and might well have been the first display of the diadem outside the Argead line. However, it was not the first use of the regal title. If Plutarch's text is sound, then Ptolemy had been termed king for some time before the battle of Salamis. It was an 'unofficial' designation. As Plutarch (*Demetr.* 18. 2) explicitly notes, the formal proclamation came later, as a response to Antigonus' public assumption of the diadem, but it does not exclude the informal use of the title. Ptolemy's courtiers could have addressed him as king as a matter of routine flattery.

We should now examine two controversial inscriptions. The first is directly relevant to Ptolemy's campaign in Asia Minor, and deals with the surrender of the Carian city of Iasus. It comprises a dossier, first the agreements which secured the initial capitulation and two later letters from Ptolemaic officials in the area.[105] The capitulation came late in 309, for the negotiations were directed by Polemaeus, the renegade nephew of Antigonus, who had originally captured the city in the Antigonid interest back in 314 and came to join Ptolemy in Cos.[106] Polemaeus negotiated for his new

---

[104] The sarcasm would be all the more telling if it were already accepted doctrine that 'the ability to command an army' was a necessary condition of kingship (*Suda*, s.v. βασιλεία (2); cf. Müller 1973: 110–12; Sherwin-White and Kuhrt 1993: 119–20; Gehrke 1982: 253–4.

[105] Blümel 1985: nos. 2–3. First published by Pugliese Carratelli 1967/8: no. 1 ('Iasus in libertatem vindicata'), with improved readings by Garlan 1972, 1975. See also Mastrocinque 1979: 30–2, 43–7; Hauben 1987*b* (bibliography n. 1); Billows 1989: 192; 1990: 201 n. 31, 209–10.

[106] Diod. 19. 75. 5; 20. 27. 3. On the career of Polemaeus see, most conveniently, Billows 1990: 426–30, no. 100. At Iasus Polemaeus apparently secured an agree-

master, and after a complex exchange the city of Iasus was offered freedom, autonomy, and immunity from tribute and garrison in return for perpetual alliance with Ptolemy and his descendants.[107] As yet Ptolemy is not termed king, but the dynastic implications are clear; his descendants are expected to inherit his position. However, the political situation changed rapidly. Polemaeus did not endear himself to his new patron, and was poisoned on suspicion of disloyalty early in 308 (Diod. 20. 27. 3). In consequence the negotiations he had brokered were reviewed. There is a letter by Ptolemy's viceroy in the area, a certain Aristobulus, who is surely identical with the Aristobulus who represented Ptolemy in the Peace of 311.[108] He enjoyed a position parallel to that of Leonides at the Isthmus, administering the little empire which Ptolemy had created on the coast of Asia Minor. When approached by the delegates of Iasus, he confirmed the city's rights to its own revenues (hence autonomy!), but referred the delicate question of the city's payments (*syntaxis*) to the Ptolemaic war chest to his master. Aristobulus' letter does not mention Ptolemy by name, but it twice refers to him as *the king*.[109] Now, it is difficult to date the letter to the period after Ptolemy's official assumption of the regal title in 305/4. By then his fleet had been destroyed at Salamis; he had beaten back an Antigonid invasion of Egypt with some difficulty, and Demetrius' invasion of

---

[107] ment from the mercenaries he had installed, that they would surrender the ἄκραι if they received a satisfactory response from Ptolemy within fifteen days (Blümel 1985: no. 2, lines 7–18).

[107] σ[υμμάχους] ἔσεσθαι Πτολεμαίωι καὶ τοῖς ἐγγόνοις αὐτοῦ ε[ἰς] τὸν ἀεὶ χρόνον (Blümel 1985: no. 2, lines 31–2). This is the language of the Corinthian League (Tod 1948: 177, lines 12–13) and the League of Antigonus and Demetrius (Moretti: *ISE*, no. 44, lines 141–2).

[108] Blümel 1985: no. 3, lines 1–18. On the interpretation see Hauben 1987*b*: 4. The inscription continues (lines 19–28) with an identical oath by another Ptolemaic official, an otherwise unknown Asclepiodotus. The Iasians prudently called upon him to endorse the settlement made by his colleague.

[109] Blümel 1985: no. 3, lines 7–8 (ἀνενέγκαι εἰς τὸ[ν] βασιλέα), line 15 (ἣν ἂν ὁ βασιλεὺς συντάξηι). In the earlier document of surrender there is no regal titulature (Blümel 1985: no. 2, lines 16, 30–1, 38, 41, 47, 49, 52), and it has been almost universally assumed (against historical probability) that there was a considerable interval between the surrender of Iasus and Aristobulus' ruling, which (it is thought) cannot have preceded Ptolemy's official adoption in Egypt of the diadem and title of king.

Rhodes, launched from Loryma in the *peraea*,[110] was in full swing. It is hard to see how a Ptolemaic enclave in Caria and Lycia could remain in existence under such circumstances, and there is no Ptolemaic activity in the area on record for some decades. The first explicit documentation comes from Limyra in south-east Lycia, which attests that in 288/7 the city was under the regime of two Caunian administrators appointed by Ptolemy.[111] There is, however, no evidence for any involvement in Caria, and Plutarch places the region under Lysimachus as late as 286.[112] In any case, if the letter of Aristobulus is dated so late, it becomes very difficult to identify the author as the courtier and diplomat who was active in Ptolemy's service at the time of the Peace of 311.[113] It is surely preferable to date Aristobulus' letter to 308, after Ptolemy's departure for the Isthmus. Then the Iasians will have been concerned about their precise status after the demise of their patron, Polemaeus, and Aristobulus was the obvious person to approach. They demanded confirmation of their free, autonomous, and independent status, which Aristobulus was ready to grant after they gave confirmation of their good faith. Their immunity from tribute presumably remained; the only dispute related to the payment (*syntaxis*) for the defence of the area, which was something different and separate from the tribute (*phoros*) which symbolized subjection.[114] Aristobulus' letter is surely close to the time of Iasus' submission to Polemaeus, and it is

[110] Diod. 20. 82. 4. This marks the latest date for the Antigonid recapture of Iasus. Billows 1990: 147 argues plausibly that 'during the latter part of 309 and 308 Demetrius must certainly have recaptured the cities of Karia and Lykia that Ptolemy had conquered in the first half of 309'.

[111] Wörrle 1977.

[112] Plut. *Demetr.* 46. 4–5. The only other evidence adduced in favour of a Ptolemaic presence in Caria in the mid-280s is a chronographic note of Porphyry (*FGrH* 260 F 42) which mentions Ptolemy's occupation of Caria along with many islands, cities, and regions. But the reference to Caria comes immediately after a note on the victory at Gaza and the restitution of Seleucus in Babylon (312/11). What is clearly at issue is Ptolemy's earlier, well-attested activities in 309/8.

[113] See Welles 1934: no. 1. 50; Hauben 1987*b*.

[114] Contra Billows 1990, 193, who interprets the *syntaxis* as tribute proper. However, the situation seems to parallel that of Asia Minor in 334/3 where the demands for tribute and military contributions were separate (Arr. 1. 26. 3, 27. 4), and the famous Priene inscription seems to distinguish *phoros* from *syntaxis* (see, however, Sherwin-White 1985: 84–6; I cannot accept her view that *syntaxis* is simply a synonym for tribute).

thematically related to it.[115] The most plausible context is the campaign of 309/8, and there is an important consequence. We now have a documentary example of the informal use of the regal title before Ptolemy officially adopted the royal diadem and royal nomenclature. Whatever his public pretensions, he was acknowledged as king by his court, and his friend and viceroy styled him 'the king', as though there were no other claimant to the title.

Similar problems arise in a famous inscription from Aspendus in Pamphylia. This is a decree of the assembly in recognition of help from a contingent of Pamphylians, Lycians, Cretans, Hellenes, and Pisidians, who were under the command of [Phil]ocles and Leonides and proved of service 'to king Ptolemy and to the city'.[116] The regal titulature has hitherto imposed a *terminus ante quem non* of 305,[117] and scholars have looked in vain for evidence of Ptolemaic activity in Pamphylia after that date. There is no evidence, and the inscription has been used to provide that evidence. Mario Segre, for instance, argued that Ptolemy had territory in Lycia and perhaps part of Pamphylia allocated to him after Ipsus,[118] but, given the very low profile Ptolemy played in that campaign, it is unlikely that his allies were particularly generous.[119] Whereas the inscription is very difficult to locate in the early third century, most of the details chime in particularly well with the campaign of 309/8. Although the

[115] Note particularly the form of the oath: 'by Zeus, Earth, Poseidon, Apollo, Demeter, Ares, Athena Areia, all the gods and goddesses, and Tauropolos'. The curious appendage of the name of Tauropolos is consistent throughout the dossier and apparently unique to it; in the 3rd cent. the name is absorbed more fully into the list of deities, after Athena Areia (Robert 1936: no. 52. 22–3 = Billows 1989: 204, no. 1; *OGIS* 229. 61, 71; 266, 25, 52).

[116] *SEG* 17. 639. *Editio princeps* by Paribeni and Romanelli 1914: 116–20, no. 83. The principal discussions are those of Segre 1934; Merker 1970: 146–7; Seibert 1970: 344–50 (with text); Bagnall 1976: 111–13; Mastrocinque 1979: 45–7. On the mechanisms of assuming citizenship see now Gauthier 1990.

[117] Heichelheim 1925: 75, 83, did date the inscription to 310/9, without any appreciation of the difficulty it involved.

[118] Segre 1934: 256–61, contested at length by Seibert 1970, 347–50, who denied that the restoration of Philocles' name was justifiable. Further scepticism in Bagnall 1976: 112–13: 'indeed any time after 294 (Ptolemy's recapture of Cyprus) seems to me possible'.

[119] Cf. Diod. 21. 1. 5: Ptolemy complained that he was denied the fruits of victory (οὐδὲν αὐτῷ μετέδωκαν . . . τῆς δορικτήτου χώρας), and Seleucus was adamant that the spoils of battle belonged only to those present on the battlefield. That surely rules out any territorial assignment to Ptolemy.

reading of the name of the first of the Ptolemaic commanders is not absolutely certain, there is overwhelming
agreement that traces consistent with a lambda are visible,
and the restoration of Philocles is practically certain.[120] In
that case Philocles can hardly be anybody other than the
trusted lieutenant of Ptolemy who captured Caunus for
him[121] and later made donations for the restoration of
Thebes. The capture of Caunus which Polyaenus ascribes to
Philocles does read like the episode recorded by Diodorus.
There the Ptolemaic forces take the city before serious siege
action at the two citadels; in Polyaenus it is explained that
the outer walls were stripped of defenders because of treacherous collusion by the city magistrates. As so often, we have
two different perspectives on the same event. Caunus, then,
was captured by Ptolemy in 309, and there is every reason to
think that Philocles was the officer in charge of the assault.

Philocles is associated with Leonides, who had begun
operations in Rough Cilicia and was with Ptolemy throughout his stay in Asia Minor and Greece.[122] Both he and
Philocles were present to command a force of mercenaries
and local irregulars in 309/8. No source records that
Aspendus came over to Ptolemy at that period, but there
were Ptolemaic forces operating to the east and west, first
when Leonides began his campaign in Rough Cilicia and
then when Ptolemy invaded Lycia in person. His base at
Phaselis was strategically placed for intervention in Pamphylia, and it was at the point of intersection between Lycia,

[120] See the observations of Merker 1970: 146 n. 24 and Bagnall 1976, 113 n. 119,
contra Seibert 1970: 345–6. The photograph published by Paribeni and Romanelli
1914 (Tav. II) appears to justify Merker's claim that 'there is room for Φιλ and the
lambda seems visible'.

[121] Polyaen. 3. 16; cf. Diod. 20. 27. 2. The action against Caunus by Philocles,
'the general of Ptolemy', is usually held to be identical with Ptolemy's capture of
the city in 309 (Holleaux 1938: 33, 419–20; Merker 1970: 146; Seibert 1970: 339).
Bean 1953, 18 n. 34, contests the hypothesis, arguing that Philocles attacked by
land (an inference from προσεστρατοπέδευσε in Polyaenus). That is a misapprehen-
sion. προσστρατεύεσθαι can with perfect propriety be used of an expedition by sea
(Polyb. 5. 3. 4–5). Presumably Philocles (and Ptolemy) established a camp near
Caunus, where negotiations could take place in secret with the treacherous
σιτόμετροι. Then, when the walls were stripped of defenders, the Ptolemaic fleet
could take the city proper from the sea. The subsequent attack on the citadels is not
described by Polyaenus, who is interested solely in the stratagem which gave access
to the city.

[122] Diod. 20. 19. 4; *Suda*, s.v. Δημήτριος. See above, p. 217.

Pisidia, and Pamphylia.[123] The troops under the command of Philocles and Leonides could easily have been recruited locally for intervention in favour of Aspendus. Every detail in the inscription suits the dating to 309/8. We can readily assume that the governing party at Aspendus welcomed Ptolemy when he arrived in Lycia and concluded an alliance on much the same terms as Iasus. Subsequently there may have been a retaliatory attack by Antigonid forces, perhaps led by the young Demetrius, fresh from his successful defence of Halicarnassus.[124] Alternatively there could have been internal dissension in Aspendus with a party bent on revoking the treaty with Ptolemy.[125] In either case the city needed strengthening, and Ptolemy sent a large body of mercenaries, supplemented by locally raised forces, to intervene before it was lost to the Antigonids. The honorary decree proves that the intervention was successful—for a time at least.

The honorary decree followed the intervention, and is best dated to 308, roughly the same time as Aristobulus' letter to the Iasians. In both documents Ptolemy is designated king, and it would seem best to assume that it was regular practice to address him as such. The Aspendians were demonstrating their loyalty and appreciation and naturally used the most flattering terms, while Aristobulus was referring to his master in language of studied deference. Ptolemy may not as yet have assumed the diadem or used the regal title in his official correspondence, but it would seem that his associates regularly used the term, and allied cities found it diplomatic to refer to him as king. According to Plutarch the Athenians were to do the same in 307, when they solemnly proclaimed Demetrius and Antigonus to be kings.[126] They had not as yet publicly declared themselves,

---

[123] For the occupation of Phaselis see Diod. 20. 27. 1, and for its excellent strategic site Livy 37. 23. 1.   [124] Plut. *Demetr.* 7. 5; see above, p. 216.

[125] As suggested by Seibert 1970: 350: 'Aber der Angreifer auf die Stadt muß nicht unbedingt unter den Diadochen gesucht werden. Es könnten die Nachbarn von Aspendos gewesen sein.' So Bagnall 1976: 112–13.

[126] Plut. *Demetr.* 10. 3: πρῶτοι μὲν γὰρ ἀνθρώπων ἁπάντων τὸν Δημήτριον καὶ Ἀντίγονον βασιλεῖς ἀνηγόρευσαν. The passage is usually accepted at face value (cf. Müller 1973: 56–8), even though it is technically incorrect. Antigonus had offered regal honours since 316 as the acknowledged lord of Asia (Diod. 19. 48. 1), and at best the Athenians were the first in the Greek mainland to take the step. As

but the reality was that they had regal powers—and the Athenians were nothing if not realists.

The Rhodians were involved with Ptolemy, and in 309/8 he wooed them in his propaganda. It therefore comes as no surprise to find a tradition in which they supported his aspirations to kingship. This is the fragmentary papyrus (*P. Colon.* 247),[127] which preserves part of a historical narrative documenting Ptolemy's assumption of the kingship, or, rather, the decision of his friends to dignify him with the regal title. As so often, there is no internal evidence to date the transaction, but, given that it concerns kingship, the first editors understandably assigned it to 306, the traditional 'Jahr der Könige'. The papyrus refers explicitly to Antigonus' regal ambitions: '[Antigonus], son of Philippus, entitled (had entitled?) himself king first (?), convinced that he would easily remove all the people in positions of distinction, and would himself have leadership of the entire world, and acquire control of affairs just like Alexander' (col. I, lines 18–26). In the next column there is a reference to a letter apparently sent by Ptolemy to the *demos* of Rhodes, in which he responded to complaints and perhaps referred to a proclamation as king (col. II, lines 6–18). Then the regal title is conferred: 'His friends, in whose number were the Rhodians, considered him worthy of the royal appellation, anticipating that the increase of Antigonus would be burdensome; in opting for Ptolemy they thought that he would remain within the bounds of his hegemony, and act independently (??) in no business in so far as it concerned themselves' (col. II, lines 28–37). It was natural enough to date these transactions to 306 and to see the papyrus as confirmation of the literary record that Ptolemy's proclamation as king came hard on the heels of Antigonus' crowning ceremony after Salamis: Antigonus assumed the title to promote his ambitions of world empire, and Ptolemy responded out of self-defence.

The situation, as with the *Liber de Morte*, is complicated

---

yet there is no epigraphical confirmation, but it is highly unlikely that after showering divine honours upon the Antigonids the Athenians would have scrupulously refrained from addressing them as kings.

[127] Maresch 1987. See now Lehmann 1988.

by the presence of the Rhodians. In the context of 306 they are a positive embarrassment. At that time Ptolemy was in Egypt, and it is hard to see why he should have taken such pains to communicate with them and seek their approval. This might be a Rhodian forgery, by writers such as Zeno who were prone to exaggerate their island's importance in the scheme of things. The papyrus echoes some of the claims in Diodorus' famous chapter on the prominence of the Rhodians after Alexander, and we could be faced with simple propaganda, valueless as historical evidence.[128] However, the overlap with Diodorus concerns the revenues which accrued to Rhodes from trade with Egypt, and this seems to be historical fact, reflected in the provisions of Alexander's supposed Will.[129] What is more, there is no reason, as we have seen, to anchor the transactions of the papyrus to 306. The statement that Antigonus had declared himself king is provided without context. It might form part of allegations made by Ptolemy and his advisers, and not be an authorial statement by the compiler of the narrative. In fact Antigonus' rivals had entertained suspicions of his ambitions from a very early date, and Diodorus uses language very similar to that of the papyrus to describe his ambitions as early as 319.[130] From 316 at least he had been hailed by his Asiatic subjects as king,[131] and according to Diodorus' narrative of the campaign of Gaza (which surely derives from Hieronymus of Cardia, a participant in the events), Demetrius was addressed as king by the Nabataeans,[132] and when his train is captured by Ptolemy and Seleucus, it is

[128] So Billows 1990: 351–2.

[129] Col. III, lines 24–8. Cf. Diod. 20. 81. 4. For the provisions of the Will, providing an annual supply of Egyptian grain, see *Metz Epit.* 108; Ps.-Call. 3. 33. 8; Wolohojian 1969: 272, p. 154. Ptolemy is attested to have sent consignments of grain during the siege of Rhodes (Diod. 20. 96. 1, 98. 1), and the donations may have begun somewhat earlier.

[130] Diod. 18. 50. 2 (περιβαλλόμενος δὲ ταῖς ἐλπίσι τὴν τῶν ὅλων ἡγεμονίαν ἔγνω μὴ προσέχειν μήτε τοῖς βασιλεῦσι μήτε τοῖς ἐπιμελήταις αὐτῶν). The passage continues with an explicit reference to the role of the historian Hieronymus (50. 4 = *FGrH* 154 T 4). Cf. Plut. *Eum.* 12. 1–2.   [131] Diod. 19. 48. 1; cf. Polyaen. 4. 6. 13 fin.

[132] Diod. 19. 97. 3. The speech is almost certainly the composition of Hieronymus (J. Hornblower 1981: 177–80), and the address is what he considered would be appropriate for Demetrius in 312/11. It is most unlikely that he was working from a *procès-verbal* of an actual transaction, and gave the Greek equivalent of the Arabic 'King' without realizing that it had a different connotation (so Müller 1973: 49).

explicitly defined as 'royal baggage'.[133] This comes close to self-proclamation, and might have been represented as such by Antigonus' enemies. Nothing in the papyrus, then, excludes a context early in 308, on the eve of Ptolemy's crusade in Greece. At that time, he was in close proximity to Rhodes, and the most plausible interpretation of the propaganda of the *Liber de Morte* suggests that he was taking considerable pains to win over the island. It is far from impossible that he communicated his regal aspirations and was duly recognized by a formal acknowledgement by the *demos* of Rhodes. They did not go so far as to ally themselves with Ptolemy, but they considered the earlier treaty with Antigonus void and took a neutral stance. It cost them nothing (and gained them considerable advantages) to support Ptolemy's regal pretensions. The transactions recorded in the papyrus could well be historical.

The events of 309/8 are of crucial importance in the history of the Successors. It was the first serious attempt to exploit the demise of the Argead house. Ptolemy intervened as the champion of Greek autonomy, the principle enshrined in the Peace of 311, and simultaneously promoted himself as the proper successor to Alexander's monarchy. To that end he liberated a string of cities from Antigonid garrisons, and established himself at Cos, where the Greek world could admire the pomp of his court and his wife could produce a possible heir. At the same time he negotiated for the hand of Cleopatra, the senior surviving Argead princess, and encouraged his courtiers and the representatives of friendly cities to address him as king.[134] By the spring of 308 he was ready to display himself in his new role, demonstrating to

---

[133] Diod. 19. 85. 3. For other references to Demetrius' regal pretensions see 19. 81. 4, 93. 4. It seems certain that the Antigonids were promoting themselves as a royal dynasty and did so for almost a decade before their formal assumption of the diadem.

[134] That was admittedly a radical change from his position after Perdiccas' murder in 321, when he had rejected an offer to assume the regency of the kings (Arr. *Succ.* F 1. 29–30; Diod. 18. 36. 6–7), but then the political climate was very different. The army which he would command was mutinous, heavily influenced by the fearsome, contumacious Silver Shields, and he would have to negotiate with Antipater who was forging through Asia Minor at the head of a strong army of Macedonians (so Billows 1990: 67). He resigned the poisoned chalice to Arrhidaeus and Peithon, who drained it with gusto—with the predictable consequences. By the time they reached Triparadeisus their authority was in tatters, thanks to the

the Greek world that he was the champion of freedom and that they had nothing to fear from his regal aspirations. The celebration of the Isthmian Games was to provide a visible symbol, and subsequently, so he hoped, the Peloponnesian cities would spontaneously expel Cassander's garrisons. At this stage things went wrong. Antigonus took the risk of having Cleopatra murdered, and deprived Ptolemy of his Argead bride. At much the same time the Peloponnesian cities showed reluctance to support the material cost of their liberation. There is probably more to the story, but the evidence fails us. At all events Ptolemy made peace with Cassander and left the Isthmus under the oversight of his regent, Leonides. His regal pretensions remained, but he had no adequate base to exploit them and challenge Cassander in Macedonia.

As we have seen, Ptolemy's ambitions provide the ideal context for the propaganda embedded in the various versions of our *Liber de Morte*, and it is likely enough that the nucleus of that remarkable document emanates from Ptolemy himself. The period after Alexander was rife with political forgeries. Our sources mention explicitly Eumenes' fake letter with its disinformation about Cassander's death, and Cassander himself made Machiavellian use of a purported letter summoning him to Macedon.[135] It was a similar, if more elaborate stratagem to produce a supposed Will of Alexander which flattered the Rhodians and emphasized Ptolemy's services to the dead king. Fifteen years had elapsed since the death of Alexander, but the production of wills *post mortem* was a feature of Attic inheritance cases[136] and well known throughout the Greek world. And it

ambitions of Eurydice, and they wisely resigned in favour of Antipater (Diod. 18. 39. 1–2; Arr. *Succ.* F 1. 31; Polyaen. 4. 6. 4; *Heidelberg Epit., FGrH* 155 F 1 (4)). To decline the regency under those circumstances was hardly the great refusal. Ptolemy had no lack of ambition and little respect for the Argead kings and their minders, as he showed the following year, when he invaded Syria and wrested it from its appointed satrap. In 309/8, when the opportunity offered, he had no ideological scruples, and aimed directly at the vacant kingship with Cleopatra as his intended consort.

[135] For Eumenes' forgery see Diod. 19. 23. 2–3; Polyaen. 4. 8. 3; Bosworth 1992: 62–4, and for Cassander's fake letter Polyaen. 4. 11. 2 with Bosworth 1994*a*: 64–5.

[136] MacDowell 1978: 100–5. The will of Demosthenes' father was apparently not extant and a matter of dispute over ten years after his death.

would not have seemed beyond belief that the Will of Alexander had been suppressed. Perdiccas, who was able to produce material from the archives to illustrate and quash Alexander's last ambitions, was in a position to conceal documents which undermined his own position. The *Liber de Morte* seems to emphasize the weak link that prevented publication of the Will. It was not to be taken to Rhodes by Holcias (who was indispensable at Alexander's side), but entrusted to Ismenias the Theban, who might never have reached Rhodes to discharge his errand.[137] Accidents were multifarious and unpredictable, and it need not have occasioned much surprise when Ptolemy produced a Will in the name of Alexander and in the interest of Rhodes.

Ptolemy perhaps did not represent himself as the principal agent in the recovery of the Will. It is a popular and probable assumption[138] that the author of the document is the mysterious Holcias who shares Alexander's last confidences alongside Perdiccas, Ptolemy, and Lysimachus, receives the Illyrians as his subjects,[139] and has a sister betrothed to Leonnatus.[140] Holcias presumably passed into the service of Ptolemy,[141] and produced a document which served the interests of his master, while giving himself a central position in the transmission of power. Relations with the Illyrians should have been his preserve; the actions of Cassander, who had recently transplanted the Illyrian Autariatae to northern Macedonia,[142] were therefore unjustified. His sister should have been married to a Bodyguard of Alexander, one of the leading figures after the king's death. Holcias, then, wrote himself into early Hellenistic history. At the same time Cassander's and Antigonus' positions were undermined; they were implicitly denounced as the anti-

[137] See above, n. 50.

[138] Ausfeld 1895: 365; Heckel 1988: 79–81.

[139] *Metz Epit.* 122; Ps.-Call. 3. 33. 23; Wolohojian 1969: 274, p. 155; Jul. Val. 3. 30 (1427–8).

[140] *Metz Epit.* 116; Ps.-Call. 3. 33. 14; Jul. Val. 3. 30 (1390–1).

[141] For his opposition to Antigonus in Asia Minor see Polyaen. 4. 6. 6. If he returned to Macedon in 320/19 with his insurgent troops, he could have left the turbulent political scene there to take service with Ptolemy at any time before 309.

[142] Diod. 20. 19. 1; Just. 15. 2. 1–2. For the earlier campaigns against Glaucias and the Taulantians see Diod. 19. 67. 6–7; Polyaen. 4. 11. 4 with Diod. 19. 70. 7, 78. 1, 89. 1–2.

thesis of what Alexander intended for themselves and the empire. The Will might have stood alone; but it is quite possible that it was accompanied by a pamphlet which gave a tendentious account of Alexander's death. It accused Antipater of contriving the poisoning of his king, with the collusion of senior marshals, who included acolytes of the Antigonids such as Nearchus, and it also showed Rhoxane as the true and devoted wife of Alexander. How far this original nucleus was developed we cannot say. Some later sensational stories, such as Alexander's attempt to disappear into the Euphrates,[143] may have been blended in;[144] and at the same time the original version of the Will was contracted and distorted by gross textual corruption. However, it cannot be denied that much of the *Liber de Morte* has a precise political relevance. It is replete with detail, tendentious and misleading, anchored to historical personages. There is demonstrable, directed malice which enhances Ptolemy's reputation at the expense of his rivals. The events of 309/8 provide what seems to me a historical setting which gives a pointed subtext to virtually every clause in the Will and to much of the narrative of Alexander's death. The conclusion is, I think, compelling. Much of the *Liber de Morte* emanates from propaganda hatched at the court of Ptolemy and is designed to promote his regal ambitions. Fiction it may be, but it has clearly defined political ends. The document was not meant to change history, nor did it do so. However, it appealed to its readers' curiosity, and, even if they rejected the individual details, there was a strong subliminal message: Ptolemy was the true heir to the legacy of Alexander and deserved the kingship.

---

[143] *Metz Epit.* 88–92, 101; Ps.-Call. 3. 30. 1–16, 32. 4–7; Wolohojian 1969: 259, pp. 147–50, 268, pp. 151–2; Jul. Val. 3. 30 (1277–1319); Leo 30 (cf. Arr. 7. 27. 3)

[144] The horrendous portent which precedes Alexander's death has been thought an obvious late fiction, but even this (as Liz Baynham argues, below, pp. 242–62) can be given a sharp political focus in the period after the murder of Alexander IV.

8

A Baleful Birth in Babylon

The Significance of the Prodigy in the *Liber de Morte*—An Investigation of Genre

ELIZABETH BAYNHAM

> The rat, the cat and Lovell our dog
> Rule all England under the hog.

Through a vivid play on names and family coats of arms, William Colyngbourne's epigram is a sour allusion to the leading supporters of King Richard III during the Wars of the Roses; namely, Sir Richard Ratcliff, Sir William Catesby, and Lord Lovell.[1] Colyngbourne posted the lines on the door of St Paul's in the summer of 1483; he was caught, tried—and hanged, drawn, and quartered in the autumn of 1484. Of course the use of such evocative symbolism was hardly unique to the fifteenth century; nor was its scathing import lost on its contemporaries, particularly the subjects of the couplet. But sometimes the meaning of symbolic visual or literary images may not be so obvious to us today.

One of the more intriguing documents in the extant corpus of ancient literature on Alexander is a fictitious account of his last days and Will, which was originally appended to a late Latin history known to us as the *Metz Epitome*. We can be reasonably certain that the real Alexander did not make a Will, but references to such a document are found in two of our main historical sources. Quintus Curtius, the Roman historian, claims (10. 10. 5) that an alleged Testament of the king had purported to distribute his empire amongst his generals, but he emphatically

I am grateful to Professor A. B. Bosworth for the reference and for comments made on earlier drafts of this paper.

[1] See Hillier 1985: 101–8.

rejects the validity of its existence and the tradition. According to Diodorus Siculus, Alexander admired the Rhodians so much that deposited his Will with them (20. 81. 3). Historically, this does not seem very likely in view of Alexander's treatment of the island; he had installed a garrison on it and at his death the Rhodians removed their Macedonian overlords.[2]

Within this volume, A. B. Bosworth has put forward a Ptolemaic context for the *Liber de Morte* and proposed a date of 309 BC. He has also strengthened the case for the pamphlet as political propaganda and demonstrated that it accords well with Ptolemy Soter's own royal aspirations at that time and his rivalry with Seleucus and Antigonus, especially in relation to courting the favour of Rhodes.

Yet one salient aspect of the composition as a whole is its false representation of actual historical events surrounding Alexander's death and its intersection with the clearly fabulous Alexander Romance. The narratives of both the *Liber de Morte* and Pseudo-Callisthenes (the basis of the Alexander Romance) are very close in content and tone. It is easy to assume that both were intended for the same purpose: entertainment. Thus the issue of the document's genre requires some further investigation, since this has often deterred scholars from treating its content or significance with the respect it very likely deserves—especially in relation to its place in the corpus of early Alexander historiography.[3]

I shall use the gruesome portent preceding Alexander's death as a pivot for this discussion.[4] Most scholars have explained this prodigy as a late, bizarre interpolation chiefly because it did not fit the earlier, political contexts proposed.

[2] The Macedonians had imposed a garrison, possibly from 332 BC, which may have been removed (cf. Curt. 4. 8. 12–13) but Curtius is not explicit that it was. Hauben 1977: 307–39, especially 311, suggested that Alexander responded to complaints about the behaviour of the garrison, without removing it. A garrison was still there in 323 when the Rhodians expelled it by force, Diod. 18. 8. 1. See also Bosworth 1980a: 242–3; Atkinson 1980: 372, 468. On the political organization of Rhodes during this period, see Fraser 1952: 192–206.

[3] For recent arguments that the *Liber de Morte* is pure fiction, see Seibert 1984; also his review of Heckel 1988 in *Gnomon* 62 (1990), 564–6.

[4] The monstrous portent; *LDM* 90; cf. Ps.-Call. 3. 30 ff. (Kroll); Wolohojian 1969: 147, translated from the Armenian; Syrian derivative, cf. Budge 1889 (repr. 1976): 134–5.

The imagery of a dead human male child joined to five large, aggressive animals simply did not seem to make any historical sense. Therefore it seemed appropriate to dismiss it as sensationalist fabrication—merely a shoddy special effect, intended only to create a frisson of horror—which was added to an already shoddy story. However, if Bosworth's date of composition of 309 BC is correct, the meaning of the omen may assume a startling clarity. It fits this context, but no other. The omen therefore becomes an integral part of the text. I will argue that it is designed, with maximum literary and emotive impact in mind, as a symbol of the historical distribution of the early Successor kingdoms. This in turn may cast some light on not only the document's purpose as propaganda, but the reasons for its compositional format. Why did the pamphlet take the form of part narrative and part Testament, for what audience was it written, and was it meant to be 'believed' as a genuine expression of Alexander's last wishes?

It may be helpful to outline a general background. The literary genre of the *Liber de Morte* is very puzzling. An exact equivalent to its type is difficult to find, but the *Liber de Morte*'s closest model would possibly be Xenophon's quasi-historical and Utopian *Cyropaedia*; in itself a multi-faceted composition which eludes classification into any one category.[5] One major difference between the two texts is that the *Liber de Morte* deals with a specific event. Nevertheless, there are some interesting parallels between Xenophon's depiction of the death of Cyrus and the death of Alexander in the latter. Both kings expire in Babylon. Like Alexander, Cyrus is given advance warning of his death, although in the form of a dream, rather than a birth prodigy.[6] It is true that there is nothing in the Alexander traditions which accords with Cyrus' lengthy, moralizing, death-bed speech to his sons and followers. Yet his instructions for the distribution of his empire and other dispositions possibly could have influenced the fabrication of Alexander's Will. In particular, Cyrus (*Cyrop.* 8. 7. 8) explicitly names Cambyses, his eldest son, as his successor on the throne and defines (8. 7. 11) which satrapies are to be given to his younger son. He also

---

[5] See Tatum 1989: xv.   [6] Xenophon, *Cyrop.* 8. 7. 2; cf. Hdt. 7. 12.

gives directions for his burial. Alexander in the Testament (LDM 115) is faced with the dilemma of not having an obvious successor at hand, since Rhoxane's child was still *in utero*. Nevertheless, he designates his preferences clearly. If Rhoxane bears a son, he will be king, but in the interim, Alexander's brother, Philip Arrhidaeus, is to be king and in the event of Rhoxane giving birth to a baby girl, the kingship is to be conferred through election by the Macedonians. Alexander also distributes the governorship of the satrapies among his generals and leaves instructions as to the transportation and burial of his body. A pointed contrast between the two texts on this latter aspect is that Xenophon's Cyrus requests a simple burial in keeping with his austere habits, whereas Alexander provides 200 talents of gold for his own sarcophagus and an additional 3,000 talents in silver for the casting of statues of himself, his family, and various divinities which were to be set up at Olympia and in Egypt. This tradition is only represented in the Will (LDM 119, 122) and the Alexander Romance (Ps.-Call. 3. 33. 16, also Wolohojian 1969: 274). Yet historically, Alexander's reign in general was marked by fabulous ostentation.

The king's love of generosity, opulence, display, and sheer showmanship is well documented. Partly the degree of this representation was determined by literary and rhetorical genre. By the Roman Imperial period, Alexander had become such a yardstick for excess of any sort, that it was inevitable that erudite intellectuals like Plutarch or Athenaeus could choose appropriate exempla from an abundance of material. However, is also true that much of the anecdotal evidence had its roots in the earliest accounts and should not always be dismissed as late embroidery.

According to Plutarch (*Alex.* 23. 9), Alexander regularly spent nearly two talents (about 10,000 drachmae) on a dinner party and expected his friends to do the same; one might compare Suetonius' story (*Vit.* 13. 3) about the Emperor Vitellius who expected meals four times daily from four different hosts, where each was expected to outlay no less than 400,000 HS. a time. Both of these occurrences would not be beyond credibility if one takes into account the rapid transport costs involved with rare and perishable items like certain types of fruit or seafood, or the importation of exotica from remote locations.

There were also the showy mass-marriages at Susa between the king's Macedonian followers and the Iranians, where some nine thousand people took part in a wedding celebration; each guest being presented with a gold cup for the libations.[7] It is not hard to find other instances of either supposed or historical extravagant excess in Alexander's reign. One might recall the proposed scheme of Deinocrates[8] to carve Mt. Athos in Thrace into a massive statue of Alexander himself, vividly described by Plutarch (*Mor.* 335c–f). The sources agree that Alexander turned the suggestion down, but at least one tradition (Vit. *De Arch.* 2. praef. 1–4) depicts the king as being so impressed with the architect's bold vision as to offer him permanent employment.[9] Hephaestion's funeral pyre or his monument was another extravaganza, which allegedly cost either ten or twelve thousand talents.[10] In short, the opulent provision of Alexander's fictitious Will is not inconsistent with the king's extravagance in the historical traditions.

We know that the *Cyropaedia* was a well-known text for the historical Alexander and his contemporaries. It influenced Onesicritus, who is said to have imitated it in style and content,[11] and may have had some impact on the narrative of Alexander's last illness in the so-called Royal *Ephemerides*. The *Cyropaedia*'s description is non-specific about Cyrus' decline, beyond a reference that he lost all appetite for food, whereas the *Ephemerides* clinically relates the course of Alexander's fever. But the correspondence between the two texts is the repetition of the same behaviour of the patient over a number of days and his increasing weakness.

[7] Plut. *Alex.* 70. 3; cf. Arrian 7. 4. 4–5; Just. 12. 10. 10; Diod. 17. 107. 6; Curt. 10. 3. 11–12; Athen. 12. 538b–539a = Chares, *FGrH* 125 F 4; Aelian, *VH* 8. 7.

[8] On Deinocrates, see Fraser 1972: 4 with n. 1. The artist's name is also reported as Stasicrates, Deinochares (Pliny, *NH* 7. 125), Dinocrates (Solinus 32. 41, 40. 5), or Cheirocrates (Strabo 14. 1. 23, 641).

[9] On the scheme to carve Mt. Athos, see Stewart 1993: 28, 37.

[10] See Plut. *Alex.* 72. 4; Arr. 7. 14. 8; Diod. 17. 115. 5; Just. 12. 2. 2; for recent discussions of the traditions, see McKechnie 1995: 418–32 and Palagia, 'Hephaestion's Pyre and the Royal Hunt of Alexander', within this volume.

[11] See *FGrH* 134 T 1.

This is not the place to explore the historicity of the *Ephemerides*;[12] however, paradoxically, if the account of Alexander's death in the Journal was a deliberately selective and circulated, if not fabricated, document, its purpose offers an interesting comparison with that of Xenophon. By describing Cyrus' death in Babylon from natural causes, Xenophon was clearly contradicting Herodotus and Ctesias in which the Persian king died a violent death fighting against the Massagetae. It did not suit his purpose to have his just and wise king who appropriated empire in order to save it from misrule and then devoted himself to its proper management, die as the aggressor in another war. Yet Xenophon was hardly offering a diatribe against war. The author and his audience would undoubtedly have known the alternative versions of Cyrus' death, but were prepared to suspend credibility for the sake of literary propriety. Xenophon's selective romance was offering an exposition of not only how to live, but how to lead. The *Cyropaedia* is a symbolic fable.

On the other hand, while the historical Alexander may well have died from disease, it is also likely that those who circulated the alleged official archive of his last illness wished to counter other, early and well-known traditions on the king's death which suggested alcoholism, or poisoning. The point is that Xenophon did not necessarily aim at creating historical belief, whereas the author (or authors) of the *Ephemerides* wanted precisely that very conviction.

The *Liber de Morte* contains narrative which may appear to us as sensationalist, clumsy, and perhaps suggestive of interpolation. Previous commentators have pointed to the role of the Rhodians as being anachronistic in a context of 321 or 317.[13] There are other passages which suggest romantic embroidery. Alexander is repeatedly poisoned in unknowing acquiescence by the sinister Iolaus, despite having received at the latter's hand the initial cup which so violently disagreed with him. However, the author of the

[12] See Bosworth 1988a: 158 ff., who gives a comprehensive summary of the problem with full bibliography.

[13] On the problem of Rhodian interpolation, see Heckel 1988: 70, n. 29: also Hauben 1977: 307–39, esp. 312 ff., and now Bosworth, 'Ptolemy and the Will of Alexander', above, pp. 213–14, 236–40.

pamphlet may have wished to stress the pathos of a king's
trust in insidious followers who should have owed him the
utmost loyalty. Such betrayal also enforces a similar, overall
theme of the document and its anti-Cassander tone. Moreover, the dying king secretly tries to throw himself into the
Euphrates, but is prevented by Rhoxane. The latter story
was known to Arrian (and emphatically discredited by
him).[14] But within the structure of the work the story serves
a purpose by presenting Rhoxane as a devoted wife. More
problematic is the suggestion that Alexander wished to
commit suicide secretly by throwing himself into the
Euphrates. In the Armenian version of Pseudo-Callisthenes
(Wolohojian 1969: 268) the king's attempt is depicted as
worthy of his great courage, whereas in the extant *Liber de
Morte* (102) he reproaches Rhoxane for robbing him of his
immortality—without giving any reason why. The explanation that Arrian provides of Alexander's motive is that the
king wanted his disappearance to be taken as a sign of his
divine paternity and that he had gone away to join the gods,
and such an interpretation may well have been part of an
earlier version of the *Liber de Morte*. Conceivably the
allusion could be a veiled tilt at Alexander's cult; however,
this would seem inconsistent with the document's overall
promotion of the king's divine paternity. Ptolemy very likely
interred Alexander's body in Alexandria and at least
acknowledged his heroic status; he may also have established
his cult.[15] But Ammon is consistently honoured; one of the
final clauses of the Will (122) is Alexander's order that
Holcias and Ptolemy are to erect gilded statues (*statuas
inauratas*) to Alexander, Ammon, Minerva, Hercules,
Olympias, and 'my father Philip' (as Alexander's mortal
father) in Olympia and Egypt respectively. Since elsewhere
the *Liber de Morte* stresses Ptolemy's readiness alone to

[14] See Ps.-Call. 3. 32. 4–6; Wolohojian 1969: 151–2; Budge 1889: 137. Cf.
Arrian, *Anab.* 7. 27. 3; see also Bosworth 1988a: 75 ff. on Arrian's critique of past
historiographical errors.

[15] On Ptolemy's burial of Alexander's body, see Curt. 10. 10. 20; cf. Diod. 18.
28. 3–4; Arrian, *FGrH* 156 F 9 25, 10. 1; Strabo 17. 1. 8; Pausanias 1. 6. 3 (who says
Alexander's body was buried at Memphis). On Ptolemy's seizure of the king's
funeral train and related activities, see Seibert 1969: 112 ff., also Billows 1990:
112 ff. Ptolemy's establishment of Alexander's cult is controversial: on the *sema* of
Alexander, cf. Strabo 17. 1. 8; Fraser 1972, 225–6.

honour the king's wishes, we need not doubt his compliance in this request also.

I return now to the baleful portent which heralds the king's approaching demise in both the *Liber de Morte* and the Alexander Romance. When Alexander is in Babylon, a peasant woman comes to him, bearing a hybrid monster to which she had just given birth. It consisted of the body of a male child to its loins with the lower part made up of five wild animals. The child was dead and in a state of advanced decomposition but the animals were very much alive. The description of the monster is elaborate and consistent in both the pamphlet and the early versions of the Alexander Romance: the beasts include a lion, a wolf, a panther, a dog, and a wild boar. The composition is deliberately evocative and the number and types of animals carefully specified. The author of the *Liber de Morte* likens the monster to representations of a similar creature in contemporary painting, and perhaps a reference to Scylla was in the original. The text is very corrupt at this point; however, the comparison of its appearance to Scylla also appears in Pseudo-Callisthenes (3. 30. 2; cf. Wolohojian 1969: 259). I shall return to the issue of iconographic representation presently.[16]

In the *Liber de Morte*, Alexander, terrified by the monstrosity, orders the magi and Chaldean seers (on pain of execution) to interpret the portent. The initial response is favourable; they suggest that as the human body was growing above the bodies of the wild animals, so Alexander himself was to rule the wild and barbarous tribes of the world. However, an additional seer, who also appears to have been one of the Chaldeans (named as Phippus in the *Liber de Morte*)[17] arrives and upon showing great distress at the sight,

[16] In the LDM, Scylla is an addition by Wagner. Heckel 1988: 9 n. 7, who accepts it, uses the comparison as evidence of a Macedonian origin and 4th cent. date for the Testament, in view of Pliny's reference (*NH* 35. 109) to the painting of Scylla by Nicomachus, who may have also worked on the Macedonian tombs; given the problems of artistic attribution, such a hypothesis may be taking the evidence too far. Scylla was usually depicted as a beautiful young woman, with a belt or girdle of dogs' heads below the waist; cf. *LIMC* viii Suppl. 1137–45, with some 4th cent. reproductions.

[17] The seer is one of the Chaldeans in Pseudo-Callisthenes (Wolohojian 1969: 259); cf. LDM 92. But the text is corrupt: Phippus is the reading supplied by the

interprets the omen adversely. According to the Chaldean,
the nature of the portent is twofold; the dead child represents Alexander himself who will die shortly. In Pseudo-
Callisthenes, the Chaldean says the animals represent
Alexander's soldiers, who will slaughter each other after the
king's death. Also, each seer predicts upheaval; a change
in world power structure (LDM) or a catastrophic event
(Ps.-Call.).

The role of birth omens in predicting events of individual,
regional, or world importance has a long tradition in the
ancient world. Interpreting the significance of abnormal
births of every type was a substantial part of Babylonian
and Assyrian divination, recorded at length in exhaustive,
specialist texts, which were intended for the instruction of
practitioners. The general underlying principle was that the
greater the abnormality, the greater the significance attached
to it.[18] The practice of interpretation originally derived from
observation and freakish malformation obviously did and
still does take place. Although there appears to be no direct
parallel to the *Liber*'s monster baby in Babylonian lists of
birth-omens, it is important that the author knew enough
about Babylonian texts and mantic practices to create veri-
similitude. Since Alexander at that time was the greatest
king in the known world, it was only appropriate that any
dire birth omen would be spectacularly weird.

The process of creating certain animal hybrids like mules
was regularly practised in antiquity; in fact, because of the
degree of human management required to produce them,
mules were normally more expensive than donkeys and
sometimes even horses. Malformation also offered the intrin-
sic appeal of the marvellous. The Roman general Pompey, no
less a consummate showman himself, decorated his theatre
with images of celebrated freaks (so Pliny, *NH* 7.3.34). Likewise, bogus marvels were evidently produced—the ancient
equivalents of Sideshow Alley. Pliny (*NH* 7. 3. 35) refers to

Codex Mettensis. Thomas follows Wagner's emendation of 'Phippus' to
'Philippus', but both editors appear to have ignored the context. It seems more
plausible to interpret 'Phippus' as a corrupted form of a Babylonian name, rather
than any attempt to make the figure Greek.

[18] See Jastrow 1914: 6.

a dead 'centaur' preserved in honey, which was brought to Rome from Egypt by the command of Claudius. If the anecdote is based on fact, one imagines that perhaps part of a human foetus had been skilfully sewn to the preserved body of a new-born foal.

Given limited understanding of the actual biological processes involved, it only needed imagination for certain cultures to popularly suppose the conception and birth of bizarre hybrids. These creatures could be literally part one creature and part another. They could also be offspring of different species born from totally unrelated mothers, such as a ewe bearing a lion, or women giving birth to animals as diverse as snakes and even elephants. According to Pliny (*NH* 7. 3. 34), the latter should be considered portents, as one of these monstrous births was associated with the outbreak of the Marsian War. Aristotle in the *De Generatione Animalium* (769b) argued at length against not only misinterpretation of malformation at birth, but also against the possibility of one species giving birth to another on the grounds of varying periods of gestation. Nevertheless, the appearance of such prodigies as omens foretelling great events is prominent in Roman traditions: indeed the Latin word *monstrum* is derived from 'a sign'. The gods were showing one something which demanded interpretation.

Birth omens are comparatively rare in extant Greek historiography and in some contexts are used as symbolic devices to enhance a narrative. Herodotus (7. 57) refers to two (biologically impossible) birth omens at the time of Xerxes' invasion of Greece; a mare gave birth to a hare and a mule dropped a hermaphrodite foal (in this case a baby mule). The historian explains that the former obviously meant that Xerxes was going to lead an army into Greece amid great pomp and circumstance, but would come running for his life back to the place he had started from. In view of Herodotus' (and the audience's) hindsight, the portent is used to anticipate historical reality. He pointedly explains the connection between the birth omen and its interpretation.

Plutarch refers to two birth portents where the political significance is also only too apparent. The first tradition is derived from Theopompus and occurs within the context of omens foretelling the collapse of Dionysius II's regime. A sow gave birth to a litter of earless piglets, which Dion's seers interpreted in his favour; the Syracusans would no longer heed the orders of the tyrant (*Dion* 24. 4).

In another example, a one-horned ram which was born on Pericles' farm was interpreted by the celebrated soothsayer Lampon as a sign that mastery over the two political parties in the city would fall into the hands of one man. The prophecy was initially discredited by Anaxagoras, who explained the abnormality in scientific terms, but when Pericles' opponent Thucydides was exiled and Pericles *did* assume control, Lampon regained the respect of the community (*Per.* 6). Robert Garland suggests that at an official or community level, the Greeks do not seem to have attached a great deal of significance to abnormal births as portents and he may be right.[19] However, although Plutarch acknowledges the anecdote as a story, he also explains that both science and divination have their place—particularly in the latter's relation to artificial symbols created by mankind.

The symbolism in other references is sometimes more arcane. In general, while portents of one sort or another abound in Alexander historiography, birth omens are not prominent—with one interesting exception. Again, according to Plutarch (*Alex.* 57. 4), just prior to Alexander's crossing of the Hindu Kush in the spring of 327 BC, a sheep allegedly gave birth to a lamb which had upon its head a malformation resembling a tiara with testicles on either side of it.[20] The king was disturbed by the omen; not so much for his own sake, as for the succession, since upon his death his power might fall upon an ignoble and impotent heir. We are not told why the birth is interpreted as symbolic of impotence. One might assume that misplaced genitalia would naturally be ineffective, but such an explanation is not explicit.[21] This is a curious episode and it is possible that Plutarch may have overlooked its full import, since he uses it

[19] See Garland 1995: 65.

[20] The omen is connected with the portent of oil at the Oxus.

[21] In Babylonian birth-omen texts there are many references to animals with misplaced genitals and their significance. They are normally interpreted as a bad sign; for examples, see Leichty 1970.

within a context of Alexander's initial depression at one omen and then joy at another.

The royal symbolism in relation to the tiara is obvious; moreover the sequential passage suggests that Alexander clearly identified the sheep as indicative of himself as a parent. But who might the lamb represent? According to the *Metz Epitome* (70), Rhoxane gave birth to a boy in India, who died while still a baby. There is no other reference to this child; however, even if he was born, the date would be more likely to have been 326. Yet there may have been a son who was born in 327—the fruit of Alexander's liaison with Barsine, the widow of Memnon, who may have still been present in the king's entourage. According to Diodorus (20. 20. 2), this child, Heracles, was about 17 in 310,[22] which could fit Plutarch's context. There could be no other more moving symbol of an impotent kingship than the young Heracles, who was first ruthlessly exploited by Polyperchon and Antigonus under the pretext of restoring him to his ancestral throne (*patria basileia*), and was then coldly put to death by Polyperchon in 309/8,[23] at the contrivance of Cassander, who promised Polyperchon he would restore his Macedonian estates and give him command of the Peloponnese, if he would eliminate his Argead rival.

This interpretation may be no more than speculation; yet what is apparent from the traditions on the Successors is that they and their attendants were a highly educated and literary group, as much at home with witty repartee, allusion, and riddle as any gentleman at a fashionable Athenian symposium. Seleucus was dubbed the 'elephant master' (*elephantarches*) by his rivals and Lysimachus was deeply angered by the courtiers of Demetrius Poliorcetes calling him a Persian *gazophylax* (a treasury official) because these men were usually eunuchs.[24] The cryptic symbolism of the sheep's malformed progeny may have been more

---

[22] On Heracles, see Berve 1926: no. 353: also Justin 15. 2. 3, who gives his age as 15 years. On Heracles' claim to the throne, see Tarn 1921: 18–28: contra Brunt 1975: 22–34.

[23] On the chronology of these events, see Wheatley 1998a.

[24] For Seleucus as the *elephantarches* and Lysimachus as *gazophylax*, see Plut. *Dem.* 25. 7–8, cf. Plut. *Mor.* 823 c–d, Athen. 6. 261b = Phylarchus *FGrH* 81 F 31. On the wit of the Diadochoi, see Lund 1992: 12–13; Billows 1990: 10–11.

apparent to Alexander's contemporaries than it was at a later time.

Portents heralding the king's death in Babylon appear in all the main Alexander historians but feature prominently in Arrian, Plutarch, and Appian. Alexander is warned by Chaldean astrologers not to enter Babylon,[25] Peithagoras the seer on carrying out a little entrail inspection exercise on behalf of his nervous brother, Apollodorus, finds an omen which bodes ill for Hephaestion and Alexander,[26] Calanus the Indian Brahman on his way to his self-immolation tells Alexander that he would soon see the king in Babylon,[27] Alexander loses his diadem on a boating expedition,[28] and a half-crazed stranger sits on the king's throne.[29] These are the stories with the largest distribution in our sources. Arrian openly states that Alexander was fated to die in Babylon and in his sophisticated literary fashion, ironically and cleverly interspaces the appearance of successive portents against a background of Alexander's intense activity and his plans for the future. But also striking is the symbolic use of the omens in the other historical traditions. Not one of them mentions a birth prodigy; yet there are several aspects of these accounts which find a curious correlation with the birth omen of the *Liber de Morte* and Alexander Romance.

Chaldean astrologers play a key role in both the historical and fictitious traditions, perhaps not surprisingly as the local experts in divination. According to Plutarch (*Alex.* 73. 2), Alexander on arriving at Babylon saw ravens fighting each other outside the city's walls and several of them fell dead at his feet. Ravens appear in Mesopotamian omen lists and fighting between birds was considered a sign of approaching turmoil.[30] The animals in the Alexander Romance are described as enemies to mankind and to each other; apart from the use of animal imagery, the common motif is the prediction of coming warfare. Moreover, the largest and

[25] See Arrian 7. 16. 5 ff.; Diod. 17. 112; Plut. *Alex.* 73; Just. 12. 13. 3; App. *BC* 2. 153.

[26] Arrian 7. 18. 1 ff.; Plut. *Alex.* 73; App. *BC* 2. 152.

[27] Arrian 7. 18. 6; Plut. *Alex.* 69. 3; cf. Cic. *De Div.* 1. 47; Val. Max. 1. 8. ext. 10.

[28] Arrian 7. 22; App. *Syr.* 9. 56: cf. Diod. 17. 116. 5.

[29] Arrian 7. 24. 1; Diod. 17. 116. 2; Plut. *Alex.* 73. 7–9. For a survey of these versions, see Montgomery 1969: 1–19; cf. Smelik 1978: 92–111.

[30] See Smelik 1978: 98 n. 24.

handsomest lion in Alexander's menagerie was kicked to death by a tame donkey (Plut. *Alex.* 73. 6). Stories concerning lions and asses are fairly common in the tales of Aesop and this anecdote may have ultimately derived from a similar tradition. But the lion is also in particular an Asiatic symbol of kingship.[31] Within its context, the inference of this anecdote is clear; the king will die at the hand of a lowly or less noble creature, possibly one of his servants. This automatically seems to point towards the role of Iolaus, Alexander's cupbearer who was instrumental in the alleged conspiracy to poison him. It is also evident that the symbolism of another portent was exploited by at least one of the Successors; in some versions the identity of the man who retrieved Alexander's diadem from the reeds and swam back with it bound around his head was said to be Seleucus.[32]

It is also commonly known that artistic representation could also offer images with symbolic messages. The Parthenon, an obvious example, proclaimed the glory of the Athenian *demos* in its elaborate sculptural decoration. In terms of Alexander iconography, one need only think of the remarkable Alexander Sarcophagus with its sides showing Macedonians and Persians engaged first in conflict and then taking part together in a royal hunt, where the quarry is a lion and a stag. The figure in the main battle scene who has been recognized as Alexander wears a lion-skin helmet and an eastern style of chiton, with tight-fitting sleeves and an overfall which was similar to Persian costume. The king's mixed dress is also depicted on another Macedonian in the centre of the battle scene, who is usually identified with Hephaestion. Whether the sarcophagus was commissioned by Abdalonymus of Sidon or not, it seems to commemorate Alexander's policy of mixed attire and co-operation between Persians and Macedonians—and interestingly has been assigned an anachronistic context. Historically, Alexander did not adopt aspects of Persian attire until after his last battle against the Persians and the death of Darius (330 BC).[33]

[31] See Palagia in this volume; also in Amm. 23. 5. 8, the killing of a lion foretells the death of a king.

[32] Arr. 7. 22; cf. Just. 15. 3. 11–14 and *Script. Hist. Aug. Sept. Sev.* 1. 9.

[33] See in particular Palagia's discussion of this important sculpture above, pp. 186–9.

I believe the monster baby in the *Liber de Morte* was meant as a literary device to symbolize an actual situation. The omen is extremely nasty; in fact comparable examples in Graeco-Roman literature are hard to find. The birth of a child would normally symbolize joy and hope for the future; the fact that the child is dead and decayed is not only horrific in itself but creates a terrible uncertainty. The identity of the dead child is straightforward. The five animals—the lion, the boar, the panther, the wolf, and the dog are more difficult to interpret. Assuming that the number itself is symbolic, it is possible that the beasts are meant to represent the five Successor kingdoms and their rulers, Ptolemy, Cassander, Lysimachus, Antigonus, and Seleucus. All of these generals had emerged as clear contenders by 309 (and also all appear in the text). Such an interpretation does not suit proposed earlier contexts of the pamphlet (either under Perdiccas or Polyperchon) as the eventual kingdoms were not defined by 321 or 317. But they were by about 311 when Antigonus was forced to recognize the sovereignty of Ptolemy, Lysimachus, and Cassander. Seleucus had just established himself in Babylon—with Ptolemy's support. Significantly, Seleucus' restricted authority of Babylon and its adjoining territory is explicitly provided for in the Testament (117) and the Alexander Romance.[34]

A historical context of 309 would also enhance the symbolism of the dead child. It becomes double; undoubtedly Alexander III, but also his son, Alexander IV, lately murdered by Cassander—who in the *Liber de Morte* and Pseudo-Callisthenes is one of the conspirators. One telling aspect about the narrative of the pamphlet is that Ptolemy is painted with nothing but the rosiest, glowing colours. He alone hears Alexander's last whispered words (LDM 111) and of all Alexander's Successors he tried to carry out the wishes outlined in his Will—such as seeking a marriage with the king's sister, Cleopatra (LDM 117). An obvious question one might pose is that if the document is Ptolemaic and aimed at denigrating Antigonus and Cassander, why would

---

[34] Ps.-Call. 3. 33. 15; cf. Jul. Val. 3. 58; Leo 33; Exc. Barb., p. 272, Dexippus, *FGrH* 100 F 8. 6. On Seleucus' settlement, see Bosworth, 'Ptolemy and the Will of Alexander', above, pp. 209–10.

their sovereignty be acknowledged at all? The answer is that Alexander's Will is a document concocted to display his alleged wishes which were blatantly flouted by the designs of his ambitious generals. The pamphlet presents Rhoxane as a faithful, loving wife and Olympias as a devoted mother, whose equally caring son intended to leave her to the protection of the Rhodians. The provisions for Alexander's wife and sisters as set out in his Testament were ignored by the marshals (with the exception of Ptolemy, as noted earlier). In the *Liber de Morte*, the portent thus becomes symbolic of the reality—that Alexander's empire was broken up into five kingdoms after his death.

Another pertinent question is that if one assumes that the animals are meant to represent the Successors, which beast symbolizes whom? The literary and iconographical evidence for any kind of association between the Diadochoi and animals is scanty and often obscure. This means that any proposal for the most part, is invariably speculative and difficult to pin down. The coinage is not particularly helpful; Alexander's image dominates the satrapal issues of the Diadochoi and the use of animals is fairly limited. Three of the Successors used a lion motif. A lion appears on Lysimachus' early coinage which was minted at Lysimacheia and possibly as his own personal seal; the lion may also have been used as a seal by Alexander.[35] In *circa* 240 BC, Ptolemy, son of Lysimachus, minted a coin showing a lion with one forepaw upraised, which supports the idea of the lion as a dynastic symbol in the family. In view of the legend that Lysimachus had supposedly saved Alexander's life by killing a lion, his promotion of his association with the animal in his propaganda is not surprising. His flagship was even named *Leontophoros*—the Lion Bearer.[36] We need not doubt that Lysimachus wanted to convey a leonine image.

A lion and anchor also featured on the silver staters of

[35] See Baldus 1978: 195–9, esp. 196–8; cf. Lund 1992: 160.
[36] For Lysimachus and the lion, see Curt. 8. 1. 14–17. A similar story is also told of Craterus (cf. Plut. *Alex.* 40. 5, Pliny, *NH* 34. 64). Craterus also offered a dedication at Delphi; see Moretti, *ISE* no. 73 and Palagia's discussion above, Ch. 6 n. 71. On Lysimachus' ship, *Leontophoros*: see Lund 1992: 160 n. 26. Alexander also may have encouraged comparisons between himself and a lion; cf. Kiilerich 1988: 56–7.

Seleucus[37] which were issued at Babylon in 310 BC and on some of Cassander's coinage.[38] However, as a royal symbol, the lion was obvious property for any general who wanted to underscore his associations with Alexander, if not his own aspirations, even though Hellenistic kingship was in its embryonic stage. The use of the lion by one Successor need not preclude it from being used by any of the others, or even necessarily mean that the lion represents Lysimachus, Seleucus, or Cassander in the omen of the *Liber de Morte*. Allowing for a little more incongruity in a prodigy that is already downright incongruous, the animal that one might obviously expect for Seleucus would be the elephant. But the mocking epithet of 'elephant master' may be anachronistic for a context of 309. The date of Seleucus' famous treaty with Chandragupta is difficult to determine, but it was not before 308 and is usually placed around 303/2 BC. This gave him a stable of 500 elephants, yet the animals would have taken some time to transport and acclimatize. They did not prove their decisive power until the battle of Ipsus.[39]

There is some evidence to link the wild boar with Cassander of Macedon, since it was a Macedonian rite of passage for an aristocratic youth to kill a boar before he could take his place with grown men. According to a certain Hegesander (via Athenaeus 1. 18a), Cassander was already a mature 35-year-old before his full credentials in this matter were established. The implied insult would be all too apparent to his contemporaries, and since Cassander is one of the main villains in the pamphlet, very appropriate.

The symbolism of the remaining animals, the wolf, the panther, and the dog is even more arcane. If the lion does not stand for Lysimachus then possibly he may be designated in this context by the panther. The cult of Dionysus was important at the Macedonian court, Thrace was significant either for the origin or youth of the god, and the

[37] A silver stater of Seleucus I issued in Babylon around 310 BC showing a lion and anchor is in the British Museum, Cunningham Collection CM 1888-12-8; BMC 51.

[38] See Miller 1991: 49–55; Cassander adopted earlier issues of Amyntas III and Perdiccas III which showed a walking lion carrying a spear in his jaws.

[39] On Seleucus' negotiations with Chandragupta, see Hauben 1974: 105–17; also Grainger 1990: 107–8, Schober 1981: 155–93.

panther was an animal primarily associated with him. A well-known pebble mosaic from Pella depicts Dionysus riding on a panther. Dionysus appeared on the coinage from Callatis, a city on the west Pontus with a large wine industry and some scholars have suggested that Lysimachus' great silver tetradrachms of Alexander display certain Dionysiac aspects.[40] But once again, the other Successors also made use of Alexander's strong links with Dionysus: Seleucus' coinage depicted Alexander wearing a panther skin.[41]

In European folklore wolves can symbolize theft and pillage; in 309 Antigonus was probably Ptolemy's most dangerous rival and again it seems fitting for the author of the pamphlet to use a pejorative image to represent him. Yet there is no direct evidence. We are left with the image of the dog, and again no satisfactory linkage can associate dogs with either Seleucus or Antigonus.[42] The symbolism of dogs varies enormously according to culture and context and they can have both positive and negative associations. Interestingly in an Egyptian Demotic text there is a reference commemorating 'the Ionians and the dogs who have come to Egypt and the Great Hound'. One German commentator has identified the dogs as Macedonians and the Great Hound as Alexander, but how much, if anything, can be made from this obscure material is debatable.[43] It is possible that there was some kind of evidence which may have clarified each animal's association with each Diadoch, but which has since been lost. However, my feeling is that the author may not have intended any specific attribution. Instead the number of the animals, their strength and savagery are the most important factors. These are not gentle or passive creatures, but violent and territorial. Moreover, the presence of the lion suggests that the document

---

[40] On the coinage of Callatis, see Lund 1992: 35. For the Dionysiac aspects of Lysimachus' coinage of Alexander, see Davis and Kraay 1973: pl. 6 with adjacent discussion.

[41] See Davis and Kraay 1973: pl. 52, dating Seleucus' coins depicting Alexander in a panther skin to 300 BC, but see also Kritt 1997: *passim*, and esp. 1–2, 108, who argues that Alexander appears in a panther skin after 306 BC.

[42] A reader for OUP has suggested that the author of the pamphlet may have been implying that Seleucus was 'Ptolemy's dog'. This is an intriguing and clever interpretation which might fit a context shortly after Seleucus' seizure of Babylon. But Seleucus' ambitions soon gave Ptolemy cause for concern.

[43] See Spiegelberg 1914: col. 6, p. 21.

was indicating that only one of the contenders deserved royal status.

In conclusion, I turn to the questions I raised earlier. Who were the audience for whom the document was composed? If one accepts that the Rhodian passages were not interpolated, the high prominence of the Rhodians, both in terms of Alexander's generosity to them and their role as guardians of his Will and his mother, almost guarantees that they were meant as the primary audience. However, it is also very likely that the text remained in circulation in Ptolemy's Egypt and was eventually absorbed into the tradition of Pseudo-Callisthenes, which itself was probably first compiled in Alexandria.

Why is the document part-narrative and part-Testament and was it meant to be believed? These are difficult problems. We have to remember that the *Liber de Morte* in its extant state is incomplete and we do not know at what point in Alexander's reign the original commenced. The dramatic narrative is meant to interest the audience, to create a 'human face', and to enhance the context of the Will. Testaments and their perversion feature in Attic inheritance cases; as an obvious example, Demosthenes' guardians exploited his father's Will and property to their own advantage.[44] Also, in the past fictitious Wills have been composed which were obviously intended to be convincing. The tradition that Alexander was poisoned, which is exploited by the *Liber de Morte* and Alexander Romance, was very early and well distributed.[45] The Rhodians (and others) may have known from reports from surviving eyewitnesses a certain amount of what had actually happened in Babylon after Alexander's death, but may have been ready to accept as genuine a document which claimed to be a transcript of what the king

---

[44] See most recently, the discussion by Sealey 1993: 247–8.

[45] The Athenian orator Hypereides sardonically proposed honours for Iolaus, son of Antipater, Alexander's cupbearer and the alleged assassin. Cf. the *Lives of the Ten Orators* attributed to Plutarch, *Vit. X Orat.* 9 = *Mor.* 849f; also Oikonomides 1987: 169–82, who identifies *IG* ii² 561 with Hypereides' decree. However, see Heckel 1992: 285. Curtius (10. 10. 14, 18), notes the contemporary credence of the rumour, even though like most of the main, ancient Alexander historians, he discounts the allegations himself. Yet in 317 Olympias, claiming she was avenging Alexander's death, executed Antipater's son Nicanor and destroyed the tomb of Iolaus (cf. Diod. 19. 11. 8; Plut. *Alex.* 77. 1).

really wanted. There have been notorious forgeries in our own times, like the Hitler Diaries—which deceived even experts—for a while. Also at that time, full knowledge of the events surrounding Alexander's death must have been restricted to a very few; interest among outsiders would have still been high and speculation rife. We need only point to the conspiracy theories surrounding the assassination of President Kennedy and the accidental death of the Princess of Wales. 'Was Diana Pregnant?' screamed an inside head-line of the *Times* recently in its promotion of a new book investigating the events leading to the fatal car-crash. 'Con-spiracy to murder' theories have remained an unfortunate if not inevitable explanation.[46]

However, I think the issue is more complicated than this. Historiography, like historical fiction is a creative process. As a general principle, historians set out to write what they believe to be true; the element of creativity comes into their individual interpretation of evidence and their presentations of it. On the other hand, the author of historical fiction writes either what could be true, or what most definitely is not true. In the latter case, as with the *Cyropaedia*, some-times didacticism, rather than historical reconstruction, is the writer's purpose. Xenophon's Cyrus is meant to be seen as a model king. It does not matter that he was nothing like the real man. In the same way, the author of the *Liber de Morte* is saying to his audience that Ptolemy is the best and noblest of Alexander's generals, beloved of the late king, the only one who tried to fulfil his wishes and the obvious choice as his royal Successor.

It is true that entertainment is very relevant here, and once more, the varying degrees of knowledge that the audience would hold. In fact, historical fiction plays upon this very aspect. How much one can separate fact from fiction depends on individual knowledge or research—but in the meantime we are entertained and intrigued. Signifi-cantly, the author of the *Liber de Morte* deliberately mentions (97–8) one of Alexander's eyewitness historians, Onesicritus, who he claims was 'too frightened' to name

---

[46] For more examples of 'conspiracy theories' see the incisive discussion by E. Badian within this volume.

certain marshals as conspirators against the king. But the mysterious author himself suffers from no such inhibitions.[47]

We do not know how many histories of Alexander, especially from those men who had been on the expedition, were already in circulation. It is possible that Nearchus' work was available as well as Onesicritus' and since the former had attached himself to Antigonus' court by 312, it is not surprising that he is named among those who knew of the conspiracy to poison the king.

As for Ptolemy—the composition of the *Liber de Morte* in 309/8 suited his immediate purpose of flattering Rhodes and his regal ambitions. At that time he was a formidable challenge to Antigonus and the other former generals of Alexander. He had achieved some stunning successes in Asia Minor and central Greece and could well present himself as the heir to Alexander's mantle. The situation was to radically alter shortly afterwards: Ptolemy suffered a disastrous defeat in Cyprus in 306 BC at the hands of Demetrius and Antigonus and his policy became more separatist. But this need not preclude earlier ambitions or his approval of a skilful, propagandist piece of fiction.

One modern and surprisingly durable view on Soter's composition of his own history suggests that the sober, factual, 'soldier' Ptolemy (to use Pearson's term)[48] wrote late in life 'to set the record straight', and to correct all the nonsense which had been circulated about the great Alexander. It is something of a poetic justice, I think, that this view should have derived from Arrian's summation, some five centuries later; 'Ptolemy was himself a King, and it is more disgraceful for a King to tell lies than anybody else': ὅτι καὶ αὐτῷ βασιλεῖ ὄντι αἰσχρότερον ἤ τῳ ἄλλῳ ψεύσασθαι ἦν.

---

[47] Cf. LDM 97–8 = *FGrH* 134 F 37; see also Bosworth 1971a: 116; Heckel 1988: 2.

[48] See Pearson 1960.

9

Artifice and Alexander History

Elizabeth Carney

Although I have never cared for musicals, when I was a graduate student I once tried, unsuccessfully, to persuade a group of my friends who all worked in the Carolina Coffee Shop in Chapel Hill, North Carolina, to break into joint song and perhaps a little bit of dance as they negotiated their way among tables full of coffee drinkers reading the Sunday *New York Times*. My plan for the coffee house failed because we couldn't agree on what song they would launch into in such implausible unison and because my cronies, whose fellowships had run out, were afraid that acting on my plan would cost them their jobs. Introducing artifice into real life is a tricky business. In fact, what I don't like about musicals is their unapologetic artificiality. How do those people all know they should break into the same song at the same moment and why don't those around them react with astonishment when they do so? Perhaps because of the inherent difficulty involved in combining the contrived with the un-contrived, obvious artifice, the very thing that puts me off as a movie-goer, intrigues me as an historian.

Distinctions between the real and what is represented as real are not always easy to draw, primarily because the relationship between them is complex, sometimes symbiotic rather than oppositional. In recent times, representation has received more attention than reality in many areas of scholarship. Indeed, my notion that both exist or are discussable as somewhat separate entities is probably an old-fashioned one. None the less, my interest here is in the intersection between the real, the lived event, and its representation.

Our sources for the reign of Alexander the Great are full of set pieces, occasions in which the usually transparent ropes moving people and scenery about in ordinary narrative become evident and we recognize that we are being manipulated. Some of these set pieces are so obvious that they constitute no real problem for the historian. We are not, for instance, really tempted to believe that Alexander got chummy with any Amazons (Plut. *Alex.* 46. 1–2). Other set pieces are not in themselves fictional but rather quite real events like the great battles which the historians of Alexander relate with varying degrees of artifice.

In this chapter, however, I intend to look at two themes in Alexander history in which it is not so easy to draw the line between what happened and what did not, between the real and the significantly augmented event. I want to look at the series of anecdotes about the advice—mostly meant to seem bad—that Parmenio gave Alexander and at the series of occasions on which Alexander isolated himself and the rest of the army, usually, then sought to persuade him to return.

My interest in these two series of events is not primarily source criticism. I want to look at the problem of how an historian should treat narrative material which is, at best, of somewhat dubious historicity and to reflect on the implications for historians of the image of Alexander constructed in these two themes.

When one looks carefully at its constituent elements, the theme of Parmenio's advice proves more nuanced than has often been recognized. While the series of incidents generally portrays Parmenio as rational, cautious, and fearful of risk-taking and Alexander as impulsive, daring, and even fond of risks, Arrian (1. 18. 6–9) tells one story that reverses the standard characterization of the pair. In this case, Parmenio is the one who advocates a risky policy, the continuation of a Graeco-Macedonian fleet despite the fact that the Persian naval forces dramatically outnumber it. Parmenio even expresses his willingness to share personally in the danger of the expedition. Alexander rejects the project as too dangerous as well as impolitic.

While a number of anecdotes picture Alexander as a person who makes the heroic choice by rejecting Parmenio's more cautious advice, only some of these incidents provide truly negative, genuinely hostile portraits of Parmenio. Often, Parmenio functions merely as a foil to Alexander.

The focus of such incidents is Alexander's heroism, not Parmenio's lack of it. For instance, in the tale of Philip the doctor, in which Alexander ignores Parmenio's warning that the physician has been bribed by Darius to poison the king and takes a dose of medicine prescribed by Philip (Plut. *Alex.* 19. 1–3; Arr. 2. 4. 7–11; Just. 11. 8. 3–9; Curt. 3. 5. 1–6. 20; Diod. 17. 31. 4–6), the stress on the king's bravery, his desire for a speedy recovery in order to pursue Darius, and/or his trust in the physician is so great, that Parmenio exists in the narrative only to provide a source for the warning, an occasion for melodrama. None of the narratives displays any further interest in Parmenio or bothers to consider why he provided apparently inaccurate information.[1] Diodorus found Parmenio's role in the incident so peripheral to the episode that he chose to omit it entirely.

Although the sources generally portray Parmenio as a traditional Macedonian uninclined to see Alexander in the context of ruler of the Persian Empire,[2] on two occasions they do not. Plutarch (*Alex.* 21. 4–5) says that Parmenio urged Alexander to establish a relationship with Barsine, primarily because of the importance of her father, Artabazus, whose mother was an Achaemenid. In another incident implying a certain sensitivity to Persian views, Arrian (3. 18. 11) recounts that Parmenio urged Alexander not to burn the palace at Persepolis, arguing that it would cost him Asian support. He said that it would suggest that he did not intend to retain his Asian empire, that he was, in fact, only a conqueror, not a ruler.

Parmenio's advice was not always bad or represented as being so. On five occasions, the sources recount that Alexander, rather than rejecting Parmenio's advice, accepts it and the sources imply that the king was right to do so.[3] Arrian (3. 18. 11–12) explicitly states that Alexander should

[1] The Greek Alexander Romance (2. 8) is interested in Parmenio's motivation and provides an explanation: he had been trying to get Philip to poison the king and tried to implicate Philip when he refused to participate in the plot. According to the story, Alexander, with surprising restraint, merely fires Parmenio.

[2] For instance, they report that Parmenio urged Alexander to accept Darius' offer of his empire west of the Euphrates, to concentrate on Macedonia, and not to attempt to be an Asian ruler (Plut. *Alex.* 29. 4; Diod. 17. 54. 1–3; Curt. 4. 11. 1–15; Arr. 2. 25. 1–2).

[3] Arr. 1. 25. 4–10; 3. 9. 3–4; Curt. 4. 10. 16–17; 3. 7. 6–10; Plut. *Alex.* 21. 4–5.

have followed Parmenio's advice not to burn Persepolis.
Two other passages imply that, on occasion, Alexander
might have been better off had he followed Parmenio's
advice.[4]

Nor is the body of Parmenio advice anecdotes as mono-
lithic as is often implied. Only four incidents are reported by
three or four of the major Alexander narratives (no incident
is reported by all five)[5] and seven incidents involving
Parmenio's advice are mentioned by only one author of a
major narrative.[6] The context for Parmenio's advice often
varies from author to author, even when several sources
refer to the same incident. In some sources, Parmenio
proffers unsolicited advice, whereas in others he responds to
repeated requests of Alexander for advice.[7] Some authors
say that Parmenio spoke for a larger group, particularly
older officers, but other authors, dealing with the same
incident, picture him standing alone.[8] The sources usually
seem to understand the advice and subsequent discussion
as happening in public, but some sources imagine a formal
council meeting whereas others seem to assume a less formal
circumstance.[9] Such discrepancies reflect the generally

---

[4] Curtius (4. 12. 21) says that Alexander, early in the battle of Gaugamela, began
to fear that Parmenio's advice to accept Darius' offer had been correct. While the
incident reported by Diodorus (17. 16. 2) in which Alexander rejects the advice of
both Parmenio and Antipater to marry before his departure for Asia contains no
explicit condemnation of his decision and does stress his heroic priorities, the tone
of the narrative, granted subsequent events, seems to suggest some disapproval.

[5] The four incidents are: Parmenio's warning to Alexander about Philip the
doctor (Plut. *Alex.* 19. 1–3; Arr. 2. 4. 7–11; Just. 11. 8. 3–9; Curt. 3. 5. 1–6. 20);
Parmenio's advice to accept Darius' offer (see above, n. 2); Parmenio's advice to
attack Darius' army at Gaugamela at night (Plut. *Alex.* 31. 5–7; Arr. 3. 10. 1–2;
Curt. 4. 13. 3); and Parmenio's warning for Alexander to wake up rather than sleep
on the day of the battle of Gaugamela (Plut. *Alex.* 32. 1–2; Curt. 4. 13. 17–25; Just.
11. 13. 1–3; Diod. 17. 56. 2–4). (The reader may doubt whether this last episode is
indeed an example of advice; I have concluded, with some hesitation, that it was.)

[6] Diod. 17. 116. 2; Arr. 1. 18. 6; 1. 25. 1–4; Curt. 3. 7. 8–10; 4. 10. 16–17; Plut.
Alex. 21. 4–5; Arr. 3. 18. 11.

[7] For instance, Plutarch (*Alex.* 31. 6) and Arrian (3. 10. 1) report that Parmenio
sought Alexander out before the battle of Gaugamela to offer advice, whereas
Curtius (4. 13. 3) has Alexander call a council and ask for advice.

[8] Plutarch (*Alex.* 31. 5) and Curtius (4. 13. 4–10) say that when Parmenio
proffered advice, he was the advocate for a larger group of *hetairoi* with the same
view. Arrian, in the same incident, seems to picture Parmenio speaking alone (3.
10. 1). Plutarch (*Alex.* 16. 1–2) seems to see Parmenio as a spokesman for a larger
group at Granicus too.

[9] According to Diodorus, Parmenio and Antipater offered their marriage advice

mixed tradition preserved in our sources about the nature of the Macedonian political structure.[10]

Now we must confront the issue of the historicity of Parmenio's advice. Scholars have tended to pay lip-service to the possibility that the advice theme is not historical, and then to treat each incident separately, judging its historicity on the plausibility of the incident itself, perhaps preferring one author's account to another.[11] A number of these incidents have, in fact, been widely accepted at face value, even ones reported in only one major source. Few scholars, for instance, have doubted that Parmenio and Antipater advised Alexander to marry before he invaded the Persian Empire, an incident reported by Diodorus only (17. 16. 2).[12]

This approach to the advice theme has a fundamental flaw. Each of the incidents, looked at by itself, is plausible enough. Parmenio was Alexander's senior officer, an experienced commander with great authority among both Greek and Macedonian soldiers. One can hardly doubt that he offered advice on occasions or that Alexander asked him for advice. The ageing general may often have embraced very different views from those held by his daring young commander. The implausibility lies, as Hamilton noted,[13] not in the individual incidents but rather in the theme. Even granted the variations in the advice theme I have noted, one has a hard time believing that Parmenio and Alexander so often disagreed on basic policy and that Parmenio's advice

at a meeting of Alexander's military leaders (Diod. 17. 16. 1–2). Plutarch (*Alex.* 29. 4), Diodorus (17. 54. 3), Curtius (4. 11. 1), and Arrian (2. 25. 2) all report that Parmenio's advice to accept Darius' offer to share his empire happened at a formal meeting of the king's Companions. Curtius (4. 13. 3) also says that Parmenio's advice about Gaugamela was offered at such a council, but Arrian (3. 10. 1) notes that some sources say Parmenio went to Alexander's tent to offer this advice, but does say that others were listening. Brunt 1976: 452 suggests that Parmenio's advice to Alexander about caution at Granicus was private; the sources do not specify on this and other occasions.

[10] See further Atkinson 1980, 180.

[11] For instance, Badian 1960: 328 says 'not all stories in which Alexander successfully ignored Parmenio's advice will be true, but some go back to good sources'.

[12] e.g. Bosworth 1988*b*: 43; Hamilton 1973: 50; Green 1991: 152 accept Diodorus' report that Antipater and Parmenio advised Alexander to marry and procreate before departing for Asia.

[13] Hamilton 1969: 89.

was so often wrong. Approaching the incidents seriatim simply avoids the issue that the theme raises.

Another problem develops when one judges each advice incident individually on the basis of its plausibility. The notion of plausibility is inherently extremely subjective. What Tarn found plausible, we now do not; what Hammond considers eminently reasonable, I often do not. Certainly all scholars must use judgements of plausibility in analysing the world of Alexander. Our judgements are based and, to some degree, validated by our general understanding of Alexander, ancient Macedonia, and our sources. We must be careful, however, of excessive use of plausibility as a sole standard, particularly when we deal with anecdotal material.[14] The danger that a circular argument will develop is extreme. One begins with the assumption that Parmenio was one sort of man and Alexander another sort. On that basis, one rejects or accepts the historicity of an incident, yet one's sense for what sort of person each was is coloured often by the incident itself, or by other anecdotal material like it.

Source criticism seems to offer an alternative to the somewhat circular and certainly subjective standard of plausibility. A common, although hardly universal, view has held that the advice theme ultimately derives from Callisthenes, that it was the invention of Alexander's 'official historian' in the period immediately subsequent to the deaths of Philotas and Parmenio in 330. Callisthenes has been supposed to use the advice motif theme to exculpate Alexander in the matter of the murder of the old general.[15] Despite some difficulties inherent in identifying Callisthenes as the source for the advice theme because of the historian's own not much subsequent fall from grace,[16] the idea that much of the advice theme is apologetic, meant to justify Alexander's actions and policies, is believable, particularly since this justification often emphasizes the heroic aspect of Alexander, as we know

[14] See Saller 1980: 69–83 for salutary cautions about the dependability of anecdotal material.

[15] Although Pearson (1960: 47) and Heckel (1992: 20) have dissented, the majority of scholars have found the idea that Callisthenes was the source for the hostile portrait of Parmenio created by many elements in the advice theme convincing (Cauer 1894: 33–5; Berve 1926: 303; Hamilton 1969; Atkinson 1980: 398; Bosworth 1988*b*: 41 n. 44).

[16] See discussion in Heckel 1992: 21.

Callisthenes did. Other very negative material about Parmenio, not part of the advice theme, but associated with the battle of Gaugamela, much of it unlikely to be strictly accurate, certainly confirms the idea that our sources preserve an attempt to blacken the reputation of Parmenio.[17] Such a hostile source tradition about Parmenio can only date from the period between his fall in 330 and the death of Alexander and the demise of many of the policies Parmenio was believed to have opposed.[18] The most hostile material about Parmenio and the incidents preserved in many sources deal with the last two or so years of Parmenio's life and are heavily focused on Gaugamela. If Callisthenes was not the source for this hostile tradition, then a source from that period must be. None of the Successors had any obvious reason to blacken Parmenio's reputation; it was no longer relevant. Moreover, none of them had been involved in his death and only Craterus, dead by 320, had played a role in the elimination of Philotas.[19]

[17] The negative image is particularly strong in Plutarch (*Alex.* 33. 6), where Parmenio is accused of incompetence occasioned either by his age or by his objections to Alexander's policies.

[18] Contra Heckel 1992: 20–1, who believes that it must have originated after the deaths of both Parmenio and Alexander, partly because he believes that prior to that period too many people would have known that the stories were false and partly because no 'contemporary ever charged Alexander or Kallisthenes with blackening Parmenion's memory by alleging that he gave foolish advice or failed to perform his duties in battle'. Since Heckel grants that the tradition developed prior to Cleitarchus and Ptolemy, the first point would seem to fail because it would apply to that period too, when many of Alexander's contemporaries were still around. The second point seems to assume that we know more than we do about contemporary sources. More important, it is difficult to see why Parmenio's policies or Alexander's elimination of him would have been a significant issue after the death of Alexander. While several of Alexander's associates were implicated in the decision to eliminate Philotas, according to most accounts, the determination to kill Parmenio was Alexander's.

[19] Plutarch (*Alex.* 48. 1) says that Craterus was involved in spying on Philotas and Curtius (6. 8. 1–9, 11. 10–19) claims that Craterus was not only prominent among the accusers of Philotas, but was enthusiastically involved in his torture as well. Coenus and Hephaestion, also prominently mentioned in narratives of the death of Philotas, as well as Cleander, who was involved in Parmenio's murder, all predeceased Alexander. Parmenio and his son died because, more than anything else, they objected to Alexander's changes in the monarchy, his transformation into an eastern monarch. This issue died with Alexander. While Ptolemy's own monarchy was heavily invested in the aura and reputation of Alexander, it was his posthumous reputation as a great conqueror and leader, not his role in the nitty-gritty of obsolete political quarrels which mattered to Ptolemy. While Ptolemy certainly benefited from the collapse of the Parmenio faction, having become a

On the other hand, the entire body of incidents involved in the Parmenio advice theme cannot derive from a fairly contemporary effort to justify Alexander's elimination of his faction. Some incidents, as we have seen, are not really hostile to Parmenio but simply glorify Alexander. Callisthenes, as we have observed, might be the source of such incidents as well. But other advice incidents fit neither pattern. Arrian, for instance, claims that Alexander, acting on information from Parmenio, after consultation with other associates, arranged that Parmenio arrest the prestigious and well-connected Lyncestian Alexander (Arr. 1. 25. 1–4). This version of the arrest of Lyncestian Alexander is the mirror image of the well-known tale of Philip the doctor, where Alexander chose to ignore similar information Parmenio conveyed to him about the physician. On another occasion, Curtius reports that Alexander took Parmenio's advice and did not read to the Greeks in the army letters from Darius offering bribes for treasonable activity (4. 10. 16–17). Alexander, again according to Curtius (3. 7. 6–10), follows Parmenio's suggestion for the location of the battle of Issus. Similarly, neither Parmenio's suggestion that Alexander take Barsine as his mistress (Plut. *Alex.* 21. 4–5) nor his neglected advice about Persepolis (Arr. 3. 18. 11) are incidents which either blacken Parmenio's name or heroize Alexander.

Some of the incidents just mentioned might derive from a pro-Parmenio source, as some scholars have suggested.[20] If sources which seriously defended Parmenio and his policies once existed, they too, much like the anti-Parmenio sources, would have had their origin in the politics of Alexander's reign. Whatever the merits of belief in pro-Parmenio sources, they, if they existed, would not explain the more

Bodyguard in its aftermath, none of the sources mentions him as a participant. Arrian (3. 26. 2–4) cites him for his very brief account of the deaths of father and son. The Arrian passage does seem concerned to justify the death of Parmenio, but that is all.

[20] Heckel 1992: 21 theorizes the development of a pro-Parmenio view, primarily detectable in the vulgate. Bearzot 1987: 89, 104 reaches similar conclusions. Bosworth 1980*a*: 115 thinks that Ptolemy may have respected Parmenio's memory and invented the debate at Miletus in which Alexander not Parmenio is the cautious one (see above). Another possibility is that these incidents are essentially literary, not political fabrications, part of the continuing dialogue between pro and anti-interpretations of Alexander, not Parmenio. See further below.

matter-of-fact of these advice incidents. Could these be the result of simple, non-partisan reporting of events? Perhaps.

While we could, therefore, divide the incidents in the advice theme into three tidy piles (anti-Parmenio, pro-Parmenio, and a third small group of a non-partisan nature), the advice theme is not really so easily explained. Significant variations in the accounts of different authors of the same incident strongly suggest that subsequent embroidery as well as significant excising occurred.[21]

The nature of the extant Parmenio advice suggests to me this hypothetical development for the theme. Its origins lie in the reign of Alexander, in Alexander's efforts to change the nature of Macedonian monarchy and to become an Asian ruler, and in the opposition of Parmenio and many others in the elite to these innovations. The intense hostility of material preserved in the sources relating to the period of the Gaugamela campaign and the events leading to it suggests that this was the critical period for the controversy, whatever Parmenio did or did not do at Gaugamela.[22] Contemporary with this specifically partisan issue was a general tendency to heroize Alexander, some of it already developed by anecdotes contrasting the heroic young ruler and the overly cautious old general.

After the deaths of Alexander and Parmenio, the series of advice anecdotes acquired an increasingly literary aspect as it lost its specifically political one. The advice anecdotes began to work like the paired speeches in Thucydides, as a mode of analysis, an unsurprising development in a culture fond of conducting analysis in terms of polarities. Indeed, many of the advice anecdotes are paired mini-speeches; the line between speech, dialogue, and verbal anecdote is easily crossed.[23] The undependability of included speeches in ancient historical narratives is notorious. The advice anecdotes, which appear to preserve less-than-public utterance, deserve even less credence. Clearly, placed in this context,

---

[21] Pearson 1960: 47 argues for significant later elaboration. Atkinson 1980: 398 speaks of the advice theme becoming a topos for rhetorical essays.

[22] On the controversial role of Parmenio at Gaugamela, see Bosworth 1980a: 309–11; see also Devine 1975: 382.

[23] See Hornblower 1991: 59–60 and Walbank 1985: 242–62 on speeches in Greek historians and the issue of their dependability.

incidents in which Parmenio offers advice may have been entirely or largely invented, simply to advance or clarify the narrative, much as many speeches are believed to have been.

Once this process had begun, Parmenio was no longer a specific Macedonian aristocrat with particular political views and foibles; he became an all-purpose not-Alexander, an Alexander opposite. The anecdotes also took on the colouring of stereotypical, almost folkloric confrontations between an older and a younger generation. In a tradition going back to Homer, old age, physical weakness, and prudent wisdom (Nestor; Phoenix) formed one pole and youth, physical prowess, and passionate action (Achilles) another. In reality, conflicts at the court of Alexander did not always or even usually break down along generational lines, although our extant sources often claim they did.[24] Moreover, the theme of Parmenio's advice constitutes a variation by reversal on the theme of the 'tragic warner' found in Herodotus and, to a lesser degree, in Thucydides.[25] Ordinarily the king who is warned is shown by the narrative to be wrong, guilty of imprudent and disastrous decisions, whereas the older warner, who is usually ignored, is shown to be right,[26] but in the Parmenio advice theme, the old adviser is usually shown to be wrong and the rash young king is vindicated. The advice theme, even if turned on its head, clearly derives from Greek literary tradition.

Once the advice theme was initiated, writers who found Alexander's character sinister, as Curtius often did, might develop one sort of detail; authors like Arrian might expand or delete in the opposite direction. Such additions and subtractions, however, no longer served any political view and cannot, therefore, reasonably be described as pro or anti-Parmenio, but rather sprang from essentially literary concerns, and stock ones at that.

In the light of this reconstruction of the development of

[24] See further Carney 1980: 230–1; 1981: 151, 156–7. Of those men said to have attempted to kill Alexander (Hermolaus and his friends; those involved in the conspiracy Philotas failed to disclose; Alexander the Lyncestian), most seem either his own age or even younger.

[25] See discussion in Bischoff 1932, Lattimore 1939: 24–35, and Pelling 1991. As Lattimore 1939: 35 notes, the warnings are at best of dubious historicity, primarily because they are so obviously a contrivance.

[26] Bischoff 1932: 1–4; Lattimore 1939: 24.

the series of anecdotes about Parmenio's advice, I must conclude that none of these anecdotes provides usable historical
information. It is possible that some of the incidents preserve, at least in part, material relating to actual decision-
making in the reign of Alexander, but even in these cases,
the increasingly literary quality of the theme may still have
so distorted the preserved accounts of the incident as to
render it essentially false. While I suppose that one could
argue that those few incidents for which it is difficult to con-
ceive a reason for their invention or exaggeration (e.g.
Parmenio's advice about Barsine) could be largely historical,
the best solution is to reject the historicity of the entire
theme. The main consequence or result of the development
of the theme of the advice of Parmenio is not to increase our
understanding of Parmenio or of the king, but to contribute
to the heroization of Alexander by generating a picture of
the king in which he is always young, quick, daring, and
successful. The representation of Parmenio in the advice
theme makes him so; the figure of Parmenio becomes a kind
of straight man for Alexander. This development of characterization by means of conversational opposition was and
remains a compelling narrative technique and our students
like it, but it isn't particularly true and it is probably largely
false.

Whereas the Parmenio advice theme is, I have suggested,
largely a creation of those who wrote about the reign of
Alexander in his lifetime and after, the series of stories in
which Alexander, out of a combination of anger and pique
and real pain, isolated himself from the rest of the army and
then waited, sometimes in vain, for elements in the army to
arrive and beg him to return to them, almost certainly
derives from the actions of Alexander himself. Details of our
accounts vary and may be false and exaggerated, but no one
has really doubted that Alexander acted in similar fashion on
three occasions: the slaughter of Cleitus, the refusal of his
troops to cross the Hyphasis, and the refusal of his troops
at Opis to obey his commands. Whereas the theme of
Parmenio's advice primarily involved speech and most
ancient historians felt free to invent speeches and dialogue,
the seclusion stories involve action, both Alexander's actions

and those of groups within the army. Ancient historians were far less likely to invent actions than speeches out of whole cloth, although they not infrequently added detail to narrative of events.[27] For these reasons historians have concluded that in stories of Alexander's seclusion it is not Callisthenes or any number of other writers subsequent to him who manipulate us, but Alexander himself, however assisted by subsequent authors.

Let me begin by discussing the nature of these incidents, as preserved in extant sources. It is important to note that the response of others to Alexander's behaviour was more varied (and more variously reported) than was the royal action which precipitated the response. When, immediately after he killed Cleitus, Alexander secluded himself, his troops and associates ultimately begged him to return and, whether formally or not, essentially excused his violent act. He sulked and was rewarded; his crime was not punished and the objections of those who shared Cleitus' views were silenced (Plut. *Alex.* 50–52. 4; Arr. 4. 8. 1–9. 9; Curt. 8. 1. 19–2. 13; Just. 12. 6. 1–18). When, on the Hyphasis river, Alexander's troops indicated that they would not cross, he tried the same tactic, again secluding himself, but this time he had to concede much of what those he had opposed had wanted (Diod. 17. 93. 2–95. 2; Just. 12. 8. 10–17; Plut. *Alex.* 62; Curt. 9. 2. 1–3. 19; Arr. 5. 25. 1–29. 1; Strab. 15. 1. 27, 32). A third time, at Opis, when his troops defied his plans, Alexander punished some and then once more secluded himself and again his troops or elements within them begged him to return and be reconciled (Arr. 7. 8. 1–12. 4; Diod. 17. 108. 3, 109. 1–3; Plut. *Alex.* 71. 1–5; Just. 12. 11. 5–12. 10; Curt. 10. 2. 8–4. 2). He got most of what he wanted. So the score is Alexander 2, his army 1 or perhaps 0.5, but there can be little doubt that the artifice here, the manipulation, is Alexander's. Behaviour that would in a statesman or general of our own time be inexcusable, was for Alexander always meaningful and, as we have seen, more often than not, successful.

Homer and Achilles are central to this theme and to

---

[27] I owe this distinction to the suggestions of the original respondent for this paper, Michael Flower.

Alexander's successful use of this strategy. Other than Augustus, it is difficult to think of a figure from the ancient world who more consciously controlled his public presentation than Alexander. His father, Philip II, skilfully altered the public presentation of monarchy in Macedonia, but Alexander was a master of self-representation and Homer and the figure of Achilles furnish the vocabulary of this self-presentation.

The relationship between Alexander and Homer and particularly between Alexander and the figure of Achilles used to be seen, in rather simplistic terms, as a list of rather formulaic imitations, but recent scholarship has done much to improve our previously anachronistic reading of Alexander's relationship to Achilles. John Keegan, the military historian, spoke of the Mask of Command[28] when referring to the nature of Alexander's leadership. Andrew Stewart sees Alexander as the origin of Faces of Power[29] and a number of authors talk about Alexander as a kind of actor or performer who has become one with his role.[30] An understanding of Alexander as a man who justified and explained himself to himself and others by embracing the goals, the values of Achilles, the values of Homeric heroes has become general.

Alexander's world had specific and explicit connections to that of Homer. The clan of Alexander's mother Olympias claimed descent from Achilles through his son Neoptolemus (Eur. *Andr.* 1239–49; Paus. 1. 11. 2; Pind. *Nem.* 4. 51, 7. 35–40) and Alexander repeated and emulated many events and incidents from the career of Achilleus.[31] Believing himself the descendant of Achilles, he embodied the values of

---

[28] Keegan 1987. Unfortunately, Keegan's analysis of Alexander's public presentation is marred by many errors and fundamental misunderstanding of the Macedonian milieu. His understanding, however, of the way Alexander's public and private personalities merged remains useful.

[29] Stewart 1993.

[30] Edmunds 1971: 391; Braudy 1986: 43; Keegan 1987: 47, 91; Cohen 1995: 484.

[31] See Ameling 1988: 663–4 on the importance of the claim to descent from Achilles to Olympias' dynasty. This is not the place for a lengthy discussion of the constituent elements in Alexander's Achilles emulation, but it is important to note that it was selective, surprisingly focused on his relationship with Hephaestion and on the early stages of his career in the *Iliad*, much less interested in the image of Achilles in the later stages of the epic, when the hero became more complex and more thoughtful. The Achilles Alexander chose to imitate was a rather conventional version of Homer's construct.

Achilles. Alexander's was not a unique or peculiar obsession, although his intensity on this subject may have been unusual. As archaeology offers increasing proof, the Macedonian elite in the fourth century either retained or recreated many aspects of Homeric values.[32] Simply put, to act like Achilles was to act, not just like an ancestor, but in a way that Macedonians understood and could admire. Acting like Achilles might, however curious it may seem to us, function as effective discipline in a Macedonian context; Macedonian and perhaps Greek troops might do what a commander wanted if the commander acted like Achilles. Like Achilles, the ties that bound the army to Alexander were fundamentally personal in nature and Alexander's repeated withdrawals served to remind his troops of their personal tie to him.

Let us recall the elements of Achilles' story and character relevant to Alexander's pattern of behaviour. Dishonoured by Agamemnon, Achilles chose to seclude himself from the Greek army. When the Greeks began to do badly without his help, they sent some of their most important leaders to beg Achilles to return to battle and aid them. He, however, refused to relent, rejoining the battle only after the death of his dearest associate, knowingly embracing his own death in order to bring death to his friend's killer. Achilles was anything but a team player and lacked co-operative goals or skills. Famously subject to the force of his own anger, compelling not so much by the rightness of his action as by its force, never yielding to the advice of others, he possessed great courage and skill in battle.

Although Achilles and Homer are clearly the main models and explainers for the behaviour of Alexander on the three occasions in which he secludes himself from the rest of the army, another literary model is relevant to the understanding of the reaction of Alexander's troops, at least some of them, on these occasions. In the *Iliad* the delegation of friends sent to persuade Achilles to return spoke to him calmly and rationally. Alexander's men, our sources frequently claim, acted quite differently. They frantically wept and wailed and stayed outside their commander's door

[32] See discussion in Ameling 1988: 657–92; Cohen 1995: 487–91.

for lengthy periods, attempting to persuade him to relent. Their actions recall the theme of *paraclausithyron*, a lover's song at the beloved's door, in which the lover begs for admission. The origins of this theme lie in the culture of the male Hellenic elite, in the drinking party, a context certainly very relevant to the Macedonian elite.[33]

Describing the excluded army in terms which suggest importunate lovers is not so inappropriate as it might first seem. Sexual or sexually informed relationships between men are an important part of Greek military life, often seen, as in the case of the Theban Sacred Band, as the source for inspiration and *arete*.[34] In Macedonia, however, such relationships, as demonstrated by the connection between Alexander's father Philip and Pausanias, his assassin, did not terminate at the end of youth but persisted into adulthood; they were an important part of court life.[35] Seen in the context of Dionysiac experience, certainly appropriate for the death of Cleitus, and the sexual mores of the Macedonian court, it is not really surprising that the relationship between Alexander and his troops, while not explicitly sexual, could be characterized by sexual tensions. Alexander's behaviour pattern often produced results favourable to him partly because it was, in some sense, flirtatious and that quality, in turn, inspired loyalty and achievement in the army.[36] As we shall see, these liminal emotional scenes are a much less consistent element in the narratives of these events than Alexander's angry withdrawals from his soldiers and I do not want to overemphasize this element in these

[33] Copley 1956/1981: 1–7; Cairns 1972: 6–7; Yardley 1978: 19–20.
[34] Dover 1978: 51, 191–4; Hindley 1994: 347, 365–6.
[35] Mortensen 1997. See Carney 1983: 260–72 for a discussion of the connection between frequent conspiracies against the kings and sexual relationships at court, both between members of the elite and between the kings and members of the elite.
[36] One thinks of the incident in which the Macedonian troops, while celebrating and feasting, encouraged Alexander to kiss his lover Bagoas (Plut. *Alex.* 67. 4), as an example of the less violent ways in which same-sex relationships informed the life of the army. Michael Flower points out the incident reported by Arrian (7. 11. 5–7), in which, after the troops had begged Alexander to relent, Callines, a hipparch in the Companion cavalry, explained to Alexander that the Macedonians were grieved because some of the Persians, because they were considered kinsmen, were permitted to kiss the king, but none of his own countrymen. Alexander responded that he considered all the Macedonians his kinsmen and then Callines and all who wished to, kissed the king.

stories—Homer is much more important—but neither do I think it should be ignored.

In what way can these three incidents be used by the historian; what do they signify? If all three incidents worked on the basis of the same set of values and expectations, why are the results of Alexander's repeated behaviour so varied and what do these incidents tell us about the reign of Alexander?

The death of Cleitus is universally recognized as an unpremeditated act, the consequence of Macedonian heavy drinking, human anger, the tensions of a culture and court in transition, and of the highly agonistic nature of Macedonian life, especially within the elite.[37] Most of the sources report instant repentance on Alexander's part (Just. 12. 6. 5–8; Arr. 4. 9. 2–4; Plut. *Alex.* 51. 6–52. 1; Curt. 8. 2. 1–3). Granted the situation, royal repentance was predictable. Alexander would certainly have regretted the consequences of the killing of Cleitus. He may even have regretted the act itself.[38] Whether or not he was actually suicidal (see below), his subsequent self-imposed seclusion and the efforts by those around him to draw him back into the world of the camp and campaign[39] were probably instinctive, at least initially. Alexander had violated the laws of hospitality by killing a guest, a long-time intimate who had saved his life, and, in the course of doing so, he had questioned the loyalty of his closest associates and threatened to turn the ordinary troops against them. Despite all this, his action was con-

---

[37] See Borza 1983: 45–55 on the role of the symposium and its resulting tensions in Macedonian court life. On the career and death of Cleitus, see Carney 1981: 149–60 and Heckel 1992: 34–7.

[38] See Bosworth 1995: 52 on the theme of the neglected sacrifice to Dionysus and connection to the story of Alexander's remorse.

[39] The sources vary only slightly on the specifics of the incident; source tradition on the two subsequent episodes is noticeably less uniform. In this case, Curtius says Alexander was in seclusion, fasting, for three days before 'armigeri corporisque custodes' burst into the tent, realizing that he was determined on death (8. 2. 11). Arrian (4. 9. 4–5) reports a similar period of fasting, but that the *hetairoi* persuaded him to eat and drink again (he also mentions that some sources say Anaxarchus the sophist helped to get him to relent). Plutarch (52. 2) has Alexander fast in seclusion only a day before his friends break in. Justin (12. 6. 15–17) is the only source who reports that all the troops, not just close associates, begged him to relent after a four-day fast (he also has Callisthenes help to persuade him). Diodorus' account of the episode is lost.

doned[40] and the likelihood of another incident in which a member of the elite voiced public objections to Alexander's policies was minimized.

Scholarship has usually insisted that Alexander got what he wanted because the army could not afford to lose him;[41] they were in the middle of nowhere in Macedonian terms—Maracanda—with a Persian rebel who had slaughtered Macedonians still on the loose and the only other available Argead was mentally incompetent. I do not think that this was the primary reason Alexander's behaviour after the death of Cleitus worked. The situation of the army on the Hyphasis was similar, but, on that occasion, the army failed to respond when Alexander secluded himself. He was the one who yielded. (See below.)

The reason the king behaved in the way he did after he killed Cleitus and the reason important elements in the army accepted his behaviour was that Alexander's deed appeared to fit Homeric norms. His actions had been excessive, as those of Homeric heroes so often were, but they were big, terrible on a large scale. In Homer and in Attic tragedy Hellenic culture showed a fascination with those who demonstrated extreme behaviour.[42] Alexander's behaviour appeared to replicate that of his supposed ancestor Achilles. Arrian's diction (4. 9. 5), when in speaking of the death of Cleitus, he says that some of the prophets sang of *menis* (wrath), deliberately mimics the first line of the Iliad and explicitly reminds the reader of the wrath of Achilles.[43] Heroes were proverbially angry,[44] but the anger of Achilles was unique and godlike.[45]

---

[40] Curtius (8. 2. 12) actually says that the Macedonians decreed that Cleitus had been killed 'iure' and would have forbidden him funeral rites, had Alexander not intervened.

[41] Badian 1964: 198, more or less following Justin (12. 6. 15–16), who says that the troops begged Alexander not to let his grief destroy them all in distant barbarian territory.

[42] Griffin 1987: 85–104.

[43] Bosworth 1995: 64.

[44] Griffin 1980: 95. They often withdrew from group effort because of their anger, as Phoenix recalled to Achilles (*Il.* 9. 524–99).

[45] *Menis* is used in the *Iliad* and archaic poetry in general only of gods; Achilles is the only human exception (Schein 1984: 91) and his wrath was notoriously unrelenting and superhuman. See also references and discussion in King 1987: 248 n. 109.

The Achilles' reference suggests an analogy that was both false and true. Alexander's fondness for the *Iliad* and emulation of Achilles is well known[46] and worked for him and his audience at a self-conscious level and an unconscious one. He liked to think he was like Achilles and he really was; his army admired and feared him because of this.[47]

Alexander's behaviour in connection to Cleitus was not, in many respects, however, remotely parallel to that of Achilles when Agamemnon insulted him. There is the superficial similarity, the self-imposed separation from the rest of the army and the delegation of friends, but the differences are greater. It is debatable at best whether Cleitus dishonoured Alexander to the degree that Agamemnon did Achilles.[48] When Achilles decided to abandon his role in the expedition, he was not, although the most prominent warrior, its leader, whereas Alexander removed

[46] See discussion and full references in Edmunds 1971: 372–4; Ameling 1988: 658–92; Cohen 1995: 483–505. Edmunds understands Alexander's emulation of Achilles and other heroes as religious in origin (Edmunds 1971, 369), whereas Cohen 1995, 485 sees it as secular in origin, derived from his education. Alexander imitated specific acts and aspects of the life of Achilles (e.g. Plut. *Alex.* 5. 5; Arr. 7. 14. 4; Pearson 1960: 10 suggested that Alexander thought of himself as re-enacting incidents from Homer), but, more importantly, the world of the *Iliad* informed his life, particularly his military life. Plutarch says that he took it to Asia with him, sleeping with it under his pillow, using it as a kind of military encyclopedia (Plut. *Alex.* 8. 2), and ultimately placing it in a jewelled chest (seized from Darius) on the grounds that it was his most precious possession (Plut. *Alex.* 26. 1; Pliny, *NH* 7. 29. 108–9; Strabo 13. 1. 27). Dio Chrystostom (*Or.* 4. 39) claimed that Alexander knew the *Iliad* by heart. Arrian (7. 14. 4) observes that Alexander's emulation of Achilles began in his boyhood.

[47] As Griffin 1987: 89–98 observes, even the *Iliad* shows both a fascination with excess and a certain repulsion from it, or at least willingness to criticize it. The excess of Achilles, the size of his anger, is often labelled *deinos* (terrible) by Homer (9. 654, 16. 31, 16. 203). Men loved by gods, especially Zeus, seem marked for destruction and threaten to destroy others with them (see references in Griffin 1987: 89–92). Bosworth 1988b: 43 argued that Alexander's excess, in the context of his nearly compulsive risk-taking in battle, by generating 'widespread expectation of his imminent death', increased resistance to his regime. Like Achilles, Alexander often terrified by his willingness to embrace extreme danger.

[48] Clearly, this is a subjective judgement and the differences in the accounts of our sources further complicate the issue; in some Cleitus more obviously provokes the violent action of Alexander (Arr. 4. 8. 7–9. 1; Plut. *Alex.* 51. 1–5) than in others (Curt. 8. 1. 51–2; Just. 12. 6. 3), but the essential circumstance of the encounter (a banquet), and the fundamental fact that Cleitus had saved Alexander's life and had a lifetime relationship with him, seem to justify my judgement. Alexander was, of course, senior to Cleitus, reversing the situation of Achilles and Agamemnon, a circumstance which also affects this determination.

himself from an army for which he was entirely and quite personally responsible. Both Achilles and Alexander experienced huge anger, but Achilles did not kill Agamemnon; Athena pulled him by the hair and convinced him not to (*Il.* 1. 189–222). Alexander's close friends tried to play Athena's role with him, but failed (Curt. 8. 1. 45–50; Arr. 4. 8. 7–9; Plut. *Alex.* 51. 4–5). The actual killing of Cleitus resembles the deeds of another of Alexander's objects of emulation, another ancestor, Heracles, a hero familiar with drunken and violent excess.[49] The suicidal impulse ascribed to Alexander by some authors (Curt. 8. 2. 4–6; 51. 6; Just. 12. 6. 7–8)[50] is more like Ajax, another ancestor of Alexander's (Soph. *Aj.* 815; Plut. *Alex.* 65),[51] than Achilles.

Alexander's quarrel with Cleitus may have been somewhat like Achilles' quarrel with Agamemnon, but the death and after-effects were not. Although they were not, Alexander and his army acted as though they were. Alexander had frightened himself, his closest associates, and his army. The way they found to understand what had happened was to read it as justified anger, much like that of Achilles. One reason they, Alexander and his army, could do this, was that he was, in many respects, very like Achilles and his army to some degree shared his Homeric understanding of his role.

Alexander's second sulk was less successful and less straightforward. As others have noted, his behaviour on the Hyphasis when the troops would not agree to go on as he wanted was clearly modelled on his behaviour after the

[49] See Edmunds 1971: 374–6 for discussion and references to Alexander's imitation and emulation of Heracles. See also Palagia 1986: 137–51. Heracles killed many people. His drunkenness in the household of Admetus so embarrassed him when he discovered that Admetus' wife had just died that he used his strength to force Death to give her back. He killed his guest Iphitus by flinging him from the roof of his house (or the walls of Tiryns), perhaps having been driven mad by Hera, as he was when he killed his children by Megara and others.

[50] Arr. 4. 9. 2 reports that some sources say that Alexander tried to kill himself, but that most do not.

[51] The dynasty of Achilles' mother Olympias, the Aeacids, claimed descent from Achilles, but Ajax, son of Telemon, was Achilles' cousin and thus an ancestor as well. At Troy, Alexander sacrificed to Ajax as well as Achilles, according to Diodorus (17. 17. 3). Greek attitudes toward male suicide were, at best, mixed and were sometimes negative. See discussion and references in Carney 1993: 50 n. 56. Ajax was the best known heroic suicide. His action was treated favourably by some authors, more negatively by others (see *OCD*[3] 47–8, for references).

Cleitus incident.[52] The tradition is less unified than in accounts of the aftermath of the death of Cleitus; two shorter major narratives do not mention a second seclusion at all.[53] In two accounts, no committee, no thwarted lovers, came to beseech him at the entry to his tent;[54] in another they came, but only to beseech him to agree with them.[55] Alexander, rather than the army, had to yield. Why did the same behaviour not produce similar results on this second occasion?

There are several reasons why Alexander failed at the Hyphasis even though the analogy between him and Achilles was, in some respects, a better fit. Nature had, in effect, brought his men low; they could not keep going. Alexander, however, Achilles-like, was willing to oppose nature, human and otherwise, and endure. The first incident had simply required his men to accept his behaviour as existing within a heroic, a larger-than-ordinary-life context, but the second required them to act in an heroic way themselves. This they were too tired to do.

As we have already noted, it is often said that Alexander's men put up with his killing of Cleitus because they needed him too much. They needed him, however, no less on the Hyphasis; the threat of further armies was one of the things discouraging them. The army's dependence on Alexander

[52] Badian 1985: 466–7, followed by Bosworth 1995: 355.

[53] Diodorus (17. 94. 5) simply says that when Alexander's speech failed to persuade the army, he gave up further efforts. Since, however, Diodorus indicates elsewhere (17. 108. 3) awareness of a troubled reception for his ideas, this omission seems to derive from the need to shorten the narrative. Justin's brief account (12. 8. 16) also omits the episode; Alexander immediately relents when the men beseech him.

[54] Arrian (5. 25. 3) says that after Alexander's speech and that of Coenus, he went to his tent and refused even the *hetairoi* entrance for three days (see above for similarity in length of time to his seclusion over Cleitus). When Alexander got only anger and resentment, he relented. Curtius (9. 3. 18–19) says that Alexander secluded himself only two days and that he did give admission to 'adsuetos'. Alexander is angrier at the men and his officers in Arrian's account than he is according to Curtius, who says that Alexander secluded himself because he didn't know what to do, torn between anger at the frustration of his own goals and an inability to scold the men, apparently in response to their pitiful entreaties (Curtius does not have them wait at the door).

[55] Plutarch (*Alex.* 62. 3) says that Alexander secluded himself out of *dysthymia* and *orge* (anger), but that his friends appeased him and the soldiers crowded round the door and begged him and that he finally relented. Plutarch's account of this episode most resembles the narratives of the Cleitus affair.

did not change and was not, therefore, an important factor in their reaction to either incident.

The problem was that, on the Hyphasis, they did not consider Alexander's situation comparable to that of Achilles, much though Alexander wanted them to. As I have argued elsewhere,[56] the event on the Hyphasis was a failure in discipline brought on by problems in the personal relationship between the commander and his troops. His troops did not see his actions as Achilles-like, merely selfish.[57] He hoped they would find his seclusion compelling, but they did not.[58] It is also possible that they saw in the repetition of this previously successful behaviour a kind of calculation and a level of conscious manipulation that was not in the least like the actions of the passionately impulsive Achilles.

Alexander's final sulk, at Opis, was his most successful (Arr. 7. 8. 1–12. 3; Diod. 17. 108. 3–109. 3; Plut. *Alex.* 71. 1–5; Just. 12. 11. 5–12. 10; Curt. 10. 2. 8–4. 2). The reasons for the Opis event are, as I have discussed elsewhere,[59] rather unclear, although the precipitant for another quarrel between the king and his soldiers seems to have been his announcement of the dismissal of some veterans. When soldiers voiced objections, the king had the most vociferous executed and stalked off to his quarters, once more isolating himself. After Alexander indicated that he would substitute Asian troops for his Greek and Macedonian ones, his men begged him to relent. Arrian and Plutarch have them waiting at his door; Curtius may well have done the same, but the lacuna in the text makes it difficult to be certain. Justin and Diodorus once more fail to mention Alexander's seclusion, although they do indicate that the men begged Alexander's forgiveness.[60] Granted the nature of the source tradition, it is possible that this third episode's similarity to

---

[56] Carney 1996: 36–7.

[57] I base this assessment on the narratives of Curtius and Arrian. These fairly similar narratives have generally been preferred by scholars, partly because many believe Ptolemy was an important source for both. See Carney 1996: 33–5, esp. nn. 89 and 90.

[58] In Plutarch's account (see above), the men are moved, but not enough to relent.

[59] Carney 1996: 37–42.

[60] Arrian (7. 11. 1) reports that, as in the Cleitus episode he fasted, apparently for

the other two has been significantly exaggerated by subsequent literary tradition, but it is more likely that Alexander was in this case, as in the earlier two, largely his own auteur.

Of all three episodes, this was the most calculatingly manipulative; Alexander must have been well aware that he was duplicating his behaviour on the two earlier occasions. This time, he heightened the effect of his ploy by including Asians at the same time he excluded Greeks and Macedonians. This is not to say that he did not genuinely feel betrayed and dishonoured by the actions of his men; virtually all the narratives suggest that he did. In the end, his men did everything he wanted them to and were desperate in their attempts to reconnect him to their military community.

Let us return to the problem of the varying success of Alexander's seclusion technique. The first time, his sulking worked primarily because he and his men believed that he had done something terrible, but rather heroic. The second incident failed because they did not believe this, although he may have. The third incident got Alexander most of what he wanted, partly because his troops really did seem terrified to be cut off from their relationship with him and desperate to restore it; the men at his door at Opis seemed very like excluded lovers, jealous of their Persian rivals.[61] But the third incident also worked in his favour because the men really did need him more than on the two earlier occasions. The arrival of the *Epigonoi* had made it clear that they were expendable and Alexander called their bluff. His actions and their response were, in some degree, still

three days, and did not even admit the *hetairoi* at first. Plutarch (*Alex.* 71. 3–5) says that Alexander excluded Macedonians for two days, while they wept and beseeched him outside his door, and on the third day he relented. Curtius (10. 3. 5) says only that the European soldiers were not admitted, but Asiatics were. (The lacuna in Curtius makes it impossible to tell whether he would have said that the troops waited at Alexander's door, begging.) As in the episode on the Hyphasis, Diodorus (17. 109. 3) and Justin (12. 12. 6) do not mention Alexander's seclusion and though they do say that the soldiers repented and begged the king to forgive them, they do not put this reaction in the context of Alexander's door.

[61] Plutarch (*Alex.* 71. 3) specifically refers to their *zelotypia* (jealousy) and anger. The personal relationship between king-commander and his troops was at the centre of Macedonian discipline (see Carney 1996: 28–31) and the lover-like relationship of Alexander and his men was critical to continued success.

Homeric; in our world they would have been both too extreme and too personal to be effective. The irony is that the soldiers wrongly thought that the tactics that had worked for them at the Hyphasis could work again, even though the situation was dissimilar,[62] but that Alexander was equally and, it proved, correctly convinced that the behaviour that had saved him after the killing of Cleitus could be used effectively again, despite its lack of success on the Hyphasis.

The three incidents of Alexander's seclusion and return do signify the importance of Homeric values to Alexander and his men, but they also speak to Alexander's self-conscious manipulation of his own Homeric image and his ability to impose his unyielding will on others. Homeric values had real meaning to Alexander and his men, but Alexander's repeated implication that his situation and actions were analogous to those of Achilles constituted increasingly disingenuous manipulation, although it is certainly likely that Alexander himself was manipulated by the power of his own imposition of Homeric plot upon Macedonian reality.

Artifice in Alexander history has many sources, only some of which we can determine. The reader is controlled both by an increasingly artificial source tradition which turned the raw events of Alexander's reign into a literary construct, however political the origin of that construct may have been, and by the mind and will of Alexander himself, a man determined to have both his contemporaries and posterity see him as he chose to be seen, as he willed himself to be. He and his men knew the same song and sang it in near unison and so did the ancient writers who came after them.

[62] See further Carney 1996: 35–6.

10

Polybius and Alexander Historiography

RICHARD BILLOWS

Few, if any, persons in the ancient Graeco-Roman world have inspired as much writing, by both ancient and modern authors, as Alexander the Great. A prominent feature of modern Alexander scholarship is analysis of and/or commentary on the ancient writers about Alexander. Yet it seems to me that the voluminous modern literature on ancient Alexander historiography still shows some start-ling—if in some respects understandable—gaps. Modern scholars concerned with Alexander source criticism have concentrated their efforts on the so-called 'Alexander historians', the biographers, memoirists, and pamphleteers who centred their works on the person of Alexander himself. Largely overlooked, as a result, are the works of broader-ranging historians, memoirists, and pamphleteers who, while not focusing their works around the career and personality of Alexander, nevertheless certainly had a good deal to say about that redoubtable individual. In this chapter I shall review what our only surviving primary Hellenistic historian, Polybius of Megalopolis, had to say about Alexander, and what we can learn from Polybius about the views of such contemporaries of Alexander as Demetrius of Phalerum and, above all, Hieronymus of Cardia.

There was a notable Greek tradition of writing general histories, pioneered by Herodotus and Thucydides, and chronologically continuing their work. Such histories were often titled *Hellenika*, though from the mid-fourth century on the impact of the Macedonian conquests caused some to be called *Philippika* or *Makedonika*. There was also a tradi-tion of writing 'universal' histories, histories which covered all of known time down to the historian's own day, the pioneers of the genre being Herodotus again, along with the great fourth-century historian Ephorus. Exponents of both genres of history-writing who were contemporary with or later than Alexander naturally had much to say about him. Since all of this historiography is lost except for wretched fragments, and since our surviving Alexander sources—Arrian, Plutarch, Curtius, even Diodorus—chose to base themselves primarily on the biographical tradition rather than using the general or universal historians as their sources, we know very little about what these latter had to say about Alexander, or how they evaluated his career.

A number of general historians who were contemporaries or near contemporaries of Alexander continued the general history-writing of such fourth-century exponents of the genre as Callisthenes and Theopompus, including accounts of the career of Alexander as part of their narratives. Diyllus of Athens was probably born before Alexander's death—by about 330 according to Jacoby's guess—and wrote a general history starting at 357/6, the point where Callisthenes' *Hellenika* ended, and ending at 297/6, to be continued by Psaon of Plataea.[1] Duris of Samos wrote a work apparently called *Makedonika* which covered the period from 370 to about 281, and seems to have dealt with the time of Alexander in five, or possibly six books. Though we do not know when Duris was born, he is said to have been a student of Theophrastus, and was certainly old enough to have met and questioned men who had served under Alexander.[2] Nymphis of Heracleia, finally, wrote a book whose title is preserved as 'Concerning Alexander, the Diadochoi, and the Epigonoi'; though not much is known about this work, Nymphis was old enough to have been exiled from Heracleia as an enemy of Lysimachus, and so was certainly contemporary with

---

[1] For Diyllus see Jacoby, *FGrH*, no. 73 for testimonia (6), fragments (4), and a brief commentary. N. G. L. Hammond has seen in Diyllus a major source for Diodorus' book 17, which deals with Alexander, but for the portions of the book covering affairs in Greece rather than for Alexander's activities: Hammond 1983: 28–51, and note that at 33–4 Hammond suggests the decade 350–340 as the period in which Diyllus must have been born. In general, however, Hammond's methods and conclusions seem to me highly suspect.

[2] For Duris see Jacoby, *FGrH* 76 for testimonia (12), fragments of the *Makedonika* (frgs. 1–15 and 35–55), and commentary. Jacoby suggests that books 5–9 covered Alexander, though 5 to 10 seems possible: at any rate frgs. 4, 6, and 7 deal with Alexander's reign and are from books 7, 8, and 9. See further Kebric 1977 for details of Duris' life and career.

some of Alexander's veterans.[3] Hieronymus of Cardia and Demochares of Athens wrote histories of the decades after Alexander's death, and are very likely to have had a good deal to say about Alexander, in various asides and retrospects if in no other fashion. Polybius of Megalopolis continued this tradition of historiography, covering the period from 220 to 146, the middle decades of the third century having been treated by Phylarchus of Athens and Aratus of Sicyon.

Polybius' work is the only Hellenistic history of this type to have substantially survived, and Polybius is the earliest still extant historian to have had anything to say about Alexander. Though he claimed to be writing universal history in the manner of Ephorus, Polybius' universality was geographic rather than chronological: in the latter sense he was more of a general historian continuing the tradition of such historiography from the point where the histories of Aratus and Phylarchus ended. He can thus be seen as to some degree representative of both of the strands in the Greek 'great historiography' tradition—the universal and the general—and what he had to say about Alexander can perhaps be taken to indicate the kinds of judgement that this Greek historiographical tradition made about Alexander. This is not to suggest that Polybius had read all of the works mentioned above—though he had certainly read Phylarchus and Aratus, and of the earlier writers is likely to have been familiar with Hieronymus and Duris at least—but that as a representative of the same historiographical tradition he is likely to have had a somewhat similar outlook when it came to evaluating a figure like Alexander.

One of the most prominent features of the biographical tradition about Alexander is its tendency to be apologetic and/or adulatory and to invent marvellous stories illustrating his superhuman nature: so far as we can tell this is true, to a greater or lesser extent, of all of the 'Alexander historians'.[4] Whether the 'great historiography' shared this

---

[3] For Nymphis see Jacoby, *FGrH* 432 T 1 and F 17.

[4] The basic work on the 'Alexander historians' is still Pearson 1960; see also Pédech 1984; Bosworth 1988a; and Hammond 1983 and 1993, though the latter should be treated with great caution. The tendency of these primary sources to be apologetic and/or adulatory, and to invent marvels, is I imagine too well known to

tendency remains unclear, and Polybius is obviously our best witness on this matter. It is unfortunate and surprising, therefore, that Polybius has been almost totally neglected by scholars of Alexander historiography: to the best of my knowledge only Malcolm Errington has looked into Polybius' view of him, in his well-known article in the *Entretiens Hardt* volume on Alexander.[5]

To be sure Polybius has rather little to say about Alexander, being primarily concerned with a period more than a century after Alexander's death, but close examination shows that rather an interesting picture of him emerges from Polybius' comments, few and brief as they are. Besides five purely incidental references to Alexander,[6] there are fourteen passages in Polybius which express substantial and interesting views of or judgements concerning Alexander.[7] These passages, as can be seen from the list in note 7, are scattered throughout the surviving text of Polybius, and analysis of them reveals that there were five basic themes concerning Alexander that interested Polybius.

The most prominent, as Errington already perceived, is Alexander's destruction of Thebes, mentioned five times in the extant portions of Polybius' work.[8] In book 4 we read that Philip V was urged in 220 by some members of his council to treat Sparta as Alexander had treated Thebes at the start of his reign; that is, to destroy it (4. 23. 7–9). Philip decided, according to Polybius on the advice of Aratus, to treat Sparta more leniently, and it is clear that Polybius approved of this decision, and disapproved of Alexander's harshness. In book 5 Polybius records with approval that, though Alexander destroyed Thebes and enslaved the

require much comment. It is nicely and briefly illustrated in Bosworth's characterization of the primary sources at the end of his *Conquest and Empire* (295–300): Callisthenes is 'eulogistic and panegyrical'; Ptolemy and Aristobulus are 'court historians in that their view of Alexander is consistently favourable'; Cleitarchus is 'less eulogistic', but of course he did retail such marvels as Alexander's tryst with the Amazon queen; and so on.

[5] Errington 1976: 174–9.

[6] See Polybius 1. 4–5; 2. 41. 6, 9; 2. 71. 5; 3. 59. 3; 12. 12b.

[7] The 14 passages are: 3. 6. 4–14; 4. 23. 9; 5. 10. 6–9; 5. 55. 9–10; 8. 10. 7–11; 9. 28. 8; 9. 34. 1; 12. 17–22; 12. 23; 16. 22a; 18. 3. 5; 22. 18. 10; 29. 21; and 38. 2. 13–14.

[8] Errington analyses these passages—4. 23. 7–9; 5. 10. 6–9; 9. 28. 8; 9. 34. 1; 38. 2. 13–14—at 1976: 175–6.

Thebans, he nevertheless spared their temples and sanctuaries, and that he pursued the same policy in his war with
the Persians (5. 10. 6–9). In a speech by the Aetolian
Chlaeneas in book 9, Alexander's destruction of Thebes is
cited as a Macedonian atrocity against the freedom of the
Greeks; and in the reply to this speech by Lyciscus of
Acarnania, Alexander's destruction of Thebes is not
defended, but his conquest of the Persians is cited as a
compensating benefaction to the Greeks (9. 28. 8 and 34. 1).
Finally, the destruction of Thebes is cited in book 38 as an
example of the various disasters that have befallen the
Greeks, with in this case the mitigating factor that, since no
one felt Alexander's action to be justified, everyone pitied
the Thebans and their city was soon restored (38. 2. 13–14).

Noteworthy in all of this is the complete absence of the
apologetic tone of the 'Alexander historians': Polybius does
not suggest that the destruction of Thebes was due to the
intransigence of the Thebans in rejecting Alexander's offers
of peace as do Plutarch (*Alex.* 11. 4), Diodorus (17. 9. 4),
and Arrian (1. 7. 7–11); he does not attribute the actual
attack on Thebes to the unauthorized action of an over-
impetuous officer, as Arrian does (1. 8. 1–2); he does not
claim that the massacre of the Thebans was the work of
allied Phocians and Boeotians, rather than of Alexander and
his Macedonians, as does Arrian (1. 8. 8).[9] This absence of
apologia is clearly not accidental: if Polybius had had any
desire to excuse Alexander, Lyciscus' speech defending the
Macedonian record in southern Greece provided the perfect
occasion;[10] but for Polybius, Alexander's treatment of
Thebes was simply an unjustifiable atrocity, mitigated only
by the king's respect for the Theban sanctuaries.

Comparison of contemporary kings with Alexander,
found in four of Polybius' passages mentioning Alexander,
is another significant theme. We have seen that Polybius

[9] On all of this apologia see the comments of Bosworth 1980a: 78–84, noting
especially the prominent role of Ptolemy's memoir in generating it.

[10] The speech of Lyciscus (Pol. 9. 32. 3–39. 7)—as noted above—offered only
Alexander's benefactions to the Greeks in mitigation; it did not seek to excuse the
treatment of Thebes or exculpate Alexander in any way. Compare Polybius'
defence of the southern Greek politicians who sided with Philip II, and by implication of Philip II's record and role in southern Greece, at 18. 14.

contrasted Philip V's merciful treatment of Sparta at the start of his reign favourably with the merciless treatment of Thebes by Alexander at the start of his reign (4. 23. 9). On the other hand, Philip V's pillaging of enemy sanctuaries was contrasted unfavourably with Alexander's respect for the religious sanctuaries of his enemies, including the Thebans (5. 10. 6–9). Philip V is again compared unfavourably with Alexander in book 38, where Polybius criticizes the king for employing terror tactics rather than fighting his enemies in fair and open battle, as Alexander and his successors had been wont to do (38. 2. 13–14). In book 5, finally, Antiochus III's conquest of Media Atropatene is mentioned, with a specific statement that the region was not conquered by Alexander (5. 55. 9–10), at least implying a comparison favourable to Antiochus. Comparison with Alexander, most notably in the form of *imitatio Alexandri*, was certainly a theme in the image-building and propaganda of Hellenistic kings, not least among them of Philip V and Antiochus III.[11] Noteworthy in Polybius' treatment is that of the four comparisons he draws, the contemporary kings come out ahead in two, and Alexander in the other two: the standard adulatory view of Alexander placed him far above contemporary rulers.

Another theme taken up in four separate passages is Alexander's character and generalship. We have seen above that Polybius praised Alexander's religious scrupulousness in book 5 (5. 10. 6–9). Apropos of his famous critical analysis in book 12 of Callisthenes' account of the battle of Issus, Polybius commented that Alexander was too good a general to have attempted the manoeuvres Callisthenes ascribed to him (12. 17–22 at 22. 5), and he conceded that, while Callisthenes might be criticized for his flattery of Alexander amounting practically to deification (cf. 12. 12b), the fault was mitigated by the fact that—as all conceded—Alexander did have something superhuman in his character (12. 23). The fourth passage is more interesting. Telling in book 16 of the resistance of the Gazans to Antiochus III in 202/1, Polybius commented on this people's habitual bravery and

[11] See e.g. Billows 1995: 33–44; and above all now Stewart 1993, esp. at 325–8, for Philip V and Antiochus III.

loyalty, and specifically referred to their resistance to the Persians and to Alexander's invasion: 'when there seemed to be scarcely any hope of safety for those who opposed Alexander's impulse and force, they alone of the Syrians resisted . . .' (16. 22a. 5). Three key words in the original Greek are *soteria* (safety), *horme* (impulse), and *bia* (force). It is certainly true that this phrase can be read as an entirely innocuous military description, but these three terms give me pause.

In the ideology of Hellenistic kingship as developed by numerous philosophers, and in royal propaganda and civic petitions, the ideal king is supposed to be a *soter*, a saviour.[12] It is remarkable therefore that Alexander is here shown as the opposite of a *soter*, as a man from whom one cannot find *soteria*. The ascription to Alexander of *bia*, furthermore, inevitably calls to mind the reputed debate at Alexander's court between Callisthenes and Anaxarchus in Arrian, in which Callisthenes is made to say that it had always been the custom of the Argead kings to rule the Macedonians οὐδέ βίᾳ, ἀλλὰ νόμῳ—not by force but in accordance with custom (*Anab.* 4 . 11. 6).[13] The implication in Callisthenes' speech is clearly that Alexander was tending to rule by force, and it is therefore interesting to find the word *bia* ascribed to Alexander here. Finally, there is the word *horme*, literally meaning rapid forward movement. The term is used by Polybius in numerous passages with a wide range of meanings, including several in which it has a purely military sense of 'onrush', 'invasion', or 'attack'; however, it is worth calling to mind that the term also had a technical sense in Stoic philosophy, in which it referred to the animal impulse as opposed to reason, a sense with which Polybius was certainly familiar.[14]

---

[12] See e.g. Billows 1995: 56–70 for the Hellenistic ideology of kingship, and references to the modern literature.

[13] On the dispute of Anaxarchus and Callisthenes at Alexander's court, and the degree of authenticity of Callisthenes' speech, see Borza 1981; and cf. Bosworth 1988a: 113–23, and Billows 1995: 61–3.

[14] For Polybius' use of the term *horme* see A. Mauersberger's *Polybius-Lexikon*, s.v.; for the importance of *horme* in the sense of desire or irrational impulse in Stoic thought see e.g. Lloyd 1978: 233–46; for Polybius' use of the term in essentially the Stoic sense see e.g. 8. 10. 9 and 15. 25. 31, and cf. the various usages of the term to denote impulses and desires listed in Mauersberger's lexicon cited above.

If one reads this passage with the Stoic ideal of kingship in mind, therefore, one can find, not an innocuous description of Alexander's military assault on Gaza, but an account of Alexander as a man of violence (*bia*) rather than law (*nomos*), of animal passion (*horme*) rather than reason (*logos*), the opposite of the *soter* that an ideal king ought to be. In deciding which way to take this passage, one should bear in mind that Polybius was here praising the Gazans for their loyalty and steadfast courage, and that the heroic resistance of the Gazans to Alexander was played up in a number of historical sources: most notably Hegesias of Magnesia made the siege of Gaza the occasion for a highly ornate, not to say bombastic, display piece in which Alexander was depicted as a man of outrageous cruelty.[15] Clearly to some Greek historians the sack of Gaza was another instance, like the sack of Thebes, of Alexander's ruthlessness and cruelty; and I venture to suggest therefore that Polybius does here, in praising the Gazans' resistance to Alexander, depict Alexander in critical terms borrowed from some Stoic treatise on ideal kingship.[16] The fourth theme detectable in Polybius' references to Alexander has to do with the allocation of credit for the achievements of the Macedonians under Alexander's leadership. As is well known, the tendency of the 'Alexander historians' was to give full credit for all wise decisions and successful actions to Alexander himself, his various generals and advisers mostly appearing as rather colourless background figures carrying out the king's decisions: thus, for example, W. W. Tarn was led to comment on the greatness of Alexander in so successfully dominating men who proved unusually able, ambitious, and turbulent after Alexander's death, that during his lifetime 'all we see is that Perdiccas and Ptolemy were good brigade leaders, Antigonus an obedient satrap, Lysimachus and Peithon little-noticed members of the Staff'.[17] Polybius did

---

[15] Jacoby, *FGrH* 142 F 5 gives the relevant passage of Hegesias, from Dionysius of Halicarnassus, *De Comp. Verb.* 18. 123–6; cf. also the treatments of Arrian, *Anab.* 2. 25. 4–27. 7; Curt. 4. 6; Diod. 17. 48. 7; Plut. *Alex.* 25.

[16] Treatises *Peri Basileias* are attributed to the Stoics Zeno, Cleanthes, Persaeus, and Sphaerus: see further on this literature P. Hadot 'Fürstenspiegel', in *Reallexikon für Antike und Christentum* viii (1970), cols. 555–82.

[17] Tarn 1948: i. 124.

not share that view. Twice he emphasized that the planning
and preparation of the war against Persia were the work of
Philip, while Alexander merely put Philip's plans into
effect (3. 6. 4–14 and 22. 18. 10). The third passage is more
explicit. In discussing the way historians praise or criticize
kings and their policies, Polybius found occasion to criticize
Theopompus for his defamation of Philip's *hetairoi* (8. 10.
7–11). It is worth citing his actual words here:

> Besides their deeds under Philip, their achievements after his
> death along with Alexander established by common agreement
> their reputation for virtue (*arete*). For while a large share of the
> credit should perhaps go to Alexander as the overall commander,
> even though he was but a young man throughout, we should
> certainly give no less credit to his helpers and friends, who
> defeated the enemy in many marvellous battles, endured many
> extraordinary difficulties, dangers, and hardships, and after
> becoming masters of vast wealth and being well supplied for a full
> enjoyment of every desire, they neither lost any of their bodily
> powers as a result of this, nor practised any injustice or licentious-
> ness for the sake of mental appetites, but every one of them, one
> may say, showed himself kingly as to both magnanimity, and self-
> restraint, and daring as long as they lived with Philip and with
> Alexander. It is unnecessary to mention any by name. And after
> Alexander's death, in struggling with each other for rule over the
> greater part of the known world, they so memorably established
> their glory in numerous histories, that while the bitterness of
> Timaeus' writings against Agathocles the ruler of Sicily, as
> unmeasured as it may seem, does have some reason to it—in that
> he was accusing him as an enemy, a bad man, and a tyrant—
> Theopompus' bitterness falls beyond the bounds of reason.   (My
> translation.)

In sum, for Polybius only a share of the credit for the
Macedonian conquests belongs to Alexander, a greater share
belonging to his generals and advisers. Alexander's youth
and inexperience are emphasized, as opposed to the extensive experience of his chief underlings while serving his
father Philip. One could hardly imagine a greater contrast
than that between this attitude, and the well-known attitude
of the main Alexander sources in presenting Parmenio,
Alexander's oldest and most experienced general, as a foil to
Alexander, with Alexander always emerging as the bolder

and wiser, while Parmenio is always put in the wrong.[18] I imagine that scarcely anyone would deny, furthermore, that the view of the correct apportioning of credit for Macedonian successes espoused here by Polybius is far more plausible than the Alexandro-centric view offered by the 'Alexander historians' and uncritically endorsed by Tarn.

The final theme in Polybius' treatment of Alexander is represented by the well-known passage in book 29 in which he cites Demetrius of Phalerum's prediction in his *Peri Tyches* that the favour of Fortune, and with it imperial power, would one day pass from the Macedonians to some new people (29. 21. 1–7). The clear implication of Polybius' presentation of Demetrius' views is that Alexander's success was due primarily to the favour of Fortune. The notion of Alexander as the favourite of Fortune was fairly widespread: it is found to some degree in the portraits of Alexander in Curtius' history and in book 17 of Diodorus of Sicily, and the two Plutarchean treatises *On the Fortune or Virtue of Alexander* are surely evidence of a substantial controversial literature on this theme, much of it no doubt generated by the rhetorical schools.[19] The question is whether Polybius shared Demetrius' view that Alexander's success was due largely to the favour of Fortune, and obviously Polybius' own view of the influence of *Tyche* on history—a topic on which much has been written—is relevant here.[20] Polybius was clearly much taken with Demetrius' views on Fortune, probably indeed much influenced by them; at any rate, he saw Fortune as playing a major role in shaping historical developments. In that he endorsed Demetrius' view that it was Fortune that gave imperial power to the Macedonians, adding that just as Demetrius had predicted Fortune in due

[18] See on this e.g. Bosworth 1988*b*: 41 and n. 44, 76 and n. 159. Also see Carney, 'Artifice and Alexander History', within this volume.

[19] On these Plutarchean treatises see e.g. the literature cited by Seibert 1972: 37–8; the correct view—as it seems to me—namely that these are standard rhetorical treatises, products of the rhetorical schools which will probably have generated many more such on one side of the question or the other, is propounded by K. Ziegler in *RE* 21, 1 (1951), s.v. Plutarchos, no. 2, cols. 723–4, and cf. Badian 1958*a*: 436.

[20] This is not the place to go into this topic in detail: for an excellent brief account of the importance of Fortune in Polybius' thought see Walbank 1972: 60–5.

course took it away again, I think we must conclude that Polybius too saw Alexander as Fortune's favourite.

The upshot of this review of what Polybius had to say about Alexander, is that his judgement of Alexander was a far more nuanced and balanced one than that to be found in the 'Alexander historians'. In Polybius' view Alexander, though clearly a good general and an inspired leader, benefited greatly from his father Philip's planning and preparations, and as a young and inexperienced man had to depend heavily on the abilities of his chief subordinates; though to be praised for his religious scrupulosity and readiness to give battle, Alexander was arrogant and capable of outrageous cruelty to those who opposed him; as great as Alexander was, some more recent kings could be compared favourably with him in certain respects; and though, finally, Alexander clearly had something in his make-up that seemed super-human, it is also clear that he benefited from a very great deal of plain old good luck. It remains to consider to what degree this evaluation of Alexander is Polybius' own, and to what degree he took it from his sources.

In accordance with a rather widespread modern view, strongly propagated by Ziegler in his *RE* article on Polybius and endorsed by Walbank,[21] that Polybius was only superficially educated and had not read very widely, Errington argued that Polybius' entire knowledge of Alexander was derived from Callisthenes alone: Callisthenes is the only 'Alexander historian' mentioned by Polybius, and it hence seems reasonable to conclude 'that his chief, perhaps sole, informant was indeed Callisthenes'.[22] It is true that Polybius mentions no other 'Alexander historian', and that he mentions no episode in Alexander's career too late to have been treated in Callisthenes' book, which was left incomplete by his arrest and death *circa* 327. In point of fact Polybius mentions very few actual events of Alexander's career: the destruction of Thebes, the battle of Issus, the sieges of Tyre and Gaza, and the incomplete conquest of Media. Even so, the notion that Polybius' knowledge of

[21] K. Ziegler, *RE* 21, 2 (1952), s.v. Polybios, no. 1, cols. 1464–71; Walbank 1972: 32–3.
[22] Errington 1976: 178.

Alexander was derived solely, or even chiefly, from Callisthenes can be shown to be wrong. In fact, it is only in his discussion of Callisthenes' account of the battle of Issus in book 12 that Polybius seems to have used Callisthenes. The destruction of Thebes and Philip's planning for the invasion of Persia were widely known facts for which Polybius would have needed no specific source, and his treatment of them makes it clear that he did not depend on Callisthenes—for Callisthenes is hardly likely to have emphasized Philip's preparations, and certainly will not have evaluated Alexander's treatment of Thebes in the way that Polybius did. Polybius' reference to Alexander's treatment of Gaza shows signs of being derived from, or at any rate influenced by, a Stoic treatise, as I have argued above. Most of Polybius' other references to Alexander concern general notions—Alexander's religious scruples, his willingness to give battle, and the like—which can hardly be attributed to any given source, and are likely to be part of the general stock of commonplaces about Alexander. Only three other passages concerning Alexander look as if they may have been derived from a specific source, and in each case the source was demonstrably not Callisthenes.

In the first place, there is the notion of Alexander as Fortune's favourite, which is explicitly derived from Demetrius of Phalerum. This passage deserves further analysis, since some important implications of it seem to have been generally overlooked. Polybius' fairly long quotation is clearly of a summing-up passage, in which Demetrius assigned the credit for the Macedonians' (i.e. Alexander's) conquest of the Persian Empire to Fortune, and predicted that just as Fortune had deserted the Persians to favour the previously obscure Macedonians, so it would inevitably in due course abandon the Macedonians in favour of some new people. Polybius' introduction to the quotation, in that it specifically mentions Alexander, makes it clear that Demetrius referred explicitly to Alexander, for Polybius introduced his actual quotation of Demetrius with the following words:

For he, wishing in his treatise On Fortune to display clearly to

men her mutability, giving his attention to the time of Alexander
when he destroyed the Persian Empire, says the following . . .[23]

What Polybius meant by the term ἐπιστάς ἐπί ('giving
his attention to'), used here to indicate that Demetrius
dealt with Alexander, can be illustrated by an instructive
parallel elsewhere in Polybius' book: at 1. 65. 5 Polybius
introduced his account of the war between Carthage and her
ex-mercenaries in 241–239 BC with the announcement that
he would 'give his attention to this war' (ἐπὶ δὲ τὸν πόλεμον
τοῦτον ἐπιστῆσαι), and he proceeded to deal with this war at
length and in considerable detail (1. 66. 1 to 1. 88. 7). We
must surely understand likewise that, when Polybius says of
Demetrius that he 'gave his attention to' Alexander's
destruction of the Persian Empire, he means that Demetrius
included a fairly lengthy and detailed account of Alexander's
career, with full elaboration of the role of Fortune in it.
It seems most likely, then, that Demetrius' *Peri Tyches*
included a fairly extensive discussion of Alexander's career
in relation to Fortune as at least a major component. It is
interesting to note that Wehrli, the most notable modern
commentator on Demetrius, suggested that Demetrius' *Peri
Tyches* treated the relationship between *tyche* and *arete*—
fortune and virtue;[24] for we know from the two Plutarchean
treatises *De Alexandri Magni Fortuna aut Virtute* that the
question of whether Alexander's achievements were due to
fortune or to virtue was a topic of controversy in the
Hellenistic and Roman schools. It appears that it was
Demetrius who initiated this controversy, and that
Plutarch's treatises are in some sense a response to him.
Further, though Demetrius' *Peri Tyches* was misdated by
Wehrli to *circa* 280, in fact Demetrius was one of the first
writers to discuss Alexander after Callisthenes: for his
treatise should in fact be dated to the teens of the fourth
century BC. This is made clear by Demetrius' own statement
that the Macedonians were utterly unknown fifty years prior

---

[23] Polybius 29. 21. 2. The key words here are ἐπιστάς ἐπί; Paton in his Loeb
edition translated this 'asks them [men] to remember the times when Alexander
. . .', but this is a mistranslation, as Walbank noted in his *Commentary* (vol. iii
(1979), 394), translating the phrase as 'when he comes to deal with'; I have translated 'giving his attention to' in accordance with LSJ[9] s.v. ἐφίστημι A.VI and B.V.

[24] Wehrli 1968: 57–8.

to his time of writing, by which he must surely refer to the beginning of Philip II's reign in 360/59, implying a date for Demetrius' writing of *circa* 310. This approximate date is confirmed by Polybius' statement that Demetrius wrote nearly 150 years before the end of the Third Macedonian War, that is before 168, implying a date of composition around 318.[25] That makes Demetrius very likely to be earlier than all of the major 'Alexander historians' except Callisthenes, and suggests that if, as is commonly supposed, Curtius and Diodorus derived their emphasis on Alexander's fortune from Cleitarchus, then Cleitarchus had probably read Demetrius' treatise. It seems, therefore, that Demetrius should be accorded a place among the primary sources on Alexander, along with such other pamphleteers as Ephippus, Nicobule, and the writer who was behind the versions of Alexander's death found in the *Alexander Romance* and in the *Liber de Morte*.[26] Demetrius was evidently an influential force in shaping the Alexander tradition, and it is ironic to note that this conclusion revives, after a fashion, Tarn's notion of a Peripatetic image of Alexander, though not of course in the sense that Tarn meant it: Tarn suggested a unitary, hostile 'Peripatetic' view of Alexander for which he could not pinpoint an original source;[27] instead we find simply that one important, early Peripatetic philosopher—Demetrius of Phalerum—produced an influential interpretation of Alexander as the favourite of Fortune, rather than a man of genius.

The other two Polybian passages on Alexander which can be attributed to a specific source are his statement that Alexander had never conquered Media Atropatene (5. 55. 9–10), and his evaluation of the *hetairoi* of Philip and

---

[25] Wehrli, loc. cit., dates the work *c*.280; but it is clear that when Demetrius speaks of the Macedonians as being unknown fifty years earlier, he must mean by this before the reign of Philip II, so that a date around 310 or so is indicated; and this is confirmed by Polybius' statement at 29. 21. 9 that Demetrius foretold the end of the Macedonian *basileia* almost 150 years before it happened.

[26] See on this pamphleteer the arguments of Merkelbach 1977: 164–93; Heckel 1988; and cf. esp. Bosworth's paper 'Ptolemy and the Will of Alexander' in this volume.

[27] Tarn 1948: ii. 96–9 and 113–15. Against Tarn's notion of a unified Peripatetic view of Alexander see Badian 1958*b*: 153–7. Note that I do not suggest that Demetrius of Phalerum's portrait of Alexander was hostile per se, but merely that it pointed out how much the great king owed to *tyche*.

Alexander quoted at length above (8. 10. 5–12). Neither passage could possibly derive from Callisthenes: Media Atropatene was not a concept when Callisthenes was writing, and he would in any case not have emphasized Alexander's failure to specifically conquer particular sub-regions; and Callisthenes clearly did not play up the achievements of Alexander's subordinates in such a way as to give rise to Polybius' judgement of them.

We must ask ourselves how Polybius, or anyone else of his time, could have known that Alexander did not specifically conquer the region of north-western Media that later became known as Media Atropatene, as he apparently did not.[28] I suggest that the answer may lie in the circumstances under which Media Atropatene was created. The region is named after the satrap Atropates, who governed Media under Alexander from 328/7 (Arrian, *Anab*. 4. 18. 3); who became the father-in-law of the later regent Perdiccas in the great inter-ethnic marriage ceremony at Susa (Arrian, *Anab*. 7. 4. 5); and who received north-west Media as a kind of fiefdom from Perdiccas after Alexander's death, in the division of the Macedonian lands at the Babylon settlement in 323 as recorded by Diodorus (18. 3. 1, 3. 3 with Strabo 11. 13. 1 (522–3); also Justin 13. 4. 13). Perdiccas hereby created a new province: Media proper was granted to Peithon son of Crateuas, and this satrapy had previously included all of Media. The creation of Media Atropatene was hence a special favour to Perdiccas' father-in-law, and a diminution of the province of the prominent Macedonian officer Peithon. This may have been felt to require some special justification.

We know that Diodorus used Hieronymus of Cardia as his main source for Diadoch history, and it has been shown that Hieronymus was behind Diodorus' account of the divi-

---

[28] This was pointed out to me by Brian Bosworth, for whose comments I am grateful. When Alexander entered Media in early 330—from the south—he proceeded straight to north-east Media in pursuit of Darius, leaving Parmenio to occupy Ecbatana and pacify the region. Parmenio's instructions to carry out a campaign along the Caspian coast were apparently soon countermanded and never carried out: see Bosworth 1988*b*: 94–5 and 236. The only further significant campaigning in Media seems to have been carried out precisely by the Atropates who gave his name to the region of north-west Media we are concerned with: he crushed a nativist insurrection in 324 (Arr. 6. 29. 3).

sion of satrapies: Diodorus explicitly stated, apropos of
Eumenes' appointment as satrap of Cappadocia and Paphla-
gonia, that these regions had not been conquered by Alexander, and we know that Hieronymus had made the same
claim—possibly we have here a justification for the appointment of a non-Macedonian to such an important governorship.[29] It was hence Hieronymus who recorded the creation
of Atropates' special satrapy, and it seems plausible to suppose that he too may have stated apropos of this that Alexander had not conquered north-western Media. Hieronymus
was a friend and fellow-citizen, indeed very likely a close
relative, of Eumenes of Cardia; and Eumenes was one of the
main supporters of Perdiccas.[30] In suggesting, therefore,
that Hieronymus stated that Alexander had not conquered
north-western Media apropos of Perdiccas' ceding of that
area to Atropates after Alexander's death, I propose that he
may have meant this as a justification for that act, which was
probably unpopular with the Macedonians. At any rate, it
seems likely that Polybius derived his information, directly
or indirectly, from Hieronymus.

　　Hieronymus is not cited by name in the surviving text of
Polybius, but in closing his evaluation of the merits of the
hetairoi of Philip and Alexander, Polybius alluded to their
glorious deeds after Alexander's death as being handed
down in numerous histories (8. 10. 11). The last phrase is
interesting: it appears to be a characteristically vague source
reference, for there seems no other point to the reference to
these 'Numerous historians', given that Polybius' main object in this passage was to criticize Theopompus' *Philippika*.
His words here are best understood as implying that it was
one or more histories of the Diadoch period that informed
him of the outstanding careers and merits of the men who
had fought with Philip and Alexander and disputed control
of the empire after the latter's death; and that it was one of
these histories he followed in giving his glowing appraisal of
the merits of the men who ultimately became Alexander's
successors. Walbank, in his commentary ad loc., refers to
Hieronymus, Nymphis of Heracleia, and the anonymous

---

[29] J. Hornblower 1981: 87–9.
[30] For Hieronymus' relationship with Eumenes see J. Hornblower 1981: 5–10.

author of the Heidelberg Epitome as the only known historians of the Diadoch period. Even though one should in
fact add Duris of Samos and the Athenians Diyllus and
Demochares to this list, it is well known that Hieronymus
was the most respected and influential of the historians of
the Diadoch period, and was surely the one most likely to
have been taken up by Polybius.

This conclusion is strengthened when we consider the
actual wording of Polybius' account, for he refers to *hetairoi*
of Philip who performed noteworthy exploits with and
under Philip, who then served similarly under Alexander,
and who subsequently battled each other for the greater part
of the known world after Alexander's death. There are
actually rather few men of whom all of this could truly be
said. A number of the Diadochoi were essentially contemporaries of Alexander, too young to have been important
subordinates of Philip: this is the case with respect to
Seleucus, Lysimachus, Cassander, and even Ptolemy. On
the other hand, such notable officers as Antipater, Craterus,
and Perdiccas died too soon after Alexander's death to fit the
last part of Polybius' description. The only men who really
fit all of Polybius' words—important service under both
Philip and Alexander, and a major role in the struggle for the
succession after Alexander's death—are Antigonus the One-
Eyed and Eumenes of Cardia. It is surely no coincidence
that these two men were the friends, employers, and main
characters of Hieronymus of Cardia. Once again, therefore,
it is likely that Polybius was following Hieronymus here,
and that it was originally Hieronymus who criticized
Theopompus' intemperate abuse of Philip's *hetairoi* and
defended them in the terms we find in Polybius, incidentally
making much of their service under Alexander and assigning
them much of the credit for Alexander's achievements.
Polybius, wishing to criticize Theopompus for his own
reasons—he objected to Theopompus' decision to switch
from writing *Hellenika* to writing *Philippika* (8. 11. 3–8)—
found Hieronymus' defence of Philip's *hetairoi* useful grist
to his mill.

We know that Hieronymus had a number of other things
to say about Alexander. He is explicitly cited by Appian as

having stated that Alexander bypassed Cappadocia entirely on his march through Asia Minor in 334/3 (Appian, *Mith.* 8); and is recorded to have described at length Alexander's funeral carriage (Athenaeus 5. 206d–e), which description is presumably preserved in epitome by that of Diodorus (18. 26. 1–28. 2). Furthermore, Jane Hornblower has argued persuasively in her admirable book on Hieronymus that the so-called 'gazetteer' of Alexander's empire as it was near the end of his reign found at Diodorus 18. 5–6 has its origin in the introductory matter in Hieronymus' history.[31] She argued further that this geographical introduction included some discussion of the limits of Alexander's empire in Asia, and of his failed plan to extend his conquests to the Ganges basin. The limits of Alexander's conquests certainly seem to have been a recurrent topic of discussion in Hieronymus' work.

When the two new passages from Polybius concerning Alexander I have now identified as probably deriving from Hieronymus are added, it becomes clear that he had more than a passing interest in Alexander. That is hardly surprising in a historian who wrote about Alexander's successors; indeed Brian Bosworth has already pointed out that Hieronymus must have been an important source on Alexander.[32] But we must ask ourselves whether Hieronymus' comments on Alexander all came as asides in the course of his treatment of the Diadochoi, or whether Hieronymus' work could have included some fuller, more coherent treatment of Alexander's career. I would suggest that both are likely: Hieronymus must have had numerous occasions to refer to Alexander in casual asides; but a full treatment of Alexander's career also seems a plausible part of Hieronymus' introductory materials. It is likely that the first part of his history, covering events from Alexander's death to the battle of Ipsus in 301, was written and published soon after 301, in the 290s.[33] That would probably make it earlier than many of the 'Alexander histories': only those of Callisthenes and Onesicritus are certain to have been published earlier. It

[31] J. Hornblower 1981: 80–7.

[32] Bosworth 1988b: 298.

[33] See J. Hornblower 1981: 76–9 (somewhat sceptical); and Billows 1990: 330–1, esp. 331 n. 6.

would hence be natural for Hieronymus to offer an account of Alexander's reign as background to his history of Alexander's successors, perhaps similar in scale to Polybius' introductory accounts of the First Punic and Cleomenean wars, that is, one or two books.

We have no exact information about the overall scale of Hieronymus' history, but he is included by Dionysius of Halicarnassus in a list of historians whose works were so long and badly written that no one would read them to the end. The others on the list include Polybius (40 books), Duris (at least 23 books), Phylarchus (28 books), and Psaon (30 books), so that a scale of 20 to 30 books seems probable for Hieronymus' work, ample to allow for a one- or two-book introduction on Alexander.[34] We must also remember the tradition Hieronymus was working in: the Greek tradition of general history-writing, in which each writer generally saw himself as a continuator of one or more predecessors—as Xenophon of Thucydides, or Polybius of Aratus and Phylarchus, for instance. Now Hieronymus is unlikely to have seen himself as a continuator of one of the 'Alexander historians', who belonged to quite different strands of Greek historiography (court history, biography, and/or personal memoir). Rather he is likely to have seen himself as continuing Theopompus' *Philippika*, whence no doubt the critique of Theopompus borrowed by Polybius. This would certainly make a fairly detailed review of Alexander's career necessary.

I suggest, then, that Hieronymus' history began with a treatment of Alexander's reign in at least one or two books, the detail of treatment being no doubt fuller for the later years than for the earlier, in view of Callisthenes' already extant history of Alexander's career down to about 330. Since Hieronymus was certainly an adult for much of Alexander's career—he was most likely born about 350—and may even have accompanied Alexander on the staff of his friend and patron Eumenes of Cardia, Alexander's secretary, during the latter years of the king's life, he must

---

[34] Dionysius of Halicarnassus, *De Comp. Verb.* 4. 30; cf. J. Hornblower 1981: 97–100 arriving at the same conclusion re Hieronymus' scale by a slightly different route.

be regarded as a primary source in whatever he had to say about Alexander.[35] It is clear from the passages cited above that his view of Alexander was not apologetic or adulatory, and that he was much less impressed than many other writers by the great king's personality and achievements. That is perhaps not surprising in a friend and follower of such men as Eumenes and Antigonus, who must have had a strong sense of their own merits and achievements during the king's reign. One wonders, for example, whether it was Hieronymus' account of Alexander's reign that preserved memory of Antigonus' defeat of the Persian counter-attack in Asia Minor in 333, so briefly described by Curtius (4. 1. 34–5).[36]

Be that as it may, I venture to argue that Hieronymus should be included among the important primary sources for the reign of Alexander, yet one more indication of the overlooked importance in this respect of the Greek general history-writing tradition to which I alluded at the start of this chapter. It is very much to be regretted that Arrian, our best Alexander source, did not choose to make use of this historiography. One must always remember that the excellence of Arrian is only relative: he is much better than Curtius, Plutarch, and Diodorus, our other surviving sources. But his choice of Ptolemy and Aristobulus as his main sources, for which he is so often praised, should in fact be a source of criticism: it is very likely that he could have produced a better, more balanced account had he relied on Callisthenes, Hieronymus, and perhaps Duris or Diyllus, reserving the memoirs of Ptolemy and Aristobulus for supplemental usage.

Careful perusal of Polybius suggests, then, not only that Polybius himself had some interesting things to say about Alexander, but that some of his sources were far more influential in establishing the general tradition about Alexander than has previously been recognized. A further suggestion

[35] On the dates of Hieronymus' life, and his possible service under Alexander, see J. Hornblower 1981: 5–9.

[36] See Billows 1990: 43–5 for more detail on Curtius' account of this matter; and note that Errington 1970: 72–5 has argued very persuasively that Curtius used Hieronymus for his account of events immediately after Alexander's death in book 10, and hence that Curtius was familiar with Hieronymus' history.

along these lines could be offered: it seems conceivable that it was Hieronymus who was behind the detailed military information in the so-called 'vulgate' tradition, most fully represented in the accounts of Curtius and Diodorus, that led Tarn to hypothesize his infamous 'mercenaries' source'. Many of the former mercenaries of Darius and Alexander clearly took service in the Diadoch armies, and few men will have had better opportunities than Hieronymus—an officer successively in the armies of Eumenes and Antigonus—to meet and question such men; and we do know that both Diodorus and Curtius were familiar with Hieronymus' book.[37] I suggested at the start of this chapter that the traditions of general and universal historiography should be more closely investigated by scholars of Alexander historiography: I hope I have shown that such investigation could be fruitful enough to repay the effort.[38]

[37] Diodorus explicitly referred to Hieronymus as a historian of the Diadoch period four times—at 18. 42. 1, 18. 50. 4, 19. 44. 3, and 19. 100. 3—and for his use of Hieronymus as his main source see Hornblower 1981: *passim*, and more briefly Billows 1990: 342–6. For Curtius' probable knowledge and use of Hieronymus see n. 36 above.

[38] It is worth noting, for instance, that at five or six books in length, Duris' treatment of Alexander's reign was only slightly shorter than that of Arrian—though to be sure Duris also treated other matters occurring during Alexander's reign. Moreover, the fact that nearly half of the surviving fragments of Duris' *Makedonika*—16 out of 36, F 4–8 and 39–49 in Jacoby, *FGrH* 76—refer to the reign of Alexander suggests that his account was not without influence.

-

11

Originality and its Limits in the Alexander Sources of the Early Empire

JOHN ATKINSON

This chapter aims to contextualize the major accounts of Alexander's reign that were produced in the early Empire and to consider the writers' aspirations, their treatment of fashionable motifs and current issues, and the limits of their originality.

Momentous events invite monumental histories. The demise of the Hellenistic kingdoms and the establishment of autocracy, first by Caesar and then by Augustus, invited monumental histories. For some the civil wars lent themselves to the traditional mode of Roman historiography, and there are several fragments of contemporary or near-contemporary accounts of Augustus' battle for power.[1] But after 31 BC it clearly became more difficult to carry on with writing contemporary history. Tacitus for one understood why such historiography lost its intellectual challenge as well as its political usefulness.[2] But, if we look beyond the class which traditionally took an interest in writing history, it is not fortuitous that this period saw the production of a number of monumental histories: Timagenes' universal history,[3] Trogus' *Philippica*, Diodorus Siculus' *Bibliotheke*, and Nicolaus of Damascus' 143-book universal history; and to these we should add Dionysius of Halicarnassus' *Antiquities* and of course Livy's history of Rome.

We must of course immediately distinguish between works that were monumental simply by virtue of their scale

---

[1] For example in Plutarch, *Antony* 53. 4 and 59; *Brutus* 53. 2; Suetonius, *Augustus* 11 and 27; Strabo 11. 13. 3. 523. See also Toher 1990.

[2] *Ann.* 1. 1. 2; *Hist.* 1. 1; cf. Dio 53. 19. 3–4.

[3] Greek historians naturally added a new dimension: cf. Noe 1984: esp. 41 ff.

and length,[4] and those that were monumental in terms of an ambition to explain world history.

I. THE SEQUENCE OF WORLD EMPIRE

Universal history that sought to explain the past had to reveal patterns, turning points, and culminations. Significance lay in the geometry and laws of history. Thus it is not surprising that writers of the Augustan age went back to the tradition, whose early form can be seen in Herodotus, of the sequence of world empires or great monarchies, with the idea of four great monarchies—Assyrian, Median, Persian, and Macedonian[5]—before the emergence of Rome as the most powerful world empire. For the annexation of Egypt ended the last of the great Hellenistic kingdoms and confirmed Rome's position as the successor to the world empire created by Alexander.

The idea was clearly taken over by Trogus, who began with the Assyrians, and then dealt with the transfer of power to the Medes (Just. 1. 3. 6), who in turn yielded to the Persians. From book 7 he focused on Philip, showing first how he conquered the whole of Greece, and that led to Alexander's conquest of the Persian Empire. In Trogus' account it seems that a sort of final climax was reached when in 20 BC Augustus retrieved from the Parthians legionary standards seized from the armies of Crassus and Antony (Just. 42. 5. 11–12). Only at that point did Trogus address the *origines* of the Latins.

The root of the idea can be seen in Herodotus' account of the succession of the Assyrian, Median, and Persian empires. It found new meaning in Daniel 2: 31–45 and 7: 1–14, where the progression is the Chaldean, Median, Persian, and Graeco-Macedonian monarchies, which serves

---

[4] Henderson 1989: esp. 70 ff., argues that Livy's extension of his original plan to complete his history of Rome in 120 books (ending with the establishment of the Second Triumvirate) by adding on a further 22, to take the story down to 9 BC, effectively subverted the meaning of his earlier work. Livy abandoned closure in favour of continual history, and in the process gave up his claim to explain Rome's growth, establishment of an empire, and descent into chaos (Livy *Praefatio*). In a way Livy retreated into narrative.

[5] The sequence presented succinctly in Arr. 2. 6. 7.

to presage the emergence of a new great monarchy, that of Judas Maccabaeus. Thus the theory could be embedded in apocalyptic or messianic literature.

Swain argued that the (pre-Maccabean) model became known to the Romans through their troops who fought at Magnesia in 189 BC.[6] Swain's case rested on some dodgy chronological assumptions, as Mendels argued, proposing instead that it was only in the first century BC that the propagandistic image emerged of Rome as the fifth great empire after the four eastern ones (Assyria, Media, Persia, and Macedonia).[7] But in Lycophron's *Alexandra* we appear to have a third-century version of the succession of empires, with Rome as the power that will challenge the Macedonians. Cassandra predicts that Xerxes will lead the Persians into Greece, but will be turned to flight; the lion of Macedon (who is taken to be Alexander the Great)[8] will force the Argive leaders into submission, and six generations later his descendant, sc. Pyrrhus, will join battle by land and by sea with Cassandra's kinsmen (presumably the Romans) (*Alexandra* 1411–50). The emphasis here, at least before the introduction of Cassandra's kinsmen, on leaders rather than empires echoes the role in Assyro-Babylonian apocalyptic literature of the *palu*, which, according to Tadmor does not refer to an empire, but the rule of one king in a dynasty: thus those writers had in mind the reign of four individuals, each representing one dynasty.[9]

In the late first century BC the world empires theory was clearly a topos, found, for example, in the work of Alexander Polyhistor of Miletus, though he built the Parthians into the sequence, and presented Mithradates I (175–138 BC) as the man who advanced Parthian power (*FGrH* 273 F 81). Another example seems to be Castor of Rhodes, who certainly took his *Chronica* down to 61 BC (*FGrH* 250 F 5), and thus covered Pompey's settlement of the east.

Writers differed on the date when Rome might be said to have emerged as a world power: Dionysius of Halicarnassus

[6] Swain 1940.
[7] Mendels 1981.
[8] For example by A. W. Mair in the Loeb edition of Lycophron (*Callimachus: Hymns and Epigrams; Lycophron; Aratus* (London, 1921)), 483–6.
[9] Tadmor 1981.

made it 197 (or 168); but for many writers the relevant turning point in world history was marked by the death of Mithradates and Pompey's settlement of the east, which included the annexation of Syria as a Roman province. Velleius Paterculus was certainly aware that these were dates of traditional significance, for he interrupts his narrative at this point to sketch the history of the establishment of the provinces (2. 38–9). In the context of the battle of Actium and its aftermath Velleius makes little of the significance of the demise of the Ptolemaic dynasty, but draws in as a consequence of the pacification of the east the recovery of the standards captured by the Parthians at the battle of Carrhae (2. 91. 1), and the return was dated to 12 May 20 BC. Thus Velleius arrives at the same key date as does Trogus.

II. THE SHADOW OF POMPEY

Two interconnected themes link the work of Diodorus, Timagenes, and Trogus: first, the particular significance in world history which attached to the demise of the Seleucid kingdom and Rome's confrontation with the Parthian Empire; and secondly, Pompey's role in Rome's dealings with the powers in the east. Thus these excursions into universal history led back into position-taking on Pompey's merits.[10]

Diodorus refers to the world empires model, for example at 2. 48. 5, and the successions are duly marked off: thus the Medes take over from the Assyrians (2. 28. 8), but Astyages lost out to Cyrus, and the Persians took over (2. 34. 6), and of course Alexander's victory over Darius III is recounted in book 17. Beyond that the picture is hazy.

Diodorus praises Pompey for his military discipline and skill, his manly qualities and his governorship of Sicily,[11]

---

[10] Nicolaus of Damascus has to be considered separately, since his attachment to the court of Herod and his concern with Jewish history set him apart from the other three. A general study of Nicolaus is provided by Wacholder 1962. S. Hornblower (1994b: 50–1) suggests that Nicolaus was probably similar to Dionysius in his attitude to Rome, and thus different from Diodorus, who reveals some lack of enthusiasm for Rome.

[11] Diod. 38/39. 9. 10 and 20.

and this was no doubt his due to the patron of his home territory. Diodorus went on to deal with Pompey's victories in the east, and quoted his claim to have extended the boundaries of Rome's hegemony to the frontiers of the world (40. 4).

Diodorus' original plan seems to have been to take his story down to 59 BC, perhaps to conclude with the ratification of Pompey's settlement of the east.[12] But then he took the narrative down to 46 BC, if one can accept the date reference in 1. 5. 1, and he at least covered Caesar's campaigns in Britain.[13] The 'conquest' of Britain is mentioned because it marked a significant expansion of Roman hegemony in the west. But Diodorus presents a sympathetic picture of the Britons, as people who were free from the cunning and sleaze of the society of Diodorus' day, and free from the luxury that comes from excessive wealth, and generally lived in peace among themselves (21. 6). By implication Diodorus questions the justification for Caesar's invasion. Furthermore, in the context of Caesar's conquests in the west Diodorus three times alludes to him as Caesar, who has been hailed a god because of the scale of his achievements.[14] The repetition may be intended to irritate, for it seems that Diodorus favoured Pompey rather than Caesar, and the way in which Diodorus skirts the issue of Alexander's divine pretensions suggests that he did not mention the apotheosis of Caesar with sincere approbation.[15]

III. DIODORUS THE PHILOSOPHER

But Diodorus certainly aspired to transcend the Roman political debate, and not only by relating his work to the world empires theme. The Cape Town connection is an inducement for me to refer to Benjamin Farrington, who in

---

[12] Diod. 1. 4. 7, which read with 4. 1 implies that he began writing about 59 BC, and finished thirty years later: cf. Sartori 1983, though the reference to Tauromenium in 16. 7. 1 might post-date 30 BC.

[13] Diod. 1. 4. 7; 3. 38. 2–3; 40. 7. 2.

[14] Diod. 4. 19. 2; 5. 21. 2 and 25. 4.

[15] Rubincam 1992 notes the linkage in Diodorus' thinking between Caesar's apotheosis and the tradition of Heracles and Alexander, but it seems that Diodorus was disapproving in Caesar's case and apologist in Alexander's.

his inaugural lecture, delivered in Swansea, in 1936,[16] presented Diodorus as a progressive thinker, out of step with
his contemporaries in three significant areas: first, he
challenged the acceptability of the dependence on slave
labour: a classic text on the evils of slave labour is Diodorus'
account of the realities of mining in Spain. Secondly,
Farrington focused on Diodorus' treatment of the
Chaldeans in 2. 29, whom he saw as true philosophers,
unlike the Greeks for whom philosophy was but another
way of making money, and who were more interested in pro-
liferating schools and theories than in getting in tune with
universal truths. Diodorus emerges as a follower of Zeno
with a strong belief in a *kosmos* following its preordained
path. Thirdly, he emphasizes Diodorus' inclusion in his
work of Iambulus' account of his stay in the island utopia,[17]
where men lived to be 150, all had split tongues, which
allowed them to communicate in any two known languages
at the same time; they were all over six feet tall and perfectly
formed, and with no body hair; in their tropical paradise
they lived a simple life and practised a form of communism
in which children belonged to the community, and not to the
family (2. 55–60). Farrington saw in Diodorus' admiration
of the Chaldeans and his use of Iambulus' utopia an expression of a commitment to the notion of the brotherhood of
man.

More recently Sacks[18] has analysed Diodorus' sections on
cosmogony and the origins of human society as the product
of his age, and a serious attempt on Diodorus' part to make
his contribution to these weighty philosophical issues.

But was Diodorus as original as Farrington imagines? The
utopian ideas may owe at least something to Poseidonius,
and it is even more likely that his treatment of Spanish

---

[16] *Diodorus Siculus, universal historian*, inaugural lecture (Farrington 1937).
Farrington's experience and political development in South Africa are not
irrelevant to the understanding of his academic preoccupations. (He was a lecturer
at the University of Cape Town, and, after his conversion to Marxism, a somewhat
public intellectual in Cape Town, in the 1920s.)

[17] Possibly the legendary Chryse opposite the mouth of the Ganges (Mela 3. 7.
7), since Diodorus refers to Palibothra at 2. 60. 2. Brown 1949*b*: 72–7 discusses
Diodorus' summary of Iambulus, and relates it to Onesicritus' account of
Musicanus' utopian society (on which see Bosworth 1996*a*: esp. 84–9).

[18] Sacks 1990.

mines drew on Poseidonius, who travelled in Spain and wrote about mining in Spain in his castigation of the greed that drove men to mining and of the damage which that activity did to society.[19]

Still, Diodorus is sufficiently critical of Roman imperialism, for example in his accounts of the Punic wars, and in particular in his sympathy for Corinth and for Carthage in the Third Punic War, for one to be sure that he was consciously distancing himself from the Greek encomiastic style, such as one finds later in Dionysius of Halicarnassus.

All this might lead one to expect an original approach to the history of Alexander's campaigns. But he does not seem to build on themes which he has introduced earlier. For example, in the opening sections of book 17 he passes up the opportunity to allude again to the succession of world empires.[20] He does not include a scene with the Gymnosophists, mentions Calanus' suicide with little philosophical elaboration, and likewise does not rise to the challenge of elaborating on the clash between the philosopher Anaxarchus and the Chaldeans (112). In contrast with his treatment of Iambulus' island utopia, Diodorus' descriptions of the peoples whose territories Alexander invaded are anthropological, and he shows a preference for the more credible traditions on the more fabulous elements.[21] His sympathy for the underdog is indicated in his attack on sensationalism, where he declares that an artificially tragic presentation of human disaster is a betrayal of sympathy for the sufferers (19. 8. 4).[22] He comes close to violating this principle in his account of the massacre of the mercenaries who left Cleophis' fortress under a truce (17.

---

[19] Poseidonius on the Golden Age: T 53 and F 284; travels in Spain: T 22; on mining and its evils and mining in Spain: F 239–40. All references are to Edelstein and Kidd 1972.

[20] Opportunities are missed at 1. 3–4 and 6. 3.

[21] As in 90, where the figures he gives differ from Onesicritus'. His account of the structures of Babylon similarly show a reluctance to repeat incredible measurements.

[22] The point holds whether Diodorus was making a personal comment or echoing an observation by his source. As Duris was probably Diodorus' source for Agathocles, it is quite possible that Diodorus was criticizing Duris, as Plutarch (*Per.* 28. 2–3) criticized Duris for sacrificing truth to drama in another context.

84), but his version is considerably less sensationalist than is
Curtius'.[23]

Thus for Diodorus the world empires theory was of no
great significance in the story of Alexander's campaigns.
Furthermore, as memory of Pompey receded there was
less incentive to redraw the picture of Alexander, whom
Pompey emulated. Diodorus seems not to have attempted a
revisionist or programmatic portrayal of Alexander.

IV. TIMAGENES AND POMPEY LESS THAN MAGNUS

While Diodorus favoured Pompey, Timagenes was hostile.
He was the son of a royal moneylender in Alexandria, and
was taken prisoner when Gabinius laid siege to the city in 55
BC. The rags-to-riches version of what happened in Rome is
that he started as a cook, then became a sedan-bearer, and
finally joined Augustus' circle of friends.[24] He was for a
while in Antony's circle, but then appears in Augustus'
entourage. Laqueur suggests that he had published his great
work on the eastern dynasties before Augustus went to war
against Antony and Cleopatra, and thus was used as an
expert in much the same way as Pompey had relied on
Theophanes of Mytilene for his special knowledge.[25] But
Seneca implies that Timagenes worked on his history after
the break with Augustus, which would seem to have been
sometime after Actium.[26]

He had all the confidence of a self-made man, and was
temperamental. He is supposed to have written the *Histories
of Caesar's Achievements*, but when Augustus banished him
from his court, he burnt the work.[27] His patron was now
Asinius Pollio, himself a forthright man, whose frankness
brought him into conflict with Augustus. The *Suda* then
links him with a Caecilius—presumably the *rhetor* from
Kale Akte in Sicily.

[23] In 8. 10. 22 ff.
[24] Seneca, *Controv.* 10. 5. 22 = Jacoby, *FGrH* 88 T 2.
[25] R. Laqueur, *RE* 6a, 1 (1936), s.v. Timagenes, no. 2, col. 1063–71.
[26] Seneca, *De Ira* 3. 23. 6; Sordi 1982: 777. Horace commented before 20 BC on
Timagenes' style as one dangerous to emulate (*Epistulae* 1. 19. 15–16).
[27] Sen. *Controv.* 10. 5. 22; *De Ira* 3. 23. 6.

Timagenes was forced to give up teaching and lived out of town. He died trying to master one of the skills of polite Roman society: for he made himself vomit between courses at dinner, and choked to death.

The old orthodoxy is that Timagenes was anti-Roman, or at least hostile to Roman imperialism. This rests on the rather slender evidence of Seneca's reference to Timagenes' resentment at the *felicitas urbis* (*Epp.* 91. 13 = T 8), which has to do with the physical appearance of the city, and then there is Livy's dismissive comment on the *levissimi ex Graecis* (9. 18. 6 = T 9), who eulogized the Parthians to spite the Romans. Livy does not in fact name Timagenes, nor anyone else for that matter. These unidentified Greeks raised the question whether the Roman people would have been able to match the might of Alexander, had fate made them coevals. That Livy was referring to Timagenes has been questioned by Laqueur, Mazzarino, and L. Braccesi.[28]

The references to Timagenes' work show that it was at least in scope universal history, and under the title *Kings* he took in Alexander's reign and the sweep of Hellenistic history. There is no direct evidence that he dealt with the sequence of 'world empires', but it is likely that he did endeavour to establish an overall pattern in his material. Evidence of partisanship emerges from several of the fragments.[29]

A more personal bias appears in his treatment of Ptolemy Auletes, who, in Timagenes' opinion, left Egypt in 58 BC quite unnecessarily, and did so under the persuasion of Theophanes, whose aim was to create a situation in which Pompey could be specially commissioned to deal with affairs in the east (F 9).[30] Timagenes clearly thought that Ptolemy Auletes was feeble, and he was even more strongly prejudiced against Theophanes. In attacking Theophanes, Timagenes may simply have been following tradition in

---

[28] Laqueur, op. cit., col. 1070; Mazzarino 1966: 540 ff., n. 485; Braccesi 1976: 184 ff.

[29] As an Alexandrian he not surprisingly shows bias against Antiochus Epiphanes' despoliation of the temple in Jerusalem (F 4), and follows the Lagid magnification of the casualty figures notched up by Ptolemy Lathyrus (F 6).

[30] Plutarch cites Timagenes here to reject the idea as quite improbable, because Pompey would not have stooped to dirty tricks (*Pompey* 49).

distancing himself from an earlier historical writer. He may have delighted in the chance to score a point off Theophanes.

To make sense of Timagenes' alleged sympathy towards the Parthians one needs to consider Timagenes' attitude to Gabinius and his patron Pompey. Timagenes was taken to Rome as a prisoner of war by A. Gabinius. In October 54, a month after Gabinius arrived back in Rome from his province of Syria, he was arraigned for *maiestas*, but acquitted through the intervention of Pompey.[31] The trial came about because Gabinius, acting on Pompey's instructions, had reinstated Ptolemy Auletes as the king of Egypt, against the express wishes of the Senate and People.[32] Gabinius was immediately guilty of *maiestas* in terms of the Lex Cornelia, in that he had left his province, Syria, without permission.[33] Along the way Gabinius arrested Aristobulus in Judaea and sent him as a prisoner to Pompey.[34] Thus he restored the situation to what it had been in 63, when Pompey adjudicated in favour of Hyrcanus and deported Aristobulus. A consequence of Gabinius' switch of attention to Egypt was that he gave up on intervening in the dispute in Parthia among the sons of Phraates, who had been murdered.[35]

Timagenes took a dim view of Pompey's intervention in Egypt, and since Gabinius' actions sidetracked the Romans from addressing the situation in the Parthian Empire, Timagenes could well have passed a scathing comment on Pompey's hesitation about facing the Parthians. This would give some sense to Livy's dismissal of the *levissimi ex Graecis*, who favoured the Parthians and used to say that the Romans might have taken fright had they had to face the threat from Alexander the Great.

Thus in a roundabout way we come to the idea that Timagenes may have expressed—at least sub-textually—a prejudice against Roman rule.[36] I do not think that much

---

[31] Cicero, *Ad Q. Fr.* 3. 1. 15 with 3. 4. 1 for the date; *Ad Atticum* 4. 18. 1.
[32] Dio 39. 55. 2–3.   [33] Dio 39. 56. 3–5.   [34] Dio 39. 56. 6.
[35] Dio 39. 56. 1–2.
[36] By contrast, Alfonsi 1977–9: 169–74 argues that Timagenes was not hostile to Rome, but to Augustus, and gave expression to this personal grudge by lamenting the *felicitas urbis* (F 8).

significance can be derived from Seneca's reference to his hostility to the *felicitas urbis* (F 8).

With regard to Timagenes' treatment of Alexander little can be built on the fragments which survive, but the reference in Livy implies that his treatment was positive, and, since the progression in classical historiography tended to be dialectic, I incline to the view that, if the negative image of Alexander in Justin's work reflects Trogus' bias, then Trogus may have taken a critical line to offset a more eulogistic account in Timagenes' *Kings*.

V. TROGUS THE CYNIC

Thus Timagenes' work brings us back to Trogus, whom von Gutschmid presented as little more than a copyist of Timagenes' universal history.[37] There was little textual evidence to support this, except for the fragment of Timagenes relating to the Tectosagi, which matches Justin 32. 3. 9–11. It is indeed possible that where Curtius and Diodorus agree on an episode in the Alexander story, and both differ from Justin, their source was Cleitarchus, and Trogus followed Timagenes. But even if Trogus did depend heavily on Timagenes, he chose a title for his work, *Historiae Philippicae*, which recalled not Timagenes' history, but Theopompus', and also the works of Antipater, Anaximenes of Lampsacus, Leon of Byzantium, and Lamachus of Myrina.[38] Seel also suggests that Trogus intended an association with the Philippic orations of Demosthenes and Cicero, while R. Develin suggests that he wished to be seen to be emulating 'the caustic moralizing typified by Theopompus'.[39] Either way Trogus intended to be controversial and to take a critical line on the kings.

On the issue of Pompey, Trogus did not conceal his family's indebtedness to Pompey's patronage (43. 5. 11), and

[37] Von Gutschmid 1882. The issues are analysed and von Gutschmid's simplistic theory is rejected by Yardley and Heckel 1997 (Introduction). Heckel, however, considers that Trogus probably made considerable use of Timagenes.

[38] Seel 1955: 27; Jacoby, *FGrH* 72, 114, 116, and 132.

[39] Seel 1955: 29–31; Develin 1985: quotation from Develin's introduction to Yardley 1994: 6.

indeed seems to have taken a positive line on Pompey (Just. 40. 2). Thus it seems likely that Trogus made a point of distancing himself from Timagenes. Trogus does not pretend that the people of the universe had reached a glorious climax, or the end of history.[40] He marks the emergence of Rome as a world power at the end of book 42 with the recovery of the Roman standards from the Parthians, but Parthian history continues and two books remain, in which Trogus deals first with the origins of the states of Italy and then with events relating to Spain and Carthage. If Justin can be trusted, Trogus ended with Augustus, *perdomito orbe*, moving troops into Spain to complete its conversion into provincial status. Thus Trogus swung the focus from east to west, even though his title indicated a preoccupation with the Hellenistic kingdoms.

Set against Timagenes' work it would seem that Trogus significantly expanded the study of the peoples in and beyond the Roman Empire.[41] He finds less place for comment on Roman politics—not surprisingly, but his approach to the Alexander story differs from the standard version of Cleitarchus, and suggests that he found his own way to deal with the nature of autocracy. Alexander becomes part of the code of political discourse: we are midway between Diodorus' novelistic account of Alexander's deeds and the vitriol of Livy (9. 17 ff.). Livy too reflects a chauvinistic reaction against the ecumenism which universal history had fostered. Trogus' position is rather different, as he reduces Rome to size and presents it as a world power (41. 1. 1), rather than the world power.

We can trace a dialectic progression in the universal histories of Diodorus, Timagenes and Trogus, and they also mark stages in a decline from cautious optimism to gloomy cynicism as the Augustan autocracy dragged on.

---

[40] Alonso-Núñez 1987: esp. 65 ff., notes some of the ways in which Trogus is unflattering about Rome: Rome's empire is acquired by *fortuna*; imperialism breeds corruption; the victims articulate their criticism of the mindlessness of Roman imperialism; the sorry tale of the demise of the Republic cannot be forgotten.

[41] On the range of Trogus' sources on India, Parthia, Bactria, and Armenia see Alonso-Núñez 1988–9: 125–55.

VI. CURTIUS RUFUS: THE PERSPECTIVE
OF A *NOVUS HOMO*

This is not the place to rehearse the familiar arguments relating to the dates of Curtius Rufus, and more particularly the period of composition of his *Historiae Alexandri Magni*. My view remains that the eulogy of the new emperor in 10. 9 was written early in the reign of Claudius, though others are no less convinced that Curtius had Vespasian in mind, or even Trajan.[42] In any event, Curtius' comment on the new emperor must post-date the accession of Tiberius, and by then the world empires model had lost its topicality, and Pompey did not have the same importance as he had had in the minds of Diodorus, Timagenes, and Trogus. Curtius' preoccupations lay elsewhere.

If he was, as I think, a senator[43] and a *novus homo*, he was making a statement by the very choice of writing a substantial historical work, rather than a technical manual, a genre which was more the preserve of Equites.[44] In dealing with the history of the war started by Alexander in Asia Curtius is to some extent Herodotean in his study of the clash of diverse cultures, but there is little concern to make a serious contribution to what we might call social anthropology. The military narrative is similarly not one to inspire confidence, and, while his coverage of the administration of the satrapies includes prosaic detail that is of value, he clearly made little effort to collate names and offices and to present an accurate picture of the relevant command structures, as can be seen in the way he covers the settlement of Egypt and again of Babylonia.

But, if Curtius had a rather cavalier attitude to the military and administrative narrative, it is clear that he took more interest in the political narrative, though here too he

---

[42] The case for a Claudian date is argued in the first two volumes of my commentary on Curtius (Atkinson 1980, 1994) and in my recent *Forschungsbericht* on Curtius in *ANRW* (Atkinson 1998), and most fully by Bodefeld 1982. A Trajanic date is suggested by Bosworth 1983.

[43] He appears to associate himself with the ruling class at 10. 9. 3, and uses the vocabulary of the aristocracy to refer to the lower orders (as at 6. 8. 10; 10. 1. 32 and 7. 1).

[44] The point about social rank and genre is elaborated by Beagon 1992: 5 ff.

appears to have used his source material as a resource on which to draw where it suited his creative purpose. The value system of the *Historiae Alexandri Magni* is what one might expect of a *novus homo*, and the preoccupation with the theme of *libertas*,[45] with the responsibilities of the king's advisers, and with issues of security and judicial process would seem to reflect what Curtius brought to the narrative.

Curtius' lack of originality can clearly be seen in passages where his narrative runs *pari passu* with another source—usually Diodorus,[46] but sometimes Arrian.[47] An example of simple copying by Curtius without much understanding occurs at 9. 10. 4 ff., where Curtius covers Alexander's advance to Gedrosia and the march through the desert. Arrian gives the starting point as Patala (6. 21. 3). Curtius first states that Alexander reached the territory of the Arabites with nine camps, and then the territory of the Gedrosians with the same number of stages. 'These people met in assembly and surrendered . . . From here on the fifth day he reached a river: the inhabitants of the area call it the Arabus' (9. 10. 5–6). Curtius then refers to Alexander's invasion of the territory of the Horitae, which he follows with the story of Gedrosian disaster, but does not name the territory. At the end of the episode he indicates that this brought the army to the frontier of Cedrosia (or Gedrosia) (9. 10. 18).

The corresponding passage in Diodorus 17. 104. 3 ff. shows that Curtius was following a source which first summarized the key events and then went back to tell the story from the beginning. Diodorus did not understand his source, since he says that Alexander won over the Abritae (cf. Curtius' Arabites) and the Gedrosians, and after that marched through the desert till he reached the frontiers of Oreitis (the land of the Horitae). At 105. 3 Diodorus marks Alexander's entry into Gedrosia. Curtius was not copying

[45] e.g. 3. 2. 18; 6. 10. 26; 8. 2. 2 and 5. 20.

[46] For example Curtius 5. 6. 9–11 with Diod. 17. 71. 1–2; 6. 5. 24–32 with Diod. 17. 77. 1–3, and Curtius 6. 7. 16–21 with Diod. 17. 79. 2–4; and Curtius 9. 8. 17–28 with Diod. 17. 103.

[47] For example at 4. 5. 13–22 Curtius has much in common with Arr. 3. 2. 3–7; Curtius 9. 2. 12–34 has been linked with Arr. 5. 25. 3 ff.: Tarn 1948: ii, appendix 15 concludes that both here used Ptolemy.

Diodorus, but both appear to have used the same source, and to have misunderstood what they read.[48] Since Curtius 9. 10. 4–5 derives from a prefatory summary, as one might find in an annalistic account, little value can be attached to the temporal reference there to eighteen camps.[49]

Curtius was in other ways confused by a source which, apart from providing anticipatory summaries of key events, also used a thematic approach, quite possibly within an annalistic framework. Thus, for example, at 7. 4. 32 Curtius records that, while Alexander was camped at Bactra, news arrived of the Spartan revolt, for, as he adds, the Spartans and their allies had not been defeated when those who were to report the start of the revolt were setting out. But at 6. 3. 2 Curtius appears to attribute to Alexander awareness a whole year earlier that the Greek uprising had failed (cf. 5. 1. 41–3 with Arr. 3. 16. 9–10). Thus it is possible that at 7. 4. 32 Curtius followed a source which dealt with Alexander's receipt of news of Agis' death as a topic at the end of the account of the year 330/29.[50]

Curtius' originality surely emerges in at least some of the speeches which he attributes to characters in the story: for example in the speech at 5. 5. 17–20 which he credits to Theaetetus, supposedly one of the Greeks liberated from forced labour in Persepolis at the end of 331. The speech reflects Roman values and Roman law relating to marriage and legitimacy, which cannot have come from the Greek primary sources whom he elsewhere claims to have read.[51]

The articulation of originality and copying in Curtius' *Historiae* can be seen most clearly in book 10 where the eulogy of the new emperor stands out as an obvious insertion into the story by Curtius. The direct reference to contemporary events made it necessary for Curtius to define the limits of the comparison. His portrayal of Philip Arrhidaeus omits reference to mental infirmity, which is attested by other

[48] Prof. Bosworth has pointed out to me that Arrian appears to have a double crossing of the Arabus at 6. 21. 3–4. Thus we lack a single unambiguous account.

[49] *Pace* Brunt 1983 (ii): 480–1.

[50] Badian 1994 has reviewed the debate on the dating issues.

[51] Dr Baynham suggested to me that the historical reality of the presence of Greek prisoners of war/slaves at Persepolis and the Greek word *ergastulum* in the preceding speech of Euctemon point to Curtius' dependence on a Greek source. But here I focus more specifically on the speech which he attributes to Theaetetus.

sources.[52] The eulogy is set at what is made the pivotal point of the story, before Arrhidaeus allows himself to be used by Perdiccas to destroy Meleager.

It is true that Curtius' account is the longest and most fleshed out, and that the essentials cohere with the skeleton outline provided by the other sources. Furthermore the denigratory portrayal of Perdiccas in this final scene might reflect Cleitarchus' approach, if Cleitarchus took a partisan line in attacking the man who made war against Ptolemy in 321/20. Ptolemy accused Perdiccas of acting without orders in the assault on Thebes in 335 (Arr. 1. 8. 1) and may likewise have accused him of a failure to maintain discipline among his troops at Halicarnassus (Arr. 1. 21. 1). But, if Diodorus and Curtius drew heavily on Cleitarchus, they do not suggest that Cleitarchus took a consistently biased line against Perdiccas. According to Diodorus, Perdiccas carried out Alexander's orders at Thebes (12. 3). It appears too that Ptolemy suppressed Perdiccas' name in some episodes, while Cleitarchus gave due credit—for example, on the wounds which Perdiccas honourably received at Gaugamela.[53] Curtius mentions Perdiccas as one of the officers who met with Alexander to arrange for Philotas' arrest (6. 8. 17), but Perdiccas is not one of those whom he singles out as particularly vicious in their attack on Philotas. Thus there is no preparation in Curtius' narrative for the role which Perdiccas plays in the elimination of Meleager in book 10, and there is nothing in Curtius and Diodorus to suggest that Cleitarchus presented Perdiccas in a consistently negative way, at least before the death of Alexander.

The 'vulgate' sources agree that Alexander on his death-bed gave precedence to Perdiccas by handing him his ring.[54] Thus far no indication that Perdiccas' actions were reprehensible. Then after Philip Arrhidaeus was proclaimed king, Meleager sent agents to arrest or kill Perdiccas: Curtius presents Perdiccas' resistance in positive terms (10. 8. 2–5),

[52] Diod. 18. 2. 2; Plut. *Alex*. 77. 5; Just. 13. 2. 11.

[53] Curtius 4. 16. 32 with Diod. 17. 61. 3; contrast Arr. 3. 15. 2. Curtius mentions Perdiccas' commission at Tyre (4. 3. 1), while Arrian omits his name. The pattern is fully analysed by Errington 1969.

[54] Curtius 10. 5. 4; 6. 4–5; Diod. 17. 117. 3; Just. 12. 15. 12. Badian 1987: 605 ff. returns to the issues of the sources for, and the historicity of, this episode.

as does Justin (13. 3. 7–4. 1). But, as the story continues, the infantry and cavalry were reconciled, and Justin reports that Perdiccas, 'furious at those responsible for the mutiny', unilaterally (meaning without consulting Meleager) arranged the lustration of the army, and used that occasion to have the ringleaders of the mutiny condemned to death.[55] Diodorus (18. 4. 7) records that Perdiccas put to death the seditious and those most hostile to himself, and used a private suit and a charge of plotting against himself as the means to have Meleager punished. Arrian's account of events after Alexander's death records that Perdiccas arranged the lustration of the army, claiming that he had authority from the king, and used the occasion to arrest the leaders of the sedition; and not long afterwards liquidated Meleager (*Succ.* F 1. 4). These brief references provide the bare bones of the story.

Curtius' account is more than a simple fleshing out of this skeleton. The key word in Curtius' version is dissimulation (10. 9. 8). Perdiccas used agents provocateurs to stir up enmity against Meleager, and feigning complete ignorance of what was happening he met Meleager with a plan to root out those responsible for this trouble-making. This is not in the other sources. Then comes the *lustratio*, with the king as the key figure, speaking for Perdiccas (10. 9. 16). Meleager discovers that the troublemakers to be punished are not Perdiccas' men who had created bad feeling against himself, but his own supporters who had joined him in the earlier occupation of the royal quarters. Some thirty (or 300) were trampled to death by the elephants, Philip Arrhidaeus neither authorizing the killing nor preventing it (10. 9. 18). Curtius comments further on Arrhidaeus' failure of leadership. Meleager realizes that he has been isolated and seeks sanctuary in a temple, but is murdered there. The emphasis on Perdiccas' *dissimulatio*, the use of secret agents, the additional twist in the story, and the treatment of the king's part in the action are peculiar to Curtius' account and of a kind with Curtius' treatment of other tales of intrigue. This

---

[55] Just. 13. 4. 7–8. The phrase acknowledged is from the translation by Yardley (1994). Prof. Bosworth has pointed out to me that the phrase *repente ignaro collega* brings Justin's version closer to Curtius'.

suggests that Curtius' originality does not stop at the end of the eulogy which immediately precedes this episode.

Curtius follows the death of Meleager with the distribution of the satrapies and most senior offices, and then returns to Alexander, finishing with the transfer of the corpse from Memphis to Alexandria. But within this final section he refers to events after 319 BC,[56] and perhaps also to the situation which post-dated the completion of Cleitarchus' history. Thus he signalled that he had more to tell. The originality in the latter half of the tenth book is strikingly offset at the very end by what must be some straight copying from his source: the observation at 10. 18 about rumours suppressed by the power of the Successors echoes Diodorus 17. 118. 2 and Justin 12. 13. 10. This has to be deliberate, as he feigned to draw attention away from his own originality.

VII. EXODOS

The earlier writers considered in this chapter were affected by the demise of the last surviving Hellenistic kingdoms and the establishment of a new political order in Rome. These linked developments invited monumental histories, and it was easy for true believers to see what had emerged as the glorious culmination of a succession of world empires. The focal figure in the story of Rome's emergence as the dominant 'world' power was Pompey, but the Caesarian coups made it difficult for historians to avoid demonstrating or betraying their attitude to Pompey and his rivals. These preoccupations of the period are shown to have aroused fresh interest in the Alexander period. In this context one must see the pretensions, enthusiasms, and partisanship of Diodorus, Timagenes, and Trogus, but in writing history on a grand scale Diodorus and Timagenes seem to have found little of great originality to say about Alexander. Although Timagenes had a reputation for being a controversial writer, on the topic of Alexander Trogus took a more revisionist line.

[56] At 10. 10. 19 Curtius refers to what happened after Antipater died in 319.

With the passage of time the issues and fashionable ideas with which those writers were most familiar faded, and this shows in the differences between their work and Curtius' *Historiae Alexandri*. Curtius, writing a monograph rather than a universal history, gave himself more scope for the display of originality, at least in the composition of his narrative. Just as he enjoyed adding new twists to the phraseology, so he added new twists to the narrative. At a key point in the final book (10. 9) he directly engages with contemporary Roman politics, and this draws attention to what appear to be novel elements in the narrative in which his personal comment is embedded. The mix of copying and innovation seems intentional, to draw attention to his art and in places to render the subtext ambivalent.

Bibliography

The list below supplies publication details for all modern literature mentioned in this volume. The abbreviations are those currently in use in *L'Année Philologique*.

ADAMS, W. L. (1974) *Cassander, Macedonia and the Policy of Coalition, 323–301 B.C.* (Diss. Virginia)
——(1980) 'The Royal Macedonian Tombs at Vergina: An Historical Interpretation', *AncW* 3: 67–72
——(1991) 'Cassander, Alexander IV and the Tombs at Vergina', *AncW* 22: 27–33
Alessandro Magno (1995) *Alessandro Magno. Storia e mito* exhibition catalogue. Rome
ALFÖLDI, A. (1943) *Die Kontorniaten.* Leipzig
——(1950) 'Die Geschichte des Throntabernakels', *La Nouvelle Clio* 2: 537–66
——(1951) 'Königsweihe und Männerbund bei den Achämeniden', Festschrift K. Meuli, *Schweizerisches Archiv für Volkskunde* 47: 11–16
ALFÖLDI, A., and ALFÖLDI, E. (1990) *Die Kontorniat-Medaillons.* Berlin and New York
ALFONSI, L. (1977–9) 'Timagene di Alessandria tra Roma e anti-Roma', *ALGP* 14–16: 169–74
ALONSO-NÚÑEZ, J. M. (1987) 'An Augustan World History: The *Historiae Philippicae* of Pompeius Trogus', *G&R* 34: 56–72
——(1988–9) 'The Roman Universal Historian Pompeius Trogus on India, Parthia, Bactria and Armenia', *Persica* 13: 125–55
ALTHEIM, F. (1947) *Weltgeschichte Asiens im griechischen Zeitalter.* i. Halle
——(1953) *Alexander und Asien. Geschichte eines geistigen Erbes.* Tübingen
——(1970) *Geschichte Mittelasiens in Altertum* (with R. Stiel). Berlin
AMELING, W. (1988) 'Alexander und Achilleus. Eine Bestandsaufnahme', in W. Will and J. Heinrichs (eds.), *Zu Alexander d. Gr. Festschrift G. Wirth*, ii. Amsterdam, 657–92
ANDERSON, J. K. (1985) *Hunting in the Ancient World.* Berkeley, Los Angeles, London
ANDREOTTI, R. (1957) 'Die Weltmonarchie Alexanders des

Grossen in Überlieferung und geschichtlicher Wirklichkeit', *Saeculum* 8: 120–66

ANDRONIKOS, M. (1984) *Vergina*. Athens

—— (1994) *Vergina* II, *The Tomb of Persephone*. Athens

ATKINSON, J. E. (1980) *A Commentary on Q. Curtius Rufus' Historiae Alexandri Magni, Books 3 and 4*. Amsterdam

—— (1994) *A Commentary on Q. Curtius Rufus' Historiae Alexandri Magni, Books 5 to 7. 2*. Amsterdam

—— (1998) 'Q. Curtius Rufus' "Historiae Alexandri Magni"', *ANRW* II, 34.4: 3447–83

AUSFELD, A. (1895) 'Über das angebliche Testament Alexanders des Großen', *RhM* 50: 357–66

—— (1901) 'Das angebliche Testament Alexanders des Großen', *RhM* 56: 517–42

AUSTIN, M. (1993) 'Alexander and the Macedonian Invasion of Asia', in J. Rich and G. Shipley (eds.), *War and Society in the Greek World*. London, 197–223

BADIAN, E. (1958*a*) 'Alexander the Great and the Unity of Mankind', *Historia* 7: 425–44

—— (1958*b*) 'The Eunuch Bagoas: A Study in Method', *CQ* 8: 144–57

—— (1960) 'The Death of Parmenio', *TAPhA* 91: 324–38

—— (1961) 'Harpalus', *JHS* 81: 16–43

—— (1963) 'The Death of Philip II', *Phoenix* 17: 244–50

—— (1964) 'Alexander the Great and the Loneliness of Power', in *Studies in Greek and Roman History*. Oxford, 192–205

—— (1965) 'The Date of Clitarchus', *PACA* 8: 5–11

—— (1966) 'Alexander the Great and the Greeks of Asia', in *Ancient Society and Institutions (Studies presented to V. Ehrenberg)*. Oxford, 37–69

—— (1967) 'A King's Notebooks', *HSPh* 72: 183–204

—— (1981) 'The Deification of Alexander the Great', in H. J. Dell (ed.), *Ancient Macedonian Studies in Honor of Charles F. Edson*. Thessaloniki, 27–71

—— (1985) 'Alexander in Iran', in *The Cambridge History of Iran*, ii (ed. I. Gershevitch). Cambridge, 420–501

—— (1987) 'The Ring and the Book', in W. Will and J. Heinrichs (eds.), *Zu Alexander d. Gr. Festschrift G. Wirth*, i. Amsterdam, 605–25

—— (1989) 'History from "Square Brackets"', *ZPE* 79: 59–70

—— (1993) 'Alexander and Philippi', *ZPE* 95: 131–9

—— (1994) 'Agis III: Revisions and Reflections', in I. Worthington (ed.), *Ventures into Greek History*. Oxford, 258–92

—— (1996) 'Alexander the Great between Two Thrones and

Heaven: Variations on an Old Theme', in A. Small (ed.), *Subject and Ruler: The Cult of the Ruling Power in Classical Antiquity*. *JRA* Suppl. 17: 11–26

BAGNALL, R. (1976) *The Administration of the Ptolemaic Possessions outside Egypt*. Leiden

BALDRY, H. C. (1965) *The Unity of Mankind in Greek Thought*. Cambridge

BALDUS, H. R. (1978) 'Zum Siegel des Königs Lysimachos von Thrakien', *Chiron* 8: 195–9

BALSDON, J. P. V. D. (1950) 'The Divinity of Alexander', *Historia* 1: 363–88

BARR-SHARRAR, B., and BORZA, E. N. (1982) (eds.) *Macedonia and Greece in Late Classical and Early Hellenistic Times*. National Gallery of Art, Washington, Studies in the History of Art, 10

BAUMER, L. E. and WEBER, U. (1991) 'Zum Fries des "Philippsgrabes" von Vergina', *Hefte des Archäologischen Seminars Bern* 14: 27–41

BAYNES, N. H. (1955) *Byzantine Studies and Other Essays*. London

BAYNHAM, E. J. (1995) 'An Introduction to the *Metz Epitome*: Its Traditions and Value', *Antichthon* 29: 60–77

——(1998a) *Alexander the Great: The Unique History of Quintus Curtius*. Ann Arbor

——(1998b) 'The Treatment of Olympias in the *Liber de Morte Alexandri Magni*—a Rhodian Retirement', in W. Will (ed.), *Alexander der Grosse: Eine Welteroberung und ihr Hintergrund*. Vorträge des Internationalen Bonner Alexanderkolloquiums, 19.–21. 12. 1996: Antiquitas, Reihe 1, Bd. 46. Bonn, 103–15

BEAGON, M. (1992) *Roman Nature: The Thought of Pliny the Elder*. Oxford

BEAN, G. E. (1953) 'Notes and Inscriptions from Caunus', *JHS* 73: 10–35

BEAN, G. E., and COOK, J. M. (1952) 'The Cnidia', *ABSA* 47: 171–212

BEARZOT, C. (1987) 'La tradizione su Parmenione negli storici di Alessandro', *Aevum* 61: 89–104

BELLEN, H. (1974) 'Der Rachegedanke in der griechisch-persischen Auseinandersetzung', *Chiron* 4: 43–67

BELOCH, K. J. (1922–7) *Griechische Geschichte*², 4 vols., Strassburg, Berlin, Leipzig

BENGTSON, H. (1977) *Griechische Geschichte*⁵. Handbuch der Altertumswissenschaft III. 4. Munich

BERGER, E. (1994) 'Penthesileia', *LIMC* vii

BERTHOLD, R. M. (1984) *Rhodes in the Hellenistic Age*. Ithaca, NY, and London

BERVE, H. (1926) *Das Alexanderreich auf prosopographischer Grundlage*. 2 vols., Munich

——(1938) 'Die Verschmelzungspolitik Alexanders des Grossen', *Klio* 31: 135–68

BICKERMANN, E., and SYKUTRIS, J. (1928) *Speusipps Brief an König Philipp*. Leipzig

BIGWOOD, J. M. (1978) 'Ctesias as Historian of the Persian Wars', *Phoenix* 32: 19–41

BILLOWS, R. A. (1989) 'Anatolian Dynasts: The Case of the Macedonian Eupolemos in Caria', *ClAnt* 8: 173–206

——(1990) *Antigonus the One-Eyed and the Creation of the Hellenistic State*. Berkeley and Los Angeles

——(1995) *Kings and Colonists. Aspects of Macedonian Imperialism*. Leiden

BISCHOFF, H. (1932) *Der Warner bei Herodot*. (Diss. Marburg)

BLOEDOW, E. F. (1995) 'That Great Puzzle in the History of Alexander: Back into "The Primal Pit of Historical Murk"', in Ch. Schubert and K. Brodersen (eds.), *Rom und der Griechische Osten*. Stuttgart, 23–41

BLÜMEL, W. (1985) *Die Inschriften von Iasos*. IGSK 28. Bonn

BOARDMAN, J. (1970) *Greek Gems and Finger Rings*. London

BODEFELD, H. (1982) *Untersuchungen zur Datierung der Alexandergeschichte des Q. Curtius Rufus*. Düsseldorf

BOEDEKER, D., and SIDER, D. (1996) (eds.) 'The New Simonides', *Arethusa* 29.2

BORZA, E. N. (1981) 'Anaxagoras and Callisthenes: Academic Intrigue at Alexander's Court', in H. J. Dell (ed.), *Ancient Macedonian Studies in Honor of Charles F. Edson*. Thessaloniki, 73–86

——(1983) 'The Symposium at Alexander's Court', *Ancient Macedonia* 3: 45–55

——(1987) 'Royal Macedonian Tombs and the Paraphernalia of Alexander the Great', *Phoenix* 41: 105–21

——(1992) *In the Shadow of Olympus. The Emergence of Macedon*². Princeton

——(1995) 'Fire from Heaven: Alexander at Persepolis', in *Makedonika. Essays by Eugene N. Borza* (ed. C. G. Thomas). Claremont, NH, 217–38

BOSWORTH, A. B. (1971*a*) 'The Death of Alexander the Great: Rumour and Propaganda', *CQ* 21: 112–36

——(1971*b*) 'The Congress Decree: Another Hypothesis', *Historia* 20: 600–16

——(1971c) 'Philip II and Upper Macedonia', *CQ* 21: 93–105

——(1976) 'Arrian and the Alexander Vulgate', in *Alexandre le Grand: Image et Réalité*. Entretiens sur l'antiquité classique, 22. Geneva, 1–46

——(1980a) *A Historical Commentary on Arrian's History of Alexander,* i. Oxford

——(1980b) 'Alexander and the Iranians', *JHS* 100: 1–21

——(1983) 'History and Rhetoric in Curtius Rufus', *CPh* 78: 150–61

——(1988a) *From Arrian to Alexander*. Oxford

——(1988b) *Conquest and Empire: The Reign of Alexander the Great*. Cambridge

——(1990) 'Plutarch, Callisthenes and the Peace of Callias', *JHS* 110: 1–13

——(1992) 'Philip III Arrhidaeus and the Chronology of the Successors', *Chiron* 22: 55–87

——(1994a) 'A New Macedonian Prince', *CQ* 44: 57–65

——(1994b) 'Alexander the Great', in D. M. Lewis, J. Boardman, *et al.*, *CAH* vi². Cambridge, 791–875

——(1995) *A Historical Commentary on Arrian's History of Alexander* ii. Oxford

——(1996a) *Alexander and the East*. Oxford

——(1996b) 'Alexander, Euripides and Dionysos: The Motivation for Apotheosis', in Wallace, R. W. and Harris, E. M. (eds.), *Transitions to Empire, Essays in Honor of E. Badian*. Oklahoma, 140–66

——(1998) 'Calanus and the Brahman Opposition', in W. Will (ed.), *Alexander der Grosse: Eine Welteroberung und ihr Hintergrund*. Vorträge des Internationalen Bonner Alexanderkolloquiums, 19.–21. 12. 1996: Antiquitas, Reihe 1, Bd. 46. Bonn, 173–203

BOYCE, M. (1979) *Zoroastrians. Their Religious Beliefs and Practices*. London

BRACCESI, L. (1976) 'Livio e la tematica di Alessandro in età augustea', in *I canali della propaganda nel mondo antico*. Milan

BRANDENSTEIN, W., and MAYRHOFER, M. (1964) *Handbuch des Altpersischen*. Wiesbaden

BRAUDY, L. (1986) *The Frenzy of Renown. Fame and its History*. New York and Oxford

BRIANT, P. (1982a) *Rois, tributs et paysans*. Annales littéraires de l'Université de Besançon, 269. Paris

——(1982b) *État et pasteurs au Moyen-Orient ancien*. Cambridge

——(1991) 'Chasses royales macédoniennes et chasses royales

perses: Le Thème de la chasse au lion sur la chasse de Vergina', *DHA* 17: 211–55

BRIANT, P. (1993) 'Les Chasses d'Alexandre', *Ancient Macedonia* 5: 267–77

——(1996) *Histoire de l'empire perse de Cyrus à Alexandre*. Paris

BROWN, T. S. (1949a) 'Callisthenes and Alexander', *AJPh* 90: 225–48

——(1949b) *Onesicritus. A Study in Hellenistic Historiography*. Berkeley

——(1967) 'Alexander's Book Order (Plut. *Alex.* 8)', *Historia* 16: 359–68

BRUNT, P. A. (1965) 'The Aims of Alexander', *Greece and Rome* 12: 203–15

——(1975) 'Alexander, Barsine and Heracles', *RFIC* 103: 22–34

——(1976 and 1983) *Arrian: History of Alexander and Indica*, i–ii. Cambridge, Mass.

——(1980) 'On Historical Fragments and Epitomes', *CQ* 30: 477–94

——(1993a) 'Plato's Academy and Politics', in id., *Studies in Greek History and Thought*. Oxford, 282–342

——(1993b) 'Aristotle and Slavery', in id., *Studies in Greek History and Thought*. Oxford, 343–88

BUDGE, E. A. (1889) *The History of Alexander the Great, Syriac Pseudo-Callisthenes*. Cambridge; repr. Amsterdam, 1976

BURKERT, W. (1985) *Greek Religion*. Oxford

BURSTEIN, S. (1991) 'Pharaoh Alexander: A Scholarly Myth', *Anc Soc* 22: 139–45

CAIRNS, F. (1972) *Generic Composition in Greek and Roman Poetry*. Edinburgh

CALMEYER, P. (1980) review of D. Stronach, *Pasargardae, ZA* 70: 297–307

——(1981) 'Zur bedingten Göttlichkeit des Großkönigs', *AMI* 14: 55–60

CARLSEN, J., DUE, B., STEEN DUE, O., POULSEN, B. (1993) (eds.) *Alexander the Great, Reality and Myth*. Rome

CARNEY, E. D. (1980) 'The Conspiracy of Hermolaus', *CJ* 76: 223–31

——(1981) 'The Death of Clitus', *GRBS* 22: 149–60

——(1983) 'Regicide in Macedonia', *PP* 211: 260–72

——(1988) 'The Sisters of Alexander the Great: Royal Relicts', *Historia* 37: 385–404

——(1993) 'Olympias and the Image of the Virago', *Phoenix* 47: 29–55

——(1994) 'Olympias, Adea Eurydice, and the End of the Argead

Dynasty', in I. Worthington (ed.), *Ventures into Greek History*. Oxford, 357–80

—— (1996) 'Macedonians and Mutiny: Discipline and Indiscipline in the Army of Philip and Alexander', *CPh* 91: 19–44

CARROLL-SPILLECKE, M. (1985) *Landscape Depictions in Greek Relief Sculpture*. Frankfurt, Bern, New York

CARTLEDGE, P. (1987) *Agesilaos and the Crisis of Sparta*. Baltimore

—— (1993) *The Greeks*. Oxford

—— (1994) 'Response to Usher', in H. A. Khan (ed.), *The Birth of the European Identity: The Europe–Asia Crisis in Greek Thought 490–322 B.C.* Nottingham, 146–55

CASTRIOTA, D. (1992) *Myth, Ethos and Actuality. Official Art in Fifth-Century B.C. Athens*. Madison

CAUER, F. (1894) 'Philotas, Kleitos, Kallisthenes', *Neue Jahrbücher für classische Philologie*, Suppl. 20: 1–79

CAWKWELL, G. L. (1978) *Philip of Macedon*. London

—— (1982) 'Isocrates', in T. James Luce (ed.), *Ancient Writers: Greece and Rome*, i. New York, 313–29

—— (1994) 'The Deification of Alexander the Great: A Note', in I. Worthington (ed.), *Ventures into Greek History*. Oxford, 293–306

CHARBONNEAUX, J. (1952) 'Antigone le Borgne et Démétrius Poliorcète sont-ils figurés sur le sarcophage d'Alexandre?', *Revue des arts* 2: 219–23

CHILDS, W. A. P., and DEMARGNE, P. (1989) *Le Monument des Néréides. Le Décor sculpté, Fouilles de Xanthos*, 8. Paris

CLAIRMONT, C. W. (1993) *Classical Attic Tombstones*. Kilchberg

CLARYSSE, W., and SCHEPENS, G. (1985) 'A Ptolemaic Fragment of an Alexander History', *CE* 60: 30–47

CLAVEDESCHER-THURLEMANN, S. (1985) *POLEMOS DIKAIOS und Bellum Iustum. Versuch einer Ideengeschichte*. Zurich

CLAYTON, P. A., and PRICE, M. J. (1988) *The Seven Wonders of the Ancient World*. London

COHEN, A. (1995) 'Alexander and Achilles—Macedonians and "Myceneans"', in J. B. Carter and S. P. Morris (eds.), *The Ages of Homer, A Tribute to Emily Townsend Vermeule*. Austin, 483–505

—— (1997) *The Alexander Mosaic: Stories of Victory and Defeat*. Cambridge

COHEN, J. M. (1963) *Bernal Díaz. The Conquest of New Spain*. Harmondsworth

COLLEDGE, M. (1987) 'Greek and non-Greek Interaction in the Art and Architecture of the Hellenistic East', in A. Kuhrt and S. Sherwin-White (eds.), *Hellenism in the East*. Berkeley, 134–62

COLLON, D. (1995) *Ancient Near Eastern Art*. London

CONNOR, W. R. (1985) 'The Razing of the House in Greek Society', *TAPhA* 115: 79–102

COOK, J. M. (1983) *The Persian Empire*. London

COPLEY, F. O. (1956, 1981) *Exclusus Amator*. American Philological Monograph Series, no. 17. Baltimore

CURTIS, J. (1989) *Ancient Persia*. London

DANDAMAEV, M. A. (1976) *Persien unter den ersten Achämeniden*, trans. H. D. Pohl. Wiesbaden

DASCALAKIS, A. (1966) *Alexander the Great and Hellenism*. Institute for Balkan Studies, Thessaloniki.

DAVIS, N., and KRAAY, C. M. (1973) *The Hellenistic Kingdoms, Portrait Coins and History*. London

DELL, H. J. (1981) (ed.) *Ancient Macedonian Studies in Honor of Charles F. Edson*. Thessaloniki

DESPINIS, G., STEFANIDOU-TIVERIOU, TH., VOUTIRAS, E. (1997) *Catalogue of Sculpture in the Archaeological Museum of Thessaloniki*, i. Thessaloniki

DEVELIN, R. (1985) 'Pompeius Trogus and Philippic History', *Storia della storiografia* 8: 110–15

DEVINE, A. M. (1975) 'Grand Tactics at Gaugamela', *Phoenix* 29: 374–85

——(1994) 'Alexander's Propaganda Machine: Callisthenes as the Ultimate Source for Arrian, *Anabasis* 1–3', in I. Worthington (ed.), *Ventures into Greek History*. Oxford, 89–102

DILLERY, J. (1995) *Xenophon and the History of his Times*. London

DINTSIS, P. (1986) *Hellenistische Helme*. Rome

DOBESCH, G. (1968) *Der panhellenische Gedanke im 4. Jh. v. Chr. und der 'Philippos' des Isokrates*. Vienna

——(1975). 'Alexander der Grosse und der Korinthische Bund', *GB* 3: 73–149

DOMBART, TH. (1924) 'Esagilla und das grosse Mardukfest zu Babylon', *Journal of the Society of Oriental Research*: 8, 3–4: 103–22

DOVEr, K. J. (1978) *Greek Homosexuality*. Cambridge, Mass.

DROUGOU, S., SAATSOGLOU-PALIADELI, CH., PHAKLARIS, P., KOTTARIDOU, A., TSIGARIDA, E.-B. (1996) *Vergina. The Great Tumulus. Archaeological Guide*². Thessaloniki

EADIE, J. W., and OBER, J. (1985) (eds.) *The Craft of the Ancient Historian. Essays in Honor of C. G. Starr*. New York

EDDY, S. K. (1961) *The King is Dead. Studies in the Near Eastern Resistance to Hellenism 334–31 B.C.* Lincoln, Nebr.

EDELSTEIN, L., and KIDD, I. G. (1972) *Posidonius*, i. *The Fragments*. Cambridge

EDMUNDS, L. (1971) 'The Religiosity of Alexander', *GRBS* 12: 363–91

ELLIS, J. R. (1976) *Philip II and Macedonian Imperialism*. London

ERDMANN, K. (1960) 'Persepolis: Daten und Deutungen', *Mitteilungen der deutschen Orient-Gesellschaft* 92: 21–47

ERRINGTON, R. M. (1969) 'Bias in Ptolemy's History of Alexander', *CQ* 19: 233–42

——(1970) 'From Babylon to Triparadeisos, 323–320 B.C.', *JHS* 90: 49–77

——(1976) 'Alexander in the Hellenistic World', in *Entretiens de la Fondation Hardt* 22. Geneva, 137–79

——(1981) 'Review Discussion: Four Interpretations of Philip II', *AJAH* 6: 77–88

——(1998) 'Neue epigraphische Belege für Makedonien zur Zeit Alexanders des Großen', in W. Will (ed.), *Alexander der Grosse: Eine Welteroberung und ihr Hintergrund*. Vorträge des Internationalen Bonner Alexanderkolloquiums, 19.–21. 12. 1996: Antiquitas, Reihe 1, Bd. 46. Bonn, 77–90

FAIRMAN, H. W. (1988) 'The Kingship Rituals of Egypt', in S. H. Hooke (ed.), *Myth, Ritual and Kingship*. Oxford, 74–104

FAKLARIS (*see also* Phaklaris), P. B. (1994) 'Aegae: Determining the Site of the First Capital of the Macedonians', *AJA* 98: 609–16

FARRINGTON, B. (1937) *Diodorus Siculus, Universal Historian*. Inaugural Lecture of the Professor of Classics. Cardiff

FLEISCHER, R. (1983) *Der Klagefrauensarkophag aus Sidon*. Tübingen

FLOWER, M. A. (1997) *Theopompus of Chios. History and Rhetoric in the Fourth Century B.C.* Pb. edn. with postscript. Oxford

FRANCIS, E. D. (1992) 'Oedipus Achaemenides', *AJPh* 113: 333–57

FRANKL, V. (1962) 'Die Begriffe des mexikanischen Kaisertums und der Weltmonarchie in den "Cartas de Relación" des Hernán Cortés', *Saeculum* 13: 1–34

FRASER, P. M. (1952) 'Alexander and the Rhodian Constitution', *PdP* 7: 192–206

——(1972) *Ptolemaic Alexandria*. Oxford

——(1996) *The Cities of Alexander the Great*. Oxford

FRASER, P. M., and BEAN, G. E. (1954) *The Rhodian Peraea and its Islands*. Oxford

FREDRICKSMEYER, E. A. (1961) 'Alexander, Midas, and the Oracle at Gordium', *CPh* 56: 160–8

——(1979) 'Divine Honors for Philip II', *TAPhA* 109: 39–61

——(1991) 'Alexander, Zeus Ammon, and the Conquest of Asia', *TAPhA* 121: 199–214

FREDRICKSMEYER, E. A. (1994) 'The Kausia: Macedonian or Indian?', in I. Worthington (ed.), *Ventures into Greek History*. Oxford, 134–58

——(1997) 'The Origin of Alexander's Royal Insignia', *TAPhA* 127: 97–109

——(1998) 'Alexander and Olympias', in G. Schmeling and J. D. Mikalson (eds.), *Qui Miscuit Utile Dulci. Festschrift Essays for Paul Lachlan MacKendrick*. Wauconda, Ill., 177–83

FRYE, R. N. (1963) *The Heritage of Persia*. Cleveland and New York

——(1972) 'Gestures of Deference to Royalty in Ancient Iran', *Iranica Antiqua* 9: 102–7

——(1984) *The History of Ancient Iran*. Handbuch der Altertumswissenschaft, III. 7. Munich

FUENTES, P. DE (1993) *The Conquistadors. First Person Accounts of the Conquest of Mexico*. Norman, Okla.

GABELMANN, H. (1979) 'Zur Chronologie der Königsnekropole von Sidon', *AA*: 163–77

GARLAN, Y. (1972) 'A propos des nouvelles inscriptions d'Iasos', *ZPE* 9: 223–4

——(1975) 'Alliance entre les Iasiens et Ptolemée Ier', *ZPE* 18: 193–8

GARLAND, R. (1995) *In the Eye of the Beholder*. London

GARNSEY, P. (1996) *Ideas of Slavery from Aristotle to Augustine*. Cambridge

GAUTHIER, M. H. (1916) *Le Livre des rois d'Égypte*, iv. Cairo

GAUTHIER, PH. (1990) 'Epigraphica', *RPh* 64: 67–70

GEHRKE, H.-J. (1982) 'Der siegreiche König. Überlegungen zur Hellenistischen Monarchie', *AKG* 64: 247–77

——(1987) 'Die Griechen und die Rache: ein Versuch in historicher Psychologie', *Saeculum* 38: 121–49

GELLER, M. J. (1990) 'Babylonian Astronomical Diaries and Corrections of Diodorus', *Bulletin of the School of Oriental and African Studies* 53: 1–7

GEORGES, P. (1994) *Barbarian Asia and the Greek Experience*. Baltimore

GERMAIN, G. (1956) 'Le Songe de Xerxes et le rite babylonien du substitut royal', *REG* 69: 303–13

GEYER, A. (1993) 'Geschichte als Mythos. Zu Alexanders "Perserschlacht" auf apulischen Vasenbildern', *JdI* 108: 443–55

GHIRSHMAN, R. (1957) 'Notes Iraniennes, VII. A propos de Persépolis', *Artibus Asiae* 20: 265–78

——(1964) *Iran, Protoiranier, Meder und Achämeniden*. Munich

GIBSON, C. (1968) *The Spanish Tradition in America*. Columbia, SC

GINOUVÈS, R. *et al.* (1993) *La Macédoine*. Paris

GIOURI, E. (1978) *Ο κρατήρας του Δερβενίου*. Athens

GOUKOWSKI, P. I. (1976) *Diodore de Sicile, livre XVII*. Budé, Paris

——(1978, 1981) *Essai sur les origines du mythe d'Alexandre*, i–ii. Nancy

GRAINGER, J. (1990) *Seleukos Nikator*. London

——(1991) *Hellenistic Phoenicia*. Oxford

GRANDJOUAN, C. (1989) *Hellenistic Relief Molds from the Athenian Agora*. Hesperia, Suppl. 23. Princeton

GRANIER, F. (1931) *Die makedonische Heeresversammlung. Ein Beitrag zum antiken Staatsrecht*. Münchener Beiträge zur Papyrusforschung und antiken Rechtsgeschichte, 13. Munich

GREEN, P. (1978) 'Caesar and Alexander: Aemulatio, Imitatio, Comparatio', *AJAH* 3: 1–26

——(1991) *Alexander of Macedon. 356–323 B.C. A Historical Biography*. Berkeley

——(1996) 'The Metamorphosis of the Barbarian: Athenian Panhellenism in a Changing World', in R. W. Wallace and E. M. Harris (eds.), *Transitions to Empire. Essays in Greco-Roman History 360–146 B.C. in Honor of E. Badian*. Oklahoma, 5–36

GREENBLATT, S. (1991) *Marvelous Possessions. The Wonder of the New World*. Oxford

GREENWALT, W. S. (1993) 'The Iconographical Significance of Amyntas III's Mounted Hunter Stater', *Ancient Macedonia* 5: 509–19

GRIFFIN, J. (1980) *Homer on Life and Death*. Oxford

——(1987) 'Homer and Excess', in J. M. Bremer, I. J. F. de Jong, and J. Kalff (eds.), *Homer: Beyond Oral Poetry, Recent Trends in Homeric Interpretation*. Amsterdam, 85–104

GRIFFITHS, J. G. (1953) 'Βασιλεὺς Βασιλέων. Remarks on the History of a Title', *CPh* 48: 145–54

GROTE, G. B. (1883) *A History of Greece*, 12 vols., London

GRUEN, E. (1985) 'The Coronation of the Diadochoi', in J. W. Eadie and J. Ober (eds.), *The Craft of the Ancient Historian*. Lanham, 253–71

GSCHNITZER, F. (1968) review of H. W. Ritter, *Diadem und Königsherrschaft*, *AAHG* 21: 167–70

HABICHT, C. (1961) 'Falsche Urkunden zur Geschichte Athens im Zeitalter der Perserkriege', *Hermes* 89: 1–35

——(1970) *Gottmenschentum und griechische Städte*². Munich

338   *Bibliography*

HABICHT, C. (1977) 'Zwei Angehörige des lynkestischen Königshauses', *Ancient Macedonia* 2: 511–16
——(1995) *Athen. Die Geschichte der Stadt in hellenistischer Zeit.* Munich
HALL, E. (1989) *Inventing the Barbarian.* Oxford
——(1993) 'Asia Unmanned: Images of Victory in Classical Athens', in J. Rich and G. Shipley (eds.), *War and Society in the Greek World.* London, 108–33
HAMILTON, J. R. (1969) *Plutarch Alexander: A Commentary.* Oxford
——(1973) *Alexander the Great.* Pittsburgh
——(1977) 'Cleitarchus and Diodorus 17', in K. Kinzl (ed.), *Greece and the Eastern Mediterranean in History and Prehistory.* Berlin. 126–46
——(1988) 'Alexander's Iranian Policy', in W. Will and J. Heinrichs (eds.), *Zu Alexander d. Gr. Festschrift G. Wirth*, i. Amsterdam, 467–86
HAMMOND, N. G. L. (1937) 'The Sources of Diodorus Siculus XVI (i). The Macedonian, Greek and Persian Narrative', *CQ* 31: 79–81
——(1980) *Alexander the Great: King, Commander and Statesman.* Park Ridge, NJ.
——(1983) *Three Historians of Alexander the Great: The So-Called Vulgate Authors, Diodorus, Justin and Curtius.* Cambridge
——(1986) 'The Kingdom of Asia and the Persian Throne', *Antichthon* 20: 73–85
——(1987) 'Papyrus British Library 3085 verso', *GRBS* 28: 331–47
——(1989) *The Macedonian State.* Oxford
——(1991) 'The Royal Tombs at Vergina: Evolution and Identities', *ABSA* 86: 69–82
——(1992) 'The Archaeological and Literary Evidence for the Burning of the Persepolis Palace', *CQ* 42: 358–64
——(1993) *Sources for Alexander the Great.* Cambridge
——(1995) 'Did Alexander use one or two Seals?', *Chiron* 25: 199–203
HAMMOND, N. G. L., and WALBANK, F. W. (1988) *A History of Macedonia.* iii. Oxford
HANKE, L. (1959) *Aristotle and the American Indians. A Study in Race Prejudice in the Modern World.* Chicago
HARDING, P. (1994) *Androtion and the Atthis. The Fragments Translated with Introduction and Commentary.* Oxford
HARTMANN, H. (1937) 'Zur neuen Inschrift des Xerxes von Persepolis', *OLZ* 40: 145–60

HATZOPOULOS, M. B. (1994) *Cultes et rites de passage en Macédoine.* Athens

—— (1996) *Macedonian Institutions under the Kings,* ii. *Epigraphic Appendix. MEΛETHMATA,* 22. Athens

—— (1997) 'Alexandre en Perse: La Revanche et l'empire', *ZPE* 116: 41–52

HAUBEN, H. (1974) 'A Royal Toast in 302 B.C.', *AncSoc* 5: 105–17

—— (1977) 'Rhodes, Alexander and the Diadochoi from 333/332 to 304 B.C.', *Historia* 26: 307–39

—— (1987a) 'Philokles, King of the Sidonians and General of the Ptolemies', in *Studia Phoenicia,* v. *Phoenicia and the East Mediterranean in the First Millennium B.C.* Louvain, 413–27

—— (1987b) 'On the Ptolemaic Iasos Inscription IGSK 28.1, 2–3', *EA* 10: 3–5

HECKEL, W. (1988) *The Last Days and Testament of Alexander the Great.* Historia Einzelschr. 56. Stuttgart

—— (1992) *The Marshals of Alexander's Empire.* London

HEICHELHEIM, F. (1925) *Die auswärtige Bevölkerung im Ptolemäerreich.* Klio Beih. 18. Leipzig

HEINRICHS, J. (1987) ' "Asiens König". Die Inschriften des Kyrosgrabs und das achämenidische Reichsverständnis', in W. Will and J. Heinrichs (eds.), *Zu Alexander d. Gr. Festschrift G. Wirth,* i. Amsterdam, 487–540

HENDERSON, J. (1989) 'Livy and the Invention of History', in A. Cameron (ed.), *History as Text. The Writing of Ancient History.* London, 64–85

HERZFELD, E. (1920) *Am Tor von Asien. Felsdenkmale aus Irans Heldenzeit.* Berlin

HILL, G. F. (1922) *BMC. Arabia, Mesopotamia, Persia.* London, repr. Bologna, 1965

—— (1923) 'Alexander the Great and the Persian Lion Gryphon', *JHS* 43: 156–61

—— (1927) 'Greek Coins acquired by the British Museum', *NC* 7: 193–208

HILLIER, K. (1985) 'William Colyngbourne', in J. Petrie (ed.), *Richard III Crown and People.* London, 101–8

HINDLEY, C. (1994) '*Eros* and Military Command in Xenophon', *CQ* 44: 347–66

HINZ, W. (1975) *Altiranisches Sprachgut der Nebenüberlieferungen.* Göttinger Orientforschung, III Reihe (Iranica), 3. Wiesbaden

—— (1979) *Darius und die Perser. Eine Kulturgeschichte der Achämeniden,* ii. Baden-Baden

HIRSCH, S. W. (1985) *The Friendship of the Barbarians. Xenophon and the Persian Empire.* Hanover, NH

HITZL, I. (1991) *Die griechischen Sarkophage der archäischen und klassischen Zeit*. Jonsered
HÖGEMANN, P. (1985) *Alexander der Große und Arabien*. Zetemata, 82. Munich
HOLLEAUX, M. (1938) *Études d'épigraphie et d'histoire grecques*, i. Paris
HÖLSCHER, T. (1973) *Griechische Historienbilder*. Würzburg
HOLT, F. (1988) *Alexander the Great and Bactria*. Mnemosyne Suppl. 104. Leiden
HORNBLOWER, J. (1981) *Hieronymus of Cardia*. Oxford
HORNBLOWER, S. (1982) *Mausolus*. Oxford
——(1984) review of N. G. L. Hammond, *Three Historians of Alexander the Great*, *CR* 34: 261–4
——(1991) *A Commentary on Thucydides*, i. Oxford
——(1994a) *Cambridge Ancient History*, vi². Cambridge
——(1994b) *Greek Historiography*. Oxford
HORNUNG, E. (1966) *Geschichte als Fest: Zwei Vorträge zum Geschichtsbild der frühen Menschheit*. Darmstadt
INSTINSKY, H. U. (1949) *Alexander der Grosse am Hellespont*. Godesberg
JACOB-FELSCH, M. (1969) *Die Entwicklung griechischer Statuenbasen und die Aufstellung der Statuen*. Waldsassen
JAEGER, W. (1948) *Aristotle²*, trans. R. Robinson. Oxford
JASTROW, M. (1914) *Babylonian-Assyrian Birth-Omens and their Cultural Significance*. Giessen
JENKINS, G. K. (1972) *Ancient Greek Coins*. London
JEPPESEN, K. K. (1992) 'Tot operum opus', *JDAI* 107: 59–102
——(1998) 'Das Maussolleion von Halikarnass, Forschungsbericht 1997', *Proceedings of the Danish Institute at Athens* 2: 161–231
JONES C. P., and HABICHT, C. (1989) 'A Hellenistic Inscription from Arsinoe', *Phoenix* 43: 317–46
JUNGE, P. J. (1944) *Darios I. König der Perser*. Leipzig
KANTZIA, C. (1980) '. . . *ΤΙΜΟΣ ΑΒΔΑΛΩΝΥΜΟΥ [ΣΙΔ]ΩΝΟΣ ΒΑΣΙΛΕΩΣ*', *AD* 35, 1: 1–16
KARAGEORGHIS, V. (1969) *Cyprus*. London
——(1992) 'Μακεδονικὰ στοιχεῖα στον ἑλληνιστικό πολιτισμό της Κύπρου', *Πρακτικὰ της Ακαδημίας Αθηνών* 67: 704–12
KEBRIC, R. B. (1977) *In the Shadow of Macedon: Duris of Samos*. Historia Einzelschriften, 29. Wiesbaden
KEEGAN, J. (1987) *The Mask of Command*. New York
KENT, R. G. (1961) *Old Persian. Grammar, Texts, Lexicon²*. American Oriental Society. American Oriental Series, 33. New Haven

KENNEDY, G. (1963) *The Art of Persuasion in Greece*. Princeton

KESSLER, J. (1911) *Isokrates und die panhellenische Idee*. Paderborn

KIENAST, D. (1973) *Philipp II von Makedonien und das Reich der Achaimeniden*. Munich

KIENITZ, F. K. (1953) *Die politische Geschichte Ägyptens vom 7. bis zum 4. Jahrdt. vor der Zeitwende*. Berlin

KIILERICH, B. (1988) 'Physiognomics and the Iconography of Alexander', *Symbolae Osloenses* 63: 51–66

KING, K. C. (1987) *Achilles. Paradigms of the War Hero from Homer to the Middle Ages*. Berkeley

KLEEMAN, I. (1958) *Der Satrapen-Sarkophag aus Sidon*. Berlin

KLEIN, W. (1905) *Geschichte der griechischen Kunst*, ii. Leipzig

KOENEN, L. (1977) *Eine agonistische Inschrift aus Ägypten und frühptolemäische Königsfeste*. Beiträge zur klassischen Philologie, 56. Meisenheim am Glan

KOLDEWEY, R. (1914) *The Excavations at Babylon*. London

KOTTARIDOU, A. (1989) 'Βεργίνα 1989. Ανασκαφή στο νεκροταφείο στα βορειοδυτικά της αρχαίας πόλης', Το αρχαιολογικό έργο στη Μακεδονία και Θράκη 3: 1–3, fig. 3

KRAUT, R. (1997) (ed.), *Aristotle Politics Books VII and VIII*. Oxford

KREFTER, F. (1971) *Persepolis Rekonstruktionen*. Teheraner Forschungen, 3. Berlin

KRITT, B. (1997) *The Early Seleucid Mint of Susa*. Classical Numismatic Studies, no. 2. Lancaster, Pa.

KUHRT, A. (1987) 'Usurpation, Conquest and Ceremonial: From Babylon to Persia', in D. Cannadine and S. Price (eds.), *Rituals of Royalty*. Cambridge, 20–55

KUNST, K. (1923) *Rhetorische Papyri*. Berlin

LANE FOX, R. (1973) *Alexander the Great*. London

——(1980) *The Search for Alexander*. Boston and Toronto

——(1996) 'Text and Image: Alexander the Great, Coins and Elephants', *BICS* 41: 87–108

LATTIMORE, R. (1939) 'The Wise Adviser in Herodotus', *CPh* 34: 24–35

LAUFFER, S. (1981) *Alexander der Grosse*.[2] Munich

LEHMANN, G. A. (1988) 'Das neue Kölner Historiker-fragment (P. Köln Nr. 247) und die χρονικὴ σύνταξις des Zenon von Rhodos (FGrHist. 523)', *ZPE* 72: 1–17

LEHMANN, PH. W. (1980) 'The So-Called Tomb of Philip II: A Different Interpretation', *AJA* 84: 527–31

——(1982) 'The So-Called Tomb of Philip II: An Addendum', *AJA* 86: 437–42

LEICHTY, E. (1970) *The Omen Series Summa Izbu TCS 4.* Locust Valley, NY

LENSCHAU, T. (1932) review of U. Wilcken, *Alexander der Grosse, Berliner Philologische Wochenschrift*, 365–70

LEON-PORTILLA, M. (1962) *The Broken Spears. The Aztec Account of the Conquest of Mexico.* London

LEONARD, I. A. (1944) 'Conquerors and Amazons in Mexico', *Hispanic American Historical Review* 24: 561–79

LE RIDER, G. (1995–96) 'Histoire économique et monétaire de l'Orient hellénistique', *Annuaire du Collège de France: Résumé des cours et travaux* 96: 829–60

LEWIS, D. M. (1977) *Sparta and Persia.* Leiden

LLOYD, A. B. (1994) 'Egypt, 404–332 B.C.', in D. M. Lewis, J. Boardman, *et al.*, *CAH* vi². Cambridge, 337–60

LLOYD, A. C. (1978) 'Emotion and Decision in Stoic Psychology', in J. M. Rist (ed.), *The Stoics.* Berkeley, 233–46

LOCK, R. A. (1977) 'The Macedonian Army Assembly in the Time of Alexander the Great', *CPh* 72: 92–107

LUND, H. S. (1992) *Lysimachus.* London

MACDOWELL, D. M. (1978) *The Law in Classical Athens.* London

MCKECHNIE, P. (1995) 'Diodorus Siculus and Hephaestion's Pyre', *CQ* 45: 418–32

——(1999) 'Manipulation of Themes in Quintus Curtius Rufus Book 10', *Historia* 48: 44–60

MACURDY, G. H. (1929) 'The Political Activities and the Name of Cratesipolis', *AJPh* 50: 273–8

MAKARONAS, CH., and GIOURI, E. (1989) Οἱ οἰκίες ἁρπαγής της Ἑλένης καὶ Διονύσου της Πέλλας. Athens

MARESCH, K. (1987) *Kölner Papyri,* vi. Papyrologica Coloniensia, 7. Opladen, 96–109, no. 247

MARKLE, M. M. III (1976) 'Support of Athenian Intellectuals for Philip: A Study of Isocrates' *Philippus* and Speusippus' *Letter to Philip*', *JHS* 96: 80–99

MASTROCINQUE, A. (1979) *La Caria e la Ionia meridionale in epoca ellenistica (323–188 a.C.).* Rome

MATHIEU, G. (1925) *Les Idées politiques d' Isocrate.* Paris

MAUDSLAY, A. P. (1908–16) *The True History of the Conquest of New Spain by Bernal Díaz del Castillo, one of its Conquerors.* London

——(1928) Bernal Diaz del Castillo. *The Discovery and Conquest of Mexico 1517–1521.* London

MAYRHOFER, M. (1973) *Onomastica Persepolitana: Das altiranische Namengut der Persepolis-Täfelchen.* Sitzungsberichte der österreichischen Akademie der Wissenschaften, phil.-hist. Klasse, 286. Vienna

MAZZARINO, S. (1966) *Il pensiero storico classico*, ii. Bari

MEHL, A. (1980/81) 'Δορίκτητος χώρα: Kritische Bemerkungen zum "Speererwerb" in Politik und Völkerrecht der hellenistischen Epoche', *AncSoc* 11/12: 173–212

MEISSNER, B. (1925) *Babylonien und Assyrien*, ii. Kulturgeschichtliche Bibliothek. Erste Reihe. Ethnologische Bibliothek, 4. Heidelberg

MENDELS, D. (1981) 'The Five Empires: A Note on a Propagandistic *Topos*', *AJPh* 102: 330–7

MERKELBACH, R. (1977) *Die Quellen des griechischen Alexanderromans*². Munich

MERKER, I. L. (1970) 'The Ptolemaic Officials and the League of the Islanders', *Historia* 19: 141–60

MERLAN, P. (1954) 'Isocrates, Aristotle and Alexander the Great', *Historia* 3: 60–81

MESSERSCHMIDT, W. (1989) 'Historische und ikonographische Untersuchungen zum Alexandersarkophag', *Boreas* 12: 64–92

MILLER, M. C. J. (1991) 'The Regal Coinage of Cassander', *AncW* 22: 49–55

MILLER, S. G. (1986) 'Alexander's Funeral Cart', *Ancient Macedonia* 4: 401–12

——(1993) *The Tomb of Lyson and Kallikles: A Painted Macedonian Tomb*. Mainz

MILNS, R. D. (1969) *Alexander the Great*. New York

MILTNER, F. (1954) 'Alexander der Grosse', in F. Valjavec (ed.), *Historia Mundi*, iii. Bern, 290–304

MILTSAKAKIS, G. (1987) 'Βεργίνα. Ο μεγάλος βασιλικός τάφος. Ζωγραφική αναπαράσταση της πρόσοψης', in *Αμητός* for M. Andronikos, xxiii. Thessaloniki

MOMIGLIANO, A. (1934) *Filippo il Macedone*. Florence

MONTGOMERY, H. (1969) 'Thronbesteigung und Klagen', *Opuscula Atheniensia* 9: 1–19

MORENO, P. (1979) 'La pittura tra classicità ed ellenismo', in R. Bianchi Bandinelli (ed.), *La crisi della polis: Arte, religione, musica*. Storia e civiltà dei greci, 6. Milan, 458–520

——(1987) *Vita e arte di Lisippo*. Milan

——(1993) 'L'immagine di Alessandro Magno nell'opera di Lisippo e di altri artisti contemporanei', in Carlsen, Due *et al.*, *Alexander the Great, Reality and Myth*. Rome, 101–36

——(1995) *Lisippo. L'arte e la fortuna*. Monza

MØRKHOLM, O. (1991) *Early Hellenistic Coinage. From the Accession of Alexander to the Peace of Apamea, 336–188 B.C.* (ed. P. Grierson and U. Westermark). Cambridge

MORTENSEN, C. (1997) *Olympias: Royal Wife and Mother at the Macedonian Court*. Diss. Queensland

MOSSMAN, J. M. (1988) 'Tragedy and Epic in Plutarch's *Alexander*', *JHS* 108: 83–93

MÜLLER, O. (1973) *Antigonos Monophthalmos und das 'Jahr der Könige'*. Bonn

MUSGRAVE, J. H. (1991) 'The Human Remains from Vergina Tombs I, II and III: An Overview', *AncW* 22: 3–9

NILSSON, M. P. (1967) *Geschichte der griechischen Religion*. i³. Munich

NOE, E. (1984) *Storiografia imperiale pretacitiana*. Florence

NYLANDER, C. (1974) 'Al-Bērunī and Persepolis', *Acta Iranica* 1: 137–50

OAKLEY, J. H. (1986) 'Reflections on Nikomachos', *BABesch* 61: 71–6

OATES, J. (1986) *Babylon*. London

OBERLEITNER, W. (1994) *Das Heroon von Trysa*. Mainz

O'BRIEN, J. M. (1992) *Alexander the Great: The Invisible Enemy*. London

OIKONOMIDES, A. (1987) 'The Decree of the Athenian Orator Hyperides Honoring the Macedonians Iolaus and Medios', *PRAKTIKA B'* (Athens): 169–82

OOST, S. I. (1981) 'The Alexander historians and Asia', in H. J. Dell (ed.), *Ancient Macedonian Studies in Honor of Charles F. Edson*. Thessaloniki, 265–82

OWEN, G. E. L. (1983) 'Philosophical Invective', in J. Annas (ed.), *Oxford Studies in Ancient Philosophy*, i. Oxford, 1–25

PAGDEN, A. (1986) *Hernan Cortes. Letters from Mexico* (with an introduction by J. H. Elliott). New Haven and London

—— (1995) *Lords of All the World*. New Haven and London

PAGE, D. L. (1975) *Epigrammata Graeca*. Oxford

PALAGIA, O. (1980) *Euphranor*. Leiden

—— (1986) 'Imitation of Herakles in Ruler Portraiture: A Survey from Alexander to Maximinus Daza', *Boreas* 9: 137–51

—— (1997) 'Initiates in the Underworld', in I. D. Jenkins and G. B. Waywell (eds.), *Sculpture and Sculptors of the Dodecanese and Caria*. London, 68–73

—— (1998) 'The Enemy Within: A Macedonian in Piraeus', in O. Palagia and W. D. E. Coulson (eds.), *Regional Schools in Hellenistic Sculpture*. Oxford, 15–26

PALLIS, S. A. (1926) *The Babylonian Akîtu Festival*. Copenhagen

PANDERMALIS, D. (1997) *Δίον. Αρχαιολογικός χώρος και μουσείο*. Athens

PARIBENI, R., and ROMANELLI, P. (1914) 'Studi e ricerche archeologiche nell'Anatolia meridionale', *Monumenti antichi* 23

PARKE, H. W. (1967) *The Oracles of Zeus.* Oxford

——(1985) 'The Massacre of the Branchidae', *JHS* 105: 59–68

PEARSON, L. (1960) *The Lost Histories of Alexander the Great.* New York

PÉDECH, P. (1984) *Historiens compagnons d'Alexandre.* Paris

PEKRIDOU, A. (1986) *Das Alketas-Grab in Termessos,* MDAI(I) Beih. *32.* Tübingen

PELLING, C. B. R. (1988) *Plutarch, Life of Antony.* Cambridge

——(1991) 'Thucydides' Archidamus and Herodotus' Artabanus', in M. A. Flower and M. Toher (eds.), *Georgica: Greek Studies in Honour of George Cawkwell.* Institute of Classical Studies Bulletin, Suppl. 58. London, 120–42

——(1992) 'Plutarch and Thucydides', in P. A. Stadter (ed.), *Plutarch and the Historical Tradition,* London, 10–40

PEREMANS, W., and VAN'T DACK, E. (1995) *Prosopographia Ptolemaica.* Louvain

PERLMAN, S. (1957) 'Isocrates' "Philippus"—a Reinterpretation', *Historia* 6: 306–17

——(1967) 'Isocrates' Advice on Philip's Attitude Towards Barbarians', *Historia* 16: 338–43

——(1969) 'Isocrates' "Philippus" and Panhellenism', *Historia* 18: 370–4

——(1976) 'Panhellenism, the Polis and Imperialism', *Historia* 25: 1–30

PETSAS, P. M. (1966) *The Levkadhia Tomb.* Athens

PFISTER, F. (1946) 'Studien zum Alexanderroman', *WJA* 1: 29–66

PFUHL, E., and MÖBIUS, H. (1977) *Die ostgriechischen Grabreliefs.* Mainz

PHAKLARIS (*see also* Faklaris), P. B. (1986) 'Ἱπποσκευές ἀπό τη Βεργίνα', *ArchDelt* 41, 1: 1–57

——(1997) 'Βεργίνα. Ο οχυρωματικός περίβολος και η ακροπόλη', *Το αρχαιολογικό έργο στη Μακεδονία και Θράκη* 10A: 69–75

POPE, A. U. (1957) 'Persepolis as a Ritual City', *Archaeology* 10: 123–30

POWELL, P. W. (1944) 'Spanish Warfare against the Chichimecas in the 1570's', *Hispanic American Historical Review* 24: 580–604

PRAG, A. J. N. W. (1990) 'Reconstructing King Philip II: The "Nice" Version', *AJA* 94: 237–47

PRAG, J., and NEAVE, R. (1997) *Making Faces.* London

PRANDI, L. (1985) *Callistene Uno storico tra Aristotele e i re macedoni.* Milan

PRANDI, L. (1996) *Fortuna e realtà dell'opera di Clitarco.* Historia Einzelschriften, 104. Stuttgart

PRESTIANNI GIALLOMBARDO, A. M. (1991) 'Recenti testimonianze iconografiche sulla *kausia* in Macedonia e la datazione del freggio della caccia della II tomba reale di Vergina', *DHA* 17: 257–304.

PRICE, M. J. (1974) *Coins of the Macedonians.* London

——(1982) 'The Porus' Coinage of Alexander the Great: A Symbol of Concord and Community', in S. Scheers (ed.), *Studia Paulo Naster Oblata,* i. *Numismatica Antiqua.* Leuven, 75–85

——(1991) *The Coinage in the Name of Alexander the Great and Philip Arrhidaeus.* 2 vols. Zurich and London

PUGLIESE CARRATELLI, G. (1967/8) 'Supplemento epigrafico di Iasos', *ASAA* 45/6: 437–65

READE, J. (1983) *Assyrian Sculpture.* London

REILLY, L. C. (1993) 'The Hunting Frieze from Vergina', *JHS* 113: 160–2

REINHOLD, M. (1970) *Purple as a Status Symbol in Antiquity.* Brussels

RHOMIOPOULOU, K. (1997) Λευκάδια. Αρχαία Μίεζα. Athens

RIDGWAY, B. S. (1990) *Hellenistic Sculpture,* i. Bristol

RITTER, H. W. (1965) *Diadem und Königsherrschaft.* Vestigia. Beiträge zur Geschichte, 7. Munich and Berlin

ROBERT, J., and ROBERT, L. (1985) *Fouilles d'Amyzon en Carie,* i. Paris

ROBERT, L. (1936) *Collection Froehner,* i. Paris

ROBERTSON, M. (1982) 'Early Greek Mosaic', in B. Barr-Sharrar, and E. N. Borza (eds.), *Macedonia and Greece in Late Classical and Early Hellenistic Times.* National Gallery of Art, Washington, Studies in the History of Art, 10: 241–9

ROISMAN, J. (1984) 'Ptolemy and his Rivals in his History of Alexander', *CQ* 34: 373–85

ROMILLY, J. DE (1993) 'Les Barbares dans la pensée de la Grèce classique', *Phoenix* 47: 283–92

ROOT, M. C. (1979) *The King and Kingship in Achaemenid Art. Essays on the Creation of an Iconography of Empire.* Acta Iranica, 19. Leiden

ROTROFF, S. I. (1982) *Hellenistic Pottery. Athenian and Imported Moldmade Bowls.* Athenian Agora, 22. Princeton

——(1997) *Hellenistic Pottery. Athenian and Imported Wheelmade Tableware and Related Material.* Athenian Agora, 29. Princeton

ROUX, G. (1992) *Ancient Iraq³.* Harmondsworth

RUBINCAM, C. (1992) 'The Nomenclature of Julius Caesar and the Later Augustus in the Triumviral Period', *Historia* 41: 88–103

RUSSELL, F. H. (1975) *The Just War in the Middle Ages.* Cambridge

RUZICKA, S. (1985), 'A Note on Philip's Persian War', *AJAH* 10: 84–95

SAATSOGLOU-PALIADELI, C. (1989) 'Το ανάθημα του Κρατερού στους Δελφούς', *Egnatia* 1: 81–99

——(1994) 'Βεργίνα 1991. Ανασκαφές στο ιερό της Εύκλειας', *Το αρχαιολογικό έργο στη Μακεδονία και Θράκη* 5: 9–21

——(1995) 'Βεργίνα 1992. Ανασκαφές στο ιερό της Εύκλειας', *Το αρχαιολογικό έργο στη Μακεδονία και Θράκη* 6: 53–7

SACHS, A. (1977) 'Achaemenid Royal Names in Babylonian Astronomical Texts', *AJAH* 2: 129–47

SACHS, A., and HUNGER, H. (1988) *Astronomical Diaries and Related Texts from Babylonia*, i. *Diaries from 652 BC to 262 BC.* Vienna

SACKS, K. S. (1990) *Diodorus Siculus and the First Century.* Princeton

——(1994) 'Diodorus and his Sources: Conformity and Creativity', in S. Hornblower (ed.), *Greek Historiography*, Oxford, 213–32

SAGGS, E. W. (1969) *The Greatness that was Babylon.* New York and Washington

STE CROIX, G. E. M. DE (1972), *The Origins of the Peloponnesian War.* London

SAKELLARIOU, M. B. (1980), 'Panhellenism: From Concept to Policy', in M. Hatzopoulos and L. Loukopoulos (eds.), *Philip of Macedon.* Athens, 128–45

SALLER, R. (1980) 'Anecdote as Historical Evidence for the Principate', *G&R* 27: 69–83

SAMUEL, A. E. (1985) *From Athens to Alexandria. Hellenism and Social Goals in Ptolemaic Egypt.* Studia Hellenistica, 26. Leuven

SARRE, F., and HERZFELD, E. (1910) *Iranische Felsreliefs.* Berlin

SARTORI, M. (1983) 'Note sulla datazione dei primi libri della *Bibliotheca historica* di Diodoro Siculo', *Athenaeum* 61: 545–52

SCHACHERMEYR, F. (1920) 'Das Ende des makedonischen Königshauses', *Klio* 16: 332–7

——(1954), 'Die letzten Pläne Alexanders des Grossen', *JÖAI* 41: 118–40

——(1970) *Alexander in Babylon und die Reichsordnung nach seinem Tode.* Sitzungsberichte der österreichischen Akademie der Wissenschaften, phil.-hist. Klasse, 268. 3. Vienna

——(1973) *Alexander der Grosse: Das Problem seiner Persönlichkeit und seines Wirkens.* Sitzungsberichte der österreichischen Akademie der Wissenschaften, phil.-hist. Klasse, 285. Vienna

SCHEIN, S. (1984) *The Mortal Hero: An Introduction to Homer's Iliad*. Berkeley

SCHEPENS, G. (1989) 'Zum Problem der "Unbesiegbarkeit" Alexanders des Grossen', *AncSoc* 20: 15–53

SCHIPPMANN, K. (1971) *Die iranischen Feuerheiligtümer*. Berlin and New York

SCHMIDT, I. (1995) *Hellenistische Statuenbasen*. Frankfurt

SCHMIDT, M., TRENDALL, A. D., and CAMBITOGLOU, A. (1976) *Ein Gruppe apulischer Grabvasen in Basel*. Basel

SCHMIDT-DOUNAS, B. (1985) *Der Lykische Sarkophag aus Sidon*. MDAI(I) Beih. 30. Tübingen

SCHMITTHENNER, W. (1968) 'Über eine Formveränderung der Monarchie seit Alexander d. Grossen', *Saeculum* 19: 31–46

SCHOBER, L. (1981) *Untersuchungen zur Geschichte Babyloniens und der Oberen Satrapien von 323–303 v. Chr.* Frankfurt

SCHREINER, J. H. (1977) 'More Anti-Thukydidean Studies in the Pentekontaetia', *Symbolae Osloenses* 52: 19–38

SCHUR, W. (1934) 'Das Alexanderreich nach Alexanders Tode', *RhM* 83: 129–56

SCHWARTZ, E. (1896) *Fünf Vorträge über den griechischen Roman*. Berlin

SCHWARZ, F. F. (1980) 'Invasion und Résistance: Darstellungsmöglichkeiten in der Alexanderliteratur', *GB* 9: 79–110

SEAGER, R. (1981) 'The Freedom of the Greeks of Asia: From Alexander to Antiochus', *CQ* 31: 106–12

SEALEY, R. (1993) *Demosthenes and his Time. A Study in Defeat*. Oxford

Search for Alexander, The (1980). Washington, DC

SEEL, O. (1955) *Die Praefatio des Pompeius Trogus*. Erlangen

SEGRE, M. (1934) 'Decreto di Aspendos', *Aegyptus* 14: 253–68

SEIBERT, J. (1967) *Historische Beiträge zu den dynastischen Verbindungen in hellenistischer Zeit*. Wiesbaden

—— (1969) *Untersuchungen zur Geschichte Ptolemaios' I.* Munich

—— (1970) 'Philokles, Sohn des Apollonios, König der Sidonier', *Historia* 19: 337–51

—— (1972) *Alexander der Grosse*. Darmstadt

—— (1983) *Das Zeitalter der Diadochen*. Darmstadt

—— (1984) 'Das Testament Alexanders: Ein Pamphlet aus der Frühzeit der Diadochenkämpfe', in A. Kraus (ed.), *Land und Reich, Stamm und Nation: Festgabe für Max Spindler*. Munich, 247–60

—— (1985) *Die Eroberung des Perserreiches durch Alexander d. Gr. auf kartographischer Grundlage*. Wiesbaden

—— (1987) 'Dareios III', in W. Will and J. Heinrichs (eds.), *Zu*

Alexander d. Gr. Festschrift G. Wirth, i. Amsterdam, 437–56

SEIBERT, J. (1990) review of W. Heckel, *The Last Days and Testament of Alexander the Great, Gnomon* 62: 564–6

——(1998) ' "Panhellenischer" Kreuzzug, Nationalkrieg, Rachefeldzug oder Makedonischer Eroberungskrieg?—Überlegungen zu den Ursachen des Krieges gegen Persien', in W. Will (ed.), *Alexander der Grosse: Eine Weltoberung und ihr Hintergrund.* Vorträge des Internationalen Bonner Alexanderkolloquiums, 19.–21. 12. 1996: Antiquitas, Reihe 1, Bd. 46. Bonn, 5–58

SETHE, K. H. (1904) *Hieroglyphische Urkunden der griechischrömischen Zeit*, i. Leipzig

SHERWIN-WHITE, S. N. (1978) *Ancient Cos.* Göttingen

——(1985) 'Ancient Archives: The Edict of Alexander to Priene, a Reappraisal', *JHS* 105: 69–89

SHERWIN-WHITE, S., and KUHRT, A. (1993) *From Samarkand to Sardis.* London

SINCLAIR, R. K. (1966) 'Diodorus Siculus and Fighting in Relays', *CQ* 16: 249–55

SIMPSON, L. B. (1965) *Cortés. The Life of the Conqueror by his Secretary Francisco López de Gómara.* Berkeley

SISMANIDIS, S. (1997) Κλίνες και κλινοειδείς κατασκευές των μακεδονικών τάφων. Athens

SMALL, A. (1996) (ed.), *Subject and Ruler: The Cult of the Ruling Power in Classical Antiquity.* Ann Arbor

SMELIK, K. A. D. (1978–9) 'The "Omina Mortis" in the Histories of Alexander the Great', *Talanta* 10–11: 92–111

SMITH, R. R. R. (1991) *Hellenistic Sculpture.* London

SORDI, M. (1982) 'Timagene di Alessandria: uno storico ellenocentrico e filobarbaro', *ANRW* II, 30.1: 775–97

SPIEGELBERG, W. (1914) *Die sogenannte demotische Chronik.* Leipzig

STAMATIOU, A. (1988) 'Alexander the Great as a Lion Hunter', Πρακτικά XII διεθνούς συνεδρίου κλασικής αρχαιολογίας, Αθήνα 1983, 2: 209–17

STEPHANIDOU-TIVERIOU, TH. (1997) 'Η οχύρωση του Δίου. Από τον Κάσσανδρο ως τον Θεοδόσιο Α'. Το ιστορικό πλαίσιο', Το αρχαιολογικό έργο στη Μακεδονία και Θράκη 10Α: 215–24

STEWART, A. (1993) *Faces of Power. Alexander's Image and Hellenistic Politics.* Berkeley

STONEMAN, R. (1991) *The Greek Alexander Romance.* Harmondsworth

——(1995) 'Naked Philosophers: The Brahmans in the Alexander Historians and the Alexander Romance', *JHS* 105: 99–114

STRASBURGER, H. (1982–90) *Studien zur Alten Geschichte* (ed. W. Schmitthenner and R. Zoepffel). Hildesheim

STRONACH, D. (1978) *Pasargadae. A Report on the Excavations conducted by the British Institute of Persian Studies from 1961–1963*. Oxford

SWAIN, J. W. (1940) 'The Theory of the Four Monarchies', *CPh* 35: 1–21.

SZNYCER, M. (1980) 'La Partie phénicienne de l'inscription bilingue gréco-phénicienne de Cos', *ArchDelt* 35, 1: 17–30

TADMOR, H. (1981) 'Addendum', *AJPh* 102: 338–9

TARN, W. W. (1921) 'Heracles, Son of Barsine', *JHS* 41: 18–28

—— (1948), *Alexander the Great*. 2 vols. Cambridge

TATUM, J. (1989) *Xenophon's Imperial Fiction*. Princeton

THEMELIS, P. G., and TOURATSOGLOU, J. P. (1997) Οἱ τάφοι του Δερβενίου. Athens

THOMAS, H. (1993) *The Conquest of Mexico*. London

THOMAS, R. (1989) *Oral Tradition and Written Record in Classical Athens*. Cambridge

TIVERIOS, M. (1997) 'Die von Xenophantos Athenaios signierte grosse Lekythos aus Pantikapaion: Alte Funde neu betrachtet', in J. H Oakley, W. D. E Coulson, and O. Palagia (eds.), *Athenian Potters and Painters*. Oxford, 269–84

TOD, M. N. (1948) *Greek Historical Inscriptions*, ii. Oxford

TOHER, M. (1990) 'Augustus and the Evolution of Roman Historiography', in K. A. Raaflaub and M. Toher (eds.), *Between Republic and Empire*. Berkeley, 139–54

TOO, Y. L. (1995), *The Rhetoric of Identity in Isocrates*. Cambridge

TRENDALL A. D., and CAMBITOGLOU, A. (1982), *The Red-Figured Vases of Apulia*. ii. Oxford

TRIPODI, B. (1991) 'Il freggio della *caccia* della tomba reale di Vergina e le cacce funerarie d'oriente', *DHA* 17: 143–209

TSIMBIDOU-AVLONITI, M. (1997) 'Οἱ ταφικοί τύμβοι της περιοχής Αγ. Αθανασίου Θεσσαλονίκης: έρευνα και προοπτικές', Το αρχαιολογικό έργο στη Μακεδονία και Θράκη 10A: 427–42

TUPLIN, C. (1996) *Achaemenid Studies*. Stuttgart

USHER, S. (1994) 'Isocrates: Paideia, Kingship and the Barbarians', in H. A. Khan (ed.), *The Birth of the European Identity; The Europe–Asia Contrast in Greek Thought 490–322 B.C*. Nottingham, 131–45

VARINLIOGLU, E., et al. (1990) 'Une inscription de Pladasa en Carie', *REA* 92: 59–78

VOKOTOPOULOU, I. (1997) 'Ο Κάσσανδρος, η Κασσάνδρεια και η Θεσσαλονίκη', in Μνήμη Μανόλη Ανδρόνικου. Thessaloniki, 39–50

VÖLCKER-JANSSEN, W. (1993) *Kunst und Gesellschaft an den Höfen Alexanders d. Gr. und seiner Nachfolger*. Munich

VON DER OSTEN, H. H. (1956) *Die Welt der Perser*[2]. Stuttgart

VON GRAEVE, V. (1970) *Der Alexandersarkophag und seine Werkstatt*. Berlin

VON GUTSCHMID, A. (1882) 'Trogus und Timagenes', *RhM* 37: 548–55

VOUTIRAS, E. (1984) 'Zur historischen Bedeutung des Krateros-Weihgeschenkes in Delphi', *WJA* 10: 57–62

—— (1990) 'Ἡφαιστίων ἥρως', *Egnatia* 2: 123–73

WACHOLDER, B. Z. (1962) *Nicolaus of Damascus*. Berkeley

WADE-GERY, H. T. (1945) 'The Question of Tribute in 449/8 B.C.', *Hesperia* 14: 212–29

WALBANK, F. W. (1957–79) *A Historical Commentary on Polybius*, 3 vols., Oxford

—— (1972) *Polybius*. Berkeley and London

—— (1985) *Selected Papers. Studies in Greek and Roman History and Historiography*. Cambridge

WALSER, G. (1984) *Hellas und Iran*. Darmstadt

WAYWELL, G. B. (1978) *The Free-Standing Sculptures of the Mausoleum at Halicarnassus*. London

WEBB, P. A. (1996) *Hellenistic Architectural Sculpture*. Madison

WEHRLI, F. (1968) *Die Schule des Aristoteles: Texte und Kommentar*. Heft IV, 'Demetrios von Phaleron'. Basel and Stuttgart

WELLES, C. B. (1934) *Royal Correspondence in the Hellenistic Period*. London

—— (1983) *Diodorus of Sicily* (LCL), VIII. Cambridge, Mass.

WENDLAND, P. (1910), 'Beiträge zur athenischen Politik und Publizistik des vierten Jahrhunderts, I., König Philippos und Isokrates', *Nachrichten von der königlichen Gesellschaft der Wissenschaften zu Göttingen* 1910: 123–82

WERNER, R. (1988), 'Alexander der Molosser in Italien', in W. Will and J. Heinrichs (eds.), *Zu Alexander d. Gr. Festschrift G. Wirth*, i. Amsterdam, 335–90

WEST, M. L. (1968) 'Two Passages of Aristophanes', *CR* 18: 5–8

—— (1992), *Iambi et Elegi Graeci*[2], ii. Oxford

—— (1993) 'Simonides Redivivus', *ZPE* 98: 1–14

WETZEL, F., SCHMIDT, E., MALLWITZ, A. (1957) *Das Babylon der Spätzeit*. Berlin

WHEATLEY, P. V. (1995) 'Ptolemy Soter's Annexation of Syria 320 B.C.', *CQ* 45: 433–40

—— (1998a) 'The Date of Polyperchon's Invasion of Macedonia and Murder of Heracles', *Antichthon* 32: 12–23

—— (1998b) 'The Chronology of the Third Diadoch War, 315–311 B.C.', *Phoenix* 52: 257–81

WIDENGREN, G. (1959) 'The Sacral Kingship of Iran', *Numen*, Suppl. 4. Leiden: 242–57

WIDENGREN, G. (1960) 'La Légende royale de l'Iran antique', *Hommages à G. Dumézil*: Coll. Latomus. Berchem-Bruxelles, 225–37

——(1965) *Die Religionen Irans*. Stuttgart

WIESEHÖFER, J. (1994) *Die 'dunklen Jahrhunderte' der Persis. Untersuchungen zur Geschichte und Kultur von Fars in früh-hellenistischer Zeit (330–140 v. Chr.)*. Zetemata, 90. Munich

WILBER, D. N. (1989) *Persepolis. The Archaeology of Persia, Seat of the Persian Kings*. Princeton

WILCKEN, U. (1929) 'Philipp II von Makedonien und die pan-hellenische Idee', *Sitzungsberichte der Preussischen Akademie der Wissenschaften, phil.-hist. Klasse* 18: 291–316

——(1932) *Alexander the Great*, trans. G. C. Richards. London

——(1970) *Berliner Akademieschriften zur alten Geschichte und Papyruskunde (1883–1942)*, i. Leipzig

WILL, W. (1986) *Alexander der Grosse*. Stuttgart

WINNICKI, J. K. (1989) 'Militäroperationen von Ptolemaios I und Seleukos I in Syrien in den Jahren 312–311 v. Chr. (I)', *AncSoc* 20: 55–92

WIRTH, G. (1973) *Alexander der Grosse*. Reinbeck bei Hamburg

WOLOHOJIAN, A. M. (1969) *The Romance of Alexander the Great by Pseudo-Callisthenes*. New York and London

WOOD, M. (1997) *In the Footsteps of Alexander the Great: A Journey from Greece to Asia*. Berkeley

WÖRRLE, M. (1977) 'Epigraphische Forschungen zur Geschichte Lykiens I', *Chiron* 7: 43–66

WORTHINGTON, I. (1994) 'The Harpalus Affair and the Greek Response to the Macedonian Hegemony', in I. Worthington (ed.), *Ventures into Greek History*. Oxford, 307–30

XIROTIRIS, N. I., and LANGENSCHEIDT, F. (1981) 'The Cremations from the Royal Macedonian Tombs of Vergina', *AEph*: 142–60

YARDLEY, J. C. (1978) 'The Elegiac Paraclausithyron', *Eranos* 76: 19–34

——(1994) *Justin. Epitome of the Philippic History of Pompeius Trogus*. Atlanta

YARDLEY, J. C. and HECKEL, W. (1997), *Justin: Epitome of the Philippic History of Pompeius Trogus, Books 11–12: Alexander the Great*. Oxford

ZAHRNT, M. (1996) 'Alexanders Übergang über den Hellespont', *Chiron* 26: 129–47

ZIMMERN, H. (1926) *Das babylonische Neujahrsfest*. Der Alte Orient, 25. 3. Leipzig

Index